BORN TO BE WILD

BORN
TO BE
WILD

THE RISE OF THE
AMERICAN MOTORCYCLIST

Randy D. McBee

The University of North Carolina Press // CHAPEL HILL

© 2015 The University of North Carolina Press
All rights reserved
Manufactured in the United States of America
Set in Utopia by codeMantra, Inc.
The paper in this book meets the guidelines for permanence and durability
of the Committee on Production Guidelines for Book Longevity of the Council on
Library Resources. The University of North Carolina Press has been a member
of the Green Press Initiative since 2003.

Cover illustration: depositphotos.com/© MonaMakela

Library of Congress Cataloging-in-Publication Data
McBee, Randy D.
Born to be wild : the rise of the American motorcyclist / by Randy D. McBee.
    pages cm
Includes bibliographical references and index.
ISBN 978-1-4696-2272-9 (cloth : alk. paper) — ISBN 978-1-4696-2273-6 (ebook)
1. Motorcycling—United States—History. 2. Motorcycling—Social aspects—
United States—History. 3. Motorcyclists—United States—History.
4. Motorcycle clubs—United States—History. I. Title.
GV1059.52.M44 2015
796.7'5—dc23
2014038125

Portions of this work appeared earlier in somewhat different form in Randy D. McBee,
"A 'Potential Common Front': Hunter Thompson, the Hells Angels, and Race in 1960s
America," *International Journal of Motorcycle Studies* 1 (July 2005); and Randy D. McBee,
"Harley-Davidson's Future (Abroad)," *International Journal of Motorcycle Studies* 7,
no. 2 (Fall 2011), and are reprinted here with the permission of the publisher.

For Chloe, Dylan, and Julie

CONTENTS

ILLUSTRATIONS

ACKNOWLEDGMENTS

Many people have contributed to this project. David Roediger, Barbara Hahn, Ron Milam, Jacynda Ammons, and Cindy Willett read parts of the manuscript or helped me sort out other details. Don Troop, Michael Lichter, and Jack and Pat Jamison were kind enough to share their photographs. Sean Cunningham spoke with me on numerous occasions about politics and the Right. Thanks as well to the anonymous readers for UNC Press. Their comments and suggestions significantly helped me fine-tune the manuscript and expand its scope and argument. I also want to thank Christopher Thrasher, one of my Ph.D. students who worked for me as a research assistant. He has a real knack for finding things, and some of the evidence that appears in the manuscript would not have been discovered if not for him. Don Hennigan, another student of mine, also contributed to this project in countless ways and was always willing to share his vast knowledge of motorcycling. I also cannot imagine having a better editor than Brandon Proia. From the start he has been supportive, quick to answer any questions, and just plain smart. He not only has been a delight to work with but understands the project and helped push it in ways that made it better. Many thanks as well to Mary Carley Caviness, who helped finalize numerous details toward the end of the process, and to Brian MacDonald, whose copyediting was invaluable.

I also owe a special thanks to the many motorcyclists I talked with over the years and the motorcyclists/scholars connected to the *International Journal of Motorcycle Studies*. The journal has been up and running for a decade, and I have benefited in countless ways from the men and women who have supported it over the years. I am particularly grateful to Steven Alford and Suzanne Ferriss. Suzanne was one of the founding editors of the journal, and she and Steven have coedited the journal for most of its existence. This book has benefited enormously from their years of riding, their insightful comments, and their constant support. They both read the entire manuscript, some parts more than once, and they were also generous with their time to answer my questions, fill in details, or simply point me in the right direction. Their influence on my work is evident, and I think it's better because of them.

I also want to thank my wife, Julie Willett. Her own work in women's/gender/labor history kept me thinking differently about the project, and her comments were always spot on, even though I often struggled to recognize that. Finally, my kids, Dylan and Chloe, did little to help me with this project, except of course to provide their constant support and love.

BORN TO BE WILD

INTRODUCTION

Don't Shoot the Easy Rider

For conservatives in America, 1980 represented a moment of enormous enthusiasm and optimism. They were gearing up for Ronald Reagan's landslide victory, just as traditional political constituencies were beginning to unravel to their benefit. The leading voice of the Right, the *National Review*, actually made the case just months before the election that it was time for conservatives to make a space among their ranks for a new interest group that up until then was the most unlikely of Republicans: motorcyclists.

The *National Review* titled the article "Don't Shoot the Easy Rider," in reference to the iconic 1969 film starring Peter Fonda, Dennis Hopper, and Jack Nicholson. By referring to *Easy Rider* the author highlighted not only the extent to which the film had shaped Americans' perceptions of motorcycling but also the degree to which the motorcyclist had long stood in sharp contrast to the Right. *Easy Rider* portrayed motorcyclists as hippies, and their deaths represented a deliberate consequence of a backlash politics that was gaining ground across the country in opposition to the liberation struggles of the preceding decades and a growing antiwar movement.[1] Motorcyclists, the *National Review* made clear, were transforming, shedding the left-leaning, hippie-inspired liberalism of the 1960s to become potential constituents of the Right. A recent survey of American Motorcyclist Association (AMA) members had revealed that motorcyclists were split when it came to party affiliation, with Democrats slightly edging out their Republican counterparts 29.6 percent to 24.8 percent. But the *National Review* writer made it clear that "party politics" was no longer a "working mechanism." In the survey, about 80 percent of AMA members favored Ronald Reagan over Jimmy Carter by what the author described

A still from the movie *Easy Rider*. The film helped link motorcyclists to the counterculture when it debuted in 1969 and continues to profoundly shape our image of motorcyclists. Courtesy of Photofest, Inc.

as "the same margin that they favor Bambi over [Ugandan dictator] Idi Amin." "Next time you see a hippie on a bike," the author admonished the magazine's readers, "don't shoot the easy rider, get the hell out of his way."[2] He was going to vote for Reagan in the upcoming election and had become a member of a mainstream coalition of conservative voters.

While the *National Review*'s writer recognized a legitimate political and cultural shift, the contradiction he highlighted between the new, respectable conservative motorcyclist and the old *Easy Rider* was also too sanitized, too neat, and too forgetful of a more common (and more notorious) "outlaw" motorcyclist who dominated the public's understanding of motorcycling throughout much of the postwar period. Motorcyclists established clubs as early as the 1920s and 1930s, and some of them wore matching sweaters or jackets with their club logos or colors prominently displayed. Besides hanging out in local clubs or bars, they often took part in more organized outings or competed in formal track races and hill-climbing competitions. It was only after World War II that motorcyclists began to attract negative, nationwide attention and be labeled "outlaws."[3] They were outlaws because of their disorderly behavior on and off their bikes and because they were not officially affiliated with the AMA and guilty of engaging in non-AMA-sanctioned racing. By the second half of the 1960s, the label called to mind motorcycle clubs like the Hells Angels, whose members were generally viewed as violent and antisocial and increasingly referred to as "bikers." The fear surrounding these motorcyclists soon led to sensationalized headlines about the brutal and sadistic crimes they allegedly committed, reinforcing an image of motorcycling that exacerbated the public's fear and paranoia about all motorcyclists. The several dozen biker films released in the second half of the 1960s and 1970s only reinforced the stereotype of the violent outlaw, an image that routinely overshadowed that of the motorcyclists in *Easy Rider*, or what one scholar has described as "hippies on bikes."[4]

The rise of the image of the violent outlaw occurred during one of the most tumultuous periods in U.S. history. The period witnessed the most dramatic economic downturn since the Great Depression, and Americans faced double-digit inflation and unemployment, the collapse of the nation's manufacturing base, rising oil and gas prices, and growing international competition. Men and women across the country began to question a Cold War consensus largely based on rigid conceptions of citizenship and identity, and one that advocated an interventionist foreign policy that led the United States into a war in Vietnam. From the 1950s to the 1970s, activists from all walks of life challenged ideas about patriotism and duty, family life and conventional gender roles, and race and citizenship. The political and cultural upheaval Americans were struggling to understand, historian Natasha Zaretsky argues, challenged their long-cherished sense of exceptionalism that had been based on "the idea that the United States did not lose wars, its natural resources were boundless, its leaders wise and secure, and its economy capable of infinite expansion."[5] These struggles not only led to unprecedented conflict on America's streets, in people's homes, and in the halls of Congress but also spawned a political shift to the right that elected Ronald Reagan in 1980 and gave rise to a kind of motorcyclist worthy of the *National Review*'s attention.

The influence of the 1960s and 1970s on motorcycling cannot be overstated, but to understand the broader development the *National Review* was hoping to capitalize on, we need to explore the outlaw image's roots during the immediate postwar years and, in particular, in a 1947 motorcycle rally in the once-sleepy town of Hollister, California. The rally was intended to consist of a three-day program of AMA-sponsored races, various social activities, and a hill-climbing competition. Before the rally had even ended, newspaper reporters were describing lurid scenes. C. J. Doughty, a staff writer for the *San Francisco Chronicle*, who was the first to report on the events, described the rally as an "outburst of terrorism" that led to, among other things, the "wrecking of bars, bottle barrages into the streets from upper story windows and roofs . . . high-speed racing of motorcycles through the streets," and complaints about "indecent exposure." The "momentum of their activities," according to Doughty, "gained strength during the Fourth of July. By evening they [motorcyclists] were virtually out of control." Doughty estimated that four thousand cyclists attended the rally and nearly sixty persons were injured (three seriously). He reported that "scores of arrests were made" and that a "special night court session was convened to punish those charged with reckless driving and drunkenness."[6]

Doughty's story set the tone for subsequent coverage. In the rally's aftermath, other newspapers and magazines picked up parts of the *Chronicle* story. *Life* magazine provided its readers with only a brief caption that described the rally with the same sensationalism that characterized Doughty's initial story just below a photograph of a motorcyclist, Eddie Davenport, leaning back on his prewar Harley. Disheveled and in an apparent drunken stupor, Davenport held a beer bottle in each hand with dozens more scattered about the ground surrounding his cycle.[7] Later accounts of the rally questioned whether Davenport was actually a motorcyclist, and even claimed that the photograph was staged. The photographer had asked Davenport to pose with a cycle that was not his, and another unpublished picture showed the bottles neatly line up around the cycle. The photographer had apparently swept together the beer bottles to play on fears of drunk and disorderly conduct. Nonetheless, the picture of Davenport left an indelible mark on the public's mind about motorcycling and remains one of the most prominent images associated with Hollister and the so-called outlaw motorcyclist.[8]

Over the next three decades, the legend of Hollister only grew. The outlaw from the 1940s began to look more and more like the supposed violent biker of the 1960s and 1970s.[9] In 1979 the *San Francisco Chronicle* published an article to mark Hollister's thirty-second anniversary. The piece offered a view of the rally strikingly similar to Doughty's, the author describing it as "the worst 40 hours in Hollister's history." The streets were also "awash in beer and broken glass," more than 4,000 cyclists "swarm[ed] like hungry locusts down the main drag," and "snarling [Harley-Davidsons] charg[ed] into bars."[10]

Jack Jamison falling off his Harley at a hill-climbing competition, 1957. Courtesy of Jack and Pat Jamison.

The author claimed that the residents' memories of that fateful day were "as vivid as the vicious roar of motorcycles that caused it all in the first place," but their memories of that week were grossly exaggerated, suggesting that more nefarious activities were taking place. Besides sleeping "all over the place," one resident claimed, "there were a lot of them [motorcyclists] screwing right out there on the lawn." Mothers also kept their daughters inside, "with the doors locked," presumably because the motorcyclists were sexual predators. And the Hells Angels mysteriously became rally participants even though the club did not exist until about a year after the Hollister Rally took place.[11] "Curiously enough," the author explained, "the weekend gave a lot of people the idea, as the years passed, that it was the Hell's Angels who ran the whole show," and he quoted a motorcyclist who boasted, "Yeah man, the Angels really tore up Hollister."[12]

By connecting the Hells Angels to the original Hollister Rally, the author inadvertently evoked nearly two decades of sensationalized newspaper headlines to suggest that violence was the motorcyclist's defining characteristic at Hollister—and perhaps everywhere. The author of this article was in effect conflating two different images of motorcycling and ignoring a much more complicated story about Hollister and of motorcyclists:

some motorcyclists participated in the Hollister Rally; most did not. Most accounts written about them have focused primarily on the conflict surrounding "gangs" of motorcyclists and their alleged crimes against nonriders. Hunter Thompson's celebrated and scorned *Hell's Angels: A Strange and Terrible Saga* (originally published in 1966) is probably the best-known example of this literature. Thompson lived and rode with the Hells Angels for about a year, and his account gave the nation an "insider's" look into the drugs, sex, and violence routinely attributed to the now-famous motorcycle club.[13] Only recently have scholars begun to address motorcycling as a serious academic subject. Their work has challenged the tired and dated characterizations of motorcyclists as inherently violent and antisocial, instead engaging in a much broader and global discussion about motorcycling's culture and history. Steven Alford and Suzanne Ferriss's *Motorcycle* (2008) is one example of the exceptional scholarship that explores nearly every facet of the motorcycle—its history, design, technology, and cultural impact in the United States and abroad—from the late nineteenth century to the present.[14]

To be sure, motorcyclists at Hollister (and everywhere during the 1940s and 1950s) were often unkempt and disheveled, and sometimes rowdy and disrespectable. Nevertheless, the anxiety surrounding them had less to do with any particular behavior or violation of community standards and more to do with their unemployment and lack of community ties. The increasing attention motorcyclists received at Hollister came in the wake of nearly two decades of nationwide instability and uncertainty characterized by massive unemployment, dislocation, and war. The Great Depression compelled nearly a million people to leave their homes and communities in search of work and a better life.[15] California was a popular destination, especially by World War II, as thousands of defense jobs opened up in the region. As the war came to an end, Americans across the country were eager to finally establish the stability that had for so long escaped them, and they were particularly leery of any challenge to it. In this context, the men accused of "invading" Hollister were not simply motorcyclists but vagrants, tramps, and transients.

The growing ambivalence surrounding men who defined themselves by their disconnectedness only grew more pronounced over the next two decades. The period immediately after World War II was a time of prosperity and economic expansion that witnessed millions of Americans leaving their rural communities for jobs in urban centers, unprecedented suburban growth, and a dramatic increase in highway construction. The most notable example of the country's economic expansion was the passage of the Federal-Aid Highway Act of 1956 that paid for over 40,000 miles of highways over the next twenty years.[16] If there was ever a golden age of the automobile, it was the 1950s—an era characterized by carhops, hot rods, tailfins, and cars that one historian of the automobile describes as "longer, lower, heavier, and more powerful" than ever before.[17] But tensions over the dangers of highway travel accompanied this growth, and conflict and divisiveness tarnished suburban expansion and migration. Opportunities for homeownership reached an all-time high in the postwar years, but at the expense of black Americans, whose general exclusion from suburbia led to the segregation that still defines the divide between urban and suburban spaces.[18]

The anxiety surrounding these changes set off a whirlwind of legislative and political activity to deal with roadway travel's adverse effects and the automobile's ascendancy. Most notable was the emergence of Ralph Nader, whose assault on the automobile's design flaws continues to shape the debate about consumer protection and government regulation. Nader's and other activists' efforts to promote highway safety and protect consumers contributed to the enactment of the National Traffic and Motor Vehicle Safety Act of 1966 and the Highway Safety Act of 1966. Together these acts created the National Highway Traffic Safety Administration and empowered the government to "establish standards for State highway safety programs and provided matching funds which could be used by the States for implementing the highway safety standards."[19]

The Highway Safety Act also granted the Department of Transportation the authority to withhold federal highway funds from states that did not have a motorcycle helmet law. The majority of the nonriding public's support for helmets reflected fears of increasing fatalities in the wake of the motorcycle's unprecedented popularity (the number of registered motorcycles increased tenfold between 1945 and the end of the 1960s).[20] But the growing paranoia surrounding motorcyclists also led people to believe mistakenly that helmets would protect them from all their imagined fears about motorcyclists amid the growing debates about highway safety. In short, motorcyclists too easily and too thoroughly violated mainstream conceptions about mobility and the boundaries surrounding the movement of men, women, and machines that white Americans had established in an attempt to reclaim the security and comfort that had initially drawn them to the suburbs in the first place. Motorcyclists were neither here nor there but potentially everywhere, making them more conspicuous than their actual numbers might suggest and more of a threat than they actually were.

Though motorcyclists had faced many attempts to regulate their behavior and their machines, it was the federal support of helmet laws that led to the rise of a nationwide, grassroots motorcycle rights movement. The movement was initially episodic and lacked a particular focus or theme. The phrase "Helmet Laws Suck" was the first, best-effort to pull together an ideological framework that might unite the motorcycle community. Riders have long been divided over the helmet's efficacy, and early on, the movement was fractured along class lines: the riders most likely to oppose helmet laws were the men typically considered outlaws. Efforts to deal with the growing number of fatalities came largely from a middle-class whose ties to motorcycling accompanied the emergence and dominance of the Japanese Honda in the 1960s. By the mid-1970s the motorcycle rights movement's focus began to change and became identified with the adage "Let Those Who Ride Decide"—an ideological shift that emphasized individual rights and freedom and promoted greater unity among motorcyclists than had been evident in the preceding decade.

Motorcyclists' efforts to end federal regulation attracted widespread support from politicians, particularly by the second half of the 1970s. The motorcycle rights movement's focus on "freedom issues" and big government drew from the same rhetoric that had powered the Right since at least the rise of Barry Goldwater to national prominence during the early 1960s. Indeed, by the end of the 1970s, the AMA was spearheading a shift in favor of the Republican Party that included a broad-based effort to oust key Democratic senators linked to federal efforts to regulate personal behavior, or what the AMA (and other motorcyclists) referred to as Big Brotherism. The federal government, the AMA argued, "should do for the people only what they and their local governing bodies cannot legitimately do for themselves."[21]

Motorcyclists' relationship with the Right only grew stronger as the Reagan administration crafted a strategy to shore up support from the working class. As governor of California in the late 1960s, Reagan opposed helmet laws. As president, in 1983, he ordered an increase in tariffs that specifically targeted Japanese-made motorcycles as part of a larger effort to revive Harley-Davidson, the last American company producing motorcycles and the brand the nonriding public has generally identified with outlaws. Harley-Davidson's share of the market had been steadily declining since the introduction of Japanese Hondas and reached a low of less than 4 percent by the mid-1970s. The Reagan administration's focus on Harley-Davidson threatened to create a rift between those men and women who rode American-made Harleys and the rest of the motorcycling community, and it supported Harley-Davidson's decade-old strategy of emphasizing economic nationalism to challenge the Japanese. But Reagan's focus on Harley-Davidson also allowed him to strengthen his ties to the common man and promote the idea that the Democrats were elitist and out of touch with average, hard-working Americans.[22] Liberalism, as Jefferson Cowie cogently explains, had favored a "social agenda" in support of civil rights and other liberation struggles, and when it failed to deliver an "economic backbone," it was "the right that flowed in to fill the gap in people's politics."[23]

By the early 1990s, the impact of the relationship between motorcyclists and the Right was hard to ignore: Harley-Davidson was once again competing for the top position in the U.S. motorcycle market. The company had become a symbol of American freedom and individuality, and the ties between the Right and motorcyclists emphasized their common faith in American nationalism. Four years after ordering the tariff against the Japanese, Reagan made an appearance at a Harley-Davidson manufacturing plant, where he highlighted America's exceptionalism and the patriotism of Harley and its workers. By making an appearance with motorcyclists, he established a political tradition that future presidents and presidential wannabes adopted in their attempt to market themselves as authentic, to attract a working-class constituency, and to publicly showcase their support of "freedom issues." The most notable and recent example is John McCain's appearance at the Sturgis Motorcycle Rally in 2008.

Still, the relationship with the Right was never simply a product of the fight over helmet laws and federal encroachment. The Right grew out of a broad-based disaffection for "big government" that motorcyclists shared, beginning with the motorcycle rights movement in the latter half of the 1960s. But the country's political shift toward the Right that led to Reagan's election in 1980 also sprung from a fear of social decay embodied in struggles over feminism, racism, and sexual identity. Motorcyclists often identified with these movements as they tried to reconcile the discrimination they faced. The motorcycle rights movement appropriated the idea of "minority" as a reference point around which motorcyclists defined their own struggle. At the same time, significant evidence suggests that these same liberation movements played an important role in galvanizing the unlikely alliance between motorcyclists and conservative politicians, which has become more noticeable since the mid-1970s. The Right attracted some of its most loyal supporters in those heady days of liberation struggles, and its alliance with motorcyclists was taking shape even before state legislatures across the country had begun to pass helmet laws.[24]

The use of the term "biker," for example, emerged at the intersection of the rise of the image of the motorcyclist as violent outlaw and growing tension between motorcyclists and the counterculture. The earliest examples of "biker" in print date back to the second half of the 1960s, and its use did not become common until the early 1970s. As with the outlaw, the biker's distinguishing characteristic was his violence. Before long, a "biker type" became a stock character in popular culture and on police blotters. The biker's "propensity" for violence was particularly glaring against the backdrop of the counterculture and the rise of the hippie, who challenged conventional ideas about gender and sexuality and was attracting attention at about the same time the idea of the biker "menace" took root. Amid the political struggles of the period, bikers and hippies often formed tentative alliances, and their influence on one another is evident—"long haired" and "greasy" are typical descriptions of both. But these alliances were generally short-lived. Often impoverished and living in the same neighborhoods, bikers and hippies found themselves competing for housing and other community resources. That competition could lead to conflict. Indeed, some of the earliest examples of the use of "biker" were in reference to the so-called biker invasions into once-peaceful hippie communities, which were fading away amid the growing violence and intolerance.[25]

The roots of the relationship with the Right were also particularly noticeable in the struggle that characterized the history of motorcycling in the black community. The motorcyclist who first attracted national attention at Hollister was, simply put, a white male, and that image only grew more pronounced over the next three decades. While popular culture and the media have had a disproportionate influence on the image of the violent biker, in the black community this threat was often more real than imagined. Muhammad Ali famously threw his Olympic gold medal into the Ohio River after a brawl with a white motorcycle "gang." Such conflicts were just as likely to include motorcycle cops as vigilante bikers. Against the backdrop of the civil rights and Black Power movements, the line dividing what the black media referred to as a "white motorcycle gang" and the white motorcycle cop was, in fact, vague—both were linked to violence against black men and women and both were viewed as a challenge to the era's political struggles. The postwar years saw the motorcycle cop's role policing urban space expand at about the same time black Americans were intensifying their call for civil rights, and this convergence increased the likelihood of contact and conflict. In light of these growing struggles, the black rider was viewed not simply as a two-wheeled enthusiast but often as an explicit challenge to essentialized ideas about race that promoted the black rider's invisibility and naturalized the motorcycle rider as white. Any challenge from the black community was an act of defiance that shaped motorcycling's development and its popularity. This growing conflict guaranteed that the segregation that divided black and white communities would persist in motorcycle culture, and it helps explain the growing relationship between white motorcyclists and a Right that was ambivalent if not outright hostile to civil rights even though the larger motorcycle community was caught up in its own struggles for equality.[26]

THE FIRST HALF of this book looks broadly at the average motorcyclist from the time of the Hollister Rally in 1947 to the rise of the biker of the late 1960s and early 1970s. Chapter 1 explores the outlaw's origins in the late 1940s and identifies the conflict surrounding him and the manner in which he challenged ideas about community, social belonging, and even citizenship. It also examines the manner in which violence became associated with motorcyclists—a development that began with the rise of a signature look of rebellion during those hopeful days of economic expansion after the war and ended with a motorcyclist who defied all of our basic assumptions about common decency amid economic and political turmoil at home and abroad. The public's tendency to link motorcyclists to violence was so complete by the late 1960s and early 1970s that the motorcyclist's working-class origins were overshadowed by his antisocial behavior; a "biker type" began to shape the public's image of what crime looked like, and politicians across the country began looking for ways to regulate motorcycling and motorcyclists.

Chapter 2 looks beyond the sensational headlines about violent motorcyclists to understand the stereotypes attributed to them, paying particular attention to the growing conflict between motorcyclists and automobilists on America's highways and the rise of the middle-class rider, who made the so-called outlaw appear to be more of a problem than he actually was. Scholars have thoroughly described the automobile's ascendancy in the postwar years and how it affected transportation alternatives and the shape of urban/suburban spaces. But they have ignored the unprecedented growth in the number of registered motorcycles (from 198,000 in 1945 to around 3 million by the early 1970s) and the conflict on America's highways that accompanied their expansion. Even before the Hollister Rally, the nonriding majority was complaining about how daredevils, hounds, and motorcycle cowboys compromised their use of the country's roadways and posed a threat to highway safety. By the 1960s and 1970s, that conflict was unprecedented, and it is critical to understanding the origins of the "outlaw" rider and the push for regulation. The nonriding public's perception of the motorcycle rider as a significant threat to their safety on the road led to a national debate over highway safety, leading to the implementation of federal helmet laws.

Chapter 3 examines the rise of the middle-class motorcyclist and how his/her impact on motorcycle culture shaped the public's perception of motorcyclists. Postwar affluence and an increasingly pervasive consumer culture contributed to the 1960s "craze" for motorcycling. The middle-class motorcycle enthusiast attracted the most attention from the media because he made motorcycling respectable and family friendly and stood in sharp contrast to the traditional working-class rider. The middle-class rider was simply better at consuming motorcycles than producing them and affected a style that highlighted those differences. The growing popularity of choppers (customized motorcycles) illustrates the importance of class to motorcycling's increasing popularity, but it also reflected the technological sophistication of Japanese Hondas and the assumption that a (middle-class) rider did not have to have any mechanical competence to ride one. The middle-class rider's potential to change motorcycling culture was clear, and it translated into an increasingly bitter debate over brand-name loyalty that translated into an economic nationalism that gave rise to terms like "Jap bike" and "rice burner." The terms highlight the ways in which race shaped motorcycle culture but also reflected a deep-seated class divide that became more conspicuous as the clamor over helmets grew louder and as consumption became one of the defining issues dividing motorcyclists.

The remainder of this book explores the motorcycle rights movement that emerged in the late 1960s and the origins of the relationship between motorcyclists and the Right. Chapter 4 examines the arguments in support of helmets and the emergence of a motorcycle rights movement to oppose them. While helmet advocates struggled to establish an ideological focus during these early years, divisions among riders based on class were particularly conspicuous and responsible for the establishment of helmet regulation and the conflict that undermined effective resistance to it. Support for helmets was never simply about the loss of life but the loss of middle-class life, and opposition to helmets was never simply about freedom or individual rights.

Chapter 5 examines the end of the federal government's helmet regulation and the growing alliance between motorcyclists and the Right. It explores the motorcyclists' changing ideological struggles that gave rise to a grassroots movement, the different organizations that came together to oppose helmets, and the issues that attracted conservative politicians to the motorcycle rights movement. This alliance was by no means guaranteed. Motorcyclists directly challenged the Right's support of "law and order" and a politics of family that emphasized everything the outlaw was not, but the average motorcyclist's support of the individual and his opposition to regulation eventually attracted Republican politicians who were anxious to expand their constituency and bolster their own arguments about freedom and big government. By the mid-1970s, Reagan, in opposition to Ralph Nader, became one of the leading opponents of helmet regulation, and as president he defied his own free-trade ideology to save Harley-Davidson.

Indeed, it was during Reagan's second term as president that the rich urban biker (RUB) made his debut. The RUB emerged in the wake of the motorcycle rights movement and its struggle against helmet laws, and he challenged the image of the biker as a social outcast and proved him out to be surprisingly conventional, respectable, and patriotic. Riding a Harley still carried all the baggage, as it were, from preceding years, and the RUB's style consciously embraced that baggage, including a look strikingly similar to that of the characters in *Easy Rider* that the *National Review* had scorned at the beginning of the decade. But even as the image remained a contradiction that potentially challenged mainstream conservative political and aesthetic values, the larger ideological changes taking place in the motorcycle rights movement and the rise of a (conservative) politics that fundamentally shaped a "biker" identity also made it easier for doctors, lawyers, accountants, and other professionals to cross the rough/respectable divide that in years past seemed so insurmountable.

Chapters 6 and 7 argue that the alliance between motorcyclists and the Right was taking shape even before legislators began passing helmet laws in the late 1960s and reflected the larger struggles over gender and race throughout the postwar period. Women's and gay liberation, the counterculture, and the fight for civil rights played a particularly conspicuous role in shaping the rise of a "biker" and the success of a motorcycle rights movement. The movement used opposition to the Left to garner support for the repeal of the Highway Safety Act of 1966, and conservative politicians were equally adept at exploiting identity issues for their own political gain. The motorcyclist may have established a new standard of rebellion, but he also shared the nonriding public's conventional ideas about race and gender. Chapter 6 explores how ideas about gender and women's participation as riders and as passengers affected motorcycle culture. In the wake of the controversy at Hollister, the AMA celebrated women riders but only to highlight their domesticating influence, which posed little challenge to men's dominance of motorcycling. By the 1960s and 1970s, women's participation was growing, but it was accompanied by the rise of the scantily clad motorcycle model and the increasing commodification of women's bodies in motorcycle culture. The conflict revealed the influence and limits of feminism and the limits of the motorcycle rights movement, which challenged opposition to women's objectification as another example of regulation.

Chapter 6 also considers questions of gender and sexual identity. It argues that the clash between the Hells Angels and the antiwar movement at the Berkley-Oakland border in 1965 was not the anomaly it has generally been recognized to be but one example in a much larger history of struggle surrounding gender and sexuality. The signature look of the outlaw that emerged out of Hollister was also a style appropriated by gay men attempting to challenge charges of effeminacy. These two groups intersected with the formation of openly gay motorcycle clubs and with the rise of the stereotype that all bikers are gay. Fears about homosexuality profoundly shaped the conflict between motorcyclists and the counterculture, contributed to the motorcyclist's conventional ideas about gender and politics, and gave rise to the image of the "husky" biker who was violent but also conspicuously heterosexual.

Chapter 7 begins with the intersection of the Altamont concert in 1969 and the first blaxploitation film, *Sweet Sweetback's Baadasssss Song*, and ends with the Willie Horton ad that contributed to George Bush Sr.'s election as president in 1988.[27] *Sweet Sweetback's Baadasssss Song* focused attention on the death of Meredith Hunter, a black man killed by a motorcyclist at the Altamont concert, and the Willie Horton ad was introduced to a group of motorcyclists in Virginia months before it was released to the nation. Taken together, these events highlight the role "law and order" has played in the history of motorcycling, including the relationship between the police (that is, motorcycle cops) and motorcyclists and the opposition to the civil rights and Black Power movements. Fears about lawless motorcyclists who were generally identified as white not only grew more prevalent as the stereotypical image of the motorcyclist as criminal emerged but also intersected with the motorcycle rights movement whose members at times appropriated the term "minority" to make a case against what they considered discriminatory (helmet) legislation. Motorcyclists used race to challenge the liberation struggles of the preceding two decades, and their understanding of race promoted a conventional (and racialized) vision of freedom, politics, citizenship, and equality that has generally ignored the black community and attracted the Right.

At the same time, we cannot ignore black riders' contribution to motorcycling culture. While black men and women were as enthusiastic about motorcycles as their white counterparts, black riders also recognized that the rebelliousness that had its roots at Hollister could also unsettle racialized and gendered assumptions that have contributed to their exclusion from mainstream motorcycle culture. Indeed, by the late 1970s and early 1980s, black riders were organizing their own motorcycle rallies. Away from their white counterparts, black motorcyclists created a space in which they could affirm their identity as riders and as black men and women, and a space that had the potential to shape all of motorcycle culture once the rally came to an end.

Studies about the rise of the Right in the postwar years have ignored motorcyclists. The stereotypes about these riders and the violence attributed to them have pushed them to the margins of American society, making it easier to discount their contributions and influence on American culture. By the end of the twentieth century, those margins were increasingly difficult to find and the contradiction the *National Review* identified to draw attention to Reagan's popularity was not nearly as surprising as it was in 1980. Motorcyclists have generally preferred (and have consciously chosen) to be in the margins, but they willingly entered the political arena to defend themselves against what they viewed as an assault on their very way of life, and the Right successfully appropriated motorcycle culture, or at least the parts politicians found useful. Those in what seemed to be the margins were not only beginning to influence the core but becoming a part of it. "Don't shoot the Easy Rider," the *National Review* admonished its readers just before Reagan's election in 1980, perhaps never fully understanding that the larger shift the editor envisioned became so dominant and lasting that even today it continues to shape our public discourse about politics, culture, and society.

NO WORTHWHILE CITIZEN EVER CLIMBED
ABOARD A MOTORCYCLE AND GUNNED THE ENGINE

The Rise of the Biker, 1940s–1970s

On March 26, 1971, at the Juilliard Theater in New York City, Harold Farberman debuted *The Losers,* his new opera about a young woman who meets and falls in love with a motorcyclist. At the time, the country was in the midst of a motorcycle craze, and ten times more registered bikes were on the road nationwide than there had been in 1947, when the Hollister motorcyclists first attracted attention. But at the Juilliard Theater in 1971, the media's focus was less on the popularity of motorcycling and more on the fear that the night might turn violent. As a reporter covering the event commented, "Death and tragedy have been the stock in trade of operas over the centuries [but] a new high in shock may be in store for opera goers who attend the premiere tonight of 'The Losers.'" Farberman only added to the public's anxiety surrounding motorcyclists by describing the opera's subject as "violence" and by describing the motorcycle gang portrayed in the opera as "one of the purest manifestations of that [violence]." The opera included "a chain whip killing; a neck breaking; an initiation rite in which a boy is stripped and burned with cigarettes," and a "sensual ballet" that "ends with the off-stage gang rape of the [gang] leader's girl."[1]

The Losers was Farberman's attempt at merging the European opera tradition with the American Broadway musical, although he admitted that "no one will go away from 'The Losers' feeling [like] they have seen 'The Sound of Music'—or even 'West Side Story." Indeed, before the opera was staged, the director had to replace the actor originally cast as the boy initiated into the gang when the actor said "his religious beliefs prevented him from doing some of the things called for," and a young woman who was cast as a waitress in a "gang hangout" had to contact "her religious counselor in Arkansas to see whether she could say certain four-letter words on stage." The woman kept the part, but some of the words had to be changed. At the opera's premier, uniformed policemen were stationed at the Julliard Building and the Julliard Theater, apparently because of the fear of an "attack by a real motorcycle gang." "There was none," one journalist was glad to report later. "All the violence was on stage."[2]

This image of motorcyclists as unimaginably violent and anti-social was not uncommon in the 1960s and 1970s. By the time *The Losers* debuted, sensationalized stories about motorcyclists and their alleged crimes had graced the pages of newspapers worldwide for several years. Hollywood was churning out dozens of biker films in which the central characters were as sadistic as they were comical, and 1%er clubs like the Hells Angels were becoming the topic of best-selling exposés and conversations in newsrooms and classrooms alike.[3]

The public tagged motorcyclists as outlaws after the rally in Hollister in 1947 and after a second rally in Riverside, California, a year later. At both rallies the motorcyclists attracted attention for participating in American Motorcyclist Association (AMA)–sanctioned events without official membership in the organization and for their unruly behavior. They raced their bikes up and down the city streets, disobeyed other traffic rules and regulations, and engaged in other drunk and disorderly conduct. Scores of arrests were made in both communities, but the participants were more of a nuisance than a threat to the cities' residents, many of whom eagerly lined the streets as spectators or participated in the days' events.

In the growing numbers of stories about motorcyclists in the 1960s and 1970s, a new rider was emerging who stood in sharp contrast to his counterpart at Hollister and Riverside: he was routinely linked to drugs and guns, no longer confined to the small-town America that feared and loathed him, inclined to prey upon innocent bystanders, and linked to what Farberman suggested was a new standard of violence. Indeed, in the wake of the rise of the violent outlaw of the late 1960s and early 1970s, the word "biker" became synonymous with "motorcyclist," and a "biker type" began to shape the public's image of what a criminal looked like. For the nonriding majority, the motorcyclist's dress, his physical size, and his behavior or the crime he was accused of committing defined a "biker type," often without any mention of the motorcycle he was presumably riding and gave rise to a public perception about motorcyclists that was less likely to acknowledge distinctions among riders than in previous years.

The public's changing perception about motorcyclists also reflected their relationship to the communities in which they organized their rallies. Motorcycling was based on what riders called a "gypsying" subculture that revolved around "tours" or rallies that became increasingly popular in the pre- and postwar years.[4] The most popular rallies that today attract hundreds of thousands of riders were first organized during the first half of the twentieth century: Laconia in 1916, Hollister in 1936, Daytona in 1937, and Sturgis in 1938.[5] Organizers suspended many of these rallies during World War II, but they resumed with the end of hostilities and became the site of the controversy surrounding motorcyclists in the period immediately after the war.[6] Motorcyclists' mobility and their connection to a "gypsy" subculture encouraged the public to associate these men with transients, or any men who had a complicated and ambiguous relationship to work—bums, hoboes, tramps, vagrants. Yet the labor these men contributed economically to these small towns and their experience with wage work were familiar to these communities and to all motorcyclists who shared similar humble backgrounds. The motorcyclist's status as a transient was at the root of why some people feared him and why others embraced him. By the 1960s and 1970s, words like "tramp" were still used to describe motorcyclists, and the public remained fascinated with motorcycle culture. But violence had become such an overwhelming characteristic of the motorcyclist that the public struggled to imagine him as anything but a threat, and finding a common class experience was much more difficult than it had been when the motorcyclist first attracted national attention and when he was often accepted as a transient.

HOLLISTER

A gypsy tour is an organized motorcycle event that generally takes place over a weekend or a holiday and includes the ride to the event, often along a scenic route, and the one or two days of competitions, including races, hill climbs, dirt-track events, and field meets (stake races, plank riding, and slow races). The AMA, which was established in 1924 as an outgrowth of the Motorcycle and Allied Trades Association, sponsored gypsy tours.[7] The first gypsy tour connected to Hollister was held in 1935 at Bolado Park, ten miles south of town. Over the years the event grew from a one-day race to a three-day event with parades, dances, hill climbs, controlled stunts, and races. In an article about the Hollister Rally, *Cycle* magazine explained that the "AMA used the Hollister event as a pattern during the 1930s for other gypsy tours throughout the country" and also noted the enthusiasm with which the town's residents welcomed the cyclists.[8]

The event in Hollister was suspended in 1940 as war spread across the world. The rally in July 1947 was the first one since the war ended in 1945. The cyclists began arriving for the rally on Thursday to watch the races and to participate in the weekend of planned events. By Friday, the number of riders was estimated at about 2,000, and by Saturday, the press claimed, between 4,000 and 5,000 riders had converged on the town of fewer than 3,000 residents. Most of these motorcyclists camped on the city's edges, but about 500 gathered along the town's main street, San Benito Street, and engaged in what one historian has described as an "uproarious, drunken binge."[9] Some motorcyclists used San Benito Street as a drag strip. Others performed stunts to the roar of the crowd, and the streets became littered with beer bottles as "hundreds [of motorcyclists and spectators] loosed bottle barrages." According to *San Francisco Chronicle* staff writer C. J. Doughty, the town's seven-man police force could not contain the "riot," leading Hollister police lieutenant Roy L. McPhail to send out a formal request for backup. Forty highway patrol officers, commanded by Captain L. T. Torres, arrived shortly after dusk. "Armed with tear gas guns, the officers herded the cyclists into a block on San Benito Street, between Fifth and Sixth streets, placed a dance band on a truck and ordered the musicians to play."[10] The Highway Patrol's ploy apparently worked. With the band and the dancing distracting the motorcyclists, calm returned to Hollister as quickly and as abruptly as it had allegedly disappeared.

While the media latched on to Doughty's initial story and printed other sensational accounts, the AMA and the writers at *Motorcyclist* objected to the mainstream press's coverage. Writers at both *American Motorcycling* (the official publication of the AMA) and *Motorcyclist* admonished its readers to consider carefully the sensationalism that was rampant in newspaper and radio reports and to weigh the evidence objectively. A writer at *American Motorcycling* went so far as to explain that all mention of Hollister was withheld from the July 1947 issue because "we had to have time to secure unprejudiced first hand reports on the affair." "We know," the writer added, "that much modern newspaper practice glories in the sensational and some reporters are trained to studiously distort and varnish in order to create lurid stories for their readers."[11]

The motorcycle press also pointed to nonriders who participated in the rally and contributed to the supposed mayhem. *Motorcyclist* and *American Motorcycling* argued that local "toughies," also referred to as a "much larger group of non-motorcycling hell-raisers," shared the blame for Hollister's problems and pointed as well to "mercenary minded bar-keepers." The outside "toughies" were thought to be intentionally unruly, expecting that the cyclists would be blamed for any misbehavior, and published accounts of arrests do include Hollister residents.[12] The motorcycle press also implicated barkeepers because, reports charged, they viewed the rally merely as a way to fill their coffers and unscrupulously sold their wares with little concern for their effect on the motorcyclists or the town. Barkeepers in Hollister, the press reported, stopped selling beer as the motorcyclists became unruly to end the bottle barrages that were allegedly wreaking havoc in the downtown area, although they continued to sell whiskey under the assumption that the motorcyclists could not afford to drink it, a subtle but clear indication of the average rider's humble origins.[13]

Yet both publications accepted that something had gone awry at Hollister. Amid their protestations, they blamed a "small minority" of motorcyclists, or, as the AMA put it, a "sad band of parasites."[14] They were the "same old element that so frequently besmirches motorcycle gatherings." In the words of the writer at *American Motorcycling*, they were "hell-raisers," "real bravados," and the "few riders" who "decided to make a race track out of the street." There was a "certain type," the writer lamented, "who can only be happy when he is drinking and raising Cain."[15] "Let's be realistic in this matter," asserted the writer at *Motorcyclist*. "Unfortunately there was foundation for the story and we would be unwise to attempt to side-step the facts." The writer at *American Motorcycling* actually referred to the gypsy tour as the "Hollister holocaust," even as he urged objectivity. "We are simply doing what we should do—setting forth all of the material that has been gathered through a careful and thorough investigation based on official reports from enforcement officers."[16]

The "certain type" the AMA complained about did not receive a common name in *American Motorcycling*, *Motorcyclist*, or the *Hollister Free Lance*. It was not until a year later, after a rally in Riverside, California, attracted similar negative press coverage that the enduring label "outlaw" emerged.

The city of Riverside was actually the site of two motorcycling events that garnered negative press coverage. The first occurred on Labor Day weekend, two months after the Hollister Rally, in conjunction with the national championship races sponsored by the American Motorcycle Association and the California Highway Patrol, and the second took place a year later over the Fourth of July weekend at an amateur racing meet sponsored by the Sheriff's Training Association at the Box Spring Tourist Trophy track just five miles from Riverside.[17] The first incident attracted less media coverage, primarily in regional papers, and was not picked up by the *Los Angeles Times*. According to one report, six thousand motorcyclists were in town for the racing and an unreported number of them descended on Riverside. They "roared about the downtown streets at breakneck speeds," there was "considerable drinking and a dozen persons were jailed on charges of drunkenness, fighting or refusal to disperse," the streets "became littered with broken beer bottles, [and] chunks of rubber from screaming tires burned in impromptu 'getaway' races and 'spin-a-circle' riding." To handle the confusion downtown, the writer alleged, "the police blocked off two blocks of Eight street . . . and let the riders roar." One article concluded that the "situation was similar to a motorcycle madhouse at Hollister . . . over the July 4 holiday."[18]

The turn of events that took place a year after Hollister made the national news, and press reports suggested that the motorcyclists were even more unruly than they had been the previous year. One article described the rally as an "invasion," this time claiming that 5,000 "wild riding" motorcyclists, "most of them drunk," "thundered and roared up and down Riverside streets for three days before harried police officers finally turned the tide and restored some semblance of order." Another report claimed that many of the riders were "'veterans' of the Hollister invasion last year . . . [who] were going to make a similar night of it in Riverside." The press alleged that the trouble started after participants began "drifting back into the city" as the races wound down and gathered along 8th Street between Market and Main streets. As was the case at Hollister, the riders organized drag races down the city's streets, using traffic lights as the starting signal and blocked off traffic so they could "spin circles in the middle of main intersections." According to initial reports, motorcyclists "trampled" the hood of a car, broke some of its windows, and "manhandled" the occupants after the driver honked his horn at some cyclists who were blocking the road. Later accounts did not contradict the report but indicated that the automobilist had actually run into one of the motorcyclists.[19]

Just as it had after Hollister, the motorcycle press denounced the media's coverage as biased and argued that a "lunatic fringe" of riders were responsible for the disorder. Mainstream coverage of the Riverside incident in 1948 also described the motorcyclists as "outlaw riders" to emphasize their disorderly behavior. *Motorcyclist* actually reprinted an article from the *Pasadena California Independent* where it was reported that the "'outlaw' riders moved into town and proceeded to paint it a bright red."[20] Complaints about the motorcyclists' behavior were still prominent a month later when *Motorcyclist* attempted again to challenge negative depictions of the participants, but a motorcyclist was now an outlaw simply because he was not a member of the AMA. The "future of motorcycle sports," argued a Riverside County sheriff's report, would only be ensured if "the American Motorcycle Association–recognized motorcycle clubs and the 'outlaw' motorcycle clubs" reached "an understanding."[21]

Articles about Riverside that appeared in *Motorcyclist* also narrowed down the definition of "fringe." *Motorcyclist*'s initial article described the "trouble makers" as a "small minority" and provided a "confirmation quote" from Riverside's police chief, sheriff, and undersheriff, who characterized the offending riders as "representing not more than 2% of the cyclists."[22] A month later the county sheriff's report argued that a "change in attitude and acts of the one percent of irresponsible, intemperate and sometimes vulgar motorcyclist hiding behind the cloak of decency of the ninety-nine percent of motorcyclists must be accomplished."[23] The term "1%er" is generally linked to the AMA's 1961 public relations campaign that divided motorcyclists into two camps: the "fringe" element, whose behavior and riding habits were questionable, and the remaining "'99%' of riders who conduct themselves in a manner that brings credit to the sport."[24] But the idea of the 1%er emerged first out of the controversy surrounding Riverside in 1948 and well before the formation of most of the clubs that became infamous for their antisocial and violent behavior.

The attempt to distinguish between a minority of outlaws and a majority of law-abiding riders was not always successful. Hollister's residents and other individuals who witnessed the rally of 1947 generally failed to distinguish between different groups of motorcyclists, inadvertently challenging the idea of a fringe element. R. E. Stevenson, for example, who was from the neighboring town of Salinas (about twenty miles southwest of Hollister) and had visited the town for a day of shopping on Saturday, July 5, began his letter of complaint to the *Hollister Free Lance* by explaining that it had always been a "pleasure to come to Hollister to shop—until I came over Saturday." The town, he said, was "overrun with lawless, drunken, filthy bands of motorcycle fiends and it was impossible for law abiding citizens to drive on your streets." Stevenson claimed that he had been told that neighboring communities had loaned Hollister additional police officers to quell the disturbances, but he complained that the "noisy racing continued and drunks slept in the gutters, streets, alongside business buildings and in vacant lots." Stevenson wondered why Hollister would "tolerate such things" and why Hollister's "trustees would allow such disgraceful happenings." He concluded his letter by describing the event as a "real disgrace" and asked, "What do the home folks think?"[25]

Two days later, two responses to Stevenson appeared in the local paper and both of them took exception to his description of the motorcyclists and of the rally. "This is the answer to Mr. Stevenson of Salinas from a resident of Hollister," exclaimed Elnor Collier. "Our home," he explained, "joins the Veterans Memorial Park [where the races were held]. Our orchard was invaded, they used our open lot for parking space (without our permission), but we enjoyed every minute of it." Indeed, Collier appeared somewhat disappointed as he described the rally's aftermath and his readjustment to day-to-day life in what he suggested was the normally sleepy town of Hollister: "So now we have shaken the dust out of our drapes and rugs, Hollister has cleaned up the broken glass and gutters and our police are wearing their old smiles. Shopping is as per usual, we now have the sleep out of our eyes and the bandages off of our heads and we're waiting for a rip-roaring good time Aug. 1–3, [at] our Diamond Jubilee," a yearly festival in Hollister and just the excitement he seemed to be looking for. Collier agreed with Stevenson that the riders were often disorderly and boisterous, but in his concluding remarks proclaimed, "I, for one, say that Hollister and its residents can take it."[26]

The other letter was from Ruth Reynolds, who acknowledged some of the same problems Stevenson complained about, but she described his "account" as "a routine piece of misrepresentation." Like Collier, Reynolds admitted that the rally "was noisy" and "often annoying," and she did not blame "Mr. S" for "criticizing the demonstration." But the town was "damage free" and "not overrun" as he had suggested. "Two blocks of the main street were largely impassable," she explained, "but the remainder of our streets were free from obstacles." "Many of them [the motorcyclists] were drunk," and "some of the riders appeared to be dirty," but "many of them gave evidence of having recently taken a bath." Indeed, for all of the talk of lawlessness and disorder, Reynolds emphasized that "there were no shootings, assaults, fights, holdups, murders, incidents of arson, mayhem or rape reported. None of the citizens of Hollister was molested by the cyclists—if anyone was, he has not complained of it."[27]

To further make her case, she pointed out that the behavior of the men who participated in the yearly rodeo in Mr. Stevenson's hometown of Salinas was not all that different from the motorcyclists at Hollister and Riverside. "Our Salinas shopper," Reynolds wrote, "might well pick his hometown skirts out of the mud before he writes any more letters to the editor such as the missive, laden with adjectives that appeared in your Monday issue. While he may have been offended by the somewhat noisy mob that cluttered up his personal shopping district," she continued, "I wonder what his reactions were to the indescribable havoc that roared up and down Main Street in Salinas on a Saturday night during the recent rodeo." Reynolds confessed that she did not stay at the rodeo "long enough to vouch for the state of cleanliness, lawlessness or intoxication of the participants," but she "was impressed by the bodies that littered Main Street shortly after midnight."[28]

The Salinas rodeo came up again nearly forty years later, as residents continued to defend the motorcyclists. Johnny Lamento, a retired local racer from the Hollister area who was twenty in 1947 and participated in some of the drag racing, admitted to a reporter for *Cycle* in 1987 that some participants were tossing bottles on to the pavement and "spinning circles in the street with their machines." But, he added, "the guys weren't vicious . . . [and] it really didn't get that much out of hand." His wife (who was his girlfriend at the time of the rally) explained that whether or not someone supported the motorcyclists depended upon his or her perspective. "A lot of merchants enjoyed having the rally come [to Hollister]," she said, "because the riders brought a lot of money to town," a point made in other accounts of the gathering. "But," she added, "a lot of townspeople are 'horsey people'—ranchers and horsey people do not like motorcycles." According to the reporter, Lamento nodded in agreement and then emphasized the same point about the rodeo Reynolds made four decades earlier. "Christ," Lamento exclaimed, "I remember the rodeo they used to have in Salinas years ago. You couldn't walk down the street after the parade there were so many beer bottles."[29]

As the comparison of Hollister to the Salinas rodeos suggests, motorcyclists, much like cowboys, were part of a larger culture of sporting men that had been an identifiable part of urban and rural spaces for more than a century before the rally. Although cowboys were commonly compared to motorcyclists (who rode chrome horses), plenty of other working men participated in similar social practices and cultural forms. This culture of sporting men revolved around homosocial spaces like saloons, brothels, cigar shops, all-male schools, military camps, and sporting events. These spaces were generally dominated by working-class single men—soldiers, sailors, itinerant laborers, and run-of-the-mill bachelors. This sporting culture exhibited a rough rather than a respectable aesthetic characterized by unruly and disorderly behavior that heightened an already acute sense of invulnerability and bravado that was routinely linked to alcohol consumption. Mutuality and reciprocity were also important parts of this culture, and participants practiced them through a number of different rituals: treating one another to rounds of drinks, participating in contests of strength and skill, boasting about sexual conquests, and collectively occupying public space and transgressing it. Indeed, the collective nature of these working-class men's day-to-day lives was so common that middle-class observers linked them (often mistakenly) to gangs, as they did motorcyclists. Women, too, were generally marginal to if not entirely absent from these spaces and certainly more conspicuous than consequential.[30] At Hollister, for example, the reporter C. J. Doughty estimated that 10 percent of the participants were women, but press reports generally depicted them as passengers, not riders, and our collective cultural memory of the event has focused overwhelming on the fact that some of them were topless.[31]

The comparisons between cowboys at the Salinas rodeo and motorcyclists at Hollister also raise questions about the line dividing deviant from normative behavior. Both groups were drunken and disorderly, but comments from the participants and the town's residents suggest that cowboys were less of a threat than their two-wheeled counterparts. Lamento's wife, for example, pointed out that ranchers and "horsey people" did not like motorcyclists, no doubt because noisy machines did not mix well with horses. We cannot, however, forget the broader ties these ranchers had to the community and its economic well-being. The yearly rodeo was as drunken and disorderly as the rally at Hollister, but the response to the cowboys' rowdy behavior reflected a familiarity that motorcyclists were incapable of reproducing because of the cowboy's cultural traditions and his closer connection to the town's economy.

Indeed, throughout the discussion of the rally, the town's residents seemed to be as concerned about the motorcyclists' relationship to the community as they were about their violation of its standards. For example, the local newspaper did not simply report on the unruly behavior but noted that the police charged the attendees "on miscellaneous counts varying from vagrancy to indecent exposure" and referred to the "law-breakers" as "drunks" and "vagrants."[32] Doughty claimed that the gypsy tour "brought the largest number of transients in recent history to Hollister,"[33] and in a *Hollister Free Lance* article on the Monday after the weekend rally the author commented that the completion of the races marked the official end of the rally and by that time "complete order had been restored among the transients."[34]

The terms "motorcyclist" and "transient" were not always used interchangeably. The *Hollister Free Lance* story described participants both as transients and as "cycle enthusiasts." The motorcycle appeared as the distinguishing feature that separated the merrymakers from the other participants, but the enthusiasm these men had for motorcycles did not erase the overwhelming stigma associated with transients. A year later, the words "hoodlum" and "tramp" appeared in the county sheriff's report about the Riverside Rally, highlighting the typical negative rhetoric used to characterize motorcyclists.[35] Other accounts simply emphasized the motorcyclist's point of origin and his mobility, which inadvertently emphasized his outsider status. In the case of Hollister, California appears in every list of states from which the participants came. Neighboring states such as Arizona and Nevada were also prominent. Other riders were from as far as Oregon, and some from as far east as Michigan.[36]

The words "transient" and "tramp" have a long and complicated history of association with words like "hobo," "vagrant," and "bum"—terms that not only denote an ambiguous and insufficient relationship to work but also associate motorcyclists with long-held fears of men who generally lived on the margins or outside the typical scrutiny associated with community life. The vagrant, for example, first appeared in the late Middle Ages as a consequence of social, economic, and political changes. During this period the manorial system, which rooted peasants to the land, was in decline, pushing growing numbers of men (and women) on to the mercy of a market economy. These "vagrants," also known as masterless men, were distinct from those traditionally accepted as poor because they were mobile, able-bodied, and fit for labor, hence a "new social problem." Masterless men, argues A. L. Beier, "represented mutability when those in power longed for stability."[37] Zygmunt Bauman asserts that "social order and control in the mid sixteenth century . . . was based on the collective gaze of the small and sealed community." The rise of "masterless men" in significant numbers "made this form of control redundant and necessitated new ways of making people accountable," hence the rise of poor laws, almshouses, and prisons. The rise of "masterless men," he continues, was "at the centre of the modern state."[38]

In his history of political repression, Michael Rogin also refers to "masterless men" in the context of the economic crisis of 1873 and the national railway strike of 1877. The crisis in 1873 led to worker uprisings, state-sponsored violence against labor, and a "tramp scare," as hundreds of thousands of workers roamed the country in search of work. Contemporaries blamed the growing numbers of tramps on industrial capitalism, which led to the breakdown of homogenous, ordered communities, but Rogin argues that the growing power of centralized corporations and "their need for a national market in labor and other commodities" was to blame.[39] New Jersey passed the first "tramp law" in 1876, and more states followed its lead over the next few decades. The Connecticut law of 1905, for example, stated that "any act of begging, or vagrancy, by any person not a resident of this state, shall be *prima facie* evidence that such a person is a tramp." In some states, if an individual was convicted for vagrancy, and in essence, defined as a tramp, he or she was hired out to whoever made the highest bid or was sold into servitude for a year.[40] Tramps were an unfortunate consequence not only of the instability of the emerging capitalist order but also of the surplus pool of labor needed to sustain it.

Instability characterized the next several decades for American workers, and these so-called masterless men continued to attract considerable scrutiny and comment. In his fascinating study of hobo workers at the turn of the twentieth century, Frank Tobias Higbie thoughtfully illuminates the conflict that developed between hobos and small-town America throughout the Midwest and discusses the free speech demonstrations they organized and participated in, their association with the Industrial Workers of the World, and the history of violence against them on America's railroads.[41] By the Great Depression and World War II, as millions of men and women left their homes in search of work, migrants attracted increasing attention, particularly in California, the destination of thousands of unemployed workers. John Steinbeck memorialized these Depression-era migrants in *The Grapes of Wrath*, which tells the story of the Joad family struggling to survive its migration to California.[42] Californians, in fact, organized what were known as bum blockades at the state border with Arizona and Nevada to try to stem the flow of Dust Bowl migrants.[43] These efforts were largely unsuccessful and ultimately futile with the onset of World War II.

Higbie notes that middle-class observers viewed these men as a problem because they violated conceptions of " 'normal sex,' that is normative heterosexuality," and they "undermined workers' commitment to wage labor." Simply put, they set a bad example for workers looking for a reason to quit their jobs. While Higbie provides a more nuanced interpretation of the hobo's threat than this brief summary suggests, he argues that a "working-class consciousness often was built around a desire to escape the labor market, a desire not to be a worker." As Higbie explains, "Just as full citizenship was contingent on such factors as sex, race and length of residence, the laboring man without property would hardly refuse work without also marking himself as outside of the community; a good citizen was one who would work, start a family, and stay put."[44]

The public's reaction to motorcyclists' ill behavior at the Hollister and Riverside rallies was reminiscent of the fears surrounding masterless men from previous generations of economic dispossession and explains the nonriding majority's tendency to associate all riders with transients and tramps. The hobo or transient's violation of middle-class notions of normative heterosexuality, for example, ranged from same-sex intimacies to other acts of nonmarital sex.[45] That motorcycling was almost universally identified with single men who had no obvious ties to a domestic setting in which normative sexuality was supposed to be confined was enough in the postwar era to raise a suspicious eyebrow or two. As Elaine Tyler May has shown, heterosexuality during the Cold War was inextricably tied to maturity, breadwinning, and domesticity, and these values stood in diametric opposition not only to homosexuality but also to the motorcyclist's lifestyle.[46] Initial accounts about the Hollister Rally alleged motorcyclists' indecent exposure, even identifying one of them by name.[47] Other accounts described topless women throwing beer bottles off of rooftops and public sexuality. One longtime Hollister resident recalled motorcyclists sleeping on the courthouse lawn and in residents' front yards and "lots of them, screwing right out there on the lawn."[48]

The motorcyclists at Hollister and Riverside fared no better when it came to their ties to the community and work. Other than the motorcycles the participants rode in on, visible signs of property or the means to support themselves were inconspicuous at best, and ties to the community were just as fleeting. Likely to have a bedroll strapped to the rear of their machines, the motorcyclists tended to depart as quickly and as abruptly as they had arrived. What appeared to be their general disdain for private property only emphasized their link to vagrancy, as did their obvious indifference to road rules, regulations, and other community standards. As they were depicted, these "outsiders," represented the antithesis of the work ethic around which these communities defined themselves.

The importance of their lack of ties to work and community also cannot be overstated in light of the racial homogeneity of the motorcyclists and of the town of Hollister. While a majority of the migrant workers in the state were either Mexican or Asian, only six percent of the rural population of San Benito County was counted as "other races" or black in the 1950 census, and only 1 percent of Hollister's population of 4,903 was counted as nonwhite.[49] Published names of those arrested and injured at the rally do include men and women with Hispanic surnames, but there is no evidence to suggest that they were motorcyclists.[50] Reliable statistics regarding the numbers of black and Hispanic riders for the immediate postwar years do not exist, but anecdotal evidence suggests they were rare.[51] The AMA, in fact, prohibited black riders from joining the organization until 1954, and the San Benita Ramblers, an AMA-affiliated club, sponsored the Hollister Rally.[52]

Reporter Doughty's comments also suggest that the line dividing transients from other migrants/itinerants was not as ambiguous as he understood it to be. For example, he noted that the rally brought more transients (that is, motorcyclists) to the city than had been seen in several years, suggesting a more haphazard or random pattern to their appearance than was the case with the seasonal laborers who profoundly shaped the state's agriculture. And the indifference of motorcyclists to the community's standards and values suggests a familiarity or tolerance not generally extended to men of color by residents of Hollister. The numbers of transients were evident, Doughty reported, by the "hundreds" who "slept in 'haystacks' . . . and in the city parks and squares."[53]

Life magazine's photograph of Eddie Davenport leaning back on a prewar Harley only exacerbated fears about the motorcyclist's disconnectedness from the community he was accused of "terrorizing," and proved the assumption that he was unemployed. Davenport's posture is the epitome of the "slouch" that Susan Bordo has identified with Marlon Brando and his interpretation of masculinity that other midcentury movie icons like James Dean would emulate. Bordo points specifically to Brando's portrayal of Stanley Kowalski in *A Streetcar Named Desire* (1951). Kowalski's childlike dependence on Stella, Bordo argues, exhibited a vulnerability that made him particularly attractive to female audiences. Kowalski also wore skin-tight dungarees (or jeans) at a time when men wore them baggy, and he sported a white, tight-fitting T-shirt that normally would have been worn underneath another shirt. Kowalski's "slouch" embodied his attitude, which ranged from indifferent to contemptuous and childlike, and was accompanied by a constant and inarticulate "mumbling" and a "smirk"—a physicality and style Brando adopted again for his role as Johnny Strabler, the motorcycle club leader in *The Wild One*.[54]

While Bordo claims that Brando represented something new, Kowalskis (and Davenports) had been on the streets of working-class communities for decades. The slouch was reminiscent of other working-class rebels, like the Bowery B'hoys of New York's Lower East Side during the nineteenth century and the Mexican American and African American zoot suiters about a century later. They were able-bodied men who were presumed to be unemployed, often linked to gangs and criminal activity, and distinctive for their dress and behavior. In his book *Race Rebels*, for example, Robin Kelley argues that the conked hair and other accoutrements of the zoot suit allowed men who adhered to this style to establish an identity based on something other than wage labor and to participate in an oppositional culture that emphasized pleasure over work.[55] Indeed, in

Marlon Brando as Johnny Strabler in *The Wild One*. Courtesy of Photofest, Inc.

the case of Bowery B'hoys, zoot suiters, and motorcyclists, attitude, dress, and posture are critical to understanding the ways in which they challenged normative assumptions about men's responsibilities and gender roles. While working men's and women's outright defiance in the form of strikes, boycotts, and clashes with police is important to understanding the struggle surrounding wage work, workers' subtle day-to-day resistance to workplace authority and discipline, what Kelley calls infrapolitics, is just as crucial even if it is much more difficult to detect, or even when workers

A motorcyclist being taken into police custody at Hollister in 1947 is dressed much like Brando's Johnny Strabler in *The Wild One*. © Corbis Images.

are completely removed from the shop floor. In response to the imposition of an industrial work ethic, men and women adopted a number of tactics to defy arbitrary management rules and the monotony of wage labor, including the inappropriate posture or slouch, the ill-timed smirk, and the inarticulate mumble. The slaves, migrant laborers, factory workers, and even the fast-food workers Kelley has studied used infrapolitics to shape the workplace and their relationship with bosses who tried to dismiss their behavior as laziness, undisciplined, or insubordination.[56] This attitude and body posture may have grown out of the conflict surrounding work, but it also profoundly shaped the ways in which working men and women fiercely laid claim to leisure spaces and the manner in which they fought to preserve them.

The use of the terms "transient," "vagrant," and "tramp" to describe motorcyclists confirmed this connection even as it presented a different challenge and even if a direct connection to the workplace was missing. If the transient, as Higbie argues, was a constant reminder of the average worker's desire to escape the labor market, the motorcyclist was the example of what a successful escape looked like. The motorcyclist's slouch (on or off his bike), in other words, was not intended simply to contest control over the workplace but to reject any connection or allegiance to it. In *The Wild One*, Brando's Johnny mumbles "Whadda ya got" when he's asked What are you rebelling against? and critics/observers have used his response to characterize the outlaw's indifference.[57] But the motorcyclist's rebelliousness was much more focused than Johnny's comment suggested. The slouch that had evolved into a distinctive masculinity and rebellion had its roots in the centuries-old struggles over who controlled the workplace and remained tied to ideas about work even though the rebellion was most visible outside of it.

The broader context in which motorcyclists attracted national attention only exacerbated the fear surrounding his link to transients and increased its appeal. Because of his mobility, the motorcyclist was less likely than the working-class rebels from earlier decades to be connected to the community he was considered a threat to, and his ambivalence about work coincided with a period of exceptional economic opportunity for wage workers. While Americans feared a return to depression after World War II, the economy experienced unprecedented expansion. Union membership reached an all-time high by the early 1950s, homeownership became a reality for the first time for a significant number of working men and women, and full-time, full employment became the government's solution for ensuring economic prosperity and stability. Benjamin Kline Hunnicutt argues that during the Depression and in response to labor's push for a shorter workweek, the Roosevelt administration "committed the federal government to the emerging belief that progress was perpetual economic growth and Full-Time, Full Employment—the tenets of the new economic gospel of consumption" that had emerged after World War I. In support of this vision, the government committed its resources to stimulus spending, budget deficits, and liberal Treasury policies. This shift in the government's role profoundly shaped its response to the Depression—that is, public works projects or what were referred to as "investments in the future." And it set the stage for the Cold War—perpetual military mobilization and a renewed emphasis on domesticity, breadwinning, and national security.[58] Full employment and its corollary, consumption, then, became linked to ideas about national purpose, social belonging, and citizenship. A good citizen was a good producer, fully employed, and a good consumer. Because the motorcyclist was neither, his rebellion and the threat he posed had as much to do with what he was not—not a member of the community and not a worker—than with his rowdy and seemingly lawless behavior.

At the same time, the motorcyclist was unique because of his motorcycle and the manner in which he manipulated this technology to heighten his presence, his style, and his rebellion. Scholars who have examined the Hollister Rally have generally dismissed it without considering the motorcyclist's larger relationship to the community, and they have cited the *Life* magazine photograph as an example of the sensationalism surrounding riders because it was staged.[59] Apparently an overzealous photographer swept together the bottles of beer to play on fears of drunk and disorderly conduct. One source even claims that Davenport was not a motorcyclist but simply a passerby who was convinced to pose for the picture. Davenport thus was the unsuspecting participant in a journalistic ruse to arouse passions and to elicit the scandalous.[60] Does it really matter, though, that Davenport may not have been a motorcyclist, and (except for the beer bottles) would the picture have looked any different if it had not been staged? Davenport's legs are stretched forward past where they would normally be if he was riding the bike and he is leaning back to one side, but his posture is not all that different than the typical rider at rest in any given context. To a certain extent, the rider's body conforms to the motorcycle's design whether at rest or in motion. High, curved handlebars were standard on stock Harley or Indian motorcycles at the time, and the bike's footboards or pegs were located toward the front of the motorcycle's frame, so the rider had to stretch his legs forward to reach them. The rider's posture, the familiar slouch, further emphasized a body at rest and confirmed the motorcyclist's connection to other men (transients) whose separation from the community and unemployment were prominent.[61] Discussions about American workers during the Depression and the years following World War II—whether they be industrial workers or farmers—called to mind words like independent, strong, resilient, and hardworking—words and men who stood in sharp contrast to the motorcyclist's image at Hollister and in *Life* magazine—lazy and self-indulgent but also carefree and comfortable. The contrast helps explain why some residents described the motorcyclist as a challenge to the community and its values and why others accepted him as a welcome break from them.[62]

The motorcycle in the *Life* magazine photograph was called a "bobbed" or "chopped" cycle. In 1950 the editor of *Cycle* magazine singled out the two most popular styles that referred to the rider's dress and his cycle, the Eastern Marcel and the Western Bob. The Eastern Marcel (also referred to as a garbage wagon) was associated with "the great majority of motorcycle riders in the eastern and midwestern sections of the country." Rider and motorcycle would be conspicuously overdressed, the rider wearing

The famous *Life* magazine picture of Eddie Davenport aboard a prewar Harley at Hollister in 1947. © Corbis Images.

a shiny, chrome-studded leather jacket and a cap (often a soft, rounded cap or a muir cap), and the motorcycle weighed down with plenty of chrome-plated attachments.[63] The editor described the Western Bob or West Coast Bob as the "jackets and Levis get-up," which he claimed was the preferred attire of most West Coast riders. The rider sporting this style rode a stripped-down version of a stock model: no fenders or only

Jack Troop competing in a hill-climbing contest on a Harley in the early 1950s. Note the bobbed fenders and other modifications that helped make the bike suitable for off-road riding. Courtesy of Don Troop.

"bobbed" fenders; no factory-installed headlight, only a small, lightweight fog light; no primary chain covers; foot pegs rather than footboards; and absolutely no chrome. In a letter to *Cycle* in March of 1954, R. O. Des Marias of Lompoc, California, explained that a "chopped or bobbed motor is just what the word implies. Chop everything off that you don't need. . . . "There is no special way to do it. Just strip your motor as though you were getting it ready for competition, but still legal enough for the road." "One way to start," he noted, "is to take off the back fender and replace it with the front fender with the leading edge at the top of the wheel only in reverse. This way there is no wind resistance to the front wheel. Put the rear fender in your garage."[64]

Since bikes built specifically for off-road riding were not widely available until the 1960s,[65] chopping or bobbing the bike lightened the load and made it suitable for most riding conditions. As Des Marias put it, a rider "strips and chops [his bike] so if he wants to drag, cross-up, broadside, trail ride, hill climb, etc., he can."[66] The style was particularly suited for California, where it supposedly originated. As one rider explained, the state had "an immense amount of distance between towns of representative size," and it was "festooned with super highways from top to bottom and side to side." Riders could also take advantage of "a year-around riding climate," and the "mountains, deserts, beaches, and Hollywood" provided the "destination of countless trips."[67] A bobbed or chopped bike was simply easier to maneuver than other bikes and suitable for about any riding situation, including drag races down Hollister's and Riverside's main streets.

The riders identified with the Western Bob and a chopped bike became linked to racing and stunt riding in the postwar years, to the image of countless 1950s rebels, and to a vigorous and rebellious masculinity. Fred Traylor of Los Angeles, for example, admonished readers of *Motorcyclist* "not [to] react too hastily to the popular picture of a drunken 'hound' which appeared in 'Life' magazine." "In all fairness to 'Life,'" he argued, the "rider does accurately represent [a] strong (and noisy) minority." "There are riders who are rough and noisy—and crude, lots of them," he explained, comparing them to those who frequently appeared in AMA publications as the ideal motorcyclist, adding, "It is not the effete minority that crowds the highways (except on nice clear days) riding in pretty 'bloomer-girl' formation—their fancy pants all colorful and natty."[68]

Indeed, their rebellion was as much about their carefree attitude and the joy of riding than the unruly behavior for which they had become known. Des Marias, for example, stressed that the "chop" was "not for style and show" but for "comfort and pleasure," and Fred Traylor described the Hollister weekend as "good natured relaxation." The "horseback rider of one hundred years ago," he asserted, was the motorcyclist's nineteenth-century counterpart. He, too, would get "red-eyed and drunkenly shoot-up a saloon," which "also typified good natured relaxation, 'Western-style.'"[69] Des Marias focused more on riding his bike than Traylor did, and neither explicitly linked motorcycling to their working lives. But the nonriding public's use of the term "transient" suggests that they saw a connection. It was a connection that served as the basis for their complaints about motorcyclists' behavior and their comparison of them to other groups of single, able-bodied men. The drunk and disorderly behavior of men in Salinas was typical at the yearly rodeo, but these were men who had ties to the community and presumably (because of their link to horses) were willfully employed.

Bobbed cycles date back to the 1920s and 1930s, but Hollister marked the moment that the style attracted national attention and just as it was becoming a distinctly American one. Scholars agree that what could be defined as a motorcycle appeared in the second half of the nineteenth century, and it is generally described as a bicycle with an internal combustion engine or machine. By the early twentieth century a number of technological breakthroughs occurred in frame design, suspension, ignition, and carburation that, in addition to distinguishing the motorcycle from the bicycle and automobile, made the motorcycle more reliable and smoother running than previous incarnations. A number of inventors and companies emerged during these early years. Indian, founded in 1901, and Harley-Davidson, founded in 1903, are the two most notable examples in the United States.[70] These early cycles, or "lightweights," were slowly replaced by bigger, more powerful models, and by 1930 lightweights had practically disappeared from the American market. After World War II and with congressional efforts to liberalize trade relations, a new breed of lightweights, notably from British manufacturers—BSA, Vincent, Triumph, and Norton, to name just a few—began to have a noticeable impact on the American market.[71] They stood out from their American counterparts in two ways. British bikes were known as lightweights because they had an engine displacement of 350 cubic centimeters (ccs) or less and were considerably smaller than the American-made Harleys and Indians. Two of the basic Harleys available in the 1940s were the 61-inch and 74-inch Knuckleheads, which were 1000ccs and 1200ccs, respectively.[72] These cycles also featured a different basic design and hence required the rider to be in a different position on the bike. While the rider of an American-made Harley or Indian appeared as if he was sitting at rest or upright with a noticeable slouch, British motorcycles had flat or straight handle bars, and the foot pegs were in a high or "far-back position" that forced the rider into a "crouching-forward" posture, thus mitigating wind resistance and enhancing the motorcycles' speed. Today's sport bikes (often called "crotch rockets") require a similar position.[73]

To be sure, some British cycles more clearly embraced this posture than others. Vincent motorcycles, for example, were notorious for handlebars that were almost entirely straight or flat, and in the debates about these differences, riders had a tendency to exaggerate them. But a clear distinction between bikes was noticeable in the postwar period, and it profoundly shaped the development of motorcycle culture. In a 1952 issue of *Cycle*, James Rand, a self-described "Limey," for example, complained about what people considered the mechanical superiority of American-made products and objected to what he described as "those awful antediluvian pre-1918 handlebars." He made fun of the handlebars on American bikes, which produced a posture "known over here some thirty-odd years gone as the 'sit up and beg décor'" and derided the position of the rider's legs, which were "thrust positively before them like wax figures lain in armchairs." He added, "Surely you would not expect the winner of your Kentucky Derby to hurry past the post sitting bolt upright—albeit with bended neck—and above all with his legs thrust gawkingly before him."[74] In response to Rand, Bob Godfrey of Wilmette, Illinois, referred to English handlebars as "those stubby little back breakers" and emphasized that with flat bars a "rider's arms are in a position which is almost (mind I say almost) parallel to the front fork tubes," which meant that the "shock from the front wheel is transmitted directly to the rider's arms and shoulders." The high bars typical of American cycles placed the rider's arms "out in front of him, in a position which allows the shoulder joints to act as they were designed to function i.e., hingewise." "Tell me, sir," Godfrey asked, referring to the British, "do you relax by going into a sprint-runner crouch? You don't? Then why sit in that position on your cycle?" Godfrey concluded his letter with a jab at the size of British cycles and of the men riding them. The "non-riding masses over here," he suspected, "must be under the impression that English motorists are all of the 5 foot 2 inch 96 pound variety because of the diminutive size of the machine itself."[75]

The motorcyclists at Hollister and Riverside were certainly rowdy and at times disrespectable and loud. But the typical memory of Hollister and the supposedly violent antics in which motorcyclists participated have overshadowed the rally, its participants, and the town's response to them. Bobbed or chopped bikes date back to the 1920s and 1930s, but it was only after the war that the motorcyclist attracted greater scrutiny and after nearly two decades of depression and war that complicated day-to-day community life and work. Bobbed cycles had a particular function. They were leaner and faster, easier to maneuver on or off the road, and better suited for drag racing and stunt riding than a stock Harley or garbage wagon. The ways in which these men rode their bikes alone posed a challenge to Hollister's residents. Yet the way residents responded to the rally's participants suggests that more was at issue than motorcyclists' violation of the town's traffic rules and regulations. They were considered transients who had shaped the state's cultural and material landscape over the preceding decades. They were men Hollister's residents were most familiar with outside the workplace even though they were perceived to be a critical challenge to it. Hollister's residents were accustomed to disorderly and drunken groups of men, but only during momentary breaks from the everyday routine of making ends meet and the other obligations they associated with citizenship. The motorcyclist was as disconnected from Hollister as the transients who wandered through the town from time to time, but his unemployment was even more egregious because he had no connection to the factories or fields to which he posed a threat. Charges that the motorcyclists at Hollister were violent did occasionally creep into discussions about them in the press, but those claims were exaggerated and the broader context surrounding those few instances were generally ignored. The violence that has become the dominant characteristic associated with riders did not emerge until the mid-1960s and against the backdrop of growing concerns about law and order.

THE "OUTLAW" OF THE 1960S

The 1960s was one of the most dynamic decades in U.S. history and one of the most dynamic periods of growth and change for motorcycling. By the end of the 1960s the number of registered bikes was increasing at an unprecedented pace, dirt bikes for the first time represented a new market, foreign motorcycle manufacturers like Honda had become household names, the men and women attracted to motorcycling were more diverse than in any previous decade, and the motorcyclist increasingly became known as a biker. The biker shared many characteristics with his counterparts from Hollister and Riverside, but the most notable exception was his violence.

The violence attributed to the motorcyclist often appeared as incoherent and as irrational as the men accused of committing it, but certain patterns are noticeable, and in some cases the motorcycle played a conspicuous role. A common scenario featured two (or more) motorcycle clubs (or what were typically referred to as "gangs") battling against one another without any clear reasons or motives. In Cleveland in 1971, for example, the police charged fifty-six members of "two rival motorcycle gangs" (the Hells Angels and the Breed) with "first degree murder and [riot]" after a brawl "broke out in a hall in which a motorcycle custom and trade show was being held." The charges stemmed from what a press report called "a knife and chain-wielding [r]umble in which five cyclists were killed and injured." Lieutenant Ralph Joyce, head of the homicide squad, believed that the Breed planned the violence in a push for power against the Hells Angels. Three Breed members and two Hells Angels were stabbed to death during the brawl, and police suspected more to follow.[76]

Another increasingly common story included the innocent bystander who became the target of a motorcycle club in the pursuit of some other crime. In Long Beach, California, in 1972, for example, three motorcyclists allegedly broke into Judy Goss's apartment and tortured her sailor boyfriend, Richard Turner, so that he would transfer ownership of his new car to them. To that end, they stripped off Turner's shirt and carved " 'criss-cross' squares on his back and poured salt in his wounds."

The pain was "so acute," that Turner allegedly capitulated to their demands. Unbeknownst to the assailants, Goss was able to "slip" out of the apartment and notify a neighbor, who called the police.[77]

Prior to the 1960s and 1970s, guns and drugs had been nonexistent in articles about motorcyclists. In an article titled "Bikers & the Law," Bill Dobbins discussed his interview with Bob L'Etoile, an investigator with the Los Angeles Police Department whose primary responsibility was to keep track of Southern California "motorcycle gangs." According to L'Etoile, the most "common offense" linked to motorcyclists was "ADW, assault with a deadly weapon" as well as "narcotics [possession]; murder; [and] quite a few rapes." Dobbins responded to L'Etoile's contention by noting that an "old time biker once told me he thought the main difference between gangs in the fifties and current groups is money; back in the fifties it was hard to earn much money, while today a guy can get a pretty good job and put some bucks in his pocket." L'Etoile agreed and noted another difference: "sophistication." "Some of the crimes he ascribes to bikers," Dobbins explained, "require complex organization, like smuggling and dealing narcotics and trading in automatic weapons. This, he says, would have been unheard of only ten years ago."[78]

Other stories bring to mind the term "unimaginable" to describe the behavior attributed to motorcyclists and their alleged crimes. In 1969 Sarah Jane Stewart and Dore Anthony de Madona, who was described as "a member of the Hell's Angels motorcycle gang," were accused of selling their four-month-old baby son to a Glendale family for "$700 to buy a motorcycle."[79] In October of 1972, Los Angeles sheriff Peter Pitchess issued a bulletin warning officers "to guard against possible hazardous conditions in traffic stops of outlaw motorcycle riders. We have received information of motorcycle handlebars and foot pedals being rigged to fire shotgun shells."[80] In July of 1972, nineteen-year-old Nancy Mabel Botelho was fatally wounded after a bullet struck her in the neck. Botelho was simply driving her car by a "tavern hangout for the Hells Angels."[81] In Titusville, Florida, in 1967, three cyclists known as Spider, Super Squirrel, and Fast Frank were imprisoned for allegedly "nailing an 18-year-old-girl to a tree because she flunked a motorcycle gang prostitution assignment." In response, Florida's governor declared a war on what he called motorcycle "bums" and visited a bar called Kitty's, a known "motorcycle gang hangout," where he told the unfortunate motorcyclists who happened to be at the bar when he made his auspicious appearance that "law and order is the order of the day in Florida." Within the week, the governor "vowed" to "make living in Florida so unpleasant [for motorcyclists] that they will go back home," presuming, of course, that all motorcyclists in Florida were either from other states or just the "bums" he associated with violence.[82]

The stunt rider or motorcycle daredevil also gained national fame and notoriety at the same time the "outlaw" motorcyclist emerged. While daredevil riders have been around since the motorcycle first appeared on city streets at the turn of the century, by the late 1960s and early 1970s, the stunt rider had become the main attraction in packed auditoriums across the country; he was no longer just a carnival side show or a distraction on America's roadways.[83] The best known is Evel Knievel, who first attracted national attention when he attempted to jump over the fountains at Caesar's Palace in 1967.[84] Other, lesser known, daredevils included Wicked Ward, who in the late 1960s successfully jumped his bike over twenty cars; Super Joe Einhorn, who surpassed Knievel's 155-foot jump; and even women riders.[85] Still others remained nameless but are just as important to the growing discussion about motorcyclists. In 1972, for example, a promoter for the Sportsman's Paradise resort in Greenfield, Indiana, promised a cash prize of $10,000 to any rider who could successfully jump what at the time was the unimaginable distance of 200 feet from one ramp to another. Twenty-four motorcyclists attempted the stunt, and they all failed.[86]

The violence associated with the motorcyclist was inextricably bound to these daredevil stunts and their hazards. Photographs of successful jumps commonly showed riders suspended in flight over what seemed like an endless and insurmountable line of cars. The pictures of defeat were even more difficult to ignore. Some photographs featured the disfigured daredevil strapped helplessly to a hospital bed or lying motionless and crumpled on the asphalt floor of a stadium full of anxious onlookers. Other pictures showed the daredevil's motorcycle crashed on the ground with the rider flying aimlessly through the air. A Columbus, Georgia, reporter commenting on Bob Pleso's failed attempt to complete a 200-foot jump in 1971, said that "he just flew up in the air, his arms and legs straight out; he looked like a rag doll." Before his jump, Pleso had called Knievel a "con artist" who had never cleared more than twenty-one cars and claimed, by contrast, that he had "walked away from every jump and [had] no broken bones." After the failed jump, Pleso was pronounced dead on arrival at a local hospital.[87] Five of the riders who attempted the 200-foot jump at the Sportsman's Paradise were seriously injured, two of them "possibly paralyzed by back injuries." The resort voluntarily stopped the jumps, what Sheriff Robert Sebastian suggested were "leading young men to slaughter." But a scheduled land-to-water jump competition would still take place at the resort, and the owner, John Copenhaver, stated that twenty-six riders had agreed to try it.[88]

Knievel's violence off his bike further contributed to his notoriety (and to that of motorcyclists in general). In addition to physically attacking other motorcyclists, hippies, and an occasional reporter, Knievel brawled with the Hells Angels. A caller to a popular San Francisco radio talk show in 1970 recounted a melee at one of Knievel's jumps. Reportedly, Knievel had made an "obscene gesture at a group that had been heckling him prior to his 11-automobile jump." The group in question were Hells Angels who were on hand to witness the stunt. "On this," the caller continued, "a Hell's Angel attacked, and fights broke out all over Cow Palace." The fights were quickly broken up, but "one participant was carried away on a stretcher." At some point in the past, according to Knievel, the Hells Angels had made abusive remarks challenging his courage.[89]

The ongoing debate about what type of threat motorcyclists posed ebbed and flowed throughout the 1960s and 1970s even as the violence attributed to them seemed to be escalating, but motorcyclists have consistently disputed claims that their culture was antisocial, violent, or suicidal. One way to counter these claims was to highlight their contributions to charitable organizations. In 1948 the Lexington Eagles MC (motorcycle club) in Kentucky sponsored a TT (time trial) race "for the benefit of crippled children." "They Rode That Children May Walk," announced an article covering the event. The author explained, "There is a growing trend for motorcycle clubs to realize the opportunities they have for helping others" and added that "a number of clubs have [also] run races for [the] benefit of the American Cancer Fund, another very worthy cause."[90] Two decades later these types of activities remained popular. In 1970, the *San Francisco Examiner* described the Salinas Ramblers as a club that "doesn't make headlines through the lawlessness of its membership." The club's sixty-five members "have started participating in community affairs around Salinas," including a TT scramble racing event that was "strictly a benefit program to aid cerebral palsy victims."[91]

Another way motorcyclists countered the claims that they were violent was through their occasional appearance in the same newspapers that were guilty of sensationalizing the behavior attributed to them. In 1958, reporter Robert Ruark received a stern reprimand from Jules Goldstein of the National Outerwear and Sportswear Association Inc. for referring to some young men as "bums" and as "hoods" because of their "leather-jackets and blue-jeans."[92] In 1966 John M. Gantner sent a letter to the *San Francisco Examiner*'s editor to lodge a similar complaint about the association of leather jackets with motorcycle gangs. "When will people realize that the leather jacket, along with the safety helmet, is the motorcyclist's equivalent of the seat belt," he asked? "In case of a fall, leather protects against heavy abrasions."[93] In an interview with stunt rider Wicked Ward as he was recovering from a near-fatal stunt gone awry, he explained that nonriders had often mistaken him for an outlaw and that he had become a daredevil to counter these stereotypes. "I was a foolish kid in Buffalo, N.Y., who wanted to read my name in the papers," and "to try and change the image [of] what motorcycling should be about. Everyone that rides a motorcycle is not a hoodlum—a bum. They are good, hardworking people—with families."[94]

Still other examples of motorcyclists defending their reputation can be found in the numerous memoirs and travelogues motorcyclists have published over the years. Daniel Wolf, an anthropologist and motorcyclist who rode with the Rebels Motorcycle Club of Edmonton, Canada, specifically challenged Sheriff Pitchess's contention that motorcyclists converted parts of their bikes into concealed weapons. Wolf recalled an officer pulling him over and "very cautiously stepp[ing] around the front of my bike while 'casting out' the handlebars, and I wondered whether he had seen [the] information film that had been circulated to various police departments." Wolf added, "Knowing that exhaust pipes get hot to the point where steel and chrome discolour, [I] would get awfully nervous about riding behind a biker who had converted his pipes into a shotgun." He also wondered about hitting too big of a bump with "a 12-gauge shotgun shell [held] lightly against a homemade firing pin." Wolf was tempted to tell the cop that that part of the film was more science fiction than fact, but the "best–quickest—approach under these circumstances is to keep one's mouth shut and avoid eye contact."[95] In his recent book about his membership in the Outlaws Motorcycle Club, John Hall also challenged the assumption that motorcyclists were responsible for the drugs that were destroying working-class communities. Smith notes that "between drugs, the collapse of heavy industry, and racial violence, whole communities like Newark, New Jersey, Homestead and Norristown, Pennsylvania, and Greenpoint, Maspeth, and Ridgewood, New York, turned from being decent working-class neighborhoods into shitholes, often only in a matter of months. Bikers didn't make the shit [drugs]," he added; "they just got caught up in it like everyone else."[96]

Despite the efforts to differentiate the outlaw from the law-abiding rider, the nonriding public generally failed to accept an image of motorcycling that contradicted these stereotypes and refused to accept that the alleged crimes were perpetrated by a small minority of motorcyclists. George Adler, for example, was a BMW rider who frequently commuted the forty-one miles from New Brunswick, New Jersey, to New York and was all too familiar with the nonriding public's habit of viewing him as a violent outlaw. In a letter to *Cycle* magazine, he sarcastically explained, "I too have experienced the conflict between my presence and the drivers who fear me because I (1) might be about to rape and pillage or (2) have just completed raping and pillaging."[97] Dick Flowers of Columbus, Ohio, made a similar argument by contrasting 1%ers with what he suggested was a "typical" or "average" rider: "It's a shame when the kid on his way to school or the accountant on his way to the office, deciding to ride his bike, will suddenly find his neighbors looking with fearful eyes," asking themselves, "Isn't that Honda, Triumph or Yamaha, just like those glossy gassers?," a reference to choppers that were almost always linked to "outlaw" motorcyclists.[98]

Other riders offered explicit examples of how the nonriding public's confusion compromised their mobility or of what a writer at *Cycle* referred to as a "police mentality." In his interview with Dobbins, Bob L'Etoile explained that the police officers tasked with monitoring gang activity assisted other law-enforcement agencies by getting "to know each person [motorcyclist who was thought to be a gang member] AS a person." It broke "down the anonymous cloak of the gang," according to L'Etoile, and helped avoid what he suggested was common: "the biker . . . is pulled in by some anxious gung-ho local cop who can't tell a Hells Angel from a boy scout and decides to lock up anything and everything that looks like a motorcycle outlaw."[99] Gordon Jennings of *Cycle*, who was reacting to a headline about the police and motorcyclists at the annual motorcycle rally at Laconia (New Hampshire), shared this view. "The police were looking for 'Hell's Angels,'" he explained, "and seemed to be under the impression that anyone on or near a motorcycle could turn in to one of these fearful creatures, complete with tattoos, dangling swastika and a bone through the nose, by shouting Shazam."[100] Marvin Blown of Brooklyn, New York, began his letter to *Cycle* in January 1968 by asking, "How do I get these cops off my back?" Blown explained that he was riding down the Belt Parkway when a cop pulled up alongside him and motioned him to pull over. "He gives me a speeding ticket for doing 55 in a 50 and then tells me 'all cyclists are wise-guys anyway!'" The next night Blown was "popping along as usual" and another cop stopped him and gave him another ticket, saying, "I only stopped you because you were on a bike." Blown added, "Whenever I ride down through the Village I get stopped on every corner. They take my license and they stand there for a good 45 minutes giving me the baloney about getting fined 100 dollars for not having a motorcycle license (my license is good till 1969) and where did you get this license? . . . [I am] not a reckless driver. It's just that the N.Y. City police has [a] real thing for motorcycles." The harassment, Blown admitted, "really burns the . . . [shit?] out of me."[101]

The public's tendency to see all riders as outlaws was also noticeable in discussions about the motorcycle daredevil. Howard Cosell admitted that when he was assigned to cover one of Knievel's jumps in 1974 he did "not relish the assignment," had convinced himself "that motorcycle leaping was for kooks, and that it was beneath my dignity to report the event." He also had "a preconceived image of Evel that was distasteful. You know what I mean: the black leather jacket, the boots, the gloves, the kind of image conjured up by Marlon Brando in *The Wild One*, or by the marauding motorcycle gang called the 'Hell's Angels'; rebels without a cause, a danger to society, violent, a bad influence on young people and all the rest." When he met Knievel, Cosell was "surprised." He explained that not only was Knievel's speech "excellent" and "his grammar good," but that "he was not as I had envisioned: cocky, tough and defiant. On the contrary, I discovered he was a most attractive man with sensitive eyes, very light brown hair, a face and mouth that seemed too soft for the daredevil character he portrays, and he was dressed in white, almost carefully so."[102] Before David Lyle of *Esquire* met Knievel in 1969, about a year after he failed to stick the landing at Caesar's Palace, he had already concluded that he was about to meet a "Lee Marvin character burst full-blown," a reference to Marvin's role as the "outlaw," Chino, in *The Wild One*. When Lyle met Knievel, he must have appeared surprised because Knievel said, "I know exactly what you thought before you came out here, Dave. You thought, This is going to be some crazy long-haired son of a bitch—some Hell's Angel type."[103]

The public's increasingly vocal fear that all motorcyclists were outlaws suggests a discernable shift in the public's view of motorcycling sometime between the end of the Hollister Rally and the mid-1960s. To be sure, the leather-jacketed motorcyclist who became the face of the 1950s rebel cannot be overlooked. In her history of the teenager in America, Grace Palladino notes that "no one knew what teenage rebels looked like until Marlon Brando played the sullen leader of a motorcycle gang in the 1953 hit *The Wild One*."[104] Yet during the ten to fifteen years after the Hollister and Riverside rallies, contemporaries were just as likely to suggest that the outlaw had faded from view and that images of respectable motorcyclists were just as common if not more common than the Brando image of the rebel. Lily Phillips has noted that from 1947 to 1954, the *Reader's Guide to*

Periodical Literature "lists only technological developments . . . and racing information . . . connected to motorcycling."[105] The stories she refers to in the *Reader's Guide* typically focused on the motorcycle's utility, ignored Hollister and Riverside, and argued that the menace that was evident in previous years had all but disappeared. *American City*, a trade publication focusing on day-to-day management of cities and other urban issues, included articles about motorcycle cops and their efforts to curb traffic violations. Articles with titles like "Motorcycles Save Policeman Power" or "One Motorcycle Is Worth Six Cars in Traffic Control" emphasized the motorcycle's efficiency compared to autos and were often accompanied by photographs of police officers in neatly pressed uniforms lined up on the side of the street with their gleaming cycles.[106] Other publications featured stories about young craftsmen who had built motorbikes from scrap or had rigged up a scooter for hill-climbs or some other purpose. Stories of racing were also prominent and featured the trials and tribulations riders faced, racing's physical demands, and discussions about the mechanical know-how racers needed to keep their machines running. Young daredevils also graced the pages of *Life* magazine in the late 1940s. At the age of four, *Life* reported, "little Donny Emory took his first ride on a motorcycle and staked out his claim to be the youngest motorcyclist in the world." Two years later, he was described as a "veteran stunt rider and racing driver who can speed along standing up on the seat, skid-turn, ride sidesaddle and win races with the best of them."[107]

A *Popular Science* article in 1954 actually claimed that "Delinquency on Wheels" had been "halted." Once again, Hollister was the place it all began or what the author referred to as "a new low-watermark in [the] motorcyclists' roughneck reputation." The author complained that "more than one community suffered under the impact of roughneck cycle invasions" and that the nonriding public "almost universally disliked" motorcyclists. A "war" soon began between motorcyclists, who "traveled in groups or gangs," and cops, who "took grim pleasure in arresting riders for the slightest infractions." "Running feuds between ranchers and homesteaders," the author concluded, "never held a candle to the undeclared war in California . . . between cops and motorcyclists." Seven years later, the author contended, the tension between cops and motorcyclists was hardly noticeable. Arrests for noisy pipes and other infractions were increasingly rare, accidents and motorcycle rider fatalities had dropped significantly, and "peace prevail[ed]" between the police, motorcyclists, and the nonriding public.[108]

Narrowing down the specific moment that violence became the motorcyclist's defining characteristic is, to say the least, complicated. Renowned student of U.S. language, Peter Tamony, notes in his correspondence with Birney Jarvis, a *San Francisco Chronicle* reporter whom Tamony described as a founding member of the San Francisco chapter of the Hells Angels (1954), that the "outlaw" motorcyclist was born in 1953 with the release of *The Wild One*. According to Tamony, *The Wild One* was the "turning point in 'operation' and 'performance' of motorcyclists." After members of the Hells Angels saw the film, Jarvis argued, "many [of them] thought they should be BEATNIK, dirty types, and that tough image became the norm." Tamony who studied the origins of the name Hells Angels argued that 1957 was the year that violence became associate with the motorcycle club. He explained that a club was formed in San Francisco in 1954 with a membership of fifteen. "Until about 1957," he continued, "mention in the San Francisco press was of 'motorcyclists' and 'a motorcycle club.' After that time, the club apparently became notorious for members' criminal and antisocial activities because "depredators, disrupters of the peace, and perpetrators of deviate sexual outrages were general[ly] reported as Hell's Angels."[109] Hunter S. Thompson, on the other hand, argued that the 1965 Monterey rape case was the moment when the Hells Angels acquired the national infamy that follows the club today. "Until the Monterey rape," Thompson argued, "they were bush-league hoods known only to California cops and a few thousand cycle buffs . . . and nobody else cared."[110]

The three men's claims about the moment violence became linked to motorcyclists do not necessarily contradict one another. *The Wild One* may have been the turning point, as Jarvis suggested, although he does not describe them as violent, and the local and national press had no reason to pick up on any change in behavior until a significant single event captured their attention or until a particularly astute reporter noticed a pattern taking shape and pieced together a national trend. Either way, the defining moment or time frame they favored suggests that the Hollister and Riverside rallies did not establish the image of the uncompromising and violent outlaw who would become identified with the 1960s and be routinely mistaken for the Hells Angels and other 1%er clubs. That association emerged ten to fifteen years later with the help of a press that had a knack for sensationalizing the crimes cyclists had allegedly committed and for ignoring both the contradictory evidence that challenged the notion of motorcyclists' lawlessness and the larger population of riders who stood in diametric opposition to the outlaw.

Indeed, though the movies of the postwar years showed motorcyclists to be rebellious, the critical reception reveals that their portrayal was not without nuance. Reviewers of *The Wild One* were certainly critical of motorcyclists, describing them with the usual flare for the absurd: "be-bopping hoodlums," a "trouble-hungry sickle club of teen-age boys," and "motorized wolves" who "resent discipline and show an aggressive contempt for common decency and the police."[111] Yet critics' objections to the movie suggest that the film's motorcyclists did not elicit as much fear and loathing as discussions of *The Wild One* have assumed. One reviewer complained that the film made the town's residents out to be as much to blame for the chaos as the motorcyclists. "The script," complained another critic, "makes a couple of pious passes at point-ing a moral. . . . It says that the community—the greedy tavern keeper, a weak cop, some hotheaded and vicious citizens—is as much to blame for what happens as the young delinquents are, but it is hard to believe in such talk." "After building up such a violent case against his hell-raisers," another reviewer asserted, "Mr. Kramer's picture makes the well-meaning townspeople just as unpleasant as their visitors, thus knocking the props out from under whatever point the film has. . . . In the end, *The Wild One* says that the law, as it now exists, renders it impossible to deal with such a hoodlum outbreak and these pseudo-Fascists are allowed to ride off on their 'sickles' like so many invincible S.S. men."[112]

Did the movie blur distinctions between motorcyclists and the towns-folk, who reviewers described as vigilantes, irresponsible, violent, and out of control (as well as comical)? Or were critics upset because the blurring of those lines made the outlaw look much better than he actually was or what critics thought he should look like? Either way, criticism about *The Wild One* suggests that the film, like the Hollister and Riverside rallies, did not establish as rigid a divide between motorcyclists and the nonriding majority as some have claimed. In *The Wild One*, Marlon Brando's club was presented as the lesser of two evils when compared to Chino (Lee Marvin's character), but neither members of the club nor Chino seemed all that different from the townsfolk, who were portrayed as just as culpa-ble as the motorcyclists critics wanted to demonize.

Press coverage of motorcycle rallies in the early 1960s was also similar in tone to that of Hollister and Riverside. At the 1960 state fair in Springfield, Illinois, where a national championship motorcycle race was taking place, ninety-two cyclists were thrown into jail for "staging" what the press called a "midnight jamboree through downtown Springfield." According to one report, the motorcyclists "started racing through downtown streets, insult-ing townspeople, and fighting with one another." Reportedly, the cyclists were "rocking autos, sitting on the curb drinking, [and] dropping bottles from hotel windows." The jailed cyclists were members of the Chicago

Outlaws and among an estimated crowd of 6,000 motorcycle enthusiasts in town for the race. About 150 police had descended on the downtown area after "an estimated 300 cyclists began acting up."[113]

That the Springfield episode was reminiscent of the 1947 Hollister Rally and its film equivalent, *The Wild One*, is an understatement. With a larger population than Hollister, Springfield also hosted more motorcyclists, but the basic scenario was the same: extra police were called on to restore "order," only a small number of cyclists were implicated, and their rowdiness was confined primarily to property damage, drunk and disorderly conduct, and reckless driving. Indeed, the initial headline about the Outlaws and their jamboree referred to the evening's events as a "Reign of Terror," a phrase not all that different from C. J. Doughty's "outburst of terrorism" in reference to Hollister.[114]

Like Hollister, motorcyclists at Springfield were not as significant of a threat as the term "terror" would suggest. The sheriff claimed that his department "stopped it" before "it got too bad." Springfield police chief Charles Blume described the Outlaws as a club that "gives us trouble every year," suggesting that the motorcyclists were more of a nuisance than a threat. The sheriff described the Outlaws only as a "brazen bunch," and he noted that "the other groups [of motorcyclists] seem like good people."[115]

The timing of the unprecedented effort to regulate motorcycling also suggests that motorcyclists were not perceived to be a threat until the late 1960s and early 1970s. Even as late as 1967 only twenty-one states required a special license to operate a motorcycle. The other twenty-nine simply required a regular driver's license. By 1972, after the "violent" motorcyclist had exploded onto the scene, the number of states with a special licensing requirement had nearly doubled, to thirty-five (a 66 percent increase in five years). In 1972, *Cycle* magazine published a list of existing state laws related to motorcycling in the continental United States. All forty-eight states had legislation that targeted motorcyclists, and individual states had an average of seven laws regulating motorcycling. Wyoming had the least number (one requiring a motorcycle safety inspection), and South Carolina had the most, at nine. The most common regulations required riders to have a state-approved motorcycle safety inspection, to obtain a special motorcycle license, to keep their headlight on at all times of the day, to affix an approved rearview mirror, and to wear a helmet.[116]

Motorcycles were certainly regulated before the 1960s, but the overwhelming focus was on noise. In the October 1948 issue of *American Motorcycling*, the editor waxed eloquently about the future of the sport and the crossroads motorcyclists had come upon. One road led to the "promised land, where motorcycling and motorcycle riders are recognized as a real asset to the community they represent. The other road leads the way toward further restrictions and increased unfavorable public opinion." Choosing which road to take was easy, he continued, but only if "we can all help eliminate that terrible brand put upon us—the open muffler." The editor, in fact, traced the restrictions placed on riders directly to noisy pipes: cities were passing ordinances prohibiting motorcycles in specified sections of the city because of the noise, competitive events were being banned in Massachusetts owing "primarily to the Sunday morning noise made by some riders passing through communities on their way to tracks or hills," and "several states" were planning to "impound motorcycles not properly fitted with approved mufflers."[117]

Motorcyclists also recognized the link between the rise of the violent outlaw and the push for regulation. In a letter to *Cycle*, Dick Flowers of Columbus, Ohio, focused specifically on how the image of the violent motorcyclist led to efforts to regulate all motorcyclists when he cited the brawl among motorcyclists at the Cleveland Motorcycle Custom and Trade Show in 1971. "The cost of recognition in the case of the Cleveland episode," he noted, "was extremely high."[118] James M. Mackay of Thonotosassa, Florida, made a similar point in a letter to *Cycle* in 1968 when he explained that "the law makes no distinction and provides no measure for sorting out the baddies. It applies equally to the paperboy who whines through the early morning darkness on his Twist Grip 150, to guys like me who gingerly barge an old Ariel 650 through inhospitable traffic, dodging those 'frozen faced, blue haired old ladies' whose eyesight for the most part is no better than their insight." The "bad bikies," MacKay explained, have "added impetus to a general hue and cry demanding that bikes be legislated off the streets." "Already," MacKay insisted, "solo riding, helmet, goggle and even curfew laws are being proposed on a state-wide level. Municipals by the score are ganging up on motorcyclists, making it an increasingly hostile environment for pleasure riding."[119] After three cyclists were arrested for allegedly assaulting a young woman in Florida, in fact, the governor specifically cited the laws regulating motorcycling as the most effective method of controlling their behavior. "We'll get rid of them," the governor explained, "by enforcement of strict inspection of their vehicles, requiring that they follow the helmet and goggle law, and arrest for every traffic violation and misdemeanor."[120]

The growing scrutiny of motorcyclists also points to the public's growing concern for law and order. By the latter half of the 1960s, Michael W. Flamm argues, Americans from all walks of life were becoming convinced that their country was "coming apart at the seams" and thus the issue of law and order "emerged at the forefront of political discourse." The issue first attracted national attention with Barry Goldwater's bid for the presidency against Lyndon Johnson in 1964. Over the next few years, as fears about street crime, urban riots, and political demonstrations became more acute, law and order became the "most important domestic issue" in the 1968 presidential election.[121]

Law and order became a popular political slogan and social ideal, Flamm argues, because of its "amorphous quality"—the issue's "ability to represent different concerns to different people at different moments." The focus on law and order was a response both to civil disobedience—understood as protests for civil rights and civil liberties as well as urban riots and the antiwar protests—and to run-of-the-mill crimes—robberies, rapes, muggings, and murders—often linked to motorcyclists. Flamm argues that historians have paid too much attention to the issue of race to explain the slogan's appeal and its traction. The issue of personal security, he contends, more effectively highlights the fears that marked the era and the broader debates about liberalism and its failures. The "unraveling of liberalism," he argues, was "due . . . to the widespread loss of popular faith in liberalism's ability to ensure personal security."[122]

By the latter half of the 1960s, then, the public's understanding of motorcyclists became increasingly tied to concerns about its safety. By this time, Americans were much more inclined to see anyone who rode a motorcycle as a criminal, and a certain "type" had emerged: the stereotypical "biker" was long-haired and dirty, clad in grungy jeans and a leather jacket (or some similar variation)—almost freakish in appearance, rude to other motorists on the roadway, and violent. He was also a rebel, a wild one, and a punk. "As every little old lady in rubber soled shoes is well aware," argued reporter Wells Twombly, "no worthwhile citizen ever climbed aboard a motorcycle and gunned the engine." These "creatures," he added, "generally wear black leather jackets, smoke dope and terrorize small towns after first beating the sheriff senseless with a chain."[123] Twombly's comments suggest that Hollister and Riverside profoundly shaped his view of motorcyclists, but it was his current understanding of the motorcyclist and his potential to be violent that explains his intolerance for anyone on two wheels and his memory of motorcycling's past.

THE "BIKER"

Between World War II and the 1970s the very name the public used to describe motorcyclists had transformed. Through the first two and a half to three decades after World War II "cyclist" or "motorcyclist" had been the typical terms for riders, and their machines were often referred to as "motors," "bikes," or "cycles." "Outlaw" was a common alternative after Hollister and Riverside—but beginning in the late 1960s and early 1970s the term "biker" began to overshadow "outlaw." Slang dictionaries trace its usage to this period and define it as a synonym for motorcyclist, but especially one who is a member of a club or gang.

The word's origins are obscure. In the late nineteenth century "biker" referred to a bicycle rider (and still does today), and by the early twentieth century a bike referred to a bicycle or a motorcycle.[124] "Bike" as a synonym for motorcycle became increasingly common in the postwar period, and, by the 1960s, the term "bikie" joined "cyclist" and "motorcyclist," although with an explicit association to violent and rowdy behavior ("bikie" is still used today in Australia and New Zealand).[125]

One of the biker's two distinguishing features was that he was less likely to be linked to the working class than the motorcyclist of the 1940s and 1950s. During that period respectable, clean-cut, and hard-working men rode motorcycles, and there was little doubt about their class status. Peter Tamony described motorcyclists as "usually lower-class working men who could afford second-hand automobiles but preferred to breast the wild wind," or they were what he called "broad-bottomed manual workers."[126] In a 1954 article titled "Most Unpopular Men on the Road" in the *Saturday Evening Post* the working-class influence in motorcycling was also prominent. The article dealt broadly with the typical motorcyclist's experiences ranging from police harassment to the potential injuries and hazards riders faced, as well as the organization of motorcycle races across the country. The author asserted that, aside from the so-called experts who raced, the men taking part in endurance runs were what he called an "average bag of motorcyclists"—"a crane operator, a half dozen automobile mechanics, a one-eyed man, and a collection of red-faced teenagers out for their first timed run."[127] The working-class rank and file of the world of motorcycling was so pervasive and so complete that a writer for *Cycle* magazine in 1952 noted that if one simply mentions "the word motorcycle in a middle-aged business or professional group . . . eyebrows will be raised. Admit that you ride one and you may find yourself the subject of unpleasantly close scrutiny."[128] Working-class men rode motorcycles; middle-class men frowned upon them.

The prominence of the working class did not, however, stifle variation: there were respectable riders and rough riders. The differences between respectable and rough riders focused on the motorcyclist's appearance and roadway etiquette. Respectable cyclists were clean-cut and mindful of other motorcycles as well as their four-wheeled counterparts. Rough riders were not. "Cowboying" or "motorcycle cowboys," "roughnecks," and "muffler morons" all routinely appeared in the pages of motorcycle publications in the immediate postwar period. Motorcycle cowboys and roughnecks were notorious for the various stunts they performed on the road and their penchant for speed, while muffler morons favored the open pipe (that is, noise). All three were known for their unruly and supposedly disrespectful behavior and their blatant disregard for common courtesy. The term "cowboy" was an obvious reference to the hard-working men who drove cattle across the expanse of the West/Southwest, and "rough-necks" to the men working the oil fields of those same, often dry, dusty parts of the country, just as separate from the communities of which they were a part as any lone motorcyclist riding from town to town. And both cowboys and motorcyclists had a long-shared sentimentality for the fron-tier and western landscapes, and a feeling of ruggedness and individual-ity. Motorcyclists, like cowboys and roughnecks, also embraced a culture of leisure characterized by hard drinking, roughhousing, and everything else associated with the "sporting life," much like any upstanding outlaw whose disdain for respectability was conspicuous and celebrated.[129]

The moron's link to the working class is not as obvious as that of the cowboy or the roughneck but no less convincing. The term "moron" came into popular usage at the turn of the century with the influx of millions of immigrants from southern and eastern Europe. Native-born whites feared these immigrants because they were thought to be more foreign, more exotic, and less able to assimilate than their European predecessors from northern and western Europe. Their racial identity was neither white nor black but what historians have described as "in-between," and linked inextricably to what native-born whites understood as their "cultural back-wardness" and their "brutish, childlike behavior."[130] The word "moron," referred in particular to their supposed intellectual inferiority, and the term's popularity coincided with the rise of IQ tests in the early decades of the twentieth century that targeted these newly arrived immigrants and contributed to the discrimination they faced.[131] A significant majority of these immigrants were also poor, unskilled laborers who occupied some of the most dangerous and physically demanding jobs in the United States. As the moron's link to southern and eastern Europeans began to fade in the postwar period, it remained thoroughly attached to intellec-tual inferiority and childlike behavior which neatly fit the public's growing criticism of motorcyclists who remained prominently of modest origins.

By the 1960s and 1970s, the term was replaced by the "dumb old biker," who simply did not understand why refusing to wear a helmet placed him in serious danger.

The only acknowledged association motorcyclists had to the working class in the 1960s and 1970s was their link to cops, garages, and mechanics, who were described as notoriously greasy. A 1964 *Newsweek* article about the rise of Honda explained that although *The Wild One* "didn't exactly invent the helmeted, two-wheeled hellion, Marlon Brando's leading role in that film . . . mirrored the public's image of motorcyclists as a strange breed who hang around grimy garages and risk life and limb on their snorting mounts."[132] In another article on the growing popularity of Honda, motorcycling was described as a "realm that formerly was dominated by Hell's Angels, traffic cops and the greasy types who hung out at the local gas station."[133] Indeed, one of the most colorful and common labels for the outlaw/biker of the 1960s and 1970s was "greasy." "At one time," a contemporary explained in 1971, the "typical motorcyclist was a greasy, long-haired Hell's Angel."[134]

Ironically, even the motorcycle daredevil contributed to the disappearance of the working-class motorcyclist. Almost universally of humble origins, the stunt rider was the product of the collapse of America's manufacturing base and the loss of jobs. Joe Einhorn was working for International Harvester when he heard about the potential money a daredevil could make jumping ramp to ramp. According to one story, he jumped his motorcycle over a pickup during his lunch break to delight his coworkers and "his ego."[135] Even as a young man, Evel Knievel was able to evade wage work in his hometown of Butte, Montana. William Janhunen, a mechanic and one of Knievel's high school buddies, noted that "Knievel never worked a regular day in his life that the town can remember."[136]

A more telling example about the relationship between wage work and the motorcycle daredevil involved Wicked Ward's retirement in 1975. After plunging at seventy miles per hour to the ground after a crosswind caught his motorcycle hang glider, Ward decided to "hang up his helmet for good." With two clamps attached to his head to hold him in traction, Ward explained to a reporter that his stunt career had been the best choice of employment available to him. "I did what I did to provide a good living for [his wife and children], the best way I know how." Ward explained that "there were years [when] we made a lot of money—years we didn't, with injuries, expenses, repairs. I've made as little as $75 jumping cars and as much as $35,000." Ward was now debating what he was going to do with the rest of his life and how he was going to support his family. "I think they're ready for their daddy to come home . . . and go to work, like everybody else," he said. Ward was not sure what his future held and wondered whether anyone might "want to take a gamble with an ex-motorcycle jumper." He nonetheless admitted, "Right now I need a job" and acknowledged that he would likely end up doing wage work. "You don't have to be a daredevil to accomplish something in life," he explained. "If you dig an 8 by 10 ditch you can be proud of it." Ward anticipated a full recovery from his broken neck, "except for a possible minor motor problem—in moving his head from side to side."[137]

Yet even as the motorcycle stunt rider accompanied the growing crisis surrounding deindustrialization and was a product of it, stunt riding was more a rejection of wage work than a recognition of it. Jumping ramp to ramp was a get-rich-quick occupation that highlighted sheer guts and glory more than a work ethic or skill, and daredevils recognized this distinction. In a 1974 article titled "What Makes Evel Jump?," a psychologist interviewed linked Knievel's popularity with the idea of the American dream, albeit a postindustrial version of it. "By taking high risks with his life, using his native wit and getting a good PR man," the doctor commented, "Knievel parlayed his behavior pattern into the American dream—fame and easy millions."[138] The American dream, which for generations had been linked to homeownership and a job that ensured a comfortable economic existence, had been replaced by a postindustrial version (or nightmare) that involved sheer luck, much like winning the lottery (especially by the 1980s when state lotteries became increasingly popular) or successfully jumping ramp to ramp and surviving. Millions of Americans were attracted to stunt riding; few actually took a stab at it, and an even smaller number lived to boast about it. The stunt rider embodied the hopelessness and desperation of a working class struggling to make ends meet at a time when it was becoming obsolete, more easily exploited, and hopelessly fascinated with the stunt riders who were just as eager to escape a future of meaningless wage work as they were.

The emergence of the term "biker" in the late 1960s and its decreasing association with the working class also reflected its increasing link to violence. In a 1969 *New York Times* article about the Lower East Side, Sylvan Fox offered readers a look at the growing incidence of crime and violence because of the recent influx of "bikers." The area had become known for its hippies during the height of the "flower child craze" that reached its peak in 1967. According to the Reverend Michael Allen, then rector of St. Mark's in the heart of the East Village, "the scene had become rougher, tougher and more sordid" after the "bikers" arrived. Fox reported that attention was focused on the area the previous Monday when firemen responded to a call and found the body of a twenty-one-year-old who had been bound and set ablaze. The victim was allegedly a member of the "Pagans motor-cycle gang" and his death the result of a battle between the Pagans and the Alien Nomads. The ongoing feud, Fox reported, had turned the Lower East Side into a "world where rape, assault, gang warfare and even murder are almost commonplace."[139]

Just about two years later in a *San Francisco Chronicle* article, "biker" appeared again in quotes and in a nearly identical article about several "motorcycle gangs" and their alleged invasion of a once-peaceful hippie community. In this case it was Atlanta, Georgia, and there were two violent homicides instead of one. The neighborhood began attracting hippies in the late 1960s primarily because of cheap and plentiful housing. The "bik-ers" were soon to follow, according to the report, and before long "death & fear" had "displaced peace and love as the hallmark of a seedy hippie neighborhood." The article reported that a "shotgun blast" had recently killed a "biker" and that four young men visiting in Atlanta and touring the hippie district were beaten, tortured, and robbed. Two escaped, but one was killed and another seriously wounded. One longtime resident com-plained that "the vibes are getting so bad I can't think straight anymore" and that the place would "never be the same until the 'bikers' split."[140]

In both of these articles "biker" appeared in quotes and hippies did not, presumably because the authors recognized that their readers were famil-iar enough with hippies that no explanation was necessary—the hippie had become a recognizable part of the landscape and the biker (or at least the label) had not. But there was no mistaking who the biker was and what he represented. What stood in sharp contrast to the hippies' peace and tranquility was the bikers' violence, often random and relentlessly gra-tuitous. The bikers were either the victims of violence or more likely the ones responsible for it, and had few obvious motives or any sense of regret. Indeed, neither of these articles on hippie communities identified motor-cyclists as responsible for the use of the term "biker," and the so-called bikers' silence in the articles only increased their distance from the com-munity and the public's misunderstanding of them. The articles drew only on interviews with longtime residents or hippies. Examples of motor-cyclists referring to themselves as bikers show up about the same time, although, perhaps, with some hesitation. "Biker" first appears in *American Motorcycling* in 1972, and the first issue of *Easyriders* (June 1971) used the term only seven times. The terms "rider" or "bike rider" were more com-monly used in the magazine. Undoubtedly, the term's appearance in print lagged behind its popular usage on the streets, in people's homes, or any-where motorcyclists could be found, but the earliest use was by the main-stream media and men and women who were not bikers.

At the same time, early examples of "biker" focused more on the motor-cyclist's behavior than their motorcycles. Newspaper accounts of the "biker" were often so vague and abstract that the motorcycle is noticea-bly missing, or the press described men who were members of "motorcy-cle gangs" but they did not own any motorcycles. In the *New York Times* article on the increase in motorcyclists on the Lower East Side, for exam-ple, Fox commented, "Ironically, many of the motorcycle gangs in New York are not affluent enough to own motorcycles," although they referred to themselves as motorcycle gangs. The gangs without motorcycles were called "subway bikers."[141] A "violent brawl" in Richmond, Virginia, attracted a similar response in 1971. Five men were hospitalized and two were in custody after a fight broke out between two "youth clubs, which Richmond police call 'motorcycle gangs without bikes.'"[142] A similar usage of "biker" or "biker types" appeared in lawsuits filed at the state and fed-eral levels. "Motorcyclist" was used to identify riders in state and federal courts until 1973, when "biker" first appeared (or details of crimes did not identify whether either party rode a motorcycle). After that, both "biker" and "motorcyclist" were used, although "motorcyclist" was generally used to describe traffic problems or situations; for example, "'motorcyclist' seeking the recovery of damages after his cycle was struck by a car turn-ing left onto a road" or for "related injuries owing to the defective manu-facturing of a part" are typical examples.[143] With "biker" or "biker types," the motorcycle is once again missing, and the "biker" is linked to drugs, denim, and leather, or simply refers to a physically intimidating individ-ual: "white male, about 21 years of age, 6 feet 5 inches tall, weighing 250 pounds, a biker type" was the description of an alleged armed robbery suspect in one lawsuit.[144] The biker had become a recognizable cultural figure who stood apart not only from the other masculine tropes of the 1960s and 1970s but also from the outlaw who first attracted the public's attention after Hollister and Riverside.

THE HOLLISTER AND RIVERSIDE rallies were certainly rowdy and the attendees at times appropriately disrespectful and loud. By all accounts, male culture had run amuck, but in a fashion not all that different from that of other predominantly male, working-class gatherings common in communities across the country. Within a couple decades the outlaw who emerged at Hollister would be known increasingly as a biker and was so intimately associated with violence that he began to shape our understanding of what crime could look like. By the time the transformation was noticeable, the nonriding public routinely failed to make distinctions among riders, and the motorcyclist's working-class roots had all but disappeared. Indeed, the outlaw at Hollister was rebellious not simply because of his assumed disdain for small-town America but because he so openly complicated the community's relationship to wage labor. Motorcyclists were routinely identified with the transients who were at the heart of the wage labor system on which these communities were often dependent even as they fashioned an identity around the rejection of it. These conflicting messages account for the larger fears that shaped the rise of the outlaw and explain why the nonriding public had not abandoned the motorcyclist altogether. He had successfully imagined a day-to-day experience that found its inspiration outside the world of wage labor rather than in it.

By the late 1960s and early 1970s not only had the biker's image become synonymous with violence; it had also left an indelible mark on the public's mind about what crime looked like and why the nonriding majority failed to recognize distinctions among motorcyclists. Hollister was not forgotten by this time; it had only become more violent in the public's imagination. At the same time, motorcyclists from across the country were facing increasing scrutiny from a public that at times could prove hostile. By the mid- to late 1960s, even motorcyclists' ties to a working class that were conspicuous in the immediate postwar years were beginning to loosen as violence became the overwhelming characteristic the public identified with motorcyclists and the characteristic that continues to shape our memory of them.

HOW TO KILL A BIKER

Small-Town Invasions and the Postindustrial City

The United States has experienced riots and other forms of civil unrest throughout its history, but few decades compare to the 1960s. Civil rights demonstrations spread beyond the South, and riots also erupted in cities across the country, especially in 1968 after the assassination of Martin Luther King Jr. Far deadlier were the riots in Los Angeles (Watts, 1965), Detroit (1967), and Newark (1967). More than 100 fatalities were recorded in these three cities alone, along with millions of dollars in property damage. By the end of the decade, opposition to the war in Vietnam also led to demonstrations that turned violent. Local, state, and federal authorities often responded in kind against the participants, and politicians began to speak out in favor of "law and order."[1]

Because motorcyclists, too, were associated with riots, having been accused of starting one in Hollister in 1947, authorities were also monitoring their behavior by the 1960s. One riot that attracted national attention erupted at a gathering of motorcyclists on Weirs Beach in Laconia, New Hampshire, in June 1965. The trouble started, according to one FBI memorandum, after someone threw a smoke bomb into a crowd. Several more would follow, and as the crowd "became disorderly and noisy," motorcyclists began to "taunt" the police and interfere with traffic. The crowd quickly became what the FBI described as "an unruly mob completely defiant of police orders." Motorcyclists also fought among themselves, tossed firecrackers at passersby and the police, overturned two automobiles, and even attempted to burn down a local bowling alley. The Laconia Police Department's riot squad moved into the area and was pelted with a "barrage of flying objects," prompting the governor to call in the New Hampshire State Police to restore order.[2]

Complaints about motorcyclists, however, were not limited to the usual violence and disorderly behavior. California's Hells Angels were blamed for the riot even though the event was in New Hampshire, and the violence was linked to the motorcyclist's ability to traverse a great distance in a short time. One newspaper reported that the Hells Angels' crimes were most common when they were on "runs" and in out-of-the-way small towns. Laconia's mayor, Peter R. Lessard, was puzzled: "Why are [the motorcyclists] permitted to take part in gang assaults and property damage throughout the country? . . . Why [have] more than four hundred well known crime offenders travelled from California, more than three thousand miles, for one evening [of] entertainment and [why do they] consistently escape?"[3]

Questions about the motorcyclist's mobility and his use of the highways would continue in the months following the incident in Laconia. In August 1965 a reporter asked eight San Franciscans if the state should revoke the licenses of "rioting" motorcyclists. Copywriter Marjerie Meyer thought it was a "fine idea." "Having their wings clipped," she explained, "would let them feel the bite of justice, and give them time to ponder over the value of their licenses." In fact, those who questioned this solution did it less because of a concern that it was too severe of a penalty and more because it would not have the desired effect. Ole Tangen, who worked as a captain of a navy tanker, stated, "I guess taking licenses away from the violent ones might curb this type of activity," but "the assemblies should [also] be banned."[4] No one questioned the presence of motorcyclists in an urban riot or complained that the punishment was too severe. Motorcyclists had become an identifiable figure of the urban landscape who posed a recognizable threat that needed to be regulated.

The focus on revoking driver's licenses suggests that violence may not have been the most important issue in shaping the public's views about motorcyclists. Marjerie Meyer's comment that through such punishment motorcyclists "would realize that the use of the highways is a privilege" inadvertently blurred the line dividing the journalist's framing of violent "rioting" motorcyclists from a more mundane image of the motorcyclists who used the roads for everyday travel. The manner in which she conflated the two suggests that the motorcyclist's presence on the highways was as important to her understanding of motorcyclists as the supposed antisocial behavior for which the "outlaw" was becoming famous.[5]

Meyer's discussion of the privilege of driving speaks to the increasing importance of and tension surrounding the use of highways during the postwar years. During the late nineteenth and early twentieth centuries, American cities experienced a heterogeneous, urban public culture that would disappear in favor of the postindustrial city characterized by industrial parks, highways, the use of the automobile, detached single-family homes, and the growth of the suburbs. Suburbanization reached its peak in the years between the end of World War II and the early 1970s when the suburban population more than doubled to nearly 80 million residents and when federal and state governments paid for the construction of more than 40,000 miles of highways.[6]

Though historians have successfully highlighted the struggle over the automobile and the broader conflict over transportation, their work has focused disproportionately on the triumph of the automobile by the 1930s and on the destructive effects of highway construction on central cities and their neighborhoods after World War II.[7] Far less attention has been devoted to the struggle taking place *on* these newly built roads after the war's end.

The underlying assumption guiding our understanding of the postwar years is that alternatives to automobiles were diminishing as the freeway system was expanding and that Americans in general were content, if not outright pleased, with these changes.[8] Yet during this same period, the number of registered motorcycles was expanding to an unprecedented degree—from fewer than 200,000 after World War II to close to 3 million by 1970.[9] The dramatic rise in the number of registered motorcycles alone suggests a certain ambivalence about automobiles. But the motorcycle was not simply an alternative to four wheels. During these years of unprecedented popularity, the motorcycle was often at the center of the struggle over these new highways and was critical to understanding the frustration and anger surrounding transportation. Some contemporaries found the motorcyclist to be a nuisance, especially the motorcycle cowboy (or hound or daredevil) who was notorious for on-the-road stunts and other reckless antics. Other men and women objected to the ease with which motorcyclists violated the boundaries of the postindustrial city and challenged the security and comfort they associated with their suburban communities. All of them found that a life that revolved around automobiles was at times a frustrating one.

Concerns about roadway travel existed for decades before the massive expansion of the highway system, but conflict was increasing after World War II, and it coincided with fears about the automobile's safety and the rise of the "outlaw" motorcyclist.

THE COWBOY AND THE STUNT RIDER

In 1947, *American Motorcycling* reprinted an open letter that the Meriden (Connecticut) Motorcycle Club Incorporated sent to the editors of the city's newspapers to draw attention to its opposition to the "doubtful 'sport'

Jack Troop standing on his motorcycle (mid-1950s). His style of dress was common among riders in the 1950s and is strikingly similar to that of the typical motorcycle cop. Courtesy of Don Troop.

of 'MOTORCYCLE COWBOYING,' " in which it cited two complaints. The first was about noise that resulted either from the use of straight pipes or funnels, the product of removing the "guts" from the muffler and leaving a straight-through passage for the exhaust; or from "motor–popping or back firing," a "willful and voluntary practice" that was "produced by retarding the spark, together with some clever manipulation of the throttle control," which "causes gasses to accumulate in the muffler, and become ignited, thereby producing the explosion known as the backfire."[10]

The club's second quibble concerned boulevard riders and stunt riders. The former "tear up and down the street in general," though "going nowhere," and they "tear out at full speed the moment the light changes and slow down with a squeal of brakes when the next stop signal is reached." The latter was the type of rider who "leaves the curb in a grand sweep, with a screech of tires, and a smell of burning rubber," and delights in "cutting as close as possible when passing a car, thereby demonstrating his advantage in being on a motorcycle . . . [and] by swerving, grasping hands with adjacent riders and at times he might be even seen to stand on the seat." [11]

While riding clubs were working to differentiate themselves from reckless motorcyclists, the nonriding majority struggled to distinguish between the two. In 1954 *The Saturday Evening Post* published an article by Hal Burton titled "Most Unpopular Men on the Road" that began with the less than flattering sentence, "Nobody—except another cyclist—likes a man on a motorcycle." The article focused on racing and the particular hazards of the sport—pavement burns, sprained ankles, broken bones, and "even sudden death at a high rate of speed." When Burton tried to explain why the public disliked cyclists, he focused on the rider's fascination with the sport, which bordered on monomania, and on the issue of noise. "Motorcycles are sold with muffler attached," the author observed. But "too many purchasers, being young and high spirited, junk all such silencing devices immediately, much preferring to prickle scalps and rattle spines for miles around." The issue of noise had been at the heart of early efforts to regulate motorcycling and often the critical reason communities had banned motorcycles from certain sections of town and dirt bikes from public parks.[12]

The general public's disdain for motorcyclists, Burton argued, also reflected the rider's capacity to defy the highway's constraints. "When you have a machine that can thread its way through the thickest traffic," he explained, "it is a positive pleasure to run down the road 150 miles to buy a hot dog or to make an excursion to a nearby beach for a swim." Motorcyclists were known for riding between lanes of cars (lane splitting) when stopped at a traffic jam, a practice that often attracted scorn from his four-wheeled counterpart and contributed to the motorcyclist's reputation as the "most unpopular" man on the road. "Motorists trapped in a line of crawling cars," Burton added, "are prone to cuss fervently when a motorcycle rider worms his way through the jam, departing for parts unknown [and] with an ear-splitting roar."[13]

By the late 1950s, Rhode Island's residents were discussing the possibility of banning all motorcycles from the state's highways. At times the discussion focused on the general issue of highway safety. According to one report, Governor Christopher Del Sesto felt "that under modern day conditions motorcycles for general passenger use are too dangerous." The state had 1,200 registered motorcycles compared to 200,000 automobiles, yet motorcycles accounted for 10 percent of all highway accidents. "Anyone who has watched cyclists zip in and out of fast moving traffic on the road can understand why." Indeed, after motorcyclist Randy Wilson of Worcester, Massachusetts, complained about the possible ban, the governor backed away from a general discussion about safety and pointed more specifically to certain riders. "It was not my intention to make a specific recommendation that motorcycles be banned from Rhode Island Highways," the governor argued. "My thought was that possibly the time has come when we should consider whether they have a place on the highways and whether under present day conditions they are hazardous. . . . Motorcyclists as a group," Del Sesto added, "are looked upon as reckless because of the unsafe operation of a very few and that perhaps stricter enforcement would assist in [the] reduction of the accident frequency in this field."[14]

The media also complained about formation riding. "Gone are the days of the foxtail and the harebrained youth," argued a 1947 *Life* magazine article, which likened a group of motorcyclists to the threat of invading armies from the not-too-distant past. "Today's 200,000 'bike' riders are organized like so many Panzer units into well-disciplined clubs with costumes and emblems."[15] Formation riding could complicate a motorist's entry on to a freeway or block his exit, what was referred to as a "traffic capture." In the critiques following a rally in Riverside in 1948, a writer for the *Pasadena California Independent* cited the motorcyclist's association with "traffic capture" as one of the reasons "motorcycles are none too popular to begin with."[16] The public's negative attitude about motorcyclists thus grew out of the struggle over highways and their use, and it began before the outlaw riders attracted a national audience at Hollister.

The average motorist's complaints, however, might have been disproportionate to the problem. After all, with from 200,000 to 400,000 cyclists on the road in the 1950s, how often did the average motorist even see or hear a motorcycle, let alone be passed by one at a traffic jam?[17] Was the bitterness the product of these interactions alone, or did the day-to-day conflict between motorists and riders expose as well the frustration with a highway system that was falling short of their expectations?

As early as the 1950s, complaints about suburbs were becoming more common, and contemporaries were predicting a suburban exodus, retreat, or "back to the city" movement. The list of complaints was significant: suburban kids were too sheltered and too isolated, the suburban lifestyle was described as a "living death" that valued mediocrity, "housing areas" were "needlessly dull," and traffic was unbearable. Critics referred to the two hours of commuting as mind-numbing or what one individual described as "check[ing] our brains two hours daily while getting back and forth." One critic claimed that the number one reason for moving back to the city was that "husbands are fed up with commuting." One suburban husband explained that he was "tired of being a 'mole man,' " a "commuter who, in winter months, leaves his home in the dark of the morning, returns to it after night falls and never catches sight of the pastoral beauty that took him to the country in the first place." Wives were also "tired of eternally driving a family 'taxi' "; families in general found themselves "on the highway all the time"; and the " hazards of driving crowded highways to get to town" was cited as "another reason" for moving back to the city.[18]

The automobile's deficiencies also looked particularly galling in light of the joy of riding a motorcycle and the freedom of the open road. Simply put, motorcycling was at odds with or stood apart from the larger purpose or reason for a freeway's existence on which the average American had become dependent. While highways were functional and efficiently guided motorists from one destination to the next, wheeling out on to the open road on a motorcycle often lacked a distinct purpose, was not explicitly productive, and was more about the ride and less about the destination. Automobiles did indeed have the advantage of reproducing the privacy and comfort of the domestic setting, but drivers also consciously cut themselves off from their environment in what motorcyclists described as a steel cocoon, a cage, or a greenhouse on wheels.[19] Motorcycling provided riders with an enthusiastic engagement with their surroundings, and they routinely left the paved roadways for the numerous trails and other adventures off the beaten path. Motorcycling challenged the democratic system of highway travel that fundamentally regarded everyone as equal as long as they abided by certain road rules and the uniformity of mass movement. Underlying the popularity of freeway driving were the implicit values of individuality and mobility, which fit well with the suburban myth of the time. But a "complete surrender of will" was critic Reyner Banham's equally apt description to illustrate the discipline necessary to navigate the ever-expanding networks of highways, and it was a critique that did not take into account the growing popularity of motorcycling, which brought into even sharper relief the failure of the highway system and the attendant frustration and anger that were routinely directed at riders.[20]

Some evidence even suggests that motorcyclists also saw these differences as gendered. One historian has argued that freeway travel produced its own rigid gender conventions: men commuted back and forth to work, while women used the highways to support what Americans in the 1950s considered that most traditional of female preoccupations—shopping. Motorcyclists were apt to ignore such distinctions. In some cases, automobile critics connected the rider's safety to what they considered to be the growing numbers of female motorists on the road. "Despite claims on the contrary," argued Clark Trumbull Jr., *Motorcyclist*'s editor, there was "a large per-centage of the so-called weaker sex on the road who shall we say, are not just exactly on the ball."[21] Other critics argued that female motorists had transformed or feminized car culture. In a letter about the division between riders of American- and British-made motorcycles and women's interest in motorcycling, John G. Root of Gaithersburg, Maryland, bluntly asserted that motorcycles (and, by extension, the men who rode them) were decidedly more masculine than the four-wheeled alternative. According to Root, women had "already transformed the automobile from a highly efficient and specialized machine to a veritable living-room suite on wheels. Now they want to soften and dilute the motorcycle to the proportions of a featherbed; and they will succeed in this if given half a chance to heckle the manufacturers into including them in their ever-widening market." Root concluded that "we men have little left that we can call our own."[22]

Yet even as automobilists appeared to be sacrificing their own autonomy and freedom by committing themselves to a life on the road, they were at the same time the single-most significant threat to the motorcyclist's safety. Riders sometimes argued that automobilists were just as dangerous if not more dangerous than their two-wheeled counterparts. Mrs. Morris Roberts of Los Angeles admitted in a letter to *American Motorcycling* that motorcycling had its fair share of reckless drivers. But she was incensed that "the public doesn't seem to realize that there are just as many roughnecks driving automobiles, drinking, having accidents, killing all the passengers in their car, or hot rod drivers killing people and having accidents."[23] Other riders were much more explicit about the problems they encountered. Johnny Hruban of Central City, Nebraska, justified the open pipe because it helped stave off careless and dangerous drivers. Hruban "believe[d] in quiet motors around town and knew how much faster one can get around with a quiet bike." But "when I cruise down the highway at 70 or so a quiet bike is not in my opinion the best thing." Hruban explained, "so often a car will pull from a cross road and pull in front of a cycle. With the weak horns they have," he added, "the only thing to do is slow down quick[ly]. A loud, or anyway noisier cycle announces its coming and in a lot of cases has made motorists look and hold back till I have passed. . . . A completely silent cycle," he insisted, "would have little way to announce its coming and could prove dangerous."[24]

The editors of motorcycle publications also focused on the very real threat from automobilists. An article in *Motorcyclist* titled "It's *You*—Not the Motorcycle That Is 'Dangerous,'" Clark Trumbull Jr. begins with what appears to be another complaint about motorcyclists: "A motorcycle is a mechanical device dependent on the person riding it for all actions" and is "the safest vehicle on the road" when "properly designed." Yet he described automobilists as an ever-present and significant threat to riders.

Motorcycles were safer not only because they could accelerate quickly and could stop effectively but because they also had an overall width of about thirty inches, making it easier to "escape from many difficult situations," including the automobilist's habit of crowding motorcyclists out of their lanes. Indeed, while Trumbull admitted that it was a "rather broad assumption" that "all riders have brains," motorists had "no brains at all," and if they had some, "they are most likely concentrating on most any subject at hand other than driving." In most states, Trumbull added, "anybody can drive anything. The lack of rigid driver and car inspection laws permits all sorts of rattle-trap equipment driven by rattle-brained citizens to be loosed upon the public highways." With all the "weird types" on the road, he advised his readers to "use caution at all times for it is not what you may do but what the others may do that will bend the forks and require stitches in your scalp." The other "obvious solution" was to "anticipate the moves of the other traffic and give them a wide berth even if your pride suffers when some slope-head cuts you off with a Model T."[25]

However, the conflict on America's highways was not simply coincidental—the inevitable consequence of more vehicles occupying a limited amount of space and time. Other riders suggested that the danger facing riders was intentional and reflected the automobilist's frustration with highway travel and motorcyclists who defied it, and a larger struggle to determine who controlled the roadways. James Whiteshield of San Francisco, California, linked the dangers of highway travel to urban congestion. Whiteshield confessed that he had been ticketed for riding a borrowed cycle with a straight pipe. The ten-dollar fine convinced him to give the noise issue some thought, and he "came up with the astounding conclusion . . . that city noises might have something to do with the fact that I've found country dwellers more friendly and hospitable than their urban brethren." Whiteshield did not explain the nature of the highway inhospitality he faced from motorists—the occasional odd stare, rude comments, or the common practice of crowding riders out of their lanes—but suggested that the dangers were not simply the consequence of bad drivers—aimlessly drifting into the wrong lane or abruptly stopping on the highway. Whether their frustration was a consequence of the noise of city life or the motorcycle's straight pipe, automobilists were intentionally targeting motorcyclists.[26]

The struggle over America's roadways also influenced motorcycle culture. Some contemporaries argued that the growth of off-road riding reflected the highway's dangers. With the popularity of motocross in the late 1960s and early 1970s, trail riding would become more specialized or confined to motorcycles built specifically for off-the-road adventures. But in the immediate postwar years motorcyclists generally bobbed their cycles for what was referred to as "gully scrambling or the California style." Gully scrambling was no doubt a reflection of the joy of off-the-road riding, but the California rider's affinity for the "rough stuff" was a consequence of having been "driven from the highways" by "locust like swarms of automobiles." "Lots" of California riders did not "cavort among the cacti," but avoiding the off-road scene meant they had to "brave the streets and highways." When riders found highways dangerous, automobilists were usually to blame.[27]

Indeed, off-the-beaten path was a common theme to motorcycle culture and one that could mean trail riding or simply avoiding busy highways. A "gypsy tour," the American Motorcyclist Association (AMA) explained, "means a companionable ride to a spot away from the city where cyclists can frolic to their hearts' content."[28] Burton added that motorcyclists also "tend to draw clannishly together and to enjoy themselves in places where motorists would be hard put to go." This "clan spirit" permits "two strangers on motorcycles to become instant friends," and he added it was "an unknown thing for one cyclist to pass another without waving." He also argued that it reflected the urgency with which they avoided automobiles. "Since automobiles represent a positive hazard to the cyclist," Burton argued, "most club outings are apt to take place in a park or well off the main roads." Motorcyclists' clannishness was as much a reflection of the dangers they faced from automobilists as it was an example of the camaraderie forged through the shared joys of riding.[29]

Formation riding also may have reflected the problems motorcyclists faced from automobiles. One of motorcycling's most common images is that of the lone rider blazing a trail out into the expanse of the open road. The other typical image is that of a group of riders heading down the highway in a tightly packed and coordinated formation. On the surface, formation riding smacked of the stability, uniformity, and order associated with the suburban communities that were becoming increasingly popular across the country. But the problems riders faced also required a strength-in-numbers mentality that helped ensure the rider's safety and his or her control of the highways. What automobilists complained was a "traffic capture" did not simply complicate access on to a highway or the exit from one. It allowed motorcyclists to control the pace of movement and its flow. Burton also described how formation riding reduced the likelihood of two particular "discomforts" facing motorcyclists on America's highways: attempts by "motorists[,] observing that a cycle takes up only one third of

Motorcyclists "off the beaten path" along the Mohawk Trail, Massachusetts, 1941. Courtesy of the Library of Congress, Washington, D.C.

his lane, . . . to pass by when there are cars coming from the other direction"; and the potential hazard of running into the back of "a car that slows down suddenly."[30] The bulk and size of a formation of riders helped keep automobilists at a safer distance and hence less likely to try and push a rider out of his or her lane, and formation riding was an organized and coordinated group of riders who recognized the potential problems of a mass movement and took additional measures to guarantee its safety. The AMA's basic rules for formation riding included having "road captains" in the front and rear of the formation, maintaining appropriate speed limits, and riding in staggered formation.[31]

The frequency with which the topic of safety appeared in motorcycle publications also suggests that it was a pressing issue for motorcyclists. Accidents were such a common experience for motorcyclists that riders were suspicious when someone claimed he or she had never had one. In the January 1949 issue of *American Motorcycling*, Don Schulz of Weslaco, Texas, took exception to "Babs" Holmes, a woman rider, who "boasts about having ridden 25,000 miles without a ticket or a spill." Riding that distance without a ticket, Schulz argued, was "possible" but "not without a spill."

Schulz suggested that "Babs" could not have been going over thirty miles per hour during those 25,000 miles; that perhaps she had a side hack, which he felt made it easier to maneuver; or that she was not "an ordinary rider." "I have ridden motorcycles for almost two years" Schulz added, and "everybody I have ever met or talked to can account for several spills every thousand miles. I am not doubting her word but I am wondering how she can do it."[32] Schulz failed to explain why spills were so common. Riders were undoubtedly to blame for some of those problems, along with the general hazards of roadway travel: inexperience, slick roadways, and unsafe equipment are all potential standouts. But it is also just as likely that automobilists were responsible for some of these spills. The average motorcyclist's experience on the road was different from the automobilist's, and the conflict between the two served as the basis for the public's frustration with motorcyclists and their fears about the "outlaw" rider. These trends were conspicuous before the motorcyclist attracted attention at Hollister and would only become more noticeable as the number of riders dramatically increased over the next few decades.

ROADWAY TRAVEL IN THE 1960S AND 1970S

By the 1960s and 1970s, the roadway problems that had attracted increasing attention during the immediate postwar period became a topic for national debate. During the period from 1940 to 1974, the mileage of paved roads in the United States nearly doubled from 1,557 to 3,068 million miles, but the number of cars grew at a much more significant rate—from about 26 million in 1940 to nearly 107 million in 1974, and the number of miles traveled grew at a much faster rate than the number of miles of paved roads: from 249 billion in 1940 to nearly a trillion three decades later. Fatalities were also increasing steadily during this time. In 1945, 28,076 people were killed on America's roads.[33] A report issued by a House subcommittee on the issue of highway safety placed the figure above 56,000 for 1971 and 1972 and warned that by 1974 the nation was likely to "pass the bloody milestone of two million traffic deaths since the advent of the motor car." The committee specifically cited "sharp-pointed highway guardrails that had pierced autos and impaled the occupants; cars demolished by hitting solid concrete signs and light posts; [and] confusing or obliterated traffic signs, and slippery pavements." The report concluded that "the life that is claimed by an unnecessary roadside hazard, a concealed rural intersection or a freeway designed in such a manner that it overtaxes a responsible driver is a life lost through indifference and ineptness."[34]

Up to the early 1960s roadway accidents and fatalities had attracted little attention. In 1965 Ralph Nader noted that the "principal reason why the automobile has remained the only transportation vehicle to escape being called to meaningful public account is that the public has never been supplied the information . . . to enable it to make effective demands through the marketplace and through government for a safe, non-polluting and efficient automobile that can be produced economically." Nader argued that this oversight could have easily been avoided. "Specialists and researchers outside the industry who could have provided the leadership to stimulate this flow of information by and large chose to remain silent, as did government officials," and doctors, lawyers, engineers, and other specialists failed "to dedicate themselves to the prevention of accident injuries."[35] Nader fiercely criticized the common practice of "protective anonymity" in which academic and "commercial compilers" of data "refrain from naming makes and models."[36] The voluminous reports by Harvard professor Ross McFarland, whom Nader described as a "pioneer in the science of designing motor vehicles to fit the operational needs and safety of drivers and passengers," contained no vehicle names. Dunlap's 1959–60 study of the "differences in accident experience" for various makes of automobiles "produced reports entirely devoid of vehicle names,"[37] and in 1964 two other important studies failed to name the brands tested. A *Popular Science* article that "reported the results of brake tests for leading American car makes failed to mention any names and a test on the replacement brake linings of 19 different brands conducted by the National Association for Stock Car Advancement and Research (NASCAR) found that only five successfully met minimum traffic safety code specifications." The brands in the NASCAR study remained unnamed.[38]

By the mid-1960s the silence that had shrouded the question of automobile safety began to be lifted. After a friend of Nader's had an automobile accident that left him a paraplegic, Nader began to investigate automobile safety. His research led to a publication in 1959 that culminated in his 1965 book, *Unsafe at Any Speed*. That year, and for the first time in television history, a program titled "Death on the Highway" was shown on National Educational Television stations. Among other things, the show "connected specific design hazards with car models—Pontiac Tempest, Chrysler Newport, Ford Mustang and others." The Corvair had a particularly notorious safety record because of its tendency to flip over. In 1961 Mrs. Rose Pierini's Corvair did just that as she was driving down the street in Santa Barbara, California, and her left arm was severed. She sued, and thirty-four months later General Motors paid her a check for $70,000 rather than continue a trial that threatened to expose the Corvair's safety problems.[39] By 1965 publications like *Consumer Reports* and *Consumer Bulletin* were no longer "the only segment of the communications media which linked hazards with brand names." In a Senate investigation into traffic safety in 1965, Robert Kennedy and Abraham Ribicoff "confronted General Motors' chairman Frederic Donner and President James Roche with a November 1964 Cornell report showing a much greater door hinge failure by General Motors cars than by Ford or Chrysler vehicles." In April 1965 thirty physicians also selected the New York International Automotive Show to protest the supposed safety of autos. It was an "unprecedented action," according to Nader, and a reflection of the "measure of their desperation over the inaction of the men and institutions in government and industry who have failed to provide the public with the information to which it is entitled." These protesters included surgeons, orthopedists, pediatricians, and general practitioners.[40]

Lawsuits were filed to force automobile manufacturers to improve their designs, and various consumer groups sprang into action and began lobbying the government to establish and enforce stricter regulations.[41] The Highway Safety Act of 1966 established a coordinated program that required states to implement new standards for their highways by 1968 or risk losing federal funds. The Department of Transportation initially introduced nine safety standards, for states to follow, including mandatory vehicle inspection, periodic eye examinations for all drivers, the establishment of driver education programs, mandatory examination of fatally injured drivers and pedestrians for alcohol content, and the addition of state health officials to safety programs; two recommendations involved motorcycles, helmets for motorcycle drivers and their passengers and a new category of drivers licenses for motorcyclists (as well as school bus drivers and other specialists).[42]

The increasing pressure from the federal government to respond to highway safety compelled legislators to look more closely at drivers. Throughout the immediate postwar period, discussions about bad drivers were conspicuous. Male and female drivers and young and old drivers were routinely targeted, and poor driving was linked to everything from emotional problems to a troubled childhood.[43] In the midst of the debate over highway safety, that talk of bad drivers had turned into legislative efforts to mitigate their influence. "Are drivers the loose nuts which cause accidents?" one reporter asked in a story about driver standards. Several legislatures, the article explained, were particularly concerned about drunk drivers and were considering the revocation of the driver's license of any individual who refused to take an "alcoholic determination test." Other states were debating the use of alcohol blood tests for any riders or passengers killed in auto accidents. States that had already instituted such tests typically found that a majority of those killed in "one car smash ups" had been drinking. Other states began to focus more attention on the elderly. In Massachusetts a legislator introduced a bill to require yearly physical examinations of drivers older than seventy years of age after an eighty-year-old woman from Holyoke died from a heart attack while driving, and her car "plowed into 10 children and killed four."[44]

In this climate, motorcyclists were also attracting increased scrutiny. The federal government's recommendation in support of helmet laws in 1966 led politicians to begin discussions about legislation on the state level. As early as March 1967, proposals were underway in states like Ohio and Hawaii to "make [riders] wear crash helmets and goggles," and by year's end the first helmet laws were on the books. As 1968 came to a close, thirty-eight states had laws requiring motorcyclists to wear helmets.[45]

Motorcyclists were quick to challenge the laws in court, arguing that they limited their personal freedom to wear a particular type of clothing. Judges agreed, finding these laws unconstitutional because they were too "vague and uncertain" and regarding the issue of "regulating individual conduct" as "outside the scope" of the state's police power.

By the end of 1967, that would change. In a case in New York in August 1967, the state charged eight defendants with violating subdivision 6 of section 381 of the New York State Vehicle and Traffic Law, which made it unlawful "for any person to operate or ride upon a motorcycle unless he wears a protective helmet of a type approved by the commissioner." In Judge Alois C. Mazur's opinion, the "sole test of constitutionality" was "whether or not the requirement to wear protective helmets is within the police power of the state." To that end, Mazur defined police power, "broadly speaking," as the "right and power of the people to govern themselves" and the "inherent power of the State to enact and enforce laws for the protection of its people and the advancement of the general welfare." Mazur did admit that defining the limits of police power was complicated and quoted the maxim *sic utere tuo ut alienum non laedas* (so use your own that you do not injure that of others). "I am not prepared to say whether or not this maxim serves as a valid limitation or restriction of the 'police power' of the State," he observed. But, he added, the state's police powers were "very broad" and "comprehensive and flexible enough for the State to meet the problems of changing, social, economic and political conditions." In this case, the "massive increases in motorcycle registrations, use and accidents . . . had . . . created a new traffic safety problem" and made the motorcyclist a "real danger to other citizens." Mazur focused specifically on the possibility of a motorcyclist being "propelled off the road or into the opposite lane causing damage to other vehicles or property or injuries to passengers and pedestrians." Stones and gravel, which are often thrown up into the rider's face, could cause a "distraction or loss of controls," or a cyclist might unexpectedly veer off the road after having been struck by "hard-shelled beetles or bees." The judge suggested that the use of protective helmets might prevent such accidents from ever happening. What he concluded, however, was that helmet laws were constitutional because the motorcyclist had become a genuine threat to the safety and welfare of the nonriding majority.[46] In other words, "A motorcycle out of control is like a battering ram."[47]

Scrutiny of the highway's dangers suggested that the motorcycle had become a serious threat to the safety of automobilists, and efforts to regulate motorcycling and motorcyclists were increasingly conspicuous. Mazur justified this scrutiny by citing "special conditions, situations or occurrences" to describe motorcycling's threat to automobilists. Was Mazur reacting to the potential safety issue he attributed to the increasing numbers of registered motorcycles and the growing fears about outlaw motorcyclists? Or was he responding to the much more conspicuous decades-old conflict over the use of the highways and who controlled them that existed before the outlaw motorcyclist had attracted national attention and before complaints about traffic, congestion, and safety became a national issue? Either way, Mazur's proposed solution offered little chance of success. Unless a motorcyclist was wearing a full faced helmet or a face shield, a bee or hard-shelled beetle could still adversely affect the rider's ability to maintain control of the bike. His reasoning, in sum, was flawed, but it was a position that made sense to the nonriding majority attempting to come to terms with a transportation system and the motorcyclists who posed a threat to it.

SMALL-TOWN INVASIONS AND SUBURBAN BOUNDARIES

Gypsy tours, rallies, or overnighters have always been held in small towns or in out-of-the-way places to take advantage of a particularly scenic route and for camping and other outside activities that fit well with motorcycling. The appearance of the outlaw in 1947–48 reinforced the motorcyclist's connection to small towns and the familiar trope of "small town invasion." The idea of an invasion focused on the presence of outsiders in these communities, even though many participants were often residents of the affected locality. These stories paid far less attention to the origins of these riders and emphasized instead their marginal status and the ease with which they had violated the communities' boundaries and its standards.

By the 1960s popular culture was overrun by brawling motorcycle "gangs" and the motorcyclists' location sank further into the background. American International Pictures (AIP), more than any other production company, was responsible for the motorcyclist's image on the screen. Founded in 1954, AIP became king of the low-budget teenpic that pitted wayward teenagers against figures of authority. Often making use of the directing talents of Roger Corman, who was known as much for the speed with which he could make a film as his portrayal of modern life as "arbitrary and meaningless," the company produced about a dozen biker films and helped establish the basic plot line that resonated throughout the genre: small-town invasions and plenty of gratuitous violence. The company's first film, *Wild Angels*, for example, adopted the tagline "Their Credo is Violence; their God is Hate." In *Angels from Hell* "Violence leads Them, Fear Follows Them." *The Glory Stompers* featured a "Cycle War!" and one critic described *The Cycle Savages* as "third-rate chopper drivel made on a shoestring [budget] but with lavish helpings of crummy violence and sex." Starring Bruce Dern, Chris Robinson, and Melody Patterson, the film revolved around an artist's drawings of a motorcycle gang, which are stolen by the motorcyclists fearful the drawings might be used to apprehend them for crimes ranging from auto theft to white slavery. Of course, the gang is not content with simply stealing the paintings. The head of the gang, Bruce Dern, decides to capture the artist and torture him. As one review explained, "the audience is subjected to one of those typically sadistic scenes in which the artist who's been taken captive is given the business by having his hands crushed between the jaws of a vice (give it another turn)," which of course is preceded by the motorcycle gang slashing the artist with a razor.[48]

Or the motorcyclist was simply a threat because he was so mobile. In some films, hapless motorists were preyed upon after having taken a wrong turn and ending up off the main road. The ad for *Summertime Killer* (1972) featured a picture of a forlorn motorist who appears to have driven onto a dirt road that is obstructed with house-size boulders: the cyclist, who is literally jumping over the car, is riding one-handed and brandishing a pistol in the other. The story line is about a man who happens to ride a motorcycle attempting to avenge the death of his family at the hands of the mafia when he was a young boy. "Summertime and the driving is deadly," the ad warned would-be viewers (and motorists).[49] In other films, mobility was simply the foil around which the plot and the violence were played out. In *Chrome and Hot Leather*, the ad warned would-be viewers that the protagonist will "take his chopper and ram it down your throat." *The Peace Killers* "ride to love . . . [and] ride to kill." *The Cycle Savages* were "roaring through the streets on chopped hogs," with "hot steel between their legs," as opposed to the *Hard Rider[s]* who were "mounted on burning steel" with "only their leather between THEM and HELL." In *Naked Angels*, which was described as "an honest look at this sub-culture," the motorcyclists were "hunting down their prey" and once again "with a quarter-ton of hot steel between their legs."[50]

More common in the 1960s was the motorcyclist's increasingly conspicuous connection to urban space, which only exacerbated their distance from the small towns and communities to which they were commonly associated. The motorcycle clubs attracting attention in the late 1960s were almost always linked to a particular city. Oakland had its Hells Angels, the Outlaws were based in Chicago, and the Bandidos resided in San Antonio. The conflict attributed to these riders only reinforced an urban connection. In San Francisco in the early 1970s, Berkeley's Free Church decided to close its doors because of "brawling" by "Bay Area motorcycle gang members," whose fighting apparently disturbed the church's congregation. In Milwaukee, members of a local paper were caught in a shootout in which "one man was killed and five—including two *Milwaukee Sentinel* employees—were wounded." According to a police lieutenant, a motorcycle club called the Heaven's Devils was having a party at the Knew Boot Tavern when another "gang" called the Outlaws "showed up." The newspapermen were in a separate room from the motorcyclists when the "shots were fired." Details of what happened next were "unclear," but two of the paper's employees suffered gunshot wounds.[51]

Yet even as urban spaces began to challenge the familiar trope of small-town invasion, the postindustrial city began to shape the public's attitude about motorcyclists, our assumptions about the boundaries they routinely threatened and crossed, and the paranoia that surrounded their presence. For example, suburbs reached their peak in the years after World War II, and as they consumed more of the country's cultural and material resources, motorcyclists were increasingly identified as part of the landscape. While *Motorcyclist* claimed that "some county zoning boards" were "proposing banning them [motorcycles] from suburban areas," within a month of the end of the Hollister Rally,[52] the conflict within suburbs would not become visible until the 1960s. For example, in 1966 the governor of Wisconsin, Warren Knowles, scheduled a meeting to deal with "law enforcement problems" that he argued were created by "roving bands of young toughs and hoodlums," his reference to the Outlaws, a group of motorcyclists who the article suggested were linked to Milwaukee but had created the alleged disturbance in the nearby suburb of Cedarburg. The conflict had erupted, appropriately enough, at a gas station, further highlighting the club's outsider status and its disconnectedness from the suburban location where it had allegedly committed crimes. The press described the motorcyclists as "invading" the gas station, "defying" local police officers, and taking gasoline without paying for it. "The people of Wisconsin," the governor insisted "will not tolerate such civil disorder and flagrant violation of law," and he was "determined that the state will develop a program for dealing with and preventing such disgraceful activities in the future."[53]

In other stories the threat was more permanent and hence more of a violation of the suburb's boundaries and its inhabitants. One example implicated the motorcyclists who participated in the brawl at the Motorcycle Custom and Trade Show in Cleveland in 1971, which led to the deaths of five motorcyclists. The state had charged fifty-six of them with first-degree murder, and the police had detained another twenty-eight for questioning in an investigation that led detectives "to search a barn in suburban Brunswick in which 150 members of the Breed gang allegedly gathered before leaving" for the trade show.[54]

Amid the suburbs and the postindustrial city, motorcyclists were also more likely to cross paths with other men and women in their search for leisure. Suburbanization in general meant more time on the road going to and from work, shopping, and having fun. Suburbanites often retreated back to the central city they had originally lived in for these activities, into other suburban areas depending upon their proximity and development, or further afield to take advantage of the beaches, lakes, amusement parks, and other outdoor events that were becoming increasingly popular in the postwar years.[55] In an article about Lake Perry, a lake sixteen miles north of Lawrence, Kansas, and about an hour from Kansas City, Lynn Myers of the U.S. Army Corps of Engineers estimated that 125,000 to 130,000 visitors were expected to make the trek for the upcoming Memorial Day weekend in 1972. The expected crowd would include "campers, boating enthusiasts, water skiers, swimmers, fishermen, hikers, picnickers and beer-and soft drink guzzlers," who would also be joined by motorcyclists. In fact during the preceding weekend that had attracted an estimated crowd of around 100,000, four motorcyclists were involved in accidents, and all of them required hospitalization.[56]

Throughout the 1960s and 1970s, conflict often centered on these outdoor amusements, and motorcyclists were often blamed. At a rock festival in Watsonville, California, in 1971 a brawl broke out between motorcyclists, Mexican American youths, and surfers from the surrounding beaches. Authorities described the festival as "generally peaceful until the arrival of a motorcycle group from San Jose," and "the trouble occurred just as the festival was breaking up." Witnesses said nineteen members of a motorcycle club clashed with a group of "Mexican-American youths," and surfers from the beaches near Watson joined the melee against the motorcyclists. The fight, which lasted "more than an hour" before "being broken up by state highway patrolmen, sheriff's deputies and police," led to the death of one cyclist. Rounded up for questioning were 150 other individuals.[57]

Indeed, complaints about motorcyclists often centered on the ways in which they challenged the day-to-day organization of leisure. In the 1965 man-about-town interview with Marjerie Meyer quoted earlier, salesman Dan Littlepage made the point of leisure central to his understanding of motorcyclists and the threat they posed. When a reporter asked Littlepage if "rioting motorcyclists should lose their licenses," he replied "certainly," describing the loss of a license as a "small price" to pay. Rioting motorcyclists, Littlepage argued, "not only cause trouble and destroy property, but they prevent families that have planned and paid for expensive vacations from enjoying themselves."[58] A good example of an interrupted vacation took place in Muskegon, Michigan, the site of a National Motorcycle Hill Climb competition in the late 1960s. Besides riding "their machines through bonfires," "invading taverns," and swimming nude in Lake Michigan near the site of the sporting event, motorcyclists commandeered a motorboat for joyriding and violated the boundaries of the local country club around midnight. Sheriff's deputies "said about 20 riders invaded the private Pontaluna County Club . . . and toppled chairs, grabbed food and drinks from patrons and barged out without paying." The press reported that ten sheriff's deputies responded to the first call for assistance but were "turned back by a crowd of cycle riders who told the officers they would be shot if they entered the hill area. The officers left and returned with reinforcements, then cordoned off the area."[59]

Popular culture also took note of the motorcyclist's ability to cross boundaries, and the postindustrial city was the backdrop against which the usual sex and violence played out. An advertisement for the film *Black Angels* proclaimed "God Forgives . . . The Black Angels Don't," which was just above (and in descending order) a picture of the face of one of the Angels and a staggered triangle of a dozen motorcyclists who appear as if they are about to burst out of the poster. Except for the picture of a growling mountain lion that appears in one ad, the image of motorcyclists barreling

Promotional poster for *Black Angels* (1970). Courtesy of Photofest, Inc.

down upon the onlooker, the drawn switchblade, and a grimacing face all played upon the typical fears about violent motorcyclists. The poster image of a close-up of the star of the film did not look all that different from the poster depicting Bruce Dern, who starred in *Cycle Savages*—same hairstyle, beard, and grimace, and placed just above the same image of a dozen staggered motorcycles threatening to break out of the poster. The only obvious difference is that the Black Angel's image is a slightly darker shade of pale.[60]

The film revolves around "an ongoing gang war between two cycle mobs, the Choppers" (a black motorcycle club)—"you ain't bustin nobody whitey"—and "Satan's Serpents." The film featured the typical fights off their bikes and the gratuitous sex scenes with "a wild bunch of women," who were described as "untamed and shameless," but also high-speed chases that move from residential areas to the surrounding highways. *The Black Angels* was not advertised with the usual reference to two tons of chrome and steel between their legs. They were "exploding out of the slums [and] into the establishment," an obvious reference to the fears about urban unrest and black rebellion that captured the nation's attention in the 1960s but also to the motorcyclist's broader capacity to cross borders. Silence generally characterized the motorcyclists' connection to the inner city, and a direct link was never assumed; but it was also never denied, and their connection to the suburbs was ambiguous at best.[61] *The Black Angels* confirmed the rigid boundaries between suburb and inner city and the boundaries between security and danger, just as they broke through those boundaries with all the splendor and irreverence of a B-grade film.

As these examples suggest, the motorcyclist's ability to defy the postindustrial city contributed to the stereotypes surrounding him. The resulting conflict was often the product of a chance encounter at sites where violence was possible but generally not expected—a day at the beach or a drink at a local watering hole. The motorcyclist's mobility simply eliminated any guarantees for the nonriding public's safety, negating normal precautions such as steering clear of a notorious hangout, staying in after dark, or avoiding a certain section of town. Motorcyclists had few limits on where and when they might roam, and their interaction with the public could be unexpected and unpredictable. Motorcyclists were neither here nor there but potentially everywhere. Indeed, while the line dividing urban and suburban spaces was at times indistinct, and suburbanites would spend a considerable amount of time crossing back and forth on their way to and from work and to satiate their appetite for leisure, this configuration of space still revolved around boundaries that shaped their day-to-day lives and their understanding of motorcyclists. Highways played a critical role in the development of this system, but they were as likely to enforce those borders as to facilitate their disruption. Highways, as Eric Avila thoughtfully argues, "channeled the flow of traffic along a uniform line of movement" that shaped the public's understanding of the city and limited "the possibilities for different perspectives."[62] Thus, any violation of those boundaries threatened to disrupt them and the broader understanding of space and mobility on which this system was based— what Marjerie Meyer meant, perhaps, when she defined the use of the highway as a privilege that could be revoked. This threat included "riots," which were understood to be challenges to the boundaries of a postindustrial society and the struggle surrounding transportation.

Such stories often left out important details about the motorcyclists' role in these events, which only increased the public's fear and paranoia. One of the initial articles about the brawl between cyclists and Mexican American youth and surfers in Watsonville, California, for example, stated that the trouble began as the festival was coming to an end and as motorcyclists arrived at the "previously calm festival." The article failed, however, to explain the focus on the nineteen motorcyclists when 150 other participants were "rounded up" for questioning. Indeed, another article described the motorcyclists as belonging to a "weekend family" that "gathered for short trips and had just come from Yosemite National Park"—these were not the usual outlaws who have shaped our memory of motorcyclists and the public's reaction to them. These riders had apparently parked their bikes and "refused to let anyone near them." In response, a "youth" shouted "Let's get the riders," and the crowd began to move in on the motorcyclists. The cyclists responded by forming a circle and swinging chains above their heads to try and keep the crowd at bay. The police arrived about an hour later and used tear gas to end the melee. The paper reported that both sides blamed the other, but the police made it clear that "they (the youths) wanted to get the bikers," and they hurled apples at the police when they tried to break up the assault.[63]

Throughout the 1960s and 1970s and at public gatherings across the country, evidence suggests that motorcyclists were as likely, or perhaps more likely, to be the victims rather than perpetrators of mob violence. In Petit Rocher, New Brunswick, Canada, in 1977 motorcyclists were once again "terrorized" by members of a small community. The motorcyclists known as the Daltons had been "active" in Petit Rocher for seven years but only for the past two years had tension developed with the community's residents. The "immediate cause" was a brawl between five members of the Daltons and villagers. The Daltons were taken into custody, but close to one thousand residents including "about 50 with guns or baseball bats confronted two or three of the Daltons" at a tavern and "challenged them to a fight." Perhaps not surprising, when the motorcyclists found themselves confronting what one reporter described as a "jeering row of more than 1,000," they "fled to their clubhouse in the woods," about five miles outside of town. Roughly 300 townsfolk followed the motorcyclists, and shots were fired into their clubhouse, forcing them to retreat to the woods. The townsfolk razed the Dalton clubhouse as well as two nearby small camps, where eight of the Daltons' female friends were staying. They also destroyed "or otherwise wrecked five motorcycles, two cars, and a pickup truck," according to authorities, and killed a pet dog. The police failed to arrest any of the villagers, although some weapons had been seized and the police were still looking for the motorcyclists who fled into the woods.[64]

On their bikes, motorcyclists faced an even greater threat. "Folk wisdom has it," one writer argued about motorcycling in the early 1980s, "that there are only two types of motorcycle riders: those who have crashed and those who are about to crash."[65] The public's consensus about motorcycles was even more extreme: "If you get on a motorcycle, there's a 50-50 chance you're going to die."[66] But by the 1960s and 1970s fears about the inevitability of a crash were more urgent than in previous years. One of the best examples appeared in an Ann Landers column in the late 1970s, which ran under the title "How to Kill a Biker" from motorcyclist J.T.T. "Dear Ann Landers," the aggrieved cyclist began his letter. "On behalf of motorcycle enthusiasts across the nation, I've come up with a list of things drivers of cars can do to kill more motorcyclists this year." The list included three main topics and all were potentially fatal. "Throw things out the window, when there is a bike behind you," was the first J.T.T. addressed. "At 55 mph., cigar ashes can permanently blind a person," and "a hamburger wrapper thrown out at that speed could startle a biker and cause him to crash." "Pull out in front of bikers" was his second point. When a motorist pulled out in front of a cyclist, he noted, the motorcyclist had four options, and none of them guaranteed his safety. "He can (a) skid, laying the bike down and possibly dying, (b) run into the car ahead (instant death), (c) get clobbered by an oncoming car (also instant death), (d) hit the ditch (20 percent chance of survival)." J.T.T.'s third point focused on what had become the common practice of a motorist passing a biker and "cut[ting] in close," which J.T.T. suggested was not always accidental but often "for kicks." "They're [motorcycles] skinnier than cars, so they don't need a whole lane," he sarcastically interjected. J.T.T. concluded his letter by explaining that motorcycles were "a lot more fragile than most people think. We CAN'T stop on a dime, dodge flying objects, drive on a two-foot-wide pavement, and hope to survive long enough to see our children grow." "Please people," he beseeched the nonriding majority, "I pay my taxes . . . respect the law . . . [and] try to be considerate on the road." "If you treat me badly on the road, I will DIE, it's as simple as that. Thank you for letting me have my say."[67]

Throughout the 1960s and 1970s, contemporaries talked about the conflict J.T.T. described. A story about the middle-class rider used the term "power chauvinism" to characterize highway travel in the United States and the automobile's dominance. The numbers of motorcycle accidents and fatalities, the author argued, reflected the "attitude of U.S. auto drivers," who feel that "highways belong to cars—big cars—and grant two-wheelers their legal right-of-way with surly reluctance if at all." The author added, "with the rabbit-like proliferation of cycles on our own streets and highways (and a rocketing percentage of car drivers who are parents of cyclists), a tempering of live-and-let-live tolerance is becoming apparent here. But sheer power chauvinism—the cause of many traffic accidents of all types—still rules the U.S. highway."[68] Motorcycle cop and Captain William A. Cruber of the State Police Department at Hartford, Connecticut, knew all too well what the author meant by "power chauvinism" or what he described as "the problems faced by single-file operation when vehicles pull alongside and pass and force cycles off the traveled portion of the roadway."[69] In 1963 a motorcyclist in *American Motorcycling* explained that riding his motorcycle had convinced him "what a bully the average person is. I can drive home in my truck and cars don't pull out in front of me at all," but "if I get on my motorcycle and ride back to town," he added, "cars do pull out in front of me." It was "surprising," he remarked, "how they will do this, bully you into slowing down."[70]

In Florida in 1970 Robert H. Schultz was driving home at about five o'clock during a "peak traffic period" when a motorist in a Cadillac began to harass him and try and push him off the road. Schultz described the offending motorist as acting in an "irrational manner." He was "zipping up close and dropping back and zipping up again, blowing his horn." Schultz described the incident as the "most harrowing one he has encountered on his motorcycle," and it ended only when "he was finally able to maneuver the two-wheeler over to the edge of the curb lane on the four-lane thoroughfare." Once he pulled to the side, the Cadillac "roared by with its driver shaking his fists," a gesture most of us are familiar with but one that was particularly threatening to motorcyclists because of their greater vulnerability and history of facing disgruntled motorists who intentionally targeted them.[71]

A more troubling example and violent one took place a year earlier in Clearwater, Florida. The incident involved automobilist Andrew Davenport and members of a Tampa Bay motorcycle club known as the Lancers. One newspaper article noted that the police had denied reports that a "Bay Area motorcycle club" had "terrorized" Sun Coast residents during a Sunday afternoon ride along US 19, and they were investigating the "beating of a motorist." The police had arrested three motorcyclists for what Police Chief Frank Daniels described as a "senseless" beating, and he made it clear that his department would "take steps to see that the same type of incident doesn't occur again." The media claimed that motorcyclist, Richard Joseph Duffy, and his passenger were "knocked to the ground by the collision with Davenport's car." Clearwater detective sergeant Dave Panossian claimed that witnesses saw "Duffy [get] up, [break] the left side window of Davenport's car and [try] to drag him from the vehicle." Ten to fifteen more cyclists also approached the car and "several helped drag Davenport out of the driver's seat." After he was pulled from the car and as cyclists were beating him, "Davenport pointed a pistol in the air and fired four shots." When the police arrived, several of the motorcyclists "sped off but were later rounded up by Pinellas sheriff's deputies and local police departments." The gun was also missing from the scene and was later handed over to the police by one of the motorcyclists. Duffy was "charged with breaking and entering with intent to commit a misdemeanor—a felony" (breaking and entering Davenport's car), and another cyclist, Harry Douglas Haggard, "pleaded guilty to assault and battery." According to a hospital spokesman "Davenport suffered facial cuts, back bruises, 'two or three broken ribs' and a bleeding kidney."[72]

The incident also attracted the attention of state representative Mary Grizzle (R-Bellair Beach). She had no interest in investigating the event but rather used the occasion to seek ways to restrict motorcyclists' use of the highways to explicitly punish them. According to one article, Mrs. Grizzle had contacted the state's House Public Safety Committee to see "if there is any pending legislation that could be amended to include restrictions on cyclists." She was also considering drafting legislation that would limit the number of motorcyclists riding in formation or what she described as "riding in ganglike fashion."[73]

A twenty-one-year-old woman who was a passenger on one of the motorcycles explicitly contradicted the police's version of the day's events. The woman claimed that Davenport instigated the conflict by "cutting into our line [several times with his car]." "He almost ran three of us off the road," she explained, and at a stop light he intentionally "ran over" Duffy. The woman added that Davenport "called us bums, waved a gun around and threatened to shoot us all if we didn't get away." At that point "about five" of the motorcyclists jumped on Davenport to disarm him and "he started fighting." Davenport claimed that he "didn't fire his gun and he didn't know who did." "The gun is an automatic and a slide has to be pulled back to shove a bullet into the chamber." Davenport argued that he never kept a "slug in the chamber," and that "he wouldn't have had time to pull the gun if he wanted to." He claimed that "as soon as the cyclists pulled him out of the car, they started hitting him."[74]

A similar roadway incident occurred in Questa, New Mexico, a small town situated just north of Taos, New Mexico, that led to a gunfight between "seven carloads of area residents and a score of Colorado motorcyclists at a northern New Mexican campground"—four of the bikers were wounded, one of them seriously. The gunfight resulted from "some kind of alterca-tion" that initially started when the two were mobile and ended when the automobilist ran the motorcyclist off the road. According to one report, it "started from there," but "we don't know if there was a fist fight or what." What police do know is that the confrontation led to shooting when area residents went to the campground and "opened fire," after an "exchange of words with the motorcyclists." A "state police official" reported that "no shots were fired by the motorcycle group" during the incident, although this official emphasized that "some of them [motorcyclists] were armed and we have information that they have (fired weapons) sporadically," suggesting that the violence against the motorcyclists was legitimate or justified. The police official added, "We don't know if it was in self defense," although that was unlikely because the motorcyclists were unarmed and the town residents had gone to the campground looking for them.[75]

The outlaw's appearance at Hollister in 1947 directly reflected his mobility and his relationship to the communities he was accused of invading—hence the trope of "small-town invasion." By the 1960s and 1970s, his mobility and the fears surrounding it reflected his move from small towns to big cities and beyond. In this case, the beyond included the suburbs, to which more Americans had retreated to escape the problems they associated with cities. The real and imagined boundaries Americans tried to put in place only made the motorcyclist's mobility more of a threat and increased their dependence on the automobile at a time of growing scrutiny about its safety and usefulness.

Automobilists, in short, suffered from road rage and often blamed motorcyclists for it. The term "road rage" was first used in the late 1980s to describe the increased tension and violence on America's highways. Its emergence sent contemporaries scrambling to understand the phenome-non and the word's origins. Scholars' explanations have generally failed to account for the behavior and why it appeared at this particular time. But if we accept the contemporary definition of road rage—"violent actions directed at another motorist"—there is plenty of evidence to suggest that road rage has been around for decades and that motorcyclists, at least in the postwar years, were often singled out as the reason for it—if not one of the first groups to be victims of it.[76]

To be sure, frustration about highway travel and suburbanization accom-panied the expansion of the U.S. transportation system and the resulting con-figuration of space. But motorcyclists were never simply caught up in the rat race. Motorcycling (and motorcyclists) defied it and challenged its use and its limitations. The resulting frustration among motorcyclists contributed, and was perhaps central, to their reputation as the "Most Unpopular Men on the Road," not because of their lawless or violent behavior but because of the conflict surrounding the growth and development of this system. In his fascinating study of white flight in Los Angeles, Eric Avilla argues that Americans readily accepted Walt Disney's "representation of the new freeways as futuristic symbols of American progress and modernity" because, in part, they were "unacquainted with the inconveniences of traffic jams and the horrors of freeway shootings."[77] In our own era of road rage, it is difficult to imagine the past Avilla describes, but the motorcyclist's experience suggests that he overstates the differences between these two periods. Traffic jams were already beginning to shape the average American's experience with highway travel and, more importantly, the larger struggle over defining highway etiquette. Motorcyclists challenged it, and the resulting conflict affected the average automobilist's understanding of highway travel, and it negatively impacted the understanding of motorcyclists.

Not surprisingly, the public not only considered eliminating the privilege of roadway travel for motorcyclists but also imagined (or fantasized about) the complete destruction of their bikes. A story that circulated in the early 1970s and was captured on film in the 1977 hit *Smokey and the Bandit* focused on what a contemporary described as "trucker's revenge." The story features a trucker stopping at a roadway café for something to eat; three or four long-haired bikers in leather jackets and heavy boots enter the restaurant and harass the trucker for no apparent reason (in the film, they claimed the trucker's dog bit one of them). After having his food dumped into his lap or, in the film version, being beaten up, the trucker quietly pays his bill and leaves the café. "That truck driver isn't much of a man," one of the bikers boasts to a waitress as she watches the trucker pull out of the restaurant parking lot. "He isn't much of a driver either," she responds. "He just ran over three motorcycles."[78]

The public may have felt that the trucker's revenge was justifiable, and at screenings of *Smokey and the Bandit* the crowd cheered as the eighteen-wheeler plowed through the line of parked motorcycles.[79] But was the trucker's response proportional, and did it effectively address the issues that were at stake? Without his bike, the motorcyclist is just another thug in a leather jacket, and hence the threat he poses at the diner is as conspicuous as it was before his bike had its untimely encounter with an eighteen-wheeler. But with the decisiveness of a several-ton truck, the trucker's revenge did eliminate him from America's highways.

IN 1949 AUTOMOBILE SAFETY advocate Albert Whitney published *Man and the Motorcar* in which he equated good driving with good citizenship.

According to Whitney, "Being a good driver requires the same qualities that are needed if you are to be a good citizen, a good neighbor, a good son and a good brother. That would mean that learning to drive must be closely connected with learning to live." While Whitney's comments may resonate less today than they may have in the late 1940s, the average motorcyclist's experience suggests that the link between citizenship and driving did not extend equally to all motorists. The relationship between automobilists and motorcyclists was not only riddled with conflict. It was an unequal relationship that could be described in two ways: a relationship in which automobilists had more rights, or a relationship in which motorcyclists had none. That difference was exemplified best by what motorcyclists described as the common practice of being crowded out of their lanes by automobilists who did not see them or by automobilists who did not care. By the 1960s and 1970s, that conflict was even more difficult to ignore than in earlier decades, and the relationship between driving and citizenship was becoming more pronounced, even though highway travel was considered increasingly more dangerous.

Marjerie Meyer alluded to this relationship when she described highway travel as a privilege. While she failed to explain whose privilege she was talking about—the privilege of a legally licensed driver or one of the privileges of citizenship—the line between the two was difficult to find, and it was clear that Meyer believed some individuals had more rights than others. Her citizenship, realized daily on America's roads and freeways, then, was predicated on the absence of citizenship among others. Indeed, if Meyer was unclear about her intention and the meaning of privilege and citizenship, J.T.T. was not in his complaint to Ann Landers about the hazards that motorcyclists faced from automobilists. As J.T.T. was outlining the different dangers he confronted on the highway, he described motorcyclists as "second-class motorists" and then reminded Landers (and her readers) that "bikers have the same rights as the driver of an 18-wheel semi." By this time (the late 1970s), ideas about citizenship and its meaning had attracted considerable attention because of helmet laws and the motorcycle rights movement that emerged to challenge them. But ideas about citizenship were just as conspicuous in the aftermath of World War II and were used specifically to understand the rights and privileges of roadway travel. In other words, the motorcyclist's struggle for equality and the tension surrounding it did not begin the moment legislators began to regulate motorcycling or when the outlaw was imagined as a threat to the nonriding public. It began against the backdrop of the expansion of America's highways and the conflict over who controlled them.

YOU AIN'T SHIT IF YOU DON'T RIDE A HARLEY

The Middle-Class Motorcyclist and the Japanese Honda

"Vroom-vroom is now an established middle-class noise," claimed a 1965 *Esquire* article about the Madison Avenue Motorcycle Club (MAMC). The author described the club as one "peopled by respectable professional men who prefer two wheels to four, and it is just one manifestation of a growing sophistication of the motorcycle." The club was initially established in 1960, a year in which only 45,000 motorcycles were sold nationwide, by a group of "serious" bike-riding New York executives and professional men. Five years later, Americans were expected to purchase as many as 450,000 cycles by the year's end. Most of these new owners were casual participants in the subculture, or what the author characterized as "fair-weather riders" and "not the hard-core devotees." The picture accompanying the story showed a dozen men riding in a pack, some of them wearing sunglasses, a significant majority of them wearing helmets, and all of them in suit and tie. "Grey worsted suits in the saddle and an attaché case on the luggage carrier," the author explained, "are not the rare sight today that they were a few years ago."[1]

Stories such as this one about middle-class riders making motorcycling respectable were common in the early 1960s. Their arrival both coincided with and was the product of the introduction of the Japanese Honda into the American marketplace. Yet despite the enthusiasm that greeted the middle-class rider, ambivalence and frustration also surrounded him. These were serious riders, or so they claimed, yet their critics found it all too easy to dismiss them as "casual" motorcyclists. If anything, their struggle to overcome this claim made their impact on motorcycling more conspicuous than it might have been otherwise, and it brought the issue of class to the fore.

To be sure, there were plenty of middle-class and professional riders who did not wear a suit and tie. But just as many (if not more) did, and the image of the middle-class rider (and his Japanese-made bike) remained a conspicuous and influential issue in motorcycling in the decades to come. The trademark suit and tie was accompanied by the assumption that their bikes required little if any maintenance and that the act of buying a bike was more important than building one.

Historians have noted that these postwar years represented a period in which consumption became intimately linked to citizenship and social belonging. The middle-class rider embodied these basic ideas even as he revealed the weaknesses surrounding them. He struggled to deal with the stigma associated with the "biker" who not only had fewer resources to support his preoccupation but also promoted the idea that class consumption was more important to motorcycle culture than mass consumption.[2] In other words, the economic circumstances facing riders affected their relationship to motorcycling, and the overwhelmingly working-class constituency had more invested in its bikes than that which could be derived through the simple act of buying one.

These debates about class and consumption critically shaped what it meant to be a rider in the 1960s and 1970s. They aggravated an increasingly bitter fight about brand loyalty that gave rise to the slogan "You ain't shit if you don't ride a Harley" and formed the basis for a growing divide among riders that would influence the fight over the government's regulation of motorcyclists (through the helmet issue) and lead to a divide that is still visible today.

THE POPULARITY OF MOTORCYCLING

The growth in the number of street bikes during the 1960s and 1970s was nothing short of astounding. In 1945 there had been 198,000 registered motorcycles in the United States, and by 1950 that number more than doubled, to 454,000. Over the next decade (1950–60), this number would grow at a much more modest pace—from 454,000 to 575,000. But between 1960 and 1965 the number of registered motorcycles soared from 575,000 to 1,382,000. By 1971 the number had surpassed the 3 million mark, and as of 1974 Americans had registered a total of 5 million motorcycles for use on the country's roads and highways.[3]

The introduction of the Japanese-made Honda motorcycle is the main reason for this unprecedented uptick. The first Hondas were sold out of the back of a pickup truck in Los Angeles in 1959, and during the company's first year of operation in the United States (1959–60) it sold 2,548 cycles.[4]

Two years later (1962) the annual total had increased to about 50,000,[5] and for the 1965–66 period Honda sold 267,640 motorcycles in the United States. By this time Honda estimated that its motorcycles accounted for close to 70 percent of all American motorcycle sales and that Americans across the country were riding a total of 720,000 of them. Total sales for fiscal year 1965 were just over $77 million, while a year later the company's sales totaled over $106 million.[6] The Honda motorcycle was dubbed the "next potential Tin Lizzy."[7]

The success of Honda was largely the work of Soichiro Honda. Honda, the son of a poor village blacksmith, had always been fascinated with engines. He apprenticed as a mechanic in a Tokyo garage and at age twenty-one established an automotive repair business. He eventually started racing autos until an accident in 1935 left him without any chance of continued success. After World War II, he began building motorcycles and by 1949 had produced his fourth model, which has been described as the sire of all the Hondas that were to follow. It was capable of going about 45 miles per hour and averaged 200 miles per gallon of gas. Soichiro painted it red, black, white, and blue and called it the Dream. By 1952 Honda employed one thousand men, and his factory was about one hundred times larger than the two wooden shacks he started with.[8] By 1964, he had four factories in Japan (two in south central Honshu and two in Tokyo), a research center, and a plant in Belgium and another one set to open in Thailand.[9]

Honda was not alone in the American market. Within just over a decade of Honda's appearance in the United States, the company's share of the U.S. market dropped to around 42 percent as other Japanese companies began to sell to American consumers—Yamahas, Kawasakis, and Suzukis. Together the Japanese brands had captured more than 80 percent of the U.S. market, compelling one contemporary to note that "in no other U.S. market category do Japanese brand names hold such a commanding position."[10]

Honda's good fortune reflected the company's success at attracting a new cohort of riders—what its ads described as "the nicest people" and who were unmistakably middle class. Within a few short years of the appearance of the first Hondas, stories began to appear with titles like "New Breed of Motorcyclist," "Cycles in Social Revolution," "Cycles Swooping Up," and "Civilized Cycles: Everybody Rides 'Em Now." These articles celebrated the craze in motorcycling that was sweeping across the nation and offered vivid descriptions of the "smiling boyish faces, midriff beauties and solid commuter types," who had recently taken up cycling.[11] "Motorcycles, like pool tables," had "joined the anointed ranks of the socially acceptable."[12] Another story referred to the "growing sophistication of the motorcycle."[13] "With the endorsement of doctors, lawyers, teachers and a wide variety of other professional persons," a *New York Times* article exclaimed, "the motorcycle image has undergone a change that has contributed to the sales explosion."[14]

These new riders were also generally linked to families.[15] A 1963 *Business Week* article, for example, noted that riders of these Japanese motorcycles were swiftly changing the typical image of the "heavy leather jackets," "goggles," and "tough young men" and persuading Californians that a motorcycle can be "for family fun." About 65 percent of Honda customers were "newcomers to the sport who have never ridden a motorcycle before," and their "enthusiasm has run so high that—with the encouragement of enterprising Honda dealers—they have set up clubs and dubbed themselves 'Hondanauts.'" One such club in Eagle Rock, California, consisted of "young married couples who like to take off on weekend excursions."[16]

Motorcycling was also attracting more women riders in the 1960s. The typical picture of the middle-class motorcyclist featured comfort-conscious executives, young fashionable coeds, and even mothers gearing up for a trip to work or a weekend of fun.[17] The April 1965 issue of *American Motorcycling* featured Pat Parnell, wife and mother of two young boys, as an example of this new rider. Pat and her husband faced a "transportation problem with a home in Huffman and her job in Houston." The pair "solved it by buying a bright red motorcycle." Pat rode "40 miles a day to work in blue jeans, a long-sleeved shirt, a ski jacket, and a safety helmet over her curlers." She commented, "I think the only way you could tell I'm a girl is by my purse on the handlebars." Once she had completed her journey, she would stop at a gas station, disappear into the ladies room for a few minutes, and reappear with "blonde hair brushed, and the motorcycle outfit replaced with a pretty suit."[18]

No reliable statistics exist on the number of female riders during this era, but anecdotal evidence suggests their numbers grew considerably in the 1960s. At the time that Josephine W. Bucklew of Houston wrote a letter to *American Motorcycling* in 1949, she had been without a "motor[cycle]" for two years and had "felt lost" during that time. She explained that she had been riding horses from the time she was a "wee little one" and "was never as happy as I am on a good iron steed." Bucklew started riding a Harley 61 in 1943 and exclaimed, "There are very few days in this part of Texas that a motor cannot be ridden." The only drawback she mentioned was the scarcity of other female riders on the road: "Girl riders are still rather a novelty here in Houston—only about six or seven have their own motors even now."[19] In 1966 Honda claimed that "its women customers have doubled in number over the past two years," although the company would "not give specific figures."[20] By 1975 Yamaha would claim that 10 percent of its customers were female, up from 3 percent two years earlier. A year before the company became the first motorcycle manufacturer to buy ad space in a woman's magazine—*Cosmopolitan*. Their full-page ad was so successful that Honda followed up with its own *Cosmopolitan* ad shortly thereafter.[21]

This new middle-class rider was also African American. *Ebony* magazine's article on "50 Eligible Bachelors" for 1969 started off by highlighting motorcyclists among its featured bachelors. "If a GIRL has read up on her Afro-American history and if she doesn't object to riding on the back of a motorcycle or even in the cockpit of an airplane, she just might be able to land herself one of this year's *Ebony* eligible bachelors." The bachelors, described as men who had "much to offer," were "scattered from coast to coast," most lived in large urban communities, and they had annual incomes as high as $100,000. The article featured several photographs of men at work and at home, lounging about the bachelor pad, or standing next to their favorite sports car, and they were described in general as sophisticated and well-traveled. Many of them spoke more than one language, and almost all of them had a very clear idea of the type of woman they were looking for. The "ideal girl," *Ebony* explained, had to be "with it" on "just about everything." "Not only does she have to be intelligent, the bachelors say, but she has to be really sharp on practical sociology and politics." She also had to "have a certain grace and elegance because most of the bachelors like to entertain, and she has to be sporty enough to keep up with guys who enjoy riding motorcycles and flying airplanes." E. Gene McFadden was one such bachelor. He was twenty-nine years old and an assistant superintendent who supervised and coordinated community education for the school district of Benton Harbor, Michigan. Motorcycling was his hobby, and he wanted a "girl 'with a strong personality.' "[22]

As these examples suggest, the face of motorcycling was indeed changing in the early 1960s. White, working-class men dominated motorcycling and its image in motorcycle publications. Others riders still remained on the margins, and their impact on motorcycle culture was even less conspicuous. The lightweights that became popular in early 1960s had the potential to link these new riders together, as did their middle-class status. They were respectable and clean-cut, or what one contemporary likened to the Pepsi generation—the company's slogan in the 1960s and 1970s that emphasized the country's youth and an adventuresome spirit. Pepsi's original television ad about this generation, in fact, featured a young couple aboard a lightweight motorcycle against the backdrop of the song's lyrics and the voice-over that described the Pepsi generation as, "Just about everyone with the young view of things" who were "active livelier people with a liking for Pepsi cola."[23]

MOTORCYCLE CULTURE AND THE MIDDLE CLASS

Jack was nimble, Jack was quick,
His chopper started with one swift kick.
Jack was cool, Jack was smart,
The cheating mutha used an electric start.[24]

A 1947 *Motorcyclist* editorial about the need to sell the sport of motorcycling argued that convincing the public of the benefits of cycling should be easy because the sport combined the "American love" for "the outdoors" and the "love of mechanics."[25] Fred B. Meyers, from Roseville, California, owned a 1948 Indian Chief when he wrote a letter to *American Motorcycling* in 1950 to object to an earlier reference to motorcyclists as "grease monkeys." "Most people are under the impression that one has to be a grease monkey to ride a motor." But it "definitely is not so," he objected, even as he admitted that he kept his "motor clean" because it afforded a "better chance for closer inspection" of it, which would allow him to notice potential problems before they affected the motorcycle's performance and that he knew what problems to look for.[26] Josephine W. Bucklew of Houston carried around the "necessary tools" when she went riding and knew "enough about a motor that I can go anywhere," with only "a general overhaul on [my] 61 [OHV]" being beyond her capabilities.[27]

Other motorcyclists were much more adamant about the need for some mechanical skill. In a 1953 letter to *Cycle* Cliff Boswell highlighted the "scarcity of dependable motorcycle repair and parts shops in many western states." He claimed that "it is either necessary for a rider to carry numerous spare parts" or "chance a week or two lay-over while he sends to the nearest large city, if a break-down occurs."[28] H.E.C. from Aumsville, Oregon, described himself as a "pretty fair mechanic," and because he lived outside a major city, he had to be. When he first started riding motorcycles, he lived in southern Arizona, and the closest dealers were 128, 172, and 190 miles away in various directions. "Quite necessarily," he added, "I had to learn to repair my own."[29] Byron Lynn of Alberta, Canada, agreed that there were not enough dealers around to meet a rider's mechanical needs. "I'm living and working on a farm in central Alberta and 125 miles north of a shop and 200 miles south of another shop. Due to working and weather conditions, I wasn't always able to run into the city to have work done on my machine, so I built me a small shop that I house my machines [in] and

Jack Troop and friend looking over their bikes just before heading out for a ride, Plattsmouth, Nebraska, 1950s. Courtesy of Don Troop.

work in in my spare time." Lynn noted that he was "not a real mechanic, and I don't pretend to be [one,] but I can work on my machines and get along fine with what I have got."[30]

Jack Jamison's experience with motorcycles confirmed the need for some mechanical skill, regardless of one's proximity to a big city. Jack was born in 1940 and grew up in Brookfield, Missouri, about two hours north and east of Kansas City. He rode his first motorcycle (a 1950, 125cc Indian Vertical Twin) when he was twelve and two years later (1954) bought his first motorcycle, a 1949 125cc Harley-Davidson from a guy he met at the local motorcycle shop. "You heard of a basket case," he explained in one interview. The engine was in pieces in a bushel basket and the rest of the bike in two or three other boxes. Jamison recalled that he knew "absolutely nothing about putting a motorcycle together," but "back in those days," he added, "if you had a motorcycle or [were] interested in motorcycles you were a buddy with everyone who had one" and there were "lots of guys helping you work on it." Jamison specifically recalled trips several of his buddies would go on from time to time, and it was unusual for all of them to make it to Kansas City and back (to Brookfield). Bikes back then were unreliable, and you had to be what he described as a "half-way mechanic" because "something was going to break sooner or later."[31]

Jack Jamison (left) racing in the mid-1950s. Courtesy of Jack and Pat Jamison.

Motorcyclists also saw little difference between the mechanical reliability of an American-made Harley and that of its British counterparts.[32] Captain Joseph H. Seaman Jr. thought the nation would benefit from more competition in the cycle industry: From the "little observing I have been able to do of the English machines, the quality of the workmanship appears to be equally good as that of our own makes."[33] A. Neff from Philadelphia made a similar argument but by highlighting the deficiencies from which all motorcycles suffered. Neff had grown tired of the typical reviews he found in *Cycle* because they "seem to praise every cycle tested and find only minor things at fault but fail to point out the vast and real weaknesses of almost every model you write about." Neff added that the reviewers "never mentioned" electrical systems that "never work, voltage regulators burning out periodically, cables ever fraying, oil always leaking even on new machines, sensitive clutches needing constant adjustment, vintage design magnetos that were obsolete long ago, [and] speedometers never reaching thirty thousand miles without needing repair."[34]

British and American motorcycles were so similar mechanically that debates about different brands rarely focused on mechanical reliability or competence, favoring instead the issue of "speed" or "power."

Charles R. Grandstaff of Moundsville, West Virginia, for example, explained that he had been riding motorcycles for the past twenty-two years. For the first twenty-one, he rode only American-made Harleys and Indians. He had recently started "down the British road," and he described it as "real riding pleasure." Grandstaff noted that the "limey jobs . . . score a big count" both in operation and in upkeep, but he was particularly impressed with the comfort and power of his British cycle. "It is a great feeling to have at one's command all the power and speed of a heavy motor in one so light and easy to handle, as well as one which rides like a high priced car."[35] A.R.C. of Indianapolis also highlighted the speed of his British cycle to distinguish it from the American Harleys and Indians. A.R.C. described himself as "a man who never grew up as far as motorcycles are concerned" and counted among his playthings a 47 Triumph, a Tiger 100, and a 48 Harley "74." "Don't ask me which one I like best," he stated, "because the Harley dealers here are fine fellows. . . . I will say this, however, when some cowboy comes rattling and back firing up on an American-made job, giving me that eager-beaver look out of the corner of his eye while shouting and opening his throttle in a suspicious manner and I happen to be on my 74—I say 'wait a minute bud, till I go home and get my Triumph, then I'll take care of you.'"[36]

The success of British-made bikes was accompanied by a bitter economic nationalism, but magazine editors were quick to challenge it. In 1947, for example, L. H. Francis of Parkville, Missouri, vehemently criticized *Motorcyclist* for "devoting too much space to these damn little English machines." "This is America," he complained. "We have two good American motorcycles, let's ride them and keep our money at home." If someone wanted "English stuff," he insisted, "let them go to England and stay there."[37] The editor at *Motorcyclist* answered Francis's comment with a sharp rebuke. "With our national prosperity entirely dependent on our exports we certainly hope that foreign countries will continue to hold our products in much more liberal regard then Mr. Francis does theirs." To add insult to injury, the editor questioned Francis's own patriotism and the idea that he best represented what it meant to an American. "If you were to ask any real American (Indian) he would likely say that the most distressing importation this continent has known was the white man."[38]

Riders were just as opposed to brand-name loyalty as industry publications. "Poppy" Pringle of Oak Park, Illinois, had been "poundin'" his "kidneys on Hosses since 1926 (minus four years in the army)." During that time he had five Harleys, three Indians, one Hendy, one Super-X, one Servi-Cycle (some new and some used) and was currently riding a 350cc.

Pringle claimed that he was still looking for that "perfect bike"—"regard-less [of] who makes it!"—and noted that during his twenty years of riding he had had "a few troubles, a few minor spills—and a helluva lotta fun." Yet regardless of the brand, Pringle explained, "they're all wheels, an engine and a place to sit," and all of them had "their good and bad points." Pringle could not understand why "some of the boys are so bitter" and "steamed up" about these "'Limey' bikes!" and exclaimed "this is a free country. . . . I see a lotta [S]wiss watches, French perfume, . . . German cameras, Scotch whiskey, and Chinese Chop suey joints. . . . After all, we sell them Limeys Fords, Chevies, Indians and Harleys, don't we?" Pringle ended his letter by addressing *Motorcyclist*'s readership: "So when I see ya on the ride, I'll wave boys—I don't care what youse ride or who makes it."[39]

Over the next couple of decades and as Japanese motorcycles began to dominate the U.S. market, discussions about brand-name loyalty became increasingly acrimonious, and riders expressed that discontent with terms like "rice burner" or "Jap bike." "Jap cars, guns, aircraft, ships, tools, cloth-ing, rubber goods and especially motorcycles," argued one disgruntled rider, "are *vastly inferior* to good U.S. products," while another insisted that he had yet to see "one 'original' major engineering concept to come out of the Far East!"[40] At the Texas Hog Rally in July 1979, Eddie Maddox, a Dallas truck driver and motorcyclist, used the now familiar slogan "you ain't shit, if you don't ride a Harley" to describe his reaction to what he described as a "Japanese invasion." When a reporter asked him about the possibility of any trouble at the rally, he explained that if there was any, "it'll be over people riding Japanese motorcycles. . . . You get a bunch of Harley riders together and two or three rice burners," he said as he shook his head and pointed to his chest, "It's like the button says, you ain't (bleep) if you don't ride a Harley." He then pointed to someone walking by with a T-shirt iden-tifying Japanese motorcycles as "brought to you by the same people who brought you Pearl Harbor."[41]

These comments and the allusion to a second Pearl Harbor—in this case an invasion of consumer goods—resonated particularly due to Harley-Davidson's declining fortunes. H-D's sales of motorcycles 1000ccs or big-ger nearly tripled between 1969 and the mid-1970s—from 12,000 to 13,000 bikes a year to about 35,000. By the late 1970s, the company was selling more than 50,000 machines annually. But H-D's share of the market had experi-enced a steady decline with the arrival of the Japanese Honda.[42] The growth of British lightweights after World War II contributed to the demise of the Indian Motorcycle Manufacturing Company in 1953, and made Harley-Davidson the last American motorcycle company selling the bigger cycles

(1000ccs or bigger). H-D's dominance of the U.S. market would be conspicuous until the arrival of the Japanese whose initial interest in lightweights would lead to the company's first 750cc bike (1969) and by the end of the 1970s the introduction of the now-famous 1000cc Goldwing. By the early 1970s, Harley-Davidson's share of the U.S. market had dropped to less than 4 percent, which one contemporary compared to Volkswagen's share of the U.S. automobile market, and by the early 1980s, the number of the company's blue-collar employees declined to about half of what it had been just a few years earlier, from 4,000 in 1981 to 2,400 two years later.[43]

Yet even as the motorcycle's country of manufacture shaped the discussion about brand-name loyalty, questions about performance and mechanical competence were just as conspicuous, if not more so. While riders in the 1940s and 1950s talked about the need for some mechanical skill, Hondas were sold as a maintenance-free bike. In his article on the middle-class cyclist, journalist Michael Summer described what he perceived as the transformation taking place with the terse but apt phrase, "The old brute has been tamed. The rude beast sophisticated."[44] His comment spoke directly to the changing class dynamic that was increasingly apparent among riders. But it could just as easily have been a reference to the motorcycle itself.

Stories about the rise of the middle-class rider were just as enthusiastic about the "civilized" cycles or cycles that were undergoing a social (read "positive") revolution, as they were for the gray-flannel cyclist who had supposedly made motorcycling classy. Indeed, Soichiro Honda was described as brilliant because he realized "that the modern motorist had very little use for the noisy, heavy and hard-to-handle machines of the day—whose exposed engines were guaranteed to leave their telltale grease deposits on trousers and whose temperamental starters often called for the kicks of a karate expert." Honda introduced the "motorcycling cognoscenti to a smaller, quieter prototype with such sophisticated features as an enclosed power plant and an electric starter."[45] Lightweight two-wheelers had "gained respectability" as a means of transportation thanks to "clean, easy-to-operate designs." Hondas and other Japanese-made motorcycles were also "easy to start and operate, comfortable, and stylish." The chain was also enclosed; the muffler silenced; and an electric starter was available on some models. A clean-cut suburbanite out for some family fun simply had to get on the cycle, punch a button, and twist the throttle for hours of wholesome summertime fun and leisure.[46]

Honda riders only had praise for the brand and plenty of contempt and derision for Harley-Davidson. In a 1968 letter from "Cycle Mitch and

Doug" from Newburgh, New York, the pair referred to a Harley enthusiast as a "blow hard" and added that they had "seen many a four-stroke that just wouldn't start, including your marvelous Harley pig and when cold weather comes FORGET IT!!" In what "Cycle Mitch and Doug" called a "performance to money ratio," the pair argued that you cannot compare a Harley to a Japanese motorcycle. "A stock 350 Yamaha," they insisted, "will blow the windshield and saddle bags off of any stock Harley-Davidson. If they ever put out a 900 or even a 650 two stroke I pity your big Harley pig. . . . You Hog-Riders who go out and buy Harleys and chop 'em think you're really it, but you're nothing."[47]

Some H-D owners responded by directly challenging arguments about the brand's shortcomings. In a 1968 complaint to *Cycle* about the magazine's failure to include pictures of the Harley "74," Joe "Harley" Walker described the bike as "the biggest, sturdiest, 'safest,' longest lasting, best looking and sounding motorcycle in the world. It's also the fastest if chopped. I've had it." He complained about the shoddy quality of Japanese parts: "I've worked in a motorcycle shop mostly on Yamahas and Hondas, and they're so cheap the bolts are hollow."[48] Lawrence L. Shepler of Tacoma, Washington, made a similar comment about his Harley. Shepler made a 3,500-mile trip through Canada on his 1950 Model FL. The motorcycle carried 150 pounds of gear, a windshield, and had 125,000 miles of riding before his trip began, and after having owned the bike for two years, he had "done nothing but regular maintenance." Shepler explained that he would "like to see one of those silly foreign machines match that record."[49] Even at the Texas Hog Rally that Eddy Maddox attended, the issue of performance was just as conspicuous in the debate over brand-name loyalty. At the rally a reporter also interviewed "Fast" Eddie Camp after he had just won a grudge race on his Harley, and he "confided that he'd rather ride his Honda." Harleys, he explained, were "good bikes," but "they need too much maintenance" and were "too undependable." "Most guys who are real into Harleys," he added, "they're prejudiced," which he suggested explained their preference for the American-made bikes.[50]

Other riders focused less on disputing the claims about the Japanese-made lightweights and more on what was at the heart of the debate: What did it mean to be a motorcyclist —an issue that was particularly noticeable with the growing popularity of choppers—and to what extent was a motorcyclist also expected to be a mechanic? John Johnson of Winter Haven, Florida, had been reading *Cycle* magazine for two years when he complained about the magazine's scant coverage of "CHOPPERS!" Johnson had built a "small chopper" and appreciated the "long hours and hard work that goes into one." He assumed other riders were just as interested in these "rolling works of art. . . . After all, they are as much a part of motorcycling as trials, scrambles and the rest."[51]

Lou Ferrante of Dearborn, Michigan, made an even more explicit connection about choppers and mechanical know-how when he wondered "if the small bike people realize how much sweat, grief, and running around it takes to put a really good, solid drip free chopper on the street." Ferrante had had it up to what he called "my hubs" with all the "play on the cheapies. You know the ones I mean." He singled out the "Yamaha 250 YDS-5," which he thought "sounds like something the Air force would use to end the [Vietnam] war."[52] To make his point, Ferrante referred the editors of *Cycle* to a recent picture in their magazine: "Look at the expression on the face of your own staff man," who had earlier tested out one of the smaller bikes. "He looks as though he would rather be shoveling snow in Bangor, Maine, than be sitting on that scooter." Ferrante's real love was what he affectionately called his "1957 Harley-Davidson something glide" that he had built into a chopper. When he first "got the heap it looked like a circus looking for an empty lot." One year and "eight hundred bucks" later he had a "full chopper." "The parts on a 10 year old Hog are almost non-existent in the dealer's bins," he lamented and added, "it's all worth it." "Even being called Hell's Angel (uggah) when you wheel that 400 lb monster out on the x-way and let her loose. Man it's sheer hp," he exclaimed, "and guts. She'll shake your liver and kidneys loose. She'll give you one hell of a time starting but I guess that's part of loving a bike."[53]

Americans had been building "choppers" since at least the 1950s, but their popularity is generally linked to the 1960s and 1970s. A chopper, simply put, was the 1960s version of a bobbed or chopped motorcycle that involves a more thorough manipulation of the bike's frame and design (called raking the frame) than simply bobbing a fender or chopping off unnecessary parts. Choppers also have extended front forks to lengthen the wheelbase and raise the front end, which tilts the rider up and back and accentuates the leaning back (armchair) posture. Other conspicuous features include handlebars that are often referred to as "ape hangers" because of their extended height and curvature, chrome rails (called sissy bars) to prevent a passenger from falling off the back, a custom-designed gas tank, a small leather seat, and what Hunter Thompson described as "every conceivable kind of chrome." Many choppers were simply stripped down versions of the Harley 74; others were "rolling works of art" flawlessly painted and with plenty of chrome. All of them suggested the need for more than basic mechanical knowledge, and they also had a bad reputation for being difficult to start and keep running.[54] When Ferrante wondered aloud whether "the small bike people realize how much sweat, grief, and running around it takes to put a really good, solid drip-free chopper on the street," his discussion led invariably to the routine struggle of trying to start his chopper.[55]

As Ferrante's comments and the previous discussion suggest, the traditional working-class motorcyclist often appeared to be more of a producer than a consumer. The United States entered an era of mass consumption between World War I and World War II. During these years, as Charles F. McGovern has argued, Americans learned to associate their citizenship and the political order with consumption. Advertisers, consumerists, and other professionals used American political traditions and language to shape popular ideas about consumption and to cast it as an "important element of distinct national identity."[56] The affluence of the postwar years and the Cold War only accelerated these trends and gave rise to what Lizabeth Cohen calls a consumer republic, her term to describe the "promise of mass consumption" and the "economy, culture, and politics built around that promise."[57] Yet, like the interwar years, during which the American working class, according to Susan Porter Benson, "remained distinctly marginal to the emerging world of mass consumption because of the insufficiency and irregularity of its income," class continued to shape consumption and motorcycling.[58]

The working-class motorcyclist's spending habits reflected limited economic choices and, more importantly, their ambivalence about the trappings of a consumer society that was reflected by their embrace of a broader ethic of skill and craftsmanship. The process, in sum, was often more important than the final product. Garbage wagons, those bloated stock motorcycles that were weighed down with plenty of chrome-plated attachments, were never as influential in shaping motorcycle culture as choppers and the outlaws identified with them. A chopper, as Hunter Thompson claims, was "little more than a heavy frame, a tiny seat and a massive 1,200-cubic-centimeter (or 74-cubic-inch) engine." Class consumption, as Susan Porter Benson reminds us, was a more appropriate way to describe working men's and women's spending habits than mass consumption, and nowhere was that distinction easier to see than among motorcyclists.[59]

Indeed, discussions about choppers often highlighted how the divide between Harleys and Japanese-made bikes had a class dimension. Some riders alluded to class by simply challenging the assumption that owning a chopper automatically made the rider an "outlaw." "I am not for

Hell's Angels or any other group that gives cycling a bad name," complained John Johnson is his letter to *Cycle*. "Contrary to popular belief," he added, "[chopper riders] are not all shoddy, evil handling beats."[60] Other riders used the term "class" to directly address the differences between American- and Japanese-made bikes. When Fast Eddie Camp said, "I don't like Harleys, they're too undependable," he added: "But it's a class thing."[61] In a more explicit case, Gene Thoms wrote a scathing letter to *Cycle* to complain about the editor's bias against choppers. Thoms belittled the editor as the "High Priest" of the "motorcycle world" who was "the only one answerable for the actions and /or thinking of every motorcyclist not living or ever having lived," and complained about the magazine's coverage of choppers. "I am well aware that custom motorcycles are not 'in' on Wall Street or Park Avenue, but they are most assuredly a part of the motorcycle scene. But you insist on treating choppers as a thing from a different planet." Thoms, after admonishing the editor to "do a little better by informing the general public that not everyone who rides a motorcycle with a chrome gas tank is a dues-paying member of the Hell's Angels," asked, "Who the hell are you to pass judgment on every cyclist not conforming to your picture you are striving to paint?"[62]

The focus on performance and mechanical reliability also led to a discussion about the electric starter, which was used on motorcycles as early as the 1910s but did not become popular until the 1960s. Honda's 50cc super cub model that debuted in 1958 included an optional electric starter. By 1960, electric starters were available on all of the Honda models sold in the United States and were critical to Honda's claim about performance and reliability. Other manufactures, recognizing the demand for these starters, quickly followed suit. Norton introduced the "Electra 400" in 1963 and advertised the electric starter as standard equipment. Harley-Davidson would offer its first electric starter in 1964 with its Servi-Car, a three-wheeled motorcycle that was initially introduced during the Depression to increase sales and marketed to the service industry and to police departments, which used them until the 1960s. A year later, an electric starter appeared on the new "Electra Glide"—essentially the Duo Glide retooled with an electric starter—the first of the big twins to have one.[63]

The electric starter of the 1960s only exacerbated the divide concerning mechanical competence. An ad that appeared in *American Motorcyclist* in 1961 from the Motorcycle Parts Company of South El Monte, California, proudly announced the electric starter for the Harley 74. The starter was described as "well balanced for easy riding" and made "starting just as easy for the ladies as the men."[64] Other comments were much more explicit and suggested that the electric starter had the potential to fundamentally challenge the meaning of motorcycling. In his discussion about the Honda CB350, one rider noted that "all the movies back then had the big, bad, nasty, bad guy, motorcyclists run out to their bikes and kick start them. Now they run out and push a button."[65] Other riders questioned what constituted the definition of motorcycle. "Does a Honda qualify as a bike?" queried one rider in a 1974 *Biker News* editorial. "Oh yeah," he answered, "we took off the [electric] starter."[66] In a 1973 letter to *Cycle*, Ray Wart Taylor of Arlington, Virginia, made a similar argument about the future of motorcycling because of the technological advances that had the potential to adversely affect motorcycling. "Technical and mechanical improvements," Taylor complained, "had refined the motorcycle's performance to such extremes that it was indistinguishable from the auto," and the kick-starter was fundamental to maintaining any distinction. "At this rate there'll soon be no difference between the two-wheel and the four-wheel juggernauts, except the two wheels. If you can't kick start it," he complained, "it isn't a motorcycle."[67] Another rider argued, "It only takes a pansy to put down a Harley-Davidson," or what he referred to as "Those kind of people who have the 125cc Japanese toys with the electric starter or the 750cc 'super-toys' with a 91/2 speed transmission." These riders, he added, were "weaklings that can't handle a MAN'S machine."[68]

Still, one should not overstate the differences between Harley and Honda enthusiasts or the degree to which riding a motorcycle required some mechanical expertise. *Biker News* included a "maintenance free bike" in its 1974 list of "motorcycle myths." "You know the one," the author explained, "so perfect that its chain never needs oiling or adjusting. The air filter never needs cleaning. Nuts and bolts never need tightening. Spokes, by pure magic, never come loose. Yes sir, a motorcycle so absolutely perfect that the owner needs never to lay a wrench on it."[69] Yet throughout the 1960s and 1970s debates about bikes highlighted an economic nationalism that focused more on the rider's relationship to his motorcycle and less on its origin. Hondas were sold with the assumption that the potential (middle-class) consumer was less mechanically inclined than the traditional motorcyclist identified with grease and garages. But the introduction of Japanese bikes was also accompanied by the growing popularity of choppers, and the Harley's supposed unreliability was a feature that was critical to what it meant to be a motorcyclist, even though riders frequently complained about the bike's mechanical limitations. A poem title "The Oil Drip Blues" that appeared in the June 1982 issue of *Easyriders* was accompanied by a picture of a motorcyclist wearing a T-shirt that stated in bold red letters, "Harley's Don't Leak Oil. They Mark Their Spot."[70]

MIDDLE-CLASS STYLE AND CONSUMPTION

In the postwar years two styles of dress "evolved"—the Western Bob (or West Coast Bob) and the Eastern Marcel—and there was no clear consensus among industry writers about which style was best suited to the average motorcyclist. The editor at *Cycle* claimed the magazine's staff "favor[ed] neither outfit," even as he noted that "a leather jacket worn above a pair of clean and freshly pressed and cuffed Levis presents a trim picture. But only when the jacket is clean and unfrayed and the Levis do not display patches, torn pockets, ragged cuffs and a sickly over-all color of whitish-blue," as if the latter was more common than the trim picture of clean and neatly pressed pants and jacket.[71] The American Motorcyclist Association (AMA), on the other hand, remained committed to its mission of making motorcycling wholesome and argued that any clothing was acceptable as long as it was "clean, neat, and in good taste." There was one qualification: "There's no reason why a motorcycle rider can't dress in such a manner that he doesn't seem out of place in the best restaurants, hotels and business places." When motorcycles were in their "infancy," the AMA explained, "they were dirty and oily and all who rode them ended the trip looking the same. But modern production has eliminated the grit and grease."[72]

Riders, on the other hand, were much more likely to emphasize the utility of these styles, which often contradicted the AMA's understanding. Bob Walker of El Monte, California, defended the Bob because he favored off-road riding. On any given Sunday, Walker noted, the typical motorcyclist was "dirty and mud-splattered" and the "general public says one thing . . . what a dirty bunch of guys and gals. And look at those machines." But "little do they realize," he added, "this group has more than likely just emerged from some river bed or available cow paths." Walker wondered if a midwestern or eastern rider would "take his fancy dress and machine through what we do?"—explaining that "cleaning bills on uniforms are prohibitive enough." Walker was particularly sympathetic to wearing clean Levis and boots because they "stand up much better through sage brush, willows, and sand than any uniform I know of."[73]

Even riders who did not fit the description of the Western Bob or the Eastern Marcel admitted that these styles were functional. John Philips of New Canaan, Connecticut, explained that even though he was from the East and favored a "spotless" cycle with a "bare minimum of accessories," the Eastern Marcel was practical. "Motorcycle clothing should be . . . functional and safe," which ruled out "a business suit or even slacks and sport clothes." Motorcycling "is not like bicycling," he added. "The body needs protection especially the legs and chest. Therefore boots and leather jackets." Philips preferred "motorcycle riders" who wore "high boots and leather breeches with a leather shirt or jacket—plus a crash helmet." "There is no substitute for safe driving, but in the event of accidents leather clothing studded with metal is a lifesaver." Besides the obvious benefit to studded leather in a spill, Philips noted that "the bright spots and showy clothing are safety factors in that motorists see motorcycles more easily if the motorcyclist is dressed in shiny leather studded with chrome, and road dirt and grease and oil can be cleaned from leather pants and jackets where it would stain more 'acceptable' clothes." His conclusion: "More leather clothing on motorcyclists means safer motorcycling."[74]

Among the middle-class riders of the 1960s and in contrast to what was derisively described as the "leather jackets, tight pants set" in the "hell-for-leather era of motorcycling," this new "breed" of rider often appeared in khakis and loafers. In 1963, for example, the *Chicago Tribune* published an article titled "New Image in Motorcycling: The Score in Clothes for Men." In this version, "West Coast suburbanites" were "swinging into the saddles of motorcycles for shopping, for a quick ride to the railroad station, and for weekend fun." Although there were still "spirited daredevils who enter bruising motorcycle hill climbs" and racers known as Hot Foot Boys, who "boom into town for the annual national championship motorcycle race at Daytona Beach Florida," the typical image of the motorcyclist in black leather jacket, goggles, and crash helmet "is being rapidly replaced by the appearance of married couples out for a good time on motorized two-wheelers." To make sure the reader understood the change taking place, the article included a sketch of two suburban men riding down the street next to a young girl on a bicycle. One man was wearing "an easy-going cardigan sweater with multicolor striping in red, black, gold beige, two shades of gray and white to give it a lively look. His medium gray slacks are tapered along lean lines. His black chukka boots are right for the road." His companion sported an "Indian madras plaid odd jacket" that was a "sure scene stealer" accompanied by dark blue "slim-tapered slacks" and "well-styled slip-ons."[75]

College students were also attracted to motorcycling, and their style also contrasted with the traditional rider's. In 1963 a reporter for the *San Francisco Examiner* "swung over to Berkeley . . . to check up on the recent development of 'ivy league' enthusiasm in motorcycling." The Berkeley students had about one hundred motorcycles, and Fiji, Sigma Upsilon, or Alpha Delta Phi members owned about twenty-five of them, a fad that had been steadily increasing over the past three years. These fraternity boys were somewhat different from the typical middle-class rider in that they preferred British motorcycles, or what the reporter described as "real honest-[to]-God heavy duty, noisy motorcycles." Yet they were also distinct from the traditional outlaw. They referred to their vehicles as "bikes" to distinguish them from what they called "sickles," or American-made motorcycles, and they preferred white Levis and plaid shirts as opposed to the men they referred to as "the apes, the Marlon Brando types, the ones who wear black leather jackets, earrings, boots, silk shirts." "You know," explained one Fiji, "the Hell's Angels kind." "Originally, motorcycles were strictly for punks and animals," he added. "But now you might say we've brought a more civilized, more collegiate tone to the sport."[76]

To be sure, these new riders were often attracted to cycling for the same reasons it had become popular in previous decades. In an editorial that appeared just before the Hollister Rally of 1947, an editor at *American Motorcycling* asked, "Why Motorcycling?" The editorial touched on what might be considered the obvious: going places, "the wanderlust," or the "joy of the explorer."[77] In the premier issue of *American Motorcycling*, the editor E. W. Henn highlighted the motorcycle's popularity as a function of power. While Henn explained that he rode his first motorcycle twelve years ago (1935, a new 1918 surplus World War I military model) "right out of the crate," his interest in motorcycles became apparent when he was a young boy: "ever since I was a kid in knee pants gawking at riders and their machines and rolling down my dad's car window just to hear a motorcycle pass us on a dig out."[78] About twenty years later, a 1965 *Esquire* article on "How to Avoid Killing Yourself" admitted that cyclists were vulnerable, but the typical rider "swaps this armor for speed and maneuverability and an overwhelming enjoyment of road feel and wind-in-the-face motion," what the article's author described as "wheeling out just for the hell of it." While the motorist passively "rides inside his machine," the cyclist "sits astride his" the author commented, using a man-over-machine analogy.[79] *Esquire* published a far less subtle article more than a decade later titled "Pleasure Principle on Wheels," which reaffirmed the rider's commitment to the great outdoors, the thrill of the ride, and the motorcycle's power. "Driving a car is a mixed blessing," the author observed. "Power steering is nice, yes, but makes driving kid stuff. Lower speed limits save gas, yes, but save excitement as well. Cars are forever dry and toasty, yes, even safer than ever, and that's the problem. Let's hear it for gut churning!

Heart thumping! Head spinning! Let's hear it for the motorcycle, past and present."[80]

Yet even as contemporaries celebrated the middle-class interest in cycling, trying to find a balance between this preoccupation and the trappings of a middle-class and respectable lifestyle proved a complicated (and typical) balance to strike. A 1966 issue of *California Living*, for example, featured a picture of a young man sitting on a Bultaco—a Spanish-made cycle. The man was wearing a light colored pullover sweater and dark slacks and was looking up and smiling at a female friend. The caption beneath the photo reads, "Linda Lee Cola and Ray Soderman act out the day dream of 'machismo' that impels many a young buck to ownership of the popular Bultaco 175 Campera."[81] Riders like Soderman could appropriate the working-class identity associated with motorcycle culture or what the author described as acting "out the daydream of machismo" (apparently even on a Bultaco). But were the clothes, the neatly combed hair, and the smiling faces of the rider and his adoring companion compatible with the version of motorcycling he was attempting to imitate? Another example comes from the premier issue of *Easyriders* magazine, which featured an article on the middle-class interest in choppers, or what the editor described as the chopper's changing image from "bad" to "respectable." The article featured Jack Bell of Glendale, California, who was a sales manager of a chain of five tire stores in Southern California and the proud owner of a Knucklehead. Bell "found the bike in stock condition and built the chopper himself." *Easyriders* described Bell as "typical of the new breed of chopper owner" because of his occupation. "Now doctors, lawyers and all types of businessmen are running around on the wildest choppers available." It was "a good trend," the editor added, and it was good that "business types are moving to choppers for their kicks," because the "law can't group all chopper riders together as bad guys and dope fiends any longer." "The chopper," he added, "is replacing the sports car as the young businessman's escape— the chopper gives more kicks than a sports car—is more masculine and a helluva lot more fun."[82]

Yet the editor was also ambivalent about Bell's style. When Bell rode his chopper during the weekday, he was usually dressed in business attire and showed up for the *Easyriders* photo session wearing a pinstriped suit. The staff at *Easyriders* explained that "choppers and business suits just didn't go together" and after asking him to change, he returned in "grey flannel slacks and white buck shoes." "The chopper rider usually didn't have a shirt on," the editor quipped, "or if he did it would be only a T-shirt, leather vest or cut off. He also usually needed a shave and his Levi pants would stand up by themselves."[83]

So concerned were other middle-class apologists about the importance of class and status to the new crop of motorcycles that one author established a hierarchy that would-be motorcyclists could use to avoid certain makes of motorcycles and to cultivate and maintain a respectable image. In his 1965 *Esquire* article, Carl Gottlieb complained that during any typical discussion about motorcycling, *The Wild One* always comes to mind— specifically the scene of Marlon Brando and Lee Marvin fighting as other "punks in leather jackets stood around and drink." This image "froze the motorcycle" in "a subterranean level of the American class structure for more than a decade." Gottlieb argued that by the early 1960s the motorcycle had "begun its long uphill climb into middle-class respectability." Japanese manufacturers were responsible for popularizing the motorcycle as a "socially acceptable vehicle." They did it by "upgrading the image" and by "selling [the] hell out of our domestic market." As a result, there were more "high type, upwardly mobile riders buzzing around every year to the delight of an entire industry."[84]

Now, riders faced the fear of being identified with the wrong crowd—a problem "that never troubled motorcyclists in the good old days when if you rode on two wheels you were either a cop or a wild kid looking for trouble." With "everyone buying motorcycles this year," he wondered, "shouldn't there be some sort of yardstick to gauge caste and class?" Gottlieb explained that there "are substrates to the overall structure, and a prospective motorcyclist might well want to know whether he's buying into an elite or a lumpenproletariat."[85]

To make such a decision easier for the "prospective [middle-class] motorcyclist," Gottlieb divided motorcycles into "five classes of machine, each with a representative rider." It was important to "know what you're riding, who you'll be riding with, and where you're going." The five different categories ranged from "Class I (the Exotica and the Esoterica)," which featured the Harley XLR-TT, ridden by Roger Reiman, the only rider at the time to have won three times at Daytona National Short Track Champion and the American Motorcycle Association Grand National Champion, to Class V, which was referred to as the lowest grade. This class included "low powered, low weight, and low price machines" like the Honda Trail 90, and the featured rider was Ann Margaret, whose personal publicity frequently stressed her delight at owning and riding motorcycles.[86]

Gottlieb's ranking or class system did not discriminate against motorcycle manufacturers. Other examples of class V bikes included Yamahas,

Suzukis, Benellis, Ducatis, Bridgestones, and the Harley-Davidson M-50. But an obvious pecking order was apparent. Gottlieb dismissed the lowest-grade (V) cycles as "light lady's machines" and placed the fastest, biggest, and most unique bikes at the top of his hierarchy. The top-two levels included racing and antique bikes and the big Harleys, which were appropriate for what Gottlieb described as the "mount of both sides": the "standard-issue police motorcycle and favorite of the outlaw cycle clubs, including California's Hell's Angels."[87]

Yet even though the big Harleys appeared in Gottlieb's top-two classes, he seemed to favor the cycles in classes III and IV, which included middle-class riders. Class IV motorcycles were the ones "students, young executives, city and country hippies" favored because they were typically first-time riders. Class III cycles were "real motorcycles" for "riders who take cycling seriously." The obvious difference between the two categories was experience and perhaps money. Middle-class riders would begin in Class IV and trade up as they matured (as riders) and as their salaries increased to the point where they could afford the bigger and more expensive cycles in Class III.[88]

More telling however, are the riders representing each class. Dick Smothers, of the Smothers Brothers, was featured as a typical Class IV rider and was described as a "characteristically clean-cut youthful rider." Steve McQueen represented Class III. Gottlieb argued that McQueen was an appropriate fit for the bigger and faster cycles because he competed regularly in European and American road races and did his own movie motorcycle stunts. The difference between Dick Smothers and Steve McQueen is glaring especially when compared to the difference between a class IV 500cc Honda and its 750cc counterpart in Class III. After all, McQueen was one of the toughest action stars of the decade and bears little resemblance to Dick Smothers, who was ranked just beneath him and is known best for his dimwitted persona as part of the Smothers Brothers comedy routine.[89]

But the division Gottlieb imagined and the disparity between his two riders suited his understanding of the middle-class rider. In Gottlieb's mind, the differences among motorcyclists had less to do with the machine each representative was riding and more to do with the man. The Class IV rider may have been new to cycling, but his potential was limitless, and his claim to cycling genuine. Dick Smothers, for example, could become Steve McQueen with enough experience and the right bike. This potential transformation allowed middle-class men to make a legitimate claim to cycling without upsetting the overall structure to the caste and class system Gottlieb imagined.

Indeed, some evidence suggests that the middle-class interest in cycling had as much to do with consumption as it had with the joy of riding. The middle-class zeal for cycling should not have been surprising, because it had already "enthusiastically embraced motorboats, motorcars, motorized lawn mowers, airplanes, [and] motorscooters."[90] More motorcycles on the road coincided with the dramatic increase in the sale of recreational vehicles—travel trailers, pickup campers, camping trailers, and motor homes. Mrs. Wm. D. Venners Jr. from Jackson, Michigan, made this point evident when she complained in a letter to the AMA about the "infiltration of scum and savages into a sport that is basically meant for good clean fun and competition." The "majority of us," she added, "are no different than the people who make up the sports car, sky diving or speed boat clubs all over the county and our bikes are no more dangerous than their equipment."[91] Indeed, according to a 1967 *New York Times* article, annual sales of recreational vehicles increased 370 percent between 1961 and 1966. In 1966 alone, the industry saw a 21 percent increase over the previous year with a total retail value of nearly $600 million. Recreational vehicles' selling points included cost, comfort, and convenience, and, like motorcycles, they were also "family oriented."[92] Hondas and other Japanese-made motorcycles were celebrated because they were ideal for "off the street use" and compact and lightweight enough to "be hauled to recreation areas and riding sites in trailers or on the rear of cars and campers."[93]

In other words, the motorcycle was not necessarily part of a lifestyle but an accessory to be used at one's convenience and just as easily set aside or even discarded. While working-class motorcyclists often built or customized their own bikes (producing as opposed to consuming), their middle-class counterparts generally did not. Motorcycles were another marker of class for an already acutely class-conscious bunch whose understanding of cycling was often at odds with that of their working-class counterpart. Their different relationship should not suggest that their motorcycles had no meaning. It did not challenge their identity as consumers or as citizens, only perhaps as motorcyclists, especially if they bought a Japanese one. Motorcycles were any one of a number of status symbols that are particularly important when thinking about class and national identities in the postwar years. The culture of consumption that flourished after World War II was firmly embedded in the middle-class experience and increasingly linked to the nation's prosperity. Consumption was thus a sign of social belonging, and social belonging was fundamental to understanding citizenship.

Motorcycling was thus a means to an end but not the end itself. In the middle-class imagination or fantasy, motorcycling led to a day at the beach, a weekend at a favorite campground, or even an afternoon of fun buzzing around town on a scavenger hunt with your favorite female friend. The September 1966 issue of *Playboy*, for example, featured an article titled "Motorcycle Scavenger Hunt" that briefly recounted the history of motorcycles from Gottlieb Daimler's first motorcycle to the dramatic changes of the postwar period, a transformation of cycling that went from its "antisocial" association with "several maverick motorcycling cliques" to individuals riding on Soichiro Honda's "smaller," "quieter," and "sophisticated" cycles. This scavenger hunt was like any other scavenger hunt: couples were assigned the usual list of odd and hard-to-find items, and certain restrictions were put in place on their search. But the motorcycle's influence was prominent and potentially erotic. Photographs for the story, for example, included a close-up of a young couple stretched out on a blanket in the park kissing, with their just-out-of-focus motorcycle in the background and another rider driving down the street sandwiched between two female passengers. One of the items participants were hunting for was a live rabbit, which in this case happened to be a playmate who "got a few minutes off from her job [at the *Playboy* Club] so that guy and gal could win by a hare."[94] Motorcycles, as these examples suggest, were becoming a part of the middle-class lifestyle, even though they were rarely the focus of it. They were fun, exciting, and even glamorous but also potentially a challenge to the respectability and decorum that accompanied middle-class ideas about consumption and social belonging.

THE MIDDLE-CLASS RATIONALE

When the *Saturday Evening Post* tried to explain why motorcyclists were the "Most Unpopular Men on the Road," the magazine described the attraction as an obsession. The author argued that because most riders were preoccupied with the lifestyle during their late teens and early twenties or until marriage and domestic life distracted him from other pursuits, "the short but merry life of the average motorcyclist inspires in him an intense interest, bordering on monomania, in what the machine can do."[95] Another example comes from a letter Ann Landers received in 1956 from a wife whose husband had gone "buggy about motorcycles." The woman, who had been married for eight years and had four wonderful children, complained that her husband had spent "money on every kind of an accessory imaginable and everything that can be plated is chromed." He was starting to "hangout with 18 and 19 year-old punks who are also crazy over motorcycles" and had even joined their club. Her husband had initially justified the motorcycle for transportation and had argued that the cycle was a "way to stay youthful." But his wife quickly figured out that he wanted it for "pleasure" and that he was no longer "interested in being with friends in our age bracket." His wife was "very unhappy" and at a loss for what to do. Ann Landers knew exactly what to do, describing the "31-year-old father of four who joins a club with 18-year-olds" as "flipping his crash helmet. . . . Tell Peter Pan to hang up his black leather jacket with the eagle on the back," she insisted, "and act his age." Landers argued that "there's a vast difference between staying youthful" and acting "childish," and she suggested that "if you can't make him see it, perhaps your clergyman can."[96]

By the 1960s and 1970s fears about a preoccupation with motorcycling were still conspicuous, but it was often the middle-class rider himself expressing these concerns and not a concerned family member, acquaintance, or passerby. In the *New York Times* article about motorcycling as a "Touch of Chic," the author emphasized the interest in motorcycles at colleges across the country. In California, "where a general motion and mechanical madness prevails, they have been welcomed to the sprawling campuses," unlike the East where "some administrators, even at such institution as Bennington, have looked somewhat askance at the influx of cycles." They were nonetheless attracting attention and attracting fans at all institutions. Collegians, the reporter argued, "favor lightweights" and regarded "the bigger machines as rather gauche"; motorcycling's appeal was "based on a kind of automated nihilism." Marlon Brando in *The Wild One*, the author added, "unfailingly packs campus movie houses," and even at Yale, where "the sports page of the college newspaper features the exploits of the polo team . . . cycles have become 'in' according to an assistant professor of English who admitted to his own interest in motorcycling even as he hesitated to share it." He rode his motorcycle to work, the *New York Times* explained, "but also hides his behind a fraternity house."[97] Dr. Foster Hampton, who was a surgeon, also rode his motorcycle to work, in this case one that weighed several hundred pounds. Yet unlike the assistant professor, he did not hide his. He used it for short and long trips alike. The doctor explained that he only had to wait to buy one until after his mother died. Interestingly enough, he flew an airplane back and forth from college before he owned an automobile.[98] Another good example is George McCarty, a prosperous middle-age businessman who owned a shoe pattern factory in Haverhill, Massachusetts. McCarty liked to shed his business suit for a black leather jacket, crash helmet, and boots and "mount his Harley-Davidson motorcycle," but not everyone knew about his after-hours preoccupation. He admitted that the motorcycle and his interest in it were his "dirty little secret." "I don't tell my customers I own a motorcycle—I wouldn't dare."[99]

Motorcycles had long been the favorite plaything about which these men avoided telling not only their mothers but also their coworkers, friends, and family because motorcycling so thoroughly challenged their ideas about respectable, middle-class behavior. Though motorcycling was becoming increasingly popular, especially among middle-class men and women, a stigma was still attached to riding and to motorcyclists, and it threatened to rupture the divide between the traditional outlaw and his respectable counterpart. While this middle-class rider was soundly celebrated in the mainstream media and in the motorcycle press, a conscious effort to distinguish this rider from his working-class equivalent was nothing short of intense and all encompassing. Middle-class men were generally able to negotiate their interest in riding and had effectively kept those two different preoccupations separate and distinct. But their efforts also brought into sharp relief the boundaries surrounding class privilege and the middle-class rider's potential to disrupt them. Hampton's example is a particularly telling one. In his interview he mentioned an airplane he used for transportation when he was a student. He did not explain if his mother objected to the time he spent flying, but it was the motorcycle that had to wait until after her death. Was the motorcycle more dangerous than the plane, or was it a question of reputation and the motorcycle's potential to challenge it that made him wait?

This ambivalence also suggests that to understand the meaning of consumption we have to understand its limits. Class already limited the extent to which working-class motorcyclists accepted consumption as the key to happiness and social belonging. They had fewer resources to make ends meet and were often interested more in the process of building and maintaining a bike than in simply buying one. Indeed, for some men getting their hands dirty was fundamental to what it meant to be a motorcyclist and fundamental to what separated them from other riders. The comments from middle-class motorcyclists also suggested they feared the potential and conflicted meanings surrounding the bike itself and the men who were traditionally identified with them. Motorcycles were not simply working class but had the stain of the outlaw on them; instead of promoting social belonging, they could challenge it. The manner in which the middle-class rider dressed and the bike he rode are explicit examples of his efforts to counter the stigma he associated with the traditional working-class motorcyclist. While these efforts helped middle-class men rationalize their consumer choices, they did not always erase the anxiety with which these men were preoccupied.

The link between work and motorcycling also figured into the middle-class riders' effort to justify their preoccupation. The countless stories about the middle-class rider emphasized that he was a professional, and his status affected everything from the way he looked when riding his bike to his attitude about it. In other words, if loafers and khakis were the most common look for this new rider, grey worsted suits and attaché case, as noted by the Madison Avenue Motorcycle Club, were a close second.[100] Others described this motorcyclist as dressed in a "custom-made suit," carrying "an attaché case," and working "in a spacious Manhattan office."[101] While motorcycle clubs had traditionally chosen names that reflected their location (the Amarillo Motorcycle Club) or their interest in riding or raising hell (the Pissed Off Bastards), clubs with names that highlighted their professional standing were becoming more common. The Montgomery Street Motorcycle Club in San Francisco was featured in a 1974 *Motor Trend* article titled "The Man in the Grey Flannel Helmet." The club included about forty men, ranging in ages from their thirties to their fifties, and most of the members had families. The club's name reflected their workaday lives in and around Montgomery Street, and their professions had ties to Wall Street and Madison Avenue. The club included more than the occasional lawyer, stockholder, adman, banker, and businessman.[102]

Indeed, many of these riders were initially introduced to motorcycling for no other reason than the need for cheap, efficient transportation. Scores of "business people, suburbanites, and others" were finding that "today's lightweight, efficient models are designed more for transportation than recreation and thrills." The "emergence of the motorcycle" was "a national outgrowth for the national thirst for economy," or the same "phenomena that popularized compact cars."[103] *Motor Trend* admitted that a motorcycle's use was limited by weather, and it afforded less protection than cars in an accident. But the alternatives posed seemingly greater problems: bicycling required energy, walking was "limited by time and distance," and public transportation was "not always available." The motorcycle was the only "supplement to the car" that offered "an acceptable combination of speed, comfort, maneuverability, and economy" and was "an attractive alternative to using a car in certain travel situations," especially "short trips and commuting."[104] By the late 1960s and early 1970s, middle-class riders struggling to deal with increasing costs and an unstable economy were praising the Japanese-made Honda as a "second car."[105]

Economy would continue to fuel the motorcycle boom that lasted until the mid-1970s, and the middle-class rider remained conspicuous. With war in the Middle East in the early 1970s and the OPEC oil embargo against Europe and the United States in 1973, motorcycle registrations experienced their second greatest increase since the 1960s.[106] In 1974 Hap Jones, the nation's leading motorcycle accessory distributor explained, "The present gasoline shortage scare has flooded motorcycle dealers with the biggest influx of non-bike riders they've ever seen." Motorcycle dealer Frank Crane concurred and cited fuel shortages as the reason so many prospective buyers visited his shop. "You can tell they've never been on a motorcycle by the questions they ask," he observed. "Mostly they ask you what kind of gas mileage to expect from a given bike." Crane noted that "in ten years of selling bikes I can't remember the last time anyone ever a[s] ked me anything about fuel consumption"[107] *Cycle Sport* magazine publisher Bob Hicks even more explicitly attributed the upsurge in registrations to what he called "nonteen-age, middle class persons with little or no cycling know-how" who used "the excuse they'd been looking for" to "get their courage up and do what they wanted to do in the first place"—buy a motorcycle.[108]

The meaning of work was also increasingly attracting the attention of middle-class professionals because it had grown tedious and unrewarding. In 1952 *Cycle*'s editor asked: "Have Americans gone soft?" The editor described the United States as a " 'push button' country" and "wondered whether or not any of that original pioneer spirit still exists." The "constant struggle for existence," he claimed, "had been refined by our civilization from a physical to a mental track." The only challenge the average American faced "came in the form of a monthly quota" and what the editor called the "physical element"—handled by a "brisk walk to the office or shop" and "topped off" by a "weekly 'go' at golf or bowling." Both were fine sports, he admitted, but they also both lacked "adventure and challenge."[109] Bruce Brown, the filmmaker and director of the motorcycle racing documentary *On Any Sunday* (1971), also used the phrase "push button controlled way of life" nearly twenty years later to explain why "so many Americans are bike enthusiasts." "Everything is too easy," he protested, and argued that motorcycling "makes a person rely on his own physical prowess and self confidence."[110]

While Brown did not specifically address the workplace, his contemporaries would have certainly recognized his complaint and tied it to the day-to-day experience of being a professional. Drs. Delbert and Juannell Hughes, psychiatrists at a Veterans Administration Hospital in Dallas, not only agreed with Brown and complained about the well-ordered and disciplined nature of day-to-day life but also singled out the stress of the workplace and the need to unwind. "Our life here is regimented and disciplined," said Dr. Delbert, "and we have freedom from discipline on our vacation." "Once you learn to get into the shoes of a psychiatrist," he added, "you have to learn to get out of them too." For relaxation the pair often "drive to and from work on their super revved cycle, take weekend trips to their east Texas farm, and scoot up to Colorado as they did last year—all when the spirit moves."[111] Middle-aged businessman George McCarty also related his attraction to motorcycles with his work life. In June 1969 McCarty was one of thousands of motorcyclists who had arrived in the Loudon-Laconia, New Hampshire, area for the 100-mile national championship motorcycle race at the Bryar Motorsport Park. At the gathering were "upstanding men and women—lawyers, merchants, students, housewives—who crave the thrill of cutting through the wind astride two wheels." McCarty explained that the joy of riding was not the only reason for his participation, however. "Some guys have three Manhattans after work and that takes care of them," he commented. "I like to take a ride."[112]

Complaints from white-collar professionals about the workplace and corporate culture were increasingly common after World War II. American prosperity after the war led to the highest standard of living worldwide, but the nature of work was stifling.[113] Professionals complained about the endless monotony of shuffling papers without ever knowing why—except perhaps to please the boss. Climbing the corporate ladder had become more a question of personality—manipulating your own and your co-workers—and less of a question of your potential competence and the satisfaction derived from it. William Whyte's *The Organization Man* (1957) best represents the frustration with work and a critique of corporate culture.[114]

Unlike these other professionals who were struggling to negotiate the lifelessness of the corporate world, middle-class motorcyclists viewed riding not only as a way to deal with their workaday lives but also as an effective way to challenge stereotypes about motorcyclists and to reaffirm their identity as one. The suit and tie that had become prominent among these new riders was a public affirmation of their class standing and of an understanding of motorcycling that challenged and rejected the traditional outlaw and all the baggage associated with him. When Dick Flowers of Columbus, Ohio, complained in a letter he sent to *Cycle* in 1971 about the public's inability to differentiate between riders, he suggested that they don the suit and tie associated with the average businessman. "Everyone knows that nice guys don't ride motorcycles and especially to work,"

Flowers explained. "Nice guys ride in car pools, three abreast in black suits and striped ties and carry little black cases in their laps. Everyone knows that nice guys don't relax on weekends by donning old boots, Levis and riding cycles down back roads and dirt trails. Nice guys wear Bermuda shorts, wake up the birds on Sunday morning with their power mowers, grill steaks and drink martinis all day long. Maybe if the student on the Honda, the accountant on the Triumph or the plumber on the Kawasaki all wore black suits with striped ties and carried little black cases filled with premixed martinis the rest of the so called nice guys would accept them."[115] In his article on the Madison Avenue Motorcycle Club, Michael Sumner made this connection even more explicit when he explained that the club's "devotion to motorcycling went deeper than a casual spin around the block after work or on the weekend, and they proved it by riding (in ever increasing numbers) to work."[116] Every time a middle-class professional climbed aboard his favorite motorcycle with requisite suit, tie, and briefcase, he not only challenged the stereotypical outlaw image associated with motorcycling but also made his interest in motorcycling purposeful and utilitarian.

Indeed, the outlaw that was at the heart of all this ambivalence not only had a reputation for disrespectable and deviant behavior but also stood in sharp contrast to the wage laborer. There were plenty of hard-working motorcyclists who were not middle-class professionals, but the image of the middle-class rider who was attracting attention in the early 1960s took shape in direct opposition to an outlaw sensibility that did not recall "the nicest people" and that was defined not so much in relation to the world of work but as a rejection of it. In other words, the outlaw was a threat not simply because of his unruly behavior on and off his cycle but because he patently rejected the consumer culture that accompanied the nation's postwar affluence and the industrial ethic that valued productive and disciplined labor.[117] The look, the behavior, and the rootlessness of the motorcyclist riding from town to town with what appeared to be few cares or responsibilities first attracted national attention just as the United States was entering a period of unprecedented prosperity and as labor was reaching the peak of its strength and influence.

By the 1960s and 1970s, these ideas were especially prominent. In his recent biography about life as the president of the Oakland chapter of the Hells Angels, Sonny Barger effectively made this same argument when he explained his interest in motorcycles and a motorcycle club: "I wanted a group less interested in a wife and two point five kids in a crackerbox house in Daly City or San Jose and more interested in riding, drag racing,

Sonny Barger on the set of the movie *Hell's Angels '69*. At the time, Barger was the president of the Oakland Chapter of the Hells Angels. Courtesy of Photofest, Inc.

and raising hell."[118] A scene Thompson describes in *Hell's Angels*, highlights this idea as well. Two teenage boys "stood on the fringe of the crowd" of motorcyclists who had gathered at a bar called the El Adobe. The Hells Angels were "shouting, laughing and drinking beer" and paying no attention to the teenagers, who looked scared. One of the boys finally got up enough courage to speak to a Hells Angel named Gut. "We like your bikes, man," he said. "They're really sharp." Gut glanced at him, then at the two dozen or so stripped-down Harleys sitting in the parking lot and said, "I'm glad you like them. They're all we have."[119]

A fine line distinguishes what might be described as Barger's "they're all we want" attitude from Gut's "they're all we have." But both suggest a preoccupation with motorcycling beyond the typical middle-class rider's understanding of it, and certainly a rejection of the work ethic shaped Barger's interest in riding and being part of a motorcycle club. Barger made it clear why he was interested in motorcycling, and it is unlikely that Gut wanted anything more than the stripped-down Harleys the teenage boys were gawking at. This is not to suggest that these men had nothing more in their lives than their motorcycles, but there was little doubt about their priorities and even less of a reason to justify them. The ways in which they understood their own identity and what they wanted had little to do with their experience as workers or with workplace issues. S. Dunn inadvertently highlighted the distinction between middle-class riders and their outlaw counterparts in a 1973 article in the *Dallas Morning News* about "Motorcycle Madness." Explaining that the "madness" is here to stay, Dunn wrote: "People by the thousands escape now to the quiet woods with goat nimble trail bikes strapped to their pickup campers. Dozens of Hell's Angels tear down California freeways on fire-belching mounts and rip through the gap between cars with seemingly no regard for life, limb or the safety of anyone, [and] younger men and men in their 50s fed up with high car payments, low gas mileage and commuters' boredom spend $12,000 or more for sturdy road machines and motorcycle to work feeling much happier."[120]

Jim Pisaretz of *Biker* further emphasized the relationship between work and motorcycling, the motorcyclist's rejection of the former, how these attitudes shaped the public's perception of motorcycling, and the difference between working- and middle-class riders. "Do you ever wonder why bikers are such a disliked class of people?" Pisaretz asked. The typical reasons he suggested were all too familiar to motorcyclists: "too much damn noise," traffic hazards, "they were dirty, unwashed degenerates" and "a danger to the health and well being of every decent living person in society." But "Ain't none of those reasons the real reason Mr. Citizen comes down so hard on bikers." Motorcyclists were "disliked for one reason and one reason only. They symbolize pleasure. And Mr. Workaday Citizen can't comprehend that word." The typical middle-class male, Pisaretz argued, "just guzzled his coffee breakfast, had a fight with his wife, runs over the kid's bicycle on the way out, and has a ton of work waiting on his desk at the office. Now, when he pulls up to that light and sees this biker who has no regard for his middle-class existence, he probably feels more like taking him out than joining him." Motorcycles are for fun and enjoyment, "and enjoyment in this Puritan Ethic hung over society is the devil's word." Pisaretz explained that some middle-class men turned toward baseball and other sports to assuage the turmoil at home and at work, but they were what he called "stop gap" measures. These preoccupations were too well regulated to deal effectively with the problems endemic to a middle-class existence, and "they don't bring along an entire lifestyle based on the principle of having fun like biking does." Pisaretz argued that "some working slave who has nothing to look forward to but punching 9–5 and coming home to a wife with a headache and a bunch of ankle-biters smearing jelly on him is going to explode with indignation when he cracks open the latest issue of *Easyriders* one of his kids left on the coffee table." Critics may claim that *Easyriders*—and motorcycling in general—was offensive and disrespectful to a middle-class sensibility because it was deemed immoral, but according to Pisaretz, it actually "offends his sense of a work ethic."[121]

In hindsight, the middle-class rider, or at least this version of it, would fade away. By the second half of the 1970s, the number of registered riders took a dip, and contemporaries often blamed the middle-class rider who had enthusiastically embraced cycling for his commute to work and to save time, energy, and effort but who also quickly realized that the drive to work was easily compromised by bad weather and angry motorists who were not all that willing to share the roadways. But even before this dip began to materialize, tension was evident among middle-class riders attempting to reconcile contradictory impulses. They hoped to promote the image of respectability they had so anxiously tried to cultivate and simultaneously maintain their love of cycling without becoming too intensely attached to it. Some middle-class men handled this dilemma better than others and kept their two different lives separate. A more common approach, or at least the one attracting attention, was the middle-class rider who remained committed to his class and status at the expense of his attraction to motorcycling. What might be described as a middle-class fear of commitment shaped the rider's impact on motorcycle culture even as he attempted to maintain a safe distance from it. These men associated motorcycling with a particular purpose or reason to justify their attraction or simply understood motorcycling as another example of middle-class consumption and less as a preoccupation with riding. Indeed, what stands out about the middle-class attraction to motorcycling was why he invested so much time, energy, and effort to downplay it.

The tension surrounding middle-class riders was essentially a debate about who best represented motorcycling and what it meant to be a motorcyclist, and it explains the rise of a "mystique," which became a popular concept as the numbers of riders begins to increase in the 1960s. In some cases, mystique described a particular form of cycling and a particular rider. In 1973 mystique described motocross: "Competition, trophies and camaraderie are part of the motocross mystique," claimed a 1973 story on off-road motorcycle racing. Yet the general experience of cycling also transcended any particular attachment. The same author who described the camaraderie and competition of motocross added that "there is something about man and machine traveling together at high speed and at the edge of danger that cannot be articulated." In an article about street riding another motorcyclist made a similar claim to a mystique by describing it as "the forbidding power, the metal studded flair for the open road."[122]

Hunter Thompson came closer to describing it when he wrote about his own riding experiences: "With the throttle screwed on there is only the barest margin and no room at all for mistakes. It has to be done right . . . and that's when the strange music starts, when you stretch your luck so far that fear becomes exhilaration and vibrates along your arms."[123] The mystique, then, was not tied to a particular motorcycle or a particular rider, and it did not need to be explained or justified. It was a feeling or experience, an inarticulate relationship, a blending of man, machine, and asphalt (or mud), or perhaps a certain intangible that was difficult to define and even more difficult to understand for the uninitiated. When asked why he liked motocross, one rider responded, "you have to do it to understand it," a comment that uniquely described his particular experience on a bike but also an experience any rider could understand.[124] In Michael Sumner's 1965 interview with members of the Madison Avenue Motorcycle Club, the author distinguished these professional riders from the "casual motorcyclists" or "fair weather riders" and quoted one member's use of the term "mystique" to explain what he thought separated these men from the non-riding majority and from other riders. "If this were the day of the horse and carriage, we motorcyclists would be the people who still went everywhere on the back of the horse, instead of behind [one].[125]

The development of a "mystique" did not, however, emerge because of the popularity of motorcycling. Rather, it was a response to the challenge motorcycling (and motorcyclists) faced from the middle-class rider and his competing vision of motorcycling. At the least, these riders' experiences had little to do with, or stood in sharp contrast to, the loafer-clad suburbanite out for an afternoon of fun or a family of happy-go-lucky campers trail riding at a local park. The problem limiting the middle-class rider was his perception of his cycle, its purpose, and the rider's relationship to it. When a writer in 1947 attempted to explain why anyone would be attracted to motorcycling, he suggested the obvious—"Go places"— followed by a number of questions that offer insight into the motorcycle's popularity: "What's the big interest in going places? And why go by motorcycle? In fact, why ride one? What is there to the feel of a motor that makes a rider go throttle twistin' for six, seven hundred miles or more one weekend and turn right around and ride the same or even greater distance the next? It must be something. Something clicks."[126] In 1947, however, that certain "something" the author tried to describe had yet to be defined as a "mystique" that would later be identified with motorcyclists. Riders failed to find a label for that experience or a particular label to describe it, not because the divisions between cyclists were less intense than they would be by the 1960s. The influx of British-made lightweights caused an uproar in certain circles, but those cycles did not alter the experience of riding or dilute it: motorcycling still required a degree of more substantial mechanical knowledge than it would in later decades, and among many riders British bikes had made the sport even more robust and demanding than it already was. Motorcyclists had yet to define a mystique because there was no need to or, better yet, no obvious challenge to the sport and the common experience of riding that these enthusiasts shared. That challenge would not emerge until the introduction of the Japanese-made Honda led to the rise of the middle-class rider and his different ideas about motorcycling and its purpose.

IN 1966 the *San Francisco Chronicle* featured a story about motorcycling among middle-class riders that included a picture of a young couple riding a lightweight cycle down what looks like any average tree-lined street in suburbia. The man is dressed in slacks, a sweater, and loafers, and his female companion is wearing a skirt and sitting sidesaddle with her knees together behind her male companion. The loafers and slacks had become one of the distinctive looks of this rider (along with suit and tie) that raised questions about his understanding of motorcycling, and anyone who has been on a motorcycle would undoubtedly raise questions about riding one sidesaddle. The photograph is representative of the typical image of the middle-class rider and of the changes affecting motorcycling in the early to mid-1960s.[127]

Yet even as this image challenges our basic assumptions about motorcycling, the pair of coeds are having fun. Besides the smiling face of his passenger, the bike's speed is apparent and the eagerness with which the rider is crouched forward is unmistakable. The inherent tension between their attraction to motorcycling and their challenge to it influenced motorcycling in the1960s and 1970s and made the issue of class more conspicuous than it had been in previous years. The postwar craze in motorcycling was a consequence of a larger ethic of consumption that is fundamental to understanding a sense of national purpose that shaped an American identity and fueled its economy. But Americans' spending patterns did not necessarily promote the ideas of citizenship and social belonging that historians have attached to consumption because of the constant frustration surrounding the middle-class rider and the stigma associated with the outlaw. This class dynamic was played out in the discussion about the mechanical and technological changes identified with Japanese-made bikes that was articulated daily through the struggles that riders faced and that became identified with Harleys—starting their bikes and dealing with the leaky crankcase. This divide imagined the middle-class rider on one end and the traditional outlaw on the other.

This frustration also shaped the middle-class effort to make motorcycling purposeful. The Japanese Honda, in this line of reasoning, was not simply a motorcycle. It was the next potential Tin Lizzie, or the second car middle-class professionals relied on to ease the frustration of their workaday selves. Most of these new riders were not dressed in suit and tie, and men like Jack Bell (the chopper owner in *Easyriders*) daily challenged them (even though he wore a suit and tie). But those challenges were never consistent or forceful enough to undermine these (class) tensions, which became sharper as Harley's reputation worsened in the late 1960s and 1970s and which made the outlaw (biker) appear to be more of a threat than he actually was. The middle-class rider allowed us to imagine a different motorcyclist whose respectable, clean-cut image only increased our fears about the riders who were not.

By the early 1970s and as the issue of helmets and regulation became more conspicuous, these divisions became particularly noticeable as riders struggled to mobilize effectively against government regulation. Those efforts and the struggles to organize a grassroots political movement are the focus of the chapters to come.

THE VALUE OF A SLOW BREAK-IN

CANNOT BE OVEREMPHASIZED

The Highway Safety Act of 1966 and the End

of the Golden Age of Motorcycling

Through the 1940s and 1950s motorcycle safety attracted little attention beyond the motorcycling community, which itself focused overwhelmingly on the need for improved driver's education and on drawing attention to the incompetent automobile drivers, who were the single most significant danger facing motorcyclists. When the mainstream press focused on roadway safety, the inclusion of motorcyclists was rarely meant to draw attention to the particular experience of motorcycling so much as it was to highlight the general dangers of roadway travel or to single out the motorcycle cowboy who was often blamed for the safety problems facing automobilists. Other examples focused on the motorcycle cop, whose safety on the road was becoming more difficult to guarantee amid the expansion of the highway system after World War II and the increasing speed of highway travel. Motorcycle cops were, in fact, the first to wear helmets after World War II.[1]

As the craze for motorcycling took off in the early 1960s, the discussion about motorcycle safety shifted away from the daredevil who caused accidents to the rider who was a victim of motorcycling—often young and almost always described as inexperienced and generally linked to the Japanese Honda—the fair-weather or middle-class rider whose influence on motorcycle culture would grow throughout the decade and whose safety became the topic of discussion surrounding helmets. In other words, helmet proponents drew largely on a class-based conception of motorcycling that identified helmet safety with the need to save middle-class lives and the assumption that motorcycles were just as unpredictable and dangerous as the outlaws the public overwhelmingly identified with them—outlaws who were also the most outspoken opponents of helmet legislation. Critics viewed these arguments as a larger effort to eliminate motorcycling altogether and countered with questions about the state's power, its responsibilities, and the meaning of "freedom."

Yet just as support for helmet legislation was never simply a question about the loss of life, opposition to helmets was never simply a question of freedom or individual rights. While motorcyclists began organizing "freedom of the road" demonstrations at state capitals across the country, they also consistently blamed these fair-weather riders for the rise in the number of accidents and fatalities and for the enactment of helmet laws and other forms of regulation. The conflict surrounding helmet legislation and the riders responsible for it worsened an already glaring class schism that became even more noticeable as motorcycling took off in the early 1960s. That divide would challenge the unity that was needed to effectively oppose regulation. Indeed, by the late 1960s and early 1970s frustration characterized the motorcycle rights movement, and many riders had convinced themselves that if there ever had been a golden age of motorcycling it had long passed.

THE MIDDLE-CLASS VICTIM

On "a beautiful sunlit April afternoon" in 1963, Beth Magid was home busily preparing a casserole when the telephone rang. "There's been an accident," a stranger's voice informed her, "a motorcycle and a station wagon. Intersection of Concord and Fern Creek." Within seconds Magid was on her way to the hospital. She found her son, Ken, "lying on the receiving table where he was being given shots of novocaine and a tetanus booster." She described him as beaten and bloody. "His slacks and sport shirt were ripped . . . his white crew socks were bloodstained [and] there were jagged cuts and abrasions on his arms and legs." But it "was only when he turned his head and I saw his face," Magid explained, "that I knew how serious the accident had been." The "flesh of his firm young chin had been torn loose from his jaw and dark red blood was seeping from the corner of his misshapen mouth." When he tried to speak, she noticed that "all of his front teeth were broken off."[2]

In Mrs. Magid's account of her son's accident, she explained how she and her husband, "supposedly intelligent parents," became unwittingly part of the motor scooter and motorcycle craze. "You don't just run out and buy your son a motorcycle and turn him loose on dangerous highways." Magid explained that "it usually begins in a way that seems sensible and safe." In her case, it began with the purchase of a "motorbike" because of her son's need for reliable transportation to school. Her son had already qualified for a "Restricted Motor Vehicle Operator's License" by "taking a simple test," and once he turned fourteen he was eligible to ride his motorbike to school. As Ken began to socialize with the other boys who rode motorbikes, he became focused on a more "powerful machine" and began talking with his parents about a motor scooter. Convinced his parents would not buy one, Ken began to save his money. "For more than a year," Magid explained, "he saved from his allowance, mowed lawns, washed cars and did other odd jobs." Before long he had decided that a motor scooter was not enough to satiate his two-wheel craving and started to eye a motorcycle even though his parents tried to discourage him. He "was not to be dissuaded," Mrs. Magid recalled, and any effort to convince him otherwise only led him to "mow more laws, wash more cars, and accumulate insurance money." Magid and her husband were soon faced with a decision: "How far should parents go in refusing a son permission to buy something with money he has earned himself—especially if they are trying to develop his initiative and independence?" Magid and her husband decided to support his decision. "After all," she explained, "he was a good and responsible boy."[3]

After Mrs. Magid's son was nearly killed, she researched the licensing of motor vehicle operations. She found "widely divergent regulations" on who was eligible for a license and noted that "two-wheeled power-driven cycles are considered motor vehicles." In 1962 the American Association of Motor Vehicles asked state driver license administrators if they authorized "the operation of scooters or motorbikes by licensees who are less than sixteen years of age." Of the forty-seven replies they received, twenty seven answered yes. "This means," Magid exclaimed, "that at fourteen or fifteen years of age, youngsters in twenty-seven states can obtain restricted licenses which will permit them to ride our nation's highways on motorbikes, scooters and motorcycles." Some states, like Iowa, Kansas, and South Dakota, issued these licenses as restricted school permits only, while others, like Michigan and Utah, required the completion of a driver's training course or else limited the horsepower, the weight of the vehicle, or its top speed. But, in many states, she stressed, "there are practically no restrictions at all."[4]

Critics and concerned parents alike pointed to some efforts to provide driver education courses for motorcyclists, but instruction was generally brief and haphazard or largely unavailable. Some dealers offered new buyers instruction, but it was often limited to an "unobstructed area near the dealership for demonstrations and initial tryouts of newly purchased cycles."[5] *Readers Digest* wrote about a young man who rented a cycle at a gas station and was told how to start and stop the vehicle. "When he asked to ride around the station to familiarize himself with the controls," he was told, "Hell, no you're liable to bang into one of the pumps."[6] *Today's Health* printed a story about a dealer in the Midwest who, after becoming aware that "most of his new customers had to traverse a major multiple highway just to get home with a new cycle," moved "his place of business a few hundred yards across the six-lane thoroughfare so his neophyte buyers could get home safely." "The value of a slow break-in," one contemporary argued, "cannot be overemphasized."[7]

Motorcycle accidents and fatalities were not unique to the 1960s, nor were concerns about them, but the urgency with which contemporaries addressed the issue was more conspicuous than in earlier decades, and their concern reflected their fear that this "epidemic of injury" was affecting the middle class. Indeed, by the early 1960s stories about the dangers of motorcycling began to make their way into mainstream publications, and those stories emphasized middle-class and professional victims. Many descriptions remained nondescript: youth dead on arrival, brother and sister killed when they unexpectedly hit a rock and veered into a tree, or man killed after ramming into the back of a truck. When descriptions were more detailed they often contradicted motorcycling's typical class association. Motorcycle fatalities showed up as an eighteen-year-old University of Illinois youth, a "philosophy major who was the daughter of a prominent surgeon" who died because of injuries sustained form a motor scooter accident, a pair of newlyweds who were killed when "their lightweight was struck from the rear by an automobile," or a popular folk singer killed when "the cycle on which he was a passenger sailed over a five foot bank and plowed through two fences."[8]

More education and riding experience may have provided the training that would have saved these men and women, but education and experience were not the panaceas critics hoped for, and perhaps that was the point these writers were attempting to make. While Magid stressed the need for more emphasis on driver education, she advocated "a more general use of safety equipment, especially crash helmets." Magid cited a regulation from the Department of the Air Force dated March 1961 that read, "The wearing of protective helmets will be mandatory on all USAF installations for each person who operates or rides as a passenger on a privately-owned motorcycle, motor scooter or similar vehicle."[9] She also pointed to police departments whose use of helmets began about a decade or more earlier. The Los Angeles Police Department, for example, began requiring its motorcycle officers to wear helmets in 1955 after "police statistics showed that nearly every motorcycle officer injured in accidents suffered head injuries—some of them fatal."[10] Magid recognized that most teen-agers would object to helmets because the "other kids don't wear them" or because "I'll look like some kind of a nut or something," but she insisted that helmets were "desirable" and mistakenly suggested that, because of the current discussion about seatbelts, average Americans would welcome them. "Because of extensive publicity," Magid stressed, "most car owners recognized the importance of having seat belts installed in their cars." The same type of widespread public information, she argued, could make "protective helmets an accepted fact for motor scooter and motorcycle riders." Magid concluded by emphasizing a trope that would become familiar to the debate surrounding helmets. "If my husband and I had not been adamant about this one safety measure, it is possible that our son, Ken, who always wore a helmet while riding would have been much more seriously injured."[11]

What separated the discussion about helmets in the early to mid-1960s from that of earlier decades, was the convergence of two ideas—helmets saved lives and saving lives had become so much more urgent than in previous years because of the rise in the numbers of young, responsible, middle-class men and women who were riding motorcycles. In a 1967 edition of *Today's Health*, Harris Edward Dark made this connection explicit in an article titled "Your Youngster and the MOTORCYCLE." "WILL YOUR BOY OR GIRL RIDE A MOTORCYCLE?" he asked. "Yes," he emphatically answered, because motorcycling was "fun, glamorous," and the "most in thing to hit this country in the last 20 years." If your child is "between the ages of 10 and 20," he added, he or she is "bound to take that first ride—soon," and that was where the potential problems began. For Dark, the problem with increasing fatalities was not its effect on motorcycling but its influence on what he described as "our better families."[12] Dark contrasted these riders with the "offensive picture of the leather-jacketed motor-mobs of yesteryear." He explained that "today's motorcyclists belong to our 'better' families with good backgrounds and sufficient means to provide a toy worth several hundred dollars." The "typical teen cyclist of today," he insisted, was "intelligent, good looking, and a well-liked mixer, . . . potentially one of tomorrow's leading citizens." In other words, "losing one of these [motorcyclists] is more than a personal tragedy for family and friends—it's a real bereavement of society."[13] As Dark suggested, concerns about motorcycle fatalities reflected concerns not simply about the loss of life but about the loss of specifically middle-class life.

The public bereavement Dark imagined regularly showed up in mainstream publications throughout the 1960s as contemporaries struggled to come to terms with motorcycling and its impact. "Death and disfigurement," one physician claimed, "are seizing riders aboard the small motorcycle."[14] Another talked about a "deluge of emergency room patients" requiring "treatment for head, facial, neck, arm, leg, ankle and knee injuries." Dr. Paul Joliet of the U.S. Public Health Service (PHS) accident-prevention division called it a "serious national health problem,"[15] while a 1966 article in the *Journal of the American Medical Association* described the wave of fatalities and injuries as "a new epidemic of injury and death."[16] Other stories described the victim's wounds: "usually multiple" and "unusually severe,"[17] or what one doctor described as similar to "limb-shattering war wounds."[18]

Some invoked the specter of war abroad—helmets were needed to keep men alive to support the war in Vietnam, where they might realize the "limb shattering war wounds" doctors ascribed to motorcycle accidents. A judge in New York, for example, cited three reasons to justify protective headgear, noting that the action of an unprotected cyclist can affect the public, including its "national defense since many motorcyclists are young men."[19] Dr. John A. Perry, an orthopedic surgeon on the staff of Mercy Hospital in Pittsburgh, described these patients as "mangled and in trouble," and said he was seeing them on a "daily basis." He added, "It's been happening over the last two to three years," and it was "almost unbelievable, the loss of limbs in young people, the amputations and paraplegics, kids who won't walk again." "I absolutely hate the damn things," exclaimed Dr. Saul Haskell, an orthopedic surgeon at Michael Reese Hospital and Medical Center in Chicago. Victims often had "severe leg injuries requiring multiple blood transfusions"; others had "gone into renal shutdown," which required an "artificial kidney unit." Many recent cases, he added, "have required leg amputations," and he told the story of one young man who had to have his entire shoulder replaced "after he plowed through the rear end of a garage."[20] Dr. Robert B. Rutheford, director of emergency service at the Colorado General Hospital in Denver, noted that some physicians had noticed "a rising frequency in motorcycling accidents" and the resulting injuries, including a "shearing off of genitals."[21]

Further inflaming the fears about motorcycling and the push to contain this "epidemic" were critics who emphasized the motorcycle's response to unpredictable road conditions and the motorcycle rider's consequent vulnerability. Captain Tom Winders of the Pasadena Police complained that the numbers of fatal motorcycle crashes in part reflected the lack of education. But he was just as quick to complain about road conditions. Winders noted that road conditions that "wouldn't faze" an automobile could seriously "hinder" motorcycles and even cause them to "careen out of control." The "culprit," according to Winters, could be a "slick leaf, a splatter of grease, a pool of water on the road. . . . Even a moderately sized pebble can throw you off if you're going around a corner."[22]

Other examples were bizarre—inexplicable to say the least—and proof positive that something more drastic needed to be done to reduce the numbers of fatalities. In Tampa, Florida, two young men died in a fiery crash when the motorcycle they were riding "went out of control over a curve, skidded 118 feet, smashed into a fence gate and burst into flames." In Illinois, an eighteen-year-old was killed instantly when his motorcycle struck an auto "head on." Apparently his cycle "went out of control" as he was reaching "for something at the rear of his cycle." In Pasadena, California, a sixteen-year-old died when his motorcycle spun off a slippery leaf and smashed into the rear of a parked car.[23] In Jacksonville, Florida, two youths arrived at the hospital dead on arrival after the motorcycle they were riding suddenly "swerved off a highway, hit a guard rail and slid into a bridge abatement." A highway patrolman, the report added, found their bodies 80 feet from the impact site and the cycle 132 feet away.[24] In another example an eighteen-year-old male and his sixteen-year-old date were found dead in a gulley along a suburban railroad track. The pair, the article speculated, had apparently "ridden their borrowed motorcycle down a street that came to a dead end at the track." Stressing the word "borrowed motorcycle," the author emphasized the inexperience of the -eighteen-year-old rider who perhaps had been distracted and failed to respond quickly enough when the road came to an end. Their untimely deaths were as tragic as they were mysterious, and the motorcycle was as much to blame as the rider.[25] Other bizarre examples include "an off-duty policeman killed when his brakes locked and he was thrown into a cement divider; a man killed when his steering mechanism jammed"; "a brother and sister killed when they hit a rock [presumably in the road] and veered into a tree." The author explained that these victims were not riders who lacked experience or access to educational programs. They were "just the unlucky ones" or, better yet, the tragic victims of dangerous and unpredictable motorcycles.[26]

By the mid-1970s, it seemed as if everyone had heard of at least one fatal motorcycle crash, or so it was believed. A writer for *Today's Health* in 1975 told the story of how she fell in and out of love with a motorcycle. A close friend had convinced her one evening to go for a lakefront ride on a motorcycle. He had ridden for six years, she explained, and he had never had an accident. As soon as the pair took off, the author exclaimed, "I felt totally free." "Stars over my head, wind blowing my hair, what more could I want?" Speed was apparently what she wanted, and she assured her male companion that she would enjoy the ride more if "we went faster." Unfortunately her night ended as quickly as it began. "We hit a bump, swerved into a curb and fell over." The four-hundred-plus-pound cycle landed on her leg and broke her foot. Her friend scraped only his arm and leg. For the next few weeks, she hobbled around, and it seemed as if all she heard were stories of motorcycle wrecks and tragedies of the "if you think that's bad, listen to this" kind. The woman concluded that the riders in these stories were not reckless, just unlucky, and that "everyone knows of at least one tragic motorcycle story."[27]

Other critics talked in more detail about the differences between driving a car and riding a motorcycle to emphasize the inevitability of an accident. The average driver, according to one story, will have an accident about every five years. But "chances are . . . it will be a minor fender bender." At a speed of around ten miles an hour and especially with a fastened seat belt, "you more likely will not get hurt. Your slight mishap will be soon forgotten if not the stuff jokes are made of." The motorcycle rider's experience was never so mundane or humorous, however. "Now in your imagination," the author dared his readers to consider, "place yourself upon the seat of a motorcycle and drive into traffic." In this scenario, an auto makes a quick right turn in front of the cyclist. You brake quickly but are still going about ten miles an hour when "you impact the side of the car." Instead of the "jolting thump" and the "tug of a seat belt" that a motorist would receive before "settling back into soft upholstery," you are "catapulted high into the air literally flying right over the car your cycle hit." After the initial impact, the cyclist was likely to "smash right into a lamp pole, a street sign . . . another vehicle" and "come to a grinding, crumpling mangling collision with concrete." Your skin will "be abraded away in spots, loaded with sand, rubber, dust, and bits of dirty gravel in other places." If you happened to land on your head, not an unlikely outcome for a motorcyclist in any collision, and "strike your head on the hard surface, you don't have much chance for survival—and perhaps it's just as well because severe brain damage can ruin your life forever."[28]

The enormous success of the Japanese-made lightweight was accompanied by what contemporaries described as an alarming increase in the number of motorcycle accidents and fatalities. Discussions about accidents and efforts to minimize them had always been—and remain—a conspicuous part of motorcycle culture. What had changed were the victims. Motorcycling by middle-class riders not only challenged motorcycle culture but became the focus of the discussion about helmets and the reason riders so desperately needed them.

HELMET LAWS

In 1967 state legislators across the country began passing laws requiring helmet use, and by the end of 1968 nearly forty states had joined this effort to regulate motorcycling. The response to these laws was visible in states across the country, and helmet laws, as Will Bernard of the American Bar Association explained in 1970, ended up at the "center of a raging constitutional debate."[29] Legislators often passed helmet laws, which the courts then found unconstitutional. In Boise, Idaho, in 1969 Ada County sheriff Paul Bright and Boise police chief John Church had "ordered their men not to issue tickets based on the law as the result of a Friday decision in which 4th District Judge Merlin S. Young declared the law unconstitutional." Law Enforcement Commissioner Warner C. Mills, on the other hand, was encouraging state agencies to enforce the law, "pending an appeal of the district court decision."[30] Other states established an educational period to prepare cyclists for the enforcement of helmet laws. In May 1968 Florida State Highway Patrol officials were warning motorists that the educational period that lasted several months was over and they were "stepping up enforcement" of a new law that required motorcyclists to wear helmets and eye protection. "We feel that the educational period has been long enough to allow motorcycle riders to learn about and comply with the law and arrests are now necessary for violation," said Highway Patrol chief Col. H. N. Kirkman. In support of the law, patrol safety official Major Roger Collar added that "surveys have shown that in motorcycle accidents people who wear good quality helmets are much more likely to survive than those who do not."[31]

Questions also emerged about what constituted a "quality helmet." In Roanoke, Virginia, for example, the Roanoke police department decided not to uphold a new law "requiring motorcyclists to wear protective helmets of a type approved by State Police" because the "helmets worn by its [own] motorcycle policemen are not on the approved list."[32] Indeed, in October 1972 the National Highway Traffic Safety Administration released findings from a study of seventy-four tests of fifty-four different helmets using standards set by the industry's American National Standards Institute. Only eight of the helmets complied with the agency's standards. By this time, forty-four states required motorcyclists to wear helmets, but none had "set specific safety standards," and the federal government's proposed set of standards were not scheduled to take effect until March 1973.[33]

Meanwhile, across the country riders were challenging these laws by refusing to wear helmets. In Seattle in 1967, a police officer stopped a motorcyclist because he was not wearing his helmet presumably in violation of the state's helmet law. The law specified that a "cyclist must wear a helmet with the chin strap fastened." It did not specify where it had to be fastened and the rider had cleverly strapped the helmet to his leg. The officer released him without a ticket.[34] In Clearfield, Pennsylvania, attorney Dan P. Arnold deliberately tested the law by driving his motorcycle in Clearfield without helmet or goggles. The police ticketed him, and his challenge concluded with a Clearfield County judge ruling the law unconstitutional. Judge John A. Cherry "said the General Assembly in legislating the 1968 law went beyond its powers in making protective helmets and eye shields mandatory." According to the judge, "The general public does not require the direction or restraint imposed by this action."[35] In Columbus, Ohio, in 1970 two hundred motorcyclists held a rally on the statehouse grounds to challenge a state law requiring all riders to wear a helmet. The cyclists argued that the law was unconstitutional, and they were circulating a petition asking the Ohio General Assembly to repeal it. Dave Davis, secretary of the Columbus Soul Seekers Motorcycle Club, argued that the motorcyclists wanted the "General Assembly to give us back our constitutional right of freedom of choice."[36]

In 1968 the *Dallas Morning News* reported that within a year of Texas passing its helmet law a "group of about 60 blue denimed motorcyclists" with nicknames like "Chino" and "Big Daddy" arrived in Austin to protest against the state's helmet law. The motorcyclists had arrived from San Antonio, and the press described them as members of various Alamo City Motorcycle Clubs: the Bandidos, the Barones, and the Barrios. Some of the riders were dressed in white shirts and ties, but the ones wearing "embroidered '1 percent' badges" attracted the media's attention. One newspaper story described these motorcyclists as members of "outlaw clubs" that were "unsanctioned by the American Motorcycle Association," and most were "bearded" and "long haired." The cyclists all wore helmets "as they roared up the Capital driveway and stopped in front," where they met with Jim Crowson, one of the governor's administrative assistants. Bandito captain Jack Trudeau presented Crowson with a letter and "several petitions." While Crowson assured the motorcyclists that the governor would see the letter and the petitions, Trudeau asked for a reply and explained that "if one wasn't received in three months there might be a bigger ride on the capital," one that Trudeau warned would include as many as "1,000 motorcyclists."[37]

From the start of the debate about helmet laws two issues stood out in prominence: whether a helmet would protect the nonriding majority from cyclists who were considered a danger to automobilists, and to what extent the government was responsible for protecting its citizens from themselves—what were called "self-protection laws" and essentially a question about state power. One rider in 1967 explained that "when a person rides a motorcycle without protection from a helmet, it is a known fact he is taking chances with his own life. But, it is also a known fact that not wearing a helmet does not endanger anyone's life other than the motorcyclist's, as wearing a helmet does not help prevent accidents, but on the contrary may increase the hazards due to limited vision and hearing." His point was in essence a challenge to one of the earliest arguments about the constitutionality of helmet laws that asserted that the average motorcyclist was a danger to the nonriding public because of the potential adverse effects of hard-shelled beetles or other bugs or debris that may cause the rider to "lose control of his motorcycle and cause a collision."[38] The man behind the challenge to Nebraska's helmet law, A. P. Beyer, explained that he wore his helmet about 50 percent of the time, not for safety reasons, though, but "to cut down wind noise, keep the bugs off his teeth, and keep his hair from being rumpled." But he was opposed to helmets because "I don't feel it's anybody's business if I wear a helmet or not. . . . It saves nobody else's life if I wear a helmet, and I'm not endangering anybody else's life if I don't. It's an infringement on personal rights," he added.[39] David Nolan, a twenty-eight-year-old sales representative for a computer services firm and acting chairman of the Libertarian Party, which had just announced its formation in January 1972, summed up this position when he argued that "a man has an inalienable right to bash in his own head if he chooses—but not the head of his neighbor." Nolan explained that "it's all right to have a law requiring good brakes because if you can't stop your car you could hurt someone else. But a motorcyclist can only bash in his own head by not wearing a helmet. If he wants to run the risk to feel the wind in his hair, that's his right."[40]

Other helmet law opponents focused less on the potential danger motorists faced from riders who were helmetless and overwhelmingly on the helmet's usefulness. In a 1975 issue of *Biker*, one article concluded that the helmet law "has had *little* or *no* effect whatsoever" and that in the forty-six states that had a law in effect "slight increases in the death and injury rate percentages" were reported. "*Beware* of any reports that are *lengthy* and cite *individual* cases," the author warned. "The truth is that the death rate percentage has always remained between 1.5 percent and 3.5 percent of the total amount of accidents both *before* and *after* helmets. The only states that have lowered their actual number of fatalities are the ones that have specialized safety programs for motorcyclists, with or without mandatory helmets!"[41]

Indeed, throughout the debates over helmet legislation opponents argued that helmets increased the likelihood of injury and death. "Tell these men that you oppose the mandatory use of helmets," argued John Underwood of Clovis, New Mexico. "They have not been shown to reduce the number of fatalities in states that have passed helmet laws. Tell them helmets can cause accidents by tiring and annoying the rider. Tell them that helmets are not designed to be safe in any impact above 13.5 mph."[42] Another opponent emphasized that helmeted riders had a greater chance of being killed from a broken neck than from a concussion. In an article titled "Motorcycle Helmets CAUSE Accidents Not Prevent Them," the author cited a New York State report that argued that since a mandatory helmet law went into effect in 1967, "there was a 75 percent increase in the proportion of serious neck injuries." The report also pointed out that while broken necks were 5.8 percent of the 1966 motorcycle fatalities in New York, they accounted for nearly 38 percent of the motorcycle deaths the following year (after a helmet law was in place). The Federal Safety Board's report argued that the added weight of a two to three pound helmet puts too much strain on the neck in collisions. Helmet opponents cited studies that showed that a "six-inch thick helmet" was needed "to withstand today's speeds." Such a helmet, the author added, "would weigh about 20 pounds, and only protect the rider's head, not prevent a broken neck in an accident."[43]

Others complained about the false sense of security, the fatigue and heat exhaustion, and the difficulty in hearing and seeing associated with wearing a helmet.[44] A tragic example included the death of "a 17-year-old biker" who "was killed because he had a helmet on and couldn't hear a train coming up behind him." The young man was standing on the railroad tracks taking a picture of his father who was sitting on another motorcycle just off to the side and out of danger's way. The boy's father, Carl Scott Senior, could only "watch as the 94 car train hit his son."[45]

Another issue in the helmet debate concerned whether "the individual should be 'master of his fate and captain of his soul.'" If the government could require a helmet to "protect the man from self," it "could just as logically require everybody to be in by 10pm." Was it in "the interest of the state to have strong, robust, healthy citizens"? Some "safe-guarding of the individual is justified," because if a man "is injured, he (or his family) may become a public burden."[46] The public-burden theory was simple: motorcyclists were in accidents, they could not pay all their medical bills, and the American taxpayer had to pick up the tab. The most frequently cited quote in defense of the public-burden theory comes from a federal judge who upheld the Massachusetts helmet law in a 1972 court case: "From the moment of the injury, society picks the person up off the highway; delivers him to a municipal hospital and municipal doctors, provides him with unemployment compensation if, after recovery, he cannot replace his lost job, and, if the injury causes permanent disability, may assume the responsibility for his and his family's continued subsistence. We do not understand a state of mind that permits a plaintiff to think that only he himself is concerned."[47] In a *U.S. News and World Report* article discussing the pros and cons, Ben Kelley, senior vice president of the Insurance Institute for Highway Safety, argued that the laws requiring helmets not only protect individuals from "huge amounts of unnecessary damage— principally in damage that results in fatalities or, even worse, a lifetime of crippled inactivity and dependency—they also protect all of us in society from carrying the costs of those liabilities and of the lifetime support of people who have been totally maimed."[48]

The focus on cost and the argument that those costs were too much of a burden for the public to bear were at the heart of growing fears about a restrictive society operating under "forced self-protection laws." Kelly Wendeln, one of the leading motorcyclists opposing helmet laws, vigorously argued that "this attitude would lead to unlimited paternalism and apply to laws mandating [the] wearing of seatbelts in cars and prohibiting smoking, hang gliders, skydiving, mountain climbing, swimming, football, etc."[49] "The helmet law is the first forced self-protection law," Wendeln said. "A seat belt law will be the second."[50] After the *Wichita Eagle and Beacon* printed an article titled "Keep the Helmet Law," motorcyclist Frankie Moore followed up with a strong objection letter that asked: "If you like forced self-protection laws, why not mandatory seatbelt laws, prohibition of tobacco and alcohol, laws against 'dangerous' sports? Where do you draw the line on forced self-protection laws?"[51] Greg Anderson, the director of Cincinnati's chapter of A Brotherhood Against Totalitarian Enactments (ABATE), described the "public burden theory" as "a theory, never proven," and questioned Larry Trask, the executive secretary for the Ohio Motorcycle Dealers Association, for his support of it. "My question to him is, 'Who is going to pay for *his* final expenses, *his* widow's welfare and the upbringing of *his* orphaned children when he is killed in an auto accident, drops dead of a heart attack, dies of cancer from smoking too damn many cigarettes, or cirrhosis from too much booze: Perhaps he'll just bust his thick head in a fall in the bathtub! What I'm saying is, by his way of thinking, we are all a 'public burden' in the end. It doesn't matter how you get snuffed."[52] Bob Greene referred to the public burden theory as an "asinine presumption," which meant that the state "can protect a person against himself because any self-harm, in the abstract, involved risk of incidental harm or expense to the public." It was too "nebulous," he added, and empowered the state to "require" an individual to wear a "suit of armor or retire at sunset in the interests of his well being." In theory, Greene noted, "this could be applied to many existing sports like skiing, roller skating, football, bicycling, ad infinitum." As an example, Greene cited Canada where legislation was "brewing on a helmet law for ten-speed bicycle riders," which "surfaced" only after "an officer arrested a bicyclist in Calgary, reportedly running 85 mph down a mountainside on his ten speed!"[53] In an ironic twist, motorcyclists in the 1980s and 1990s challenged the idea that they were too significant of a burden to save by threatening to refuse to sign their organ donor cards if helmet laws were passed or not overturned.[54]

Helmet opponents also wondered why similar regulations were not being enacted to protect motorists from themselves. "I'll bet if the government had mandatory helmet laws for bicyclists, automobile occupants and pedestrians," Frankie Moore objected, "you wouldn't think it was such a great idea—but why not? If helmets are good for motorcyclists, they are good for all these others—and golfers too."[55] In a letter published in *Biker News*, Bill Tracy of Carson, California, suggested that "we (motorcyclists) should put the shoe on the other foot and push for no radio in car laws (so we'll be heard), all clear bodied car laws (so we'll have a better chance of being seen) and car operator helmet laws. Sounds crazy? Hell yes, but so is all this crap they push on us. So all you 'free and easy' bikers, no matter what you ride, make a stand. Wire your congressmen, senators, hell, even the EPA! Let them know you're fed up with this crap. Do it before a good sounding exhaust system, becomes a museum piece."[56] Bob Greene pointed to the rate of fatalities among automobilists who suffer a head injury in an automobile accident: seven out of ten, which he argued was comparable to motorcycle fatality rates. What Greene referred to as an oversight on the part of the government translated into nearly 40,000 motorists killed every year.[57] "If the car folks are too good to wear a helmet then get off the cyclists' backs." On sheer numbers, "they need it [a helmet] far worse [than motorcyclists do]." Greene suspected that the typical legislator suffered from a lack of nerve. "He doesn't seem to have the guts to jeopardize his job, let alone realize that he could be saving his own life by making helmets mandatory across the board, cars as well as bikes." Greene suspected that the legislator's wife or his fellow representatives would "never buy it" and never "go for messing their coiffeur." Why overlook 40,000 motorists "who will splatter their brains all over a windshield in the next year," while singling out "a relative handful of 2000 motorcyclists for salvation." Greene's conclusion: "If it's good for one, it's good enough for all."[58]

FRUSTRATION

While these early protests suggest the beginning of a robust grassroots political movement, activists struggled to sustain it, or to rally "1,000 motorcyclists" to the Texas capital, as Trudeau had warned. Rogue, the president of the Huns Motorcycle Club, suggested in 1974 that, except for certain parts of the country, protests were rare. He had been "getting an awful lot of letters lately on how people can do the same thing in their state that we have been doing in Connecticut," referring to the staging of protest rallies for "over 7 years."[59] Yet even in Connecticut these efforts had not succeeded. Connecticut established a helmet law in 1967. The state assembly would have repealed the law in 1972 but faced a threatened veto by Governor Thomas Meskill (against a campaign promise). Meskill explained that he was "sympathetic with those who wish to see this law repealed because of the design and weight of the safety helmets, and will work to have a more acceptable helmet approved by government officials." Connecticut, the National Highway Traffic Safety Administration explained, was facing the loss of eight million dollars in highway funds.[60]

The challenge in the courts also suggested limits to the development of a nationwide movement. In December 1972 Charles Simon had just "battle[d]" his way "through the first level of the Federal Court" in his bid to overturn Massachusetts's helmet law. At the time of the story's appearance, Simon had spent $22,000 in court costs and was in the process of filing an appeal to the Supreme Court. Of the $22,000, $15,000 was his own and $10,000 of that was borrowed on his house. Bob Greene described Simon as a "dedicated motorcyclist" and one who had "put his future on the line in a frighteningly personal way that few of us would have the guts to emulate." Greene added that the appeal to the Supreme Court had been filed as "though the nation's five million riders stood staunchly behind this crusade to guarantee their constitutional rights" but "tragically, they do not." Only seven hundred individuals had "pitched in" and that included a paltry $2,000 from the American Motorcycle Association, an organization that at the time represented 150,000 motorcyclists, or what Greene pointed out would be the "equivalent of a little over a penny a member." The rest, he sadly reported, "either don't know about the fund or don't care." Greene added that he and all motorcyclists were "lucky to have someone like him, someone who will stand there and slug it out for us while we go on about our fun." He then admonished them to get involved. "Maybe we should think about helping Charlie with that mortgage, and in so doing keep our own house in order. . . . Thank God somebody has the gumption to protect us from our protectors."[61]

Riders tried to explain the movement's slow growth by emphasizing the average rider's independent spirit. Clarence Elmore from *Motorcyclist*, for example, admitted that motorcyclists found collective efforts "distasteful," because of what he referred to as the "very nature of the motorcycling psyche" or what he also described as an "independent personality type" or "special breed." "We've got to face the fact," he added, "that the one thing all government employees and politicians understand is consensus," or what he also referred to as "blocks of constituents with common views," and "voter pressure."[62] Bob Bitchin of *Biker News* made an almost identical argument about the motorcyclist "psyche" and its impact on the movement. "Most people who ride motorcycles on the street do so because they like the feeling of freedom. They don't like to be fenced in . . . they are mavericks," which he argued "is the reason organizations to support motorcycles have such a hard time getting people to join." If Bitchin's comments were not clear enough, in another editorial he explained that "bikers are not joiners. If we were, there would not be helmet laws in 48 of the 50 states."[63] Speaking directly to the bikers, Bitchin issued his mandate: "It looks like in order to be a loner on a bike, you will have to unite to retain your freedom. DO IT NOW."[64]

Throughout these early years, the independent spirit Bitchin and Elmore described translated into different groups of motorcyclists who had little in common or at least not enough in common to promote the movement's growth. Bob Bitchin, for example, argued that riders were divided into "5 basic types of bikers," whom he described as "independent from the rest": "the so-called outlaw . . . the touring rider, the street (basically stock) rider . . . the drag racers" and dirt riders. He added that people will only ride with other motorcyclists who are the same as themselves and gave the example of dresser riders who "would form an organization and the outlaws would form an organization, but none would have true representation in the Capitol."[65] Offering an example, Bitchin explained that the Southern California Motorcycle Association (SCMA) and the Modified Motorcycle Association (MMA), what Bitchin described as the only two organizations that were having any effect in the fight against helmets, attracted different constituencies. The SCMA, according to Bitchin, "are basically families who ride mostly on the weekend," and the MMA was made up of "single men who ride all the time."[66]

Though Bitchin provided only minor details about these riders, his use of "single men who ride all the time" suggested the "outlaw" motorcyclist, whose influence on the early development of the motorcycle rights movement was as significant as his influence on the public's image of the typical motorcyclist. The "so called 'outlaw' bikers," argued Charles Clayton, "were the first to read the hand writing on the wall and realize that it meant the beginning of the end of road motorcycling." Pictures of these early rallies only seemed to confirm Clayton's contention. Riders were almost always long haired, bearded, and riding a Harley or a chopper, and the "dumb old biker" was conspicuous in derisive descriptions of helmet opponents. The use of "dumb" was no doubt the legacy of motorcyclists who were belittled as morons because of their stunt riding and noisy pipes, but also "dumb" because these riders failed to appreciate the helmet's efficacy. "There's no question [about the safety of helmets] as far as science is concerned," remarked another helmet law advocate. "Anybody who's had even high-school physics should be able to figure out that a protected head will fare better than a bare one when it hits the asphalt at 20 or 30 miles per hour."[67] Some contemporaries also automatically made the connection between outlaws and opposition to helmets. "Any motorcyclist who opposes a law requiring helmets is an outlaw rider at heart who feels superior when he kicks his machine forward with as much racket as possible, exceeds proper speed limits, and rides too close to and cuts in on other vehicles," argued Mrs. M. W. Radcliffe in a letter to the *San Francisco Chronicle* in 1967. She added, "he also favors open pipes which are against the law but unenforced by the police. In an earlier age he probably would have screamed in protest at windshields and bumpers."[68]

In contrast, helmet opponents linked the pro-helmet lobby to the Japanese-made motorcycle and its riders linked to suburbia. "There were never as many accidents before," argued Joe "HARLY" Walker from Duquesne, Pennsylvania, "until these light weight suicide motorbikes were sold."[69] Bill Tracy of Carson, California, for example, argued that "Most of the folks who want the sound level lowered are honest Joe suburbanite types who work 9–5 all week and then are set free on weekends." The suburbanite types, Carson added, were "both envious and threatened by our free and easy way of life and travel, so they start making helmet laws and lights on laws and now worse, sound laws." Carson admonished all bikers to "get involved" and warned them that, if they did not, a day will come when "your kid (though only a rug-rat now) will be sitting there and he'll ask, 'Daddy, what was a Harley-Davidson?' "[70] Concern for the suburbanites' safety sometimes seemed to correlate with a disregard for rights of the outlaw. In response to a letter about a motorcyclist who was beaten to death by the police, one rider pointed out that regardless of the controversy surrounding the violence, plenty of evidence suggested that he did not receive proper medical attention. "We all have that right (the right to medical attention)," argued the rider, "whether we're outlaw chopper [types] or John Q. Suburbia."[71]

A 1972 *Easyriders* interview with Douglas Thoms, head of the National Highway Traffic Safety Administration, also made the connection between helmets, Japanese motorcycles, and the novice or middle-class rider and revealed the limits of the unity among riders in the early 1970s. Much of the interview focused on who was responsible for motorcycle accidents and how that knowledge might resolve the helmet issue. *Easyriders*' editor was particularly interested in what Thoms thought about the typical assumption that a significant majority of fatalities took place during the novice rider's first year on a motorcycle. When Thoms was pushed on the issue, he suggested that the figure was overstated and rarely proven. He admitted that 40 to 60 percent of fatalities occurred during a rider's first year but also noted that most "people ride motorcycles to some degree before they get a license. Sometimes it's dirt riding, sometimes it's other forms of off-the-road riding, but they've almost always had some experience before they start riding on the street." Not satisfied with Thom's answer, *Easyriders* pursued the issue of finding accurate statistics "in order to pinpoint the types of people who are guilty, the types of bikes, and so on." He also asked Thoms if the "fatality rate is high primarily because of the novice rider," and if he would support a law to "prohibit sales to inexperienced, unqualified purchasers—a law that would require the buyer to show some kind of evidence that he is a capable bike rider." Thoms stated that he would "probably be opposed" to such a law because it was an "unwarranted abridgement of one's right to freedom." "But," the editor responded, "the combination of a teenager and a 750 Honda with no experience whatsoever, has got to be a hazard." The editor even suggested that helmet requirements may be justifiable in the case of certain riders. "Where it is shown that a major portion of the total fatalities are caused by the novice rider during the first year of operating a bike, doesn't it make sense that they should be the ones to have to wear the helmet, rather than the people who have been riding for years."[72] *Easyriders* failed to use the term "middle class," but the divide he used to understand the two different camps surrounding helmets was one familiar to the discussion and one that focused on the novice or middle-class rider and his "dumb old" counterpart who opposed helmets.

The ABATE update that also appeared in the June 1972 issue of *Easyriders* not only echoed the editor's points about the need to target riders who were most likely the cause of fatalities but also offered an explicit acceptance of the National Highway Traffic Safety Administration (NHTSA) and the federal government. In particular, ABATE highlighted what it called a "Sound Program for Fighting Anti-Bike Legislation" that focused on slowing the push at the state level to regulate motorcycling with the hope that the federal government would complete its safety testing and establish guidelines that favored motorcyclists—or at least would minimize the potential impact of state-by-state regulation. "It would appear that the best, most immediate way of effectively stopping enactment of antibike laws in your state is to fight a delaying action," argued ABATE, and to "wait for the results of the federal government's testing program." ABATE also reaffirmed points *Easyriders* made after its interview with Thoms: "Through cooperation," ABATE emphasized, "perhaps we can keep things under reasonable control—although it may become a matter of give and take." ABATE pointed out the NHTSA's concern about "pointed and sharp edges on sissy bars. . . . Wouldn't it be better for us to voluntarily eliminate all points and sharp edges? Would that be a cop-out? We think not, for it would be much smarter to give up useless points and sharp edges, than to lose the entire sissy bar (at least one state is proposing the outlawing of sissy bars)." "Wouldn't it [also] be better," ABATE continued, "if anyone must wear one [a helmet]—that it be the guilty, the ones causing the fatalities, who should have to wear it?" ABATE admitted that "all this may appear that we are putting a lot of naïve faith into the fact that the government is going to treat us better than individual states do. Perhaps it is naïve—but it's still better than a sharp poke in the eye with a sharp stick."[73]

Other motorcyclists were more frustrated with the marginal opposition to helmets than inclined to point fingers and found themselves asking, "Where do we go from here?" Clarence Elmore estimated that his readers had three options:

We can continue to snivel about the general public not understanding us [and] the government deliberately oppressing us about nobody representing our interests, we can continue posturing around in confusion as individuals and small groups, dissipating our energies and thus suffer the consequences of being shoved farther down the road to the abyss by better organized groups of non riders with contrary views who are superior in number and impervious to logic when it comes to motorcycles. Or we can stop bitching among ourselves polarizing the different motorcycling factions, ie street, dirt, racing, touring, etc, [and] stop looking for scapegoats like the AMA and begin to cooperate in massive concerted efforts in one direction at a time in order to overcome obstacles one at a time until we have prevailed.[74]

A year later riders were still complaining about the movement's slow start. "Once again it's time to launch into a tirade about togetherness," began Bob Bitchin's editorial in a 1974 issue of *Biker News*.[75] Bitchin explained that "we have many small organizations working [in California's Capitol] but each has a very small following." By Bitchin's counting, the largest organization in California had fewer than three thousand members. "That's right," he lamented, "LESS THAN THREE THOUSAND," even though there were three hundred thousand motorcycles registered in California. "That means less than 1 percent of the guys who are riding bikes on the street care enough about the laws to join an organization to fight unfair legislation." These paltry numbers, Bitchin suggested, not only were difficult to comprehend but also were undermining efforts to challenge helmet legislation. As Bitchin explained, "When one of these organizations walks into a state Senator's office and tries to throw some weight around the first thing the Senator will ask him is 'How many members are in your organization?' What can he tell them?" he asked. Bitchin explained that multiple organizations were working in Sacramento and Washington to help the motorcyclist, but they would accomplish very little "without the wholehearted support of bikers in the street." "Can you imagine," he added, "what kind of power we would have if all Biker organizations in Sacramento formed a coalition? Over 20,000 people would be represented instead of only 2 to 3 thousand at a time."[76]

The uncertainty surrounding helmet legislation and the problem mobilizing against it convinced motorcyclists that if motorcycling had ever had a golden age, it had passed long ago. In 1974 Laco Bob Lawrence of *Biker News* asked his readers, "What happened to the good old days?" Lawrence reminisced about the days when "you would go on a weekend ride and in your travels you would run into another biker and find a friend, in most cases." "You" and that friend shared "common interests" even "brotherhood," and both of you "understood that bikers should stand together whether it be a barroom fight or only a breakdown." It was also "common," he added, "to be invited home to be fed, or given a spot to lay-out your sleeping bag. Little thought would be given to having his tools or motorcycle ripped off," and the two motorcyclists would spend their time talking "about motorcycles, girls, the road and drinking some booze." Lawrence added that it was "rare to be broken down at the side of the road and have a motorcycle pass without stopping." "Not so today," he lamented.[77]

Lawrence's comments were not uncommon in the late 1960s and early 1970s. Nor were his fears about the loss of fraternity among motorcyclists. Hunter S. Thompson claimed that "even in the ranks of the Hell's Angels there are those who insist that the outlaw scene went over the bump in the mid-fifties, when the original faces began drifting off to marriage and mortgages and time payments."[78] Preetam Bobo was one of Thompson's examples of the outlaw's golden age, or what Thompson referred to as the "Compleat Outlaw." Bobo "is a walking monument to everything the Hell's Angels would like to stand for, but which few of them do . . . and he somehow makes it work."[79]

In a letter to *Cycle* in 1973 Bruce Marcot of Costa Mesa, California, claimed that the "seventies will destroy motorcycling." Marcot argued that motorcycling's death had "been coming for a long time," and that it was "almost here. Very soon all that will be left on the roads will be man-eating Kawasakis, ego-flaunting Harley monsters, and yes, even the subtle Honda Fours, for all the Walter Mittys among us." Marcot explained that the current trend was "toward multis . . . futuristic styling and bright colors, [and] towards SIZE." "Oh, sales will rise," he admitted, "and bikes will become like VWs, buzzing everywhere. But for those who may feel as I do, motorcycling will die." Marcot owned a 1970 CL-450 Honda. It was "not the fastest, nor the smoothest, nor the flashiest, but it doesn't have to be; it is so well built that it has withstood 45,000 miles (thus far) of wear, through every riding condition imaginable." During the summer of 1972, he rode nine thousand miles across the country, visiting friends, camping, and enjoying life. "I took my time, rode safely, and sneered at the many riders who blurred by on their screaming multis." "What I'm trying to say is that the caliber of person who will purchase the Triumph Hurricane or the Benelli Six is the type who cares more about the external benefits of biking than any such abstract enjoyment. They may be good riders, brilliant wrenchers, but they miss out on what biking can really mean." Marcot admitted that he was nineteen and had been riding for only two years. But if he could have his "wish," he would be "transported back to the motorcycling world of the

1950s when the public had yet to claim biking as its own. . . . Those who begin biking this decade will never know what it's about, and except for a few of us still around who do, the True Sport will die." Motorcycling, he finished his letter with, "is doomed."[80]

Anecdotal evidence from the 1940s and 1950s suggests that there was some truth to Thompson's and Marcot's romanticized view of a golden age. While conflict over brand-name loyalty was often as conspicuous in the immediate postwar years as it would be two decades later, it was rarely significant enough to undermine the sense of fraternity that riders would claim was disappearing by the 1960s and 1970s. For example, Tom Anderson of St. Petersburg, Florida, explained that St. Petersburg and Tampa did not have a city ordinance that would give the police the authority to "curb the cowboy motorcycle riders," and the city had some problems with motorcyclists who "gun their bikes unnecessarily—race—fan-tail and generally raise all hell." Yet he also suggested that their infractions were minor and ones with which he was familiar. In his efforts to "curb" their cowboy antics, he had "talked, pleaded and begged" them to use "good sense" and had apparently become well acquainted with them because he admitted they "are not bad fellows." Anderson estimated that there were about ten of them and admitted that they were only guilty of being noisy at the wrong time of the day. "All riders," Anderson added, "have their evening riding groups and friends." The problem was that these cowboys preferred to ride noisily "after the accepted bed-time hours" and "gun their bikes unnecessarily" when a majority of the town's citizens "want to sleep." Anderson confessed that he "thoroughly enjoy[ed] the thrills and pleasure of my Harley 61 and know that I can ride quietly during bed-time hours" as if during the rest of the day he was as noisy as his cowboy counterparts.[81]

Other cyclists simply understood differences in behavior as a reflection of a stage in the life cycle that riders in general had gone through. E. M. Gosnell of Beardstown, Illinois, admitted to his days of youthful indiscretion and his penchant for noise. Gosnell had been a motorcyclist for thirty years and cited three factors that made the "sport of motorcycling tops": "God's beautiful out of doors, cheap fuel, and America's wonderful highways." He commended the AMA's efforts to eliminate the "evils" of the sport, "noise being the worst," and then offered a confession: "There was a 'time' when I thought noise and the straight exhaust was hot stuff." Gosnell explained that he had even been among "those who have forced the judge too" and more than once had to give "a postdated check to satisfy my debt to society." While Gosnell insisted that he favored a quiet machine, he reluctantly admitted that he still found the noise of a straight stack to be "sweet music."[82]

In a letter to *Motorcyclist* Master Sergeant Everett C. Johnston of Painesville, Ohio, provided an even more insightful look at the importance of the life cycle and its stages. Johnston had just renewed his subscription to *Motorcyclist* and had sent in an additional six dollars to pay the subscription fees for his erstwhile riding companions. Johnston explained that his three friends were all "former bike riders who have somehow let their interests wander to such trivia as making homes for wives and families, planting gardens, etc." Sending each of them a subscription was one of his strategies to "fan the embers of the sport of motorcycling which are burning low indeed in their poor bewildered souls." His other strategy was to visit them occasionally on Sunday with his motorcycle roaring. "I take the end-cap out of the megaph[o]ne on my stout old Norton and thunder over to the last-named gentleman's house." Johnston noted that he would usually "get in a few sly words before his wife runs me out of the yard." He would then proceed to the second gentleman's home and repeat his performance. He would "wind up the little 500 once again in the driveway" and send his wife running for the spare set of storm windows to replace the set he just shattered. While she was away, he would "fling him on the Buddy seat and spirit him away to Harry's Tavern or some other den of iniquity." After plying him with beer, he would convince him to take a ride on his old Norton. Johnston would take him back home "with his pulse pounding and eyes shining, and fling him in the rear door without stopping." This latter trick, Johnston boasted, was "perfected on the TT Tracks of North Carolina" and a trick that worked equally well especially for a disillusioned and erstwhile bike rider who had become too preoccupied with the domestic side of life.[83]

Johnson made it clear that he did not normally ride with the end cap removed from his muffler but did so only to rekindle a desire that could never be completely snuffed out. The "sweet music" of a straight pipe was a sound they all intimately associated with memories of their former selves. The conflicting emotions these sounds produced explain the zeal with which some cyclists denounced the straight pipe, but these emotions also helped erase any easy divisions between the outlaw and his reformed counterpart, who at times cautiously tried to distance himself from his past but was never that far removed from the outlaw and his roadway antics.

The familiarity with which these men talked about each other and their riding experiences not only helped ease tensions in time of conflict or disagreement but also stands in sharp contrast to the 1960s and 1970s when riders were as likely to blame each other for the trend to regulate motorcycling than to collectively address the problems they faced. In July

1972 David L. Michel of El Segundo, California, sent a letter to *Cycle*, which appeared under the heading "Divided We Fall." Michel explained that he wrote his letter for all "road riding motorcyclists," or what he described as "those riders whose bikes' wheels never leave a paved road," to address the nonriding majority's frustration with motorcyclists. "Have you noticed an increase in the public's dissatisfaction with motorcyclists lately? Have you noticed how people are becoming much more hostile towards motorcyclists? Have you noticed how many national, state, county, and local parks are being closed to all motorcyclists? Do you have any idea what is causing this?" Michel explained that "it is not the outlaw gangs who get their name in the headlines because of their gang wars. The reason the public is becoming more irritated with motorcycles is because of the off-road, desert, and dirt motorcycles."[84]

Other riders were even more selective, and compartmentalized riders and machines into a variety of different categories. In an interview with the Wedded Wheels, a "family friendly" motorcycle club, Bob Cope described the club's members as "Road Riders" who 'like to drive along country roads, looking at the scenery" and whose interests in riding were considerably different from the other riders with whom he crossed paths. Dirt riders "ride the hill trails . . . competition riders go around in circles in tracks. Custom riders like to take their elaborate machines to shows." And outlaws were "the bad guys." In contrast, the Wedded Wheels "don't ride choppers" and called "their motorcycles machines or just plain motorcycles." Club members "don't travel in gangs or packs, and the women are not referred to as mammas. . . . They probably have more in common with the Kiwanis Club than the Hell's Angels," and club membership was linked to the AMA. As a friend of the Wedded Wheels explained, the participation of non-AMA riders was likely to lead to "knifings and drugs. You don't want to take your children to something like that."[85]

As these examples suggest, divisions from the 1960s and 1970s were not only more glaring than they were in earlier years, but the boundaries between riders were more firmly entrenched. In some cases the divide would appear artificial. Michel, for example, wrote his letter specifically for what he called the "road riding motorcycling." Such an arbitrary divide among cyclists would have been inconceivable in earlier decades. Off-road or gully scrambling was common among cyclists, and a distinct motorcycle built exclusively for off-road use would not appear until the 1960s.[86] At the same time, though, the "stage of the lifecycle" had become less prominent than in earlier decades, and relations between riders in the 1960s and 1970s were less tolerant. "Born to be Wild," Steppenwolf's 1968 hit that has become the anthem of the 1960s–70s generation of bikers, offers a terse but apt description of the changes taking place and their impact on motorcycle culture. The outlaw remained at the center of the general public's and rider's understanding of lawlessness and disorder. But divisions among riders were more common than they had been in earlier years; there were more of them, redemption was unlikely, and the conflict was affecting the success of the motorcycle rights movement. Indeed, Lawrence's response to the demise of brotherhood was "Tojo's Revenge," his euphemism for Honda's appearance and its dominance of the American motorcycle market that harkened back to the Japanese during World War II (Tojo was the general of the Japanese Imperial Army during most of World War II). In particular, Lawrence singled out what he called the "Sunday or fair weather rider" to understand this change, phrases that he associated with Hondas and these new (middle-class) riders whose connection to motorcycling had attracted increasing attention and praise. He not only pointed to that moment when the "Sunday, or fair weather rider [had] entered the picture" but also connected the two to the trend to regulate. As Lawrence explained, "This [the rise of Honda and his fair weather rider] contributed to many laws coming into effect to protect us from ourselves," or what he also described as "the laws that protect the 90 day super rider [the middle-class rider] against himself."[87]

IT IS NOT SURPRISING that the first slogan riders adopted during these early years of struggle against helmets was simple and colloquial: "Helmet Laws Suck." The slogan was especially conspicuous by late 1973 and was widely circulated in the form of bumper stickers, T-shirts, posters, and even painted on to the sides of motorcycle gas tanks.[88] This slogan said as much about the frustration facing motorcyclists as it did about their specific goals or political ideas. Motorcyclists were angry—angry with regulation, angry because of the lack of unity among riders, and angry that helmet legislation posed a broader suburban threat to their lifestyle and their freedom of the road. "Helmet Laws Suck" only seemed to highlight that anger and the broader distance between the riders who were most conspicuous in these early days of struggle (outlaws) and their supposedly respectable counterparts who were criticized as helmet advocates and the reason helmet legislation was needed.[89]

To a large degree, "Helmet Laws Suck" was simply an extension of an even more ubiquitous phrase often identified with motorcyclists and their general disdain for everyone and everything else: "Fuck Off." Throughout the 1970s *Easyriders'* readers could purchase everything they ever imagined owning with "Fuck Off" in big bold letters: T-shirts, bumper

A motorcyclist at Sturgis in 1981 flipping off the cameraman. Courtesy of Michael Lichter.

stickers, or simply have it tattooed inside the lower lip like the occasional rider who appeared in the magazine's regular pictorial feature, "In The Wind." This disillusionment has shaped historians views about the 1970s, and this attitude stood in sharp contrast to the preceding decade of activism and hope represented best by the peace sign.[90] Motorcyclists not only challenged this simple division but used that frustration and anger to try to build a consensus and a political movement. While those efforts were gaining ground during these early years, the unity needed to challenge the government effectively remained elusive. Favoring instead the short-term goal of preserving the rights of certain riders (Harley, chopper, and custom cycle riders), *Easyriders* and ABATE singled out the men and women most likely to be in an accident and the ones "guilty" of "causing the fatalities." Anti-helmet critics singled out the novice riders because of assumptions about their abysmal safety records, a suburban lifestyle, and their predilection for Japanese-made motorcycles. "Helmet Laws Suck," as the slogan goes, but not all riders were treated equally, and the solutions motorcyclists advocated only exacerbated the divisions that had become more noticeable as the need for unity became increasingly critical.[91]

LET THOSE WHO RIDE DECIDE

The Right and Age-Old Biker Values, 1940s–1990s

In the mid-1960s, artist Bob Dara produced two posters in which he imagined Lyndon Baines Johnson and Bobby Kennedy as bikers. Both were seated on custom bikes. Johnson had a stockier body than Kennedy, beer belly, and pumped up arms. The word "BULL" was tattooed across the knuckles of his left hand, and he wore a chain belt and a jacket with the sleeves torn off. Kennedy was riding a dragster with two v-twin engines, and he wore jeans and a black T-shirt. Both of their bikes had the names of their wives painted on the gas tank—"Harley Bird" and "ETHEL"[1]

The two posters provide one of the earliest moments in the postwar period where motorcyclists and politicians appeared together other than the incidental contact with a motorcycle police escort that had become routine for politicians, dignitaries, or some other special occasion or individual. But the posters of Kennedy and Johnson did not reflect a Democratic interest in motorcyclists as much as a particular attitude or style with which Dara had become enamored. Dara featured other politicians with big, brawny arms (although not as motorcyclists) and at least three other posters of motorcyclists. One was a drawing of Bob Dylan casually sitting astride a stock bike and two posters of groups of motorcyclists in typical biker attire: jeans, denim vests, sunglasses, helmets and unkempt hair, neatly shaven goatees or beards, beefy arms and bodies, and the occasional missing tooth, presumably from an accident or perhaps a brawl. Dara did not imagine them as a general threat and presented them as if they were playfully posing for a photograph to remember a weekend outing or some other get-together, but they did exude a certain toughness and resilience that apparently he also identified with Johnson and Kennedy.

The connection between politicians and motorcyclists that Dara played with in his art would be realized at about the same time that his posters became popular. In October 1972 Ed Youngblood of the American Motorcyclist Association (AMA) announced that the organization's former president, William Bagnall, had been appointed chairman of the National Committee of Motorcyclists for the Re-election of the President (Nixon). Bagnall explained that his appointment was "just one more indication that motorcyclists are being recognized as politically important citizens" and cited three reasons why they should support Nixon: "the President's recognition of motorcycling as a recreational activity of national scope," the appointment of a motorcyclist to the president's National Motor Vehicle Safety Advisory Council, and the "political recognition and respect implied in the appeal for organized support." Democrat George McGovern's camp, in contrast, had not made a "similar appeal for political involvement."[2]

Two months later the AMA admitted that the announcement had "stimulated more correspondence than any other single article . . . on the subjects of politics, legislation or ecology." But while the AMA noted that some of its readers "understand perfectly the importance of political commitment and communication," some members had "missed the point" and had allowed "their predilections toward a particular man obscure the value of political activity in the general sense." Several readers, Youngblood continued, "have confused reporting the existence of Mr. Bagnall's committee with an association endorsement of Mr. Bagnall's candidate. This should be clarified. . . . It is the intention of the American Motorcycle Association," Youngblood explained, "to encourage political activity among its members. It is not the position of the AMA to choose its members' candidates, nor should it be." Youngblood stressed that as an association, "we desire to remain neutral, though we feel it highly undesirable for the individual member and voter to remain neutral and apathetic to politics." His concern focused on those individuals "who did not or will not make choices because they do not care enough for their own future as motorcyclists and American citizens."[3]

Eight years later the AMA published an article titled "Turning the Tide" by Becky Norton Dunlop to highlight the motorcyclist's potential contribution to the congressional elections of 1980. Dunlop, a conservative activist who would work in the Reagan administration, published the article with the explicit purpose of encouraging motorcyclists to vote Republican in the upcoming elections. Dunlop described motorcyclists as a "shunned political minority" and argued that the freedom associated with a "biking lifestyle rings hollow in this era of big government." But as

Americans across the country were deciding on which candidate to vote for, Dunlop explained that the "freedom" that has always been synonymous with motorcyclists would finally be realized and that motorcyclists would become part of mainstream American politics for two main reasons: "Old age biker values have suddenly become popular among society as a whole," and motorcyclists were "helping [to] lead the backlash against Big Brother."[4]

Dunlop focused on four particular senate races: Birch Bayh (D) versus Dan Quayle (R) in Indiana, Frank Church (D) versus Steve Symms (R) in Idaho, George McGovern (D) versus Jim Abdnor (R) in South Dakota, and the race in Washington where Democrat Warren Magnuson was facing a challenge from Republican Slade Gorton.[5] Dunlop argued that these Democratic senators and senators of their "persuasion" traditionally "support[ed] the concept of massive federal government fueled by an ever-increasing claim on your income." They had "dominated the Senate" for twenty-five years and had "helped bring the country to its present plight in which a massive federal bureaucracy snarls the workings of government, stagnates the economy and pushes the American taxpayer's back to the wall." Representing the "other side," what Dunlop referred to as "the people's side," was a "growing contingent" of senators who recognized that their "constituents are sick of Washington's rabid expansionism." They "believe the Federal government should do for the people only what they and their local governing bodies cannot legitimately do for themselves." They wanted to "cut taxes, reduce the strength and authority of a multitude of Federal bureaucracies and return to states and localities much of the responsibility usurped by Washington over the past 25 years." Dunlop also emphasized their goal of getting the "government out of the marketplace, particularly in the area of energy, where America's needs are critical and bureaucrats and legislators have pursued a dead-end policy of controlling supply rather than encouraging increases in production." Dunlop noted that in all four states the population of motorcyclists was large enough to affect the outcome of each election but only if enough of them cast their votes. At the time of the article's publication, the American Motorcyclist Political Action Committee had already contributed to Republicans Abdnor and Symms, and in its final budgeting meeting before the elections, it would carefully consider a contribution to Dan Quayle.[6]

Dunlop left unacknowledged the many other issues and influences contributing to the congressional and presidential elections of 1980. She did not explain how the preceding two decades' turmoil and divisiveness had challenged motorcyclists' political efforts. But the use of "Turning the

Tide" to characterize the political moment and the role motorcyclists might play could not have been more appropriate. The more-than-a-decade-long struggle against helmets had compelled motorcyclists to ask many of the same questions about the government that conservatives were asking. The alliance between motorcyclists and the Right had begun to take shape within just a few years after the AMA had first taken exception to charges of political partisanship in the early 1970s.[7]

Protests against helmet laws began as soon as state legislatures starting passing them in 1967, but a sustained national movement would not become visible until the mid-1970s. While the strength of the movement was a result of the perseverance of dedicated activists and support from established, motorcycle organizations, its growth coincided with a broader conservative political shift that upset the American political landscape in the late 1970s and early 1980s.

Drawn to the motorcycle rights movement's frustration with government regulation and its reverence for the idea of "freedom," conservative politicians would become some of the leading voices opposing helmet laws. Those efforts translated into a relationship that is still visible today and one that has allowed the Republican Party to successfully undermine a constituency of white, working-class voters who had promoted Democratic success at the federal level since the 1930s. While this unlikely political alliance would help to win for motorcyclists a 1976 amendment to the Highway Safety Act of 1966 that would support their goals in a limited way, the Right's political ascendancy would eventually compromise motorcycle culture's underpinnings.

Political conservatism promoted an understanding of what it meant to be an American that was much more restrictive than the rebellious spirit identified with the outlaw motorcyclist from Hollister. It championed economic policies that facilitated the rise of the rich urban biker (RUB), who questioned the very "authenticity" that had initially made motorcycling so appealing to conservatives, and reinforced a divide among riders that was based on name brand loyalty. The Right's success drew inspiration from Harley-Davidson's success and the motorcycle's connection to freedom, individuality, and patriotism, ideas that were critical to an economic nationalism that became noticeable among riders as Japanese Hondas began to dominate the U.S. market in the 1960s.[8]

SUCCESS

Challenges to the Highway Safety Act of 1966 erupted as soon as state legislators began passing helmet laws, but signs of success were becoming visible only toward the end of 1974 and early 1975. Prompted by an increasingly vocal motorcycle rights movement and the growth of motorcycle rights organizations that had successfully mobilized voters, members of Congress introduced bills to challenge the Department of Transportation's authority to withhold highway funds from states without a helmet law. The debates of July and December 1975 concluded with an outcome that motorcycling rights organizers had wanted for years. A majority of the Senate voted in support of amending the Highway Safety Act (52-37), and the House of Representatives followed suit six days later with a vote of 410 to 7. President Gerald Ford would sign the bill into law in early 1976, and the battle over helmets would shift back to the states.[9]

The introduction of these bills and congressional support for them was, in part, a reflection of the culmination of the previous decade of political activity. In some cases, new organizations had joined the fight. *Easyriders* magazine established the National Custom Cycle Association (NCCA) in 1971 and formally changed its name to A Brotherhood Against Totalitarian Enactments (ABATE) a year later. Prominent in the organization's initial effort was its argument for a national organization of bikers that was "united together in a common endeavor, and in significant numbers to be heard in Washington, D.C., in the state legislatures, and even down to the city councils." *Easyriders* noted that there were numerous cases of individual bike clubs appearing before various legislative bodies to express their opposition to regulations. Still, even *Easyriders* described these efforts as "scattered, unorganized" and "unprofessional at the game of politics," which undermined their efforts and had "little effect against the power structure."[10]

In these early years ABATE established three main "projects": to amass all the information it could from members about existing and pending laws—"state by state, county by county, and city by city"—and the names and addresses of all anti-bike and pro-bike legislators. Getting the "national problem down on paper," *Easyriders* argued, would allow it to "intelligently plan our campaigns." NCCA/ABATE was also preparing a chopper to send to Washington, D.C., for the National Highway Traffic Safety Administration to test. ABATE argued that "the only way the government is really going to know [choppers are safe] is to test them, rather than taking some anti-biker's word for it." Opponents of regulation had long argued that the individual making the laws generally had no knowledge of motorcycles or any interest in them. And third, ABATE wanted to increase its membership and attract what it described as "doers." "We know there are only some of you who will get off your ass and do something—and we want that group as members."[11]

ABATE's early efforts mobilizing riders often had as much to do with individual rider's efforts as the organization's. Warren Bennett of New York, for example began to speak out against regulation around 1974. He recalled that he and another rider were "just a bunch of bikers, unorganized, not members of a club or anything." Bennett was increasingly wary of all the legislation, especially the helmet law and talk of "outlawing extended front ends." Bennett said, "We got involved and decided to put on a protest." On a visit to his sister's in California, he decided to stop by the *Easyriders'* office to explain their protest. "With that, they said, why don't you call yourselves ABATE? I said, well I didn't know you did that."[12]

In other cases, this shift in momentum reflected an existing organization's changing focus. In 1972, for example, the American Motorcyclist Association established a new youth division, a new insurance program, and a series of political workshops. These workshops, which appeared under the rubric "political frontiers," were "designed to teach concerned motorcyclists how to operate effectively in local politics." Washington-based political consultant Bill Low directed the workshops, and AMA legislative director Chet Winter coordinated them. Specific areas included the "mechanics of government, statesmanship and diplomacy and the role of the individual rider as a potentially efficient influence on politics in his locale."[13]

The AMA's shift in focus and the development of "political frontiers" also convinced some individuals who had traditionally been ambivalent about the organization to openly support it. Bob Greene of *Motorcyclist* referred to the AMA as "exploding into action, with dynamic thrust heretofore unheard-of in organized sport."[14] *Motorcyclist* began admonishing riders across the country to join the organization. In his diatribe against the federal government's efforts to regulate public land, Clarence O. Elmore reminded readers of the need not only to organize but also to support the AMA. "We were startled to say the least," Elmore exclaimed, "when we learned that, although practically every motorcyclist has something to say about the AMA, their total membership of about 200,000 represents less than 4 percent of the active motorcyclists in the country," adding that "even in California where motorcycling is most popular, there are only 28,000 AMA members, again about 4% of the state's bikers." Elmore's ambivalence about the AMA remained palpable. *Motorcyclist* had relentlessly criticized the AMA for the better part of three decades for ignoring riders' needs and for supposedly being in league with American motorcycle manufacturers. But Elmore nonetheless urged cyclists to "give them a hand for a change and see what happens," and he provided a quote from AMA national legislative director Gene Wirwahn to further encourage their support: "Think what we could do if we had only 20% of the nation's riders as members." "We say let's do more than think about it," Elmore added, and then admitted that after learning about the small percentage of AMA members, "we sent in our long overdue first AMA application."[15]

The growth of these movements and the increasing focus on the motorcyclist's role in politics also helped them refine their vision of "freedom." During the immediate post-Hollister years, the issue of noise and the motorcycle daredevil or cowboy received the most attention from the motorcycle press, which looked for ways to make motorcycling respectable—a sort of what-attracts-men-to-cycling approach that emphasized the wind in the hair and the freedom of the road. Throughout the 1960s and the 1970s riders were still talking about the freedom they associated with riding. In an article about the Washington State Penitentiary Motorcycle Association, which was described as a school, a club, and "a brotherhood that helps the biker retain his sanity," Bob Bitchin of *Biker News* asked, "What is it that makes up the biker's way of life? For most bikers," he answered, "it was Freedom," which he linked to "that great feeling you get as you putt down the street on your sled, oblivious to all the cares and worries of the regular world."[16] "Do you know anything about freedom?" asked another rider, who described it as "being out in the wind with the kick in the ass and just putting along."[17] *Easyriders* made a similar point when the magazine argued that, "short of actually riding a bike, we feel that nothing illustrates this freedom, this leaving all your problems behind you, this letting it all hang out groove—better than the sight of a guy all laid out, his feet up on highway pegs, with his girl tucked in behind him, flying down the highway with hair blowing in all directions.[18]

Freedom was never abstract for riders. It was a direct reflection of the day-to-day experience of riding. The trope of escape was critical—motorcycles represented escape from wage work, escape from the drudgery of daily life, and, if their organizing efforts paid off, escape from the increased scrutiny riders faced throughout the postwar years. As states began passing helmet laws across the country, ideas about freedom maintained a link to riding, and motorcyclists began organizing "Freedom of the Road Demonstrations."[19] The first announcement for ABATE appeared in *Easyriders* in February 1972 and described the organization as "Dedicated to Freedom of the Road."[20] Indeed, from the start of the push to end regulation, motorcyclists saw the very nature of motorcycling as fundamental to their understanding of freedom. "In my opinion," explained Bob Lawrence in *Biker News*, "the biker enjoys one of the last frontiers of freedom. To get in the wind and ride at least lets you feel free."[21]

By 1974 and 1975, however, the broader implications surrounding helmet laws assumed greater prominence, and the motorcyclist's freedom appeared as if it had as much to do with his life off his motorcycle as it did on it. Gino Sheridan described motorcycles as "fun," but they also represented "freedom," something "that Americans seems to be losing more and more of these days." Sheridan made his comment after two motorcyclists were killed while riding without helmets and in response to their doctors who speculated about the increased chance of survival had they been wearing them. "Some individuals," Sheridan argued "are simply content to live out each day relatively secure from danger, while others choose to walk that thin line between life and death." For those individuals, he added, "life does have meaning. What they do gives them strength and hope; and perhaps even makes them more thankful to be alive. But most important, they have the freedom and the right to choose."[22] Gordon Martin of the *San Francisco Chronicle* made a similar point when he attempted to explain the average cyclist's opposition to helmet laws. Martin compared the issue of head injuries between automobilists and motorcyclists and noted that if automobilists were required to wear helmets a "vast number of motorists could be saved from death or injury." But he also explained that the average rider's objection to helmets was not a question of their efficacy. "Virtually all those connected with the 10 million motorcycle riders in the country urge the use of helmets. The objection in this case is philosophical—the right of someone else to make you do something that affects only you." "Freedom it turns out," he stressed, "is in the individual right to make good decisions as well as poor ones."[23] Over two years later (1977) Harold C. Salkin wrote a letter to *Biker* to thank the magazine's editors for their support in challenging "unjust laws" and described the amendment of the Highway Safety Act of 1966 as a victory for all those who "value freedom of choice, liberty, self-determination, enjoyment of life, etc."[24]

Indeed, motorcyclists increasingly viewed themselves as not only facing a broader battle over individual rights and freedom but also spearheading a push to guarantee those rights for all Americans. Big Ed of Memphis, Tennessee, wrote a letter to *Easyriders* in the late 1970s in which he described motorcyclists as all that was "left of a dying breed of Americans who understand what freedom is all about. It's up to us," he added, "to make the decisions that affect the entire population of this country."[25]

The experience of riding remained critical to these ideas about freedom, if not the single issue shaping the rider's understanding of it, but the focus again was about making choices. Charles Clayton linked freedom to riding and to the choices individuals inevitably made. "To know what freedom is," Clayton explained, "you have to use it. You have to hold the threat and promise in your hands, wrap your legs around and gas it." "The biker," he continued "knows the way that freedom and responsibility fit together." Clayton insisted that if a motorcyclist "bends a physical law too far, it takes no vigilant policeman, judge, or executioner to chide him in the error of his ways. Crash! The sentence is carried out within split seconds of the error." Freedom was about individual choices (and mistakes), the responsibility of making those choices and sticking to them, and the right of "the individual to live his life as he pleases, so long as he doesn't harm others."[26]

These ideas about freedom and motorcycling were visible throughout the postwar years but became increasingly conspicuous by the mid- to late 1970s. They were accompanied by the slogan "Let Those Who Ride Decide," which cut against the image of the stereotypical biker too dumb and inarticulate to care about any politics beyond a violent and antisocial outlaw rebelliousness. The movement's initial slogan, "Helmet Laws Suck," had exposed a glaring divide between those riders who opposed helmet laws and the rest of the motorcycling community, especially the middle-class rider. "Let Those Who Ride Decide" consciously downplayed that divide by accepting the possibility of different positions and by reaffirming the individual's rights and freedom to choose, which became an increasingly conspicuous part of the discourse surrounding helmets, the government, and motorcyclists' rights. The frustration and anger that was apparent with "Helmet Laws Suck" was notably missing from "Let Those Who Ride Decide." Its absence increased the possibility of establishing a unity among riders that had not been visible for at least a decade.[27]

The change in tactics paid off. By the second half of the 1970s, the motorcycle rights movement had successfully attracted motorcyclists from all walks of life. Photographs of protest rallies and firsthand accounts from participants make it clear that the "outlaw" was the most prominent in the early days of organizing.[28] By the mid-1970s, a more mixed crowd of enthusiasts began to participate in these demonstrations. At what was described as California's first helmet law protest in 1975, one participant reported, "There were bikers from all walks of life. Lawyers, police (out of uniform and in), doctors, bums, families, you name it, they were all involved, and they all got along together." "One of the biggest surprises of the day," he added, was the appearance of a dirt bike "with a headlight bungie corded to the front end and a taillight strapped on the rear. He was there to help us fight."[29] In a letter that appeared in *AMA News* about year later, a dirt biker made a similar point. Sam Harris, from Glendale, California, explained that when the AMA was "fighting for the road rider in Washington [in 1976]," he was a "little bit hot" when "I saw my membership money going to fight a battle that I figured didn't involve me." But as government regulation began to catch up to off-road riding that restricted access to public lands, Harris explained, "I learned my lesson the hard way. From now on," he added, "I'm not a dirt biker, I'm a biker period. We're all in this together."[30]

By the second half of the 1970s a shift in the movement's focus was noticeable. Riders had been battling against helmet regulations since they first appeared in the late 1960s. Those efforts expanded in the early 1970s and found the support and direction needed from existing organizations and the development of new ones. The slogan "Let Those Who Ride Decide" reaffirmed the possibility that other opinions might coexist more peacefully than in previous years and promote the inclusion of other riders—even the middle-class ones who were generally linked to helmets and the push to require them. Numbers were needed to challenge legislators across the country, and the broader ideological shift this slogan represented, contemporaries argued, was essential to the movement's growth and to the larger success of attracting the positive attention needed from the nonriding majority who would play an increasingly important role in the fight against the government after 1974–75.

THE POLITICAL RIGHT

The terms of the debate about the federal government's role were emphatically set with President Roosevelt's New Deal during the Great Depression of the 1930s. Overnight his administration began establishing hundreds of government organizations that dramatically strengthened the state's regulatory capacity, and by the end of the 1930s many of the programs that gave rise to a modern welfare state were in place—Social Security, the Fair Labor Standards Act, the Federal Deposit Insurance Corporation, and the Wagner Act, to name a few. While critics have complained that these efforts idealized the white, male breadwinner, they collectively shifted the balance of power in favor of average Americans and established a coalition of voters (trade unionists, African Americans, urban Catholics, and southern Whites) that promoted success at the federal level for Democrats for the next sixty years.

During the period immediately after World War II, the federal government maintained an active and expansive role regulating the U.S. economy, and it continued to arbitrate conflicts between labor and capital, encourage domestic growth, and promote economic and military expansion abroad. Liberals viewed the country's prosperity as an affirmation of the federal government's role, and it strengthened their faith in the government's ability to resolve social and economic problems. Liberals fought to expand Social Security, increase spending on education, and promote equality for all, including, and most notably, equality for African Americans. They championed secularism, pluralism, and moral relativism as the "positive virtues" needed to balance what historian Lisa McGirr describes as "conflicting interests in a democratic society." Liberal elites, she adds, were, "not surprisingly, uncomfortable with the state's role as a regulator and guarantor of behavioral norms and virtues and, instead, advocated a new set of individual and personal freedoms." The government should promote increased opportunities for all Americans but not compromise an individual's freedom by insisting upon a set of "normative values."[31]

The prosperity of the postwar years, McGirr argues, was accompanied by "far-reaching social and cultural changes to which conservative women and men responded with deep ambivalence." The conservative movement sprang forth from a group of intellectuals and writers fearful of a centralized government. Theirs was a grassroots anticommunism that challenged the influence of the Soviet Union abroad with containment at home, a push for free markets, and activists and intellectuals who were determined to roll back New Deal liberalism. By the 1960s an alliance between normative conservatives and antistatist libertarians was taking shape. Fundamental to this alliance was a "set of beliefs whose cornerstone element was opposition to . . . the postwar federal government." The federal government had corrupted the workings of the market through regulation and had encouraged a secular culture that challenged values conservatives cherished—self-responsibility, frugality, and industriousness but also faith in God. The permissiveness conservatives identified with a liberal state challenged what McGirr describes as "moral virtue."[32]

McGirr describes the challenge of maintaining this alliance as a struggle to achieve a balance between "individual freedom" and "order and authority," and she highlights a number of outstanding "grievances" against the federal government that sustained it. Both groups found a centralized state anathema and shared a "commitment to an objective, definable, organic authority," what social conservatives accepted as God, and libertarians defined as property rights. Both groups also understood freedom as less of an individual prerogative and more of an economic imperative (economic freedom instead of individual freedom) that was accompanied by a general distaste for egalitarianism. This last point, McGirr argues, explains the Right's ambivalence about democracy and its belief in a strict interpretation of the Constitution. Conservatives viewed themselves as having a unique relationship to the founding fathers and their vision of the country and its values, what McGirr describes as a "civic religion." "They cast them-selves as the true heirs to the 'national heritage' and framed their political agenda as an effort to preserve this heritage."[33]

The political and social movements of the 1950s and 1960s and the civil disobedience and conflict that accompanied them only exacerbated the fear with which some conservatives struggled, and that fear contributed to support for conservative values and a political agenda. At the national level that support translated into the rise of Barry Goldwater. Goldwater, a Republican senator from Arizona, is the politician most often cited as the key figure in the conservative resurgence of the period. He was strongly anticommunist, opposed labor unions, was a fierce advocate of state's rights and a proponent of "law and order," advocated making Social Security voluntary, and was a persistent opponent of the New Deal's leg-acy. He would win his party's nomination for the presidency in 1964 and face Lyndon Johnson. He would lose that election in a landslide, but his influence cannot be overstated.[34]

George Wallace also upset the political establishment in the late 1960s and 1970s and also influenced modern conservatism. Wallace won the governorship in Alabama four times during the twenty-five year period from the early sixties to the late eighties and mounted four unsuccessful campaigns for president (1964, 1968, 1972, and 1976) (three as a Democrat and once on the America Independent Party ticket). Wallace struck a populist chord with a predominantly white working-class constituency and is known best for a racial demagoguery that continues to define his political career despite his best efforts for redemption during the latter years of his life. Wallace embraced the "traditional" family and Christian fundamentalism that conservatives have become identified with. He also shared in the conservative revulsion for communism, railed against big government, and became well known for his outrageous comments about hippies and protestors and for his diatribes about the abuse of centralized power, particularly government bureaucrats and federal judges, a point motorcyclists would take note of. Wallace embodied the core values that make up conservatism today, and the contradictions. The well-oiled polit-ical machine he controlled for nearly three decades in Alabama was also known for costly construction projects and other largess for his constit-uents who repaid him with their loyalty and their votes. They shared his frustration with big government but demanded a big state apparatus to protect their rights and privileges.[35]

Conservatism's rise also gained advantage from social, economic, and political changes that eroded the traditional sources of identity and power on which the working class relied, and it benefited from a privatized understanding of identity and responsibility that supplanted a collective sense of public welfare and social good. Historians have used the term "corporate liberalism" to describe the "philosophy of using the state energetically to balance the power of major interest groups and to ensure long-range stability." George Lipsitz notes that corporate liberal principles had been conspicuous since World War I, but only with the dramatic expansion of the government's role during World War II did these principles attract the support they needed to be "implemented in a comprehensive way." This approach led to a renewal of the welfare capitalism of the 1920s in the form of higher wages and fringe benefits to organized labor and government-sponsored programs in housing, education, and welfare. But these policies also limited the working class's share of the nation's wealth and political power by focusing much of that effort on expanding opportunities for private profit. Hence a disproportionate amount of government funding went to highway expansion instead of mass transit, into loans for single-detached family housing instead of for public housing or the renovation of inner cities, and into private pension plans instead of universal plans underwriting pensions, housing, and education—like the programs adopted in most other industrialized nations. As was the case with welfare capitalism in the 1920s, these programs helped build working-class support for capitalism's expansion, but they also promoted an underlying philosophy that "portrayed economic security as a private and personal matter"; promoted gender, class, and racial divisions; and idealized consumption as the root of identity, community belonging, and citizenship. Indeed, these policies disadvantaged racial minorities, who were largely excluded from the expansion of home ownership after World War II, and suburbia's growth also undercut an important source of class, ethnic, and community belonging that these older neighborhoods had promoted. Away from their former communities and without adequate mass transit, Americans increasingly found their leisure in the privacy of a single family home instead of more traditional forms of public life and amusement. In this context the family became an idealized site of consumption, and consuming commodities became more important than producing them.[36]

A postwar economic and political order that privatized day-to-day life and social well-being was particularly resonant among motorcyclists, whose support of individual rights that took shape out of the experience of riding became increasingly critical to their identity. Simply put, the decision to wear a helmet, motorcyclists and their supporters argued, was the individual's and not the federal government's. Senator Bill Meier of Euless,

Texas, described the bill he introduced to repeal a state helmet law as "one of individual freedom and choice." The question is, he added, "Should you have to be told by the government you have to wear a helmet if you're going to ride a motorcycle?"[37] "When I thought it was appropriate," argued Will Cowan, an Austin attorney who worked as the legislative director of the AMA, "yes, I'd still wear my helmet. But it's a big brother issue. It's my head, you know. And I think I should be able to do what the hell I want to with it."[38] Senator John O. Pastore (D-Rhode Island), who helped lead the push to rescind the Department of Transportation's authority, effectively summarized the same point when he said: "I never rode a motorcycle, I wouldn't ride a motorcycle and I hope I never have to ride a motorcycle. Nonetheless, the citizens of the states should be free to decide the motorcycle helmet issue."[39] Representative Frank Gaston of Dallas approached the issue from the point of safety but essentially made the same argument. Gaston admitted that helmets saved lives "but is that the role of government?" he asked. "The option [to wear one] has to remain with the individual or you lose all freedom."[40] In a letter to the National Highway Traffic Safety Administration, a highway safety representative for the state of California, L. G. Turner, explained that the state "espouses the philosophy that personal safety is the responsibility of each individual citizen and government should not attempt to protect the individual from himself."[41] At a helmet protest in Albany, New York, where about 200 motorcyclists staged a "Freedom of the Road" demonstration, one "mustachioed enthusiast" explained that the "government has no right to tell us we have to protect ourselves." He also wore a helmet and "would even if I didn't have to," but "I don't want anybody [to] tell me I have to."[42]

The focus on individual rights also translated into support for the libertarians who spoke out against helmet laws after their party was first established in 1972. In 1976 *Easyriders* featured an interview with Roger MacBride, the Libertarian Party's presidential candidate, and he wholeheartedly opposed helmet laws. "If you accept the libertarian premise that your life is your own, and not the State's," he argued, "then the government's only legitimate function is to protect people from using force and fraud against others."[43] When the AMA conducted a survey of presidential candidates in mid-1980, it found that Libertarian candidate, Ed Clark, "generated quite a bit of interest." The AMA heard from Libertarian Party members requesting additional information about Clark, and many nonmembers were just as interested. Because of that interest and because the "major" parties received the "vast majority of time and space . . . in the electronic and print media," the AMA arranged an interview with Clark and published it in its October 1980 issue. The Libertarian was the only party, the AMA asserted in the interview, that had "directly addressed the helmet law issue."[44] Riders also began to advocate in support of the Libertarian ticket. Michael H. Smith of Zion, Illinois, wrote a letter to *American Motorcyclist Magazine* in 1984 to express his disdain for government bureaucrats who "interfere with or threaten my freedom to ride." Smith explained that he believed he was "free to do anything I want, so long as I respect everyone else's rights to do the same," and there was "a name for people who think like that. They're called 'Libertarians.'" The Libertarian Party, he added, was the third largest political party in the country and had "consistently argued for the repeal of all helmet laws, bike bans, import quotas, land-use restrictions, the 55-mph speed limit, the Department of Transportation, and emissions regulations." Smith concluded by asking the AMA to endorse David Berglang, the Libertarian presidential candidate in 1984.[45]

Motorcyclists also identified with the words and deeds of notable (often historical) figures who had become well known for their critique of centralized power and its potential for abuse. Motorcyclists quoted everyone from George Wallace ("We are living in a society in which thugs and federal judges have just about taken charge")[46] to Edmund Burke ("Bad laws are the worst sort of tyranny")[47] to Louis Brandeis ("Men born to freedom are naturally alert to repel invasion of their liberty by evil-minded rulers").[48] Even Henry David Thoreau was described as a "bro from the last century [who] lived a no compromise, take-no-shit-off-anybody type of life." "Bones" of Martinez, Georgia, encouraged his fellow riders to read Thoreau's essay, *Civil Disobedience*, and described him as a "champion of individual human rights. . . . He was a dude who, in this century, would probably be a 1%er all the way!"[49]

The most common references, however, were to the founding fathers.[50] After Congress voted in support of amending the Highway Safety Act of 1966, Charles Clayton described the victory and its impact as one "for all the people and their posterity. . . . I think it was Thomas Jefferson who said it best. 'Eternal vigilance is the price of freedom.'"[51] After a reader objected to the AMA's support of the helmet law repeal, Ed Youngblood admitted in his response that he was less concerned about the reader's feelings about helmets and more "concerned about [his] apparent disregard for some basic Jeffersonian principles (such as the rights to life, liberty and the pursuit of happiness, etc.)."[52]

The American Motorcyclist Association published a mock interview with Jefferson to highlight the contradiction between the government's current policies and the founders' original intent. The AMA asked its readers, "Could it be that we have lost sight of the original goals of America's founding fathers?" and "Do modern-day bureaucrats overlook the fact that those same founding fathers did not intend for the federal government to assume the role of National Mommie?" The interview consisted of the AMA posing a series of questions and Jefferson's responses based on his writings and quotes. The AMA asked about the basis "on which you think the government should operate?' "What happens when the people in power ignore some people . . . when making decisions?" and how can a "powerful bureaucracy be brought under control?" Jefferson's assumed responses reaffirmed the positions motorcyclists had been making for years and suggest that he too would have been a friend of the motorcyclist, if not one of them. Jefferson opposed big government, "I think we have more machinery of government than is necessary." And there were limits to the government's authority: "In questions of power let no more be heard of confidence in man, but bind him down from mischief by the chains of the Constitution."[53]

The special relationship motorcyclists claimed with the founding fathers also coincided with an increasingly exuberant patriotism that became most conspicuous during the debate over helmet laws and the questions of citizenship it raised. ABATE of New York, for example, was established in 1974 and a year later began to recite the pledge of allegiance at the start of its protest rallies. One member admitted that this new "tradition" made us "look better," but when asked about the pledge, he also took exception to the capitol police who "for some reason . . . felt they shouldn't have to participate in honoring our flag." "It's kind of ironic," he added, "when a group of us so called 'bad assed' motorcyclists think more of our country than the police."[54]

The motorcyclist's patriotism did not automatically lead to a connection with veterans, even though general histories about riders have highlighted their veteran status.[55] The use of veteran or veterans in the pages of *American Motorcycling* and other publications before the 1980s almost always referred to veteran riders. Occasionally, the focus did include a Memorial Day or Fourth of July parade but not to draw attention to veterans or their service.[56] Rogue, for example, described Memorial Day as a "day set aside to honor the dead of any American War," but it focused on the "war" motorcyclists were waging against the government and highlighted the recent death of Don "Pappy" Pittsley, who died of a heart attack while arguing with a cop about the helmet law. There was no mention of veterans or of any connection between motorcyclists and veterans in Rogue's article.[57]

In another case, some of the motorcyclists who participated in a protest rally in D.C. in 1975 were veterans, but the issue came up only because a reporter noticed some of them wearing Vietnam War decorations. The arrival of the motorcyclists in D.C. coincided with Department of Transportation hearings to consider cutting off $87 million in U.S. highway funds to the last three states without helmet laws: California, Utah, and Illinois. One of the protests had occurred the day before the story was written and consisted of a parade of motorcyclists circling the White House and the U.S. Capitol, with other protests planned for each of the days the Department of Transportation was scheduled to meet to discuss each state. The reporter described the cyclists as "dressed in ragged blue jeans and vests encrusted with swastikas, skulls and crossbones and Vietnam War decorations." In the interviews that followed a protest, the motorcyclists addressed the issue as a case of "blackmail by the federal government" and discussed how helmets "cut your visibility and hearing and they can break your neck." "If I'm going to lose my life in an accident," argued Cliff English of the Wheels of Soul Motorcycle Club from Philadelphia, "what difference does it make if I break my neck or crush my skull? It's my life and my choice." The motorcyclists did not highlight their veteran status in their discussion about their opposition to helmet laws or in their complaint about government blackmail.[58]

Not until 1980 did the question of veterans begin to attract attention from motorcyclists and only after Ronald Reagan made a speech to the Veterans of Foreign Wars and referred to the Vietnam War as a noble cause. While most of his speech focused on the Soviets and his argument that peace could be guaranteed only through strength, he argued that the general public "dishonor[s] the memory of 50,000 young Americans who died in that cause when we give way to feelings of guilt as if we were doing something shameful." Reagan described Americans as "shabby" for their treatment of those veterans, and argued that they "deserve our gratitude, our respect, and our continuing concern."[59] Two months after that speech *Easyriders* magazine published "Vet Voice," a regular column about veterans and veterans' issues because the magazine explained, "We give a fuck about our gutsy vets." The article featured an image of a motorcyclist riding a chopper with a can of Coors beer in one hand, "Fuck Iran" painted on the gas tank, and in bold next to the illustration, "God, Guns, and Guts Made America Free; At Any Cost, Keep All Three." The column featured discussions about Agent Orange, the limits to benefits for incarcerated veterans, and the problems vets faced from bureaucrats who were not veterans (to name a few). *Easyriders* also began each issue with the author's memories of his experiences in Vietnam and almost always described soldiers under

Motorcyclists at City Park, Sturgis, in 1980. Courtesy of Michael Lichter.

fire: one story highlighted a "strident cry" for a medic after a soldier was shot in the hip from an AK-47, and in another the author recalled watching *Dr. Zhivago* with the Montagnards, and unexpectedly facing a barrage of mortar that left eight soldiers sprawled out on what he thought was "safe territory." The column also included up-to-date stories about veterans and the problems they faced and letters from actual vets describing their adjustment to life at home after the war ended.[60]

Easyriders not only empathized with the plight of veterans but noted that motorcyclists shared many of the problems they faced. "Are they lost, bewildered, [or] alienated? asked *Easyriders* in its first column. "Do they trust the government? Do they trust anyone?", The first issue of Vet Voice provided information to help vets get the support they needed and highlighted the experiences motorcyclists shared with them. Veterans (like motorcyclists), *Easyriders* argued, represented a disproportionate number of men in the U.S. prison system, between 25 and 33 percent. And there was no greater fraternity than that which was common between motorcyclists except perhaps the camaraderie born out of the experience of battle. "The brotherhood felt by bikers is as close as I've ever come to whatever

I felt in 'Nam. I and my vet brothers at Easyriders," the author added, "want to preserve the brotherhood this country needs. And the only way we can do that is to help our brothers—brothers make brotherhood."[61]

The attention the magazine gave vets would find a supportive audience of riders whose interest in veterans continued to grow. By the early 1980s, for example, motorcycle clubs explicitly for veterans were becoming more conspicuous. Ryan Q. Emerson from the Society of American Vietnam Veterans sent a letter to *Cycle World* in 1983 with the purpose of recruiting Vietnam veterans and other vets to form the Grunt Army Motorcycle Division. For a lifetime fee of one dollar, each veteran would get a special bike sticker, membership card, and newsletter that would "advise them of plans for motorcycle staging areas around the country." Emerson advised *Cycle World*'s readership on the need "for a conservative attitude on the part of our riders. The entire nation will always be watching," he explained.[62]

By the end of the 1980s the efforts of veterans who were also motorcyclists led to the Run for the Wall, a yearly pilgrimage of motorcyclists across the country that ends at the Vietnam Veterans Memorial in D.C. to raise awareness about those men and women killed in the war, those still missing in action, and to support U.S. military personnel across the globe. The Run began in 1989 with just a couple of motorcyclists. Today thousands participate, and the run concludes in D.C. with a parade that often includes as many as 400,000 motorcyclists.[63] More recently, motorcyclists have been some of the most conspicuous supporters of veterans of the Gulf War and the war in Iraq. In 2005 they established the Patriot Guard Riders, a volunteer group of motorcyclists who serve as funeral escorts for American servicemen and service women who died in battle in the Persian Gulf wars and for first responders and any honorably discharged veterans. Guard members also attend the funeral and provide a buffer between the family and any protestors who might try and disrupt the services. They sing patriotic songs, wave flags, and rev the engines of their cycles to drown out the protestors and "shield the mourning family and their friends." The guard most often faced off against protesters from the Westbrook Baptist Church of Topeka, Kansas, which until his recent death was led by Fred Phelps. The protestors have been disrupting the funeral services of veterans for several years, with picketers holding signs that read, "Thank God for IEDs, and "Thank God for dead soldiers." The Guard was initially organized by American Legion Riders of Post 136 in Mulvane, Kansas, and is currently supported by about five thousand riders.[64]

As these examples suggest, the motorcycle rights movement came of age against the backdrop of a broader conservative shift that upset the nation's political landscape after World War II. Unlike diehard segregationists who relied upon a race-based or states' rights agenda to challenge federal intervention, motorcyclists represented a rights-based activism that adopted a "new language that privileged their own positive rights-based claims to individual liberty and property."[65] Kevin Kruse is generally identified with this argument in his study of Atlanta in the immediate postwar years. Kruse argues that "in their own minds," conservatives "were . . . fighting for rights of their own—such as the 'right' to select their neighbors, their employees, and their children's class mates, the 'right' to do as they pleased with their private property and personal businesses, and perhaps, most important, the 'right' to remain free from what they saw as dangerous encroachments by the federal government." Modern conservatives, Kruse concludes, "did not think of themselves in terms of what they opposed but rather in terms of what they supported."[66]

There were, however, sharp differences between these conservatives and motorcyclists. Scholarship on the Sunbelt South and the environmental movement has described these political claims as rooted in a rights-based activism that reflected a "sense of middle-class entitlement" that these men and women claimed as American citizens. They were citizens—conservative, aggrieved, forgotten—but citizens nonetheless. Motorcyclists challenged these ideas in two distinct ways. While motorcyclists became increasingly embittered with federal power, their political opposition emerged out of working-class communities and a sensibility (often more rough than respectable) that would become more noticeable as the motorcycle rights movement gained ground in the early 1970s. And the struggle against helmet regulations reflected a broader disillusionment that motorcyclists complained challenged their rights as citizens. Some riders simply claimed that they had been marginalized. In a letter to *Biker* in 1978 in which R. E. Richardson of British Columbia, Canada, asked "How far do they want laws to go?" he bluntly asserted that the government was "treating bikers as second class citizens" and singled out the "special laws only for motorcycles."[67] In an article about the discrimination facing riders, David Mangeim did not simply object to the typical stereotypes attributed to motorcyclists but candidly ridiculed the "attitude that all motorcyclists are dangerous" as "archaic, and un-American."[68]

Other riders explicitly addressed the idea of citizenship and their exclusion. As early as 1948 and in the wake of the push to regulate motorcyclists after the controversy surrounding the Riverside Rally, one cyclist reminded readers, "It must be pointed out to those influential advocates of such drastic action that motorcyclists are citizens."[69] More than thirty years later this sentiment was just as prominent. In one editorial, Bob Lawrence admonished riders to "stand up for our rights as bikers." But he also asked, "How about our rights as Americans?"[70] A more telling example appeared on the side of a UPS-style van at a helmet law protest in the late 1970s. Motorcyclists had spray painted in bold white letters, "We ARE AMERICANS TOO! Weather [sic] you like it or not," just above the slogan, "Let Those Who Ride Decide."[71]

Scholars have often characterized Americans in the 1970s as disillusioned or, more recently, "Mad as Hell," and have linked them to the "silent majority" or what has also been described as the "forgotten Americans." They were the beneficiaries of the United States' postwar affluence and at the core of a developing Cold War consensus that faced increased scrutiny. Dominic Sandbrook points out that their anger gave rise to a new kind of populism that pitted what he described as the "virtuous citizen" in an epic battle "against big government, big business, and a decadent elite." While similarities existed between these Americans and motorcyclists, motorcyclists did not view themselves as "forgotten" but as Americans whose citizenship had been ignored or denied by a government that had lost its initial focus and purpose. Helmet laws and other forms of regulation, motorcyclists argued, only normalized their exclusion, even as it served as the vehicle through which they could challenge it, fashion a more cohesive sense of what it meant to be an American, and imagine a different future and perhaps even a different past.[72]

FORGING AN ALLIANCE

Politicians and motorcyclists rarely crossed paths in the years before the 1970s, and as that relationship began to materialize, the potential for conflict was always prominent. After the final passage of a bill to require motorcyclists to wear helmets was announced in the House chamber of the Iowa state legislature in 1975, an "unkempt youth [motorcyclist] yelled from the balcony, 'You're all a bunch of cowards, every one of you who voted that way. America is dead." The outburst alone attracted the media's attention, but the response from legislators was just as provocative. The bill had initially passed 57–43, but after the "outburst," Representative Floyd Millen (a Republican), who had initially voted against the bill, asked that his vote be changed. He refused to be intimidated. Eight others followed the representative's lead and the final vote in favor of the bill was 65–35.[73]

Crowds of motorcyclists in the galleries of state legislatures or at committee hearings awaiting the final decision about a helmet bill were common in the 1970s. At a 1972 senate committee hearing in California, a crowd of about one hundred Hells Angels was in attendance anxiously awaiting the decision about a helmet measure. When the eight committee members rejected it, the motorcyclists "stood up, applauded and cheered."[74] Ron Schneiders of *Cycle Guide* argued that intimidation was critical to understanding the opposition to helmet laws and the success of the campaign against them. "Giving credit where [credit is] due," he explained in his editorial, and maintained that "it was the Hells Angels who originally saved the California scene. When the California legislature met to consider the helmet question in their oak-shaded imitation of Capitol Hill, suddenly there were the Angels, as real as chains and boots. No legislator will admit to being intimidated," he added, "but that day they voted with the Angels."[75]

At a hearing on the fate of the helmet law in Texas in 1977 the presence of about seventy-five motorcyclists in the gallery "wearing dark glasses" also shaped the outcome of the day's proceedings. The cropped picture of the gallery that appeared in the *Dallas Morning News* included about a dozen and a half cyclists—some of them wearing glasses, others scratching their beards, all of them staring blankly into the camera as they awaited the announcement of the committee's findings. The caption below the picture states, "Mike Stanisci, right, president of the Fort Worth Motorcycle Club, defends the helmet law repeal as do the gallery spectators." Perhaps with little surprise, there were no position witnesses in favor of helmets.[76]

The overall political realignment that was taking shape over helmet laws, as one contemporary explained, was also "anything but clear."[77] In the U.S. Senate, for example, one of the cosponsors to amend the Highway Safety Act was Democrat Alan Cranston of California. At times, Cranston's motives were decidedly pragmatic. One contemporary described him as someone who "probably never sat on a bike in his life," and he made his mark in the Senate, in part, through his support of environmental issues. But at stake was $50 million in federal highway construction and safety funds that the federal government threatened to cut off if California did not pass a helmet law. At the time of the introduction of his bill, California was the only state without a helmet law, the state had the largest number of riders nationwide who had become politically active, and the most conspicuous ones were members of the Hells Angels.[78]

The other cosponsor of the bill was conservative Republican Jesse Helms. Like Cranston, Helms had no connection to motorcyclists, and North Carolina did not witness any helmet protests until after Congress approved of amending the Highway Safety Act.[79] But Helms was a well-established conservative, and the ideas motorcyclists embraced were ones he had already become known for championing. For example, Helms described the Highway Safety Act as a "violation of our constitutional liberties" and challenged the contention that helmet laws were a "valid exercise of the State police power." He belittled the government's motorcycle safety program as "benevolent paternalism." Citing a Case Note from the *Wisconsin Law Review*, Helms argued that the decisions upholding helmet laws "rely on a strange mixture of catchphrases. The prevention of needless additions to the welfare rolls; the protection of 'the reckless citizen against himself'; and the promotion of a healthy citizenry 'capable of self-support, of bearing arms, and of adding to the resources of the country.'" Helms concluded his speech by encouraging motorcycle manufacturers to include a helmet with the purchase of each bike in the same way that automobile manufacturers provided seat belts. "In this way," he explained, "the motorcyclist would be encouraged but not required, to wear a helmet and the decision to wear the helmet would be made by the individual rather than the Government."[80]

Yet, even as the helmet question challenged political partisanship, by the mid-1970s one contemporary identified Ronald Reagan as the conservative "turning the helmet issue into a national crusade," and he stood in diametric opposition to Ralph Nader, who one individual described as the "symbol," if not the leader, of the "pro-regulation forces." Nader, who built his reputation as an automobile safety critic, argued that the helmet safety requirement was "designed to protect not only the cyclist but the public." The public's safety and resources were at stake when a cyclist had an accident, he argued, and the rider often caused "chain reactions of secondary accidents [that] require the help of tax-financed police, ambulances, and hospitals [the public burden theory]." In a debate with Nader in 1975, Reagan focused less on these particulars and more on the government's role. Governmental regulations, he argued, were justified only to "prevent us from endangering others but not from endangering ourselves." The "government has no business to tell them to wear helmets for their own protection," Reagan argued and asked, "What is next? Do we put guards on beaches to protect surf riders? Or should we also guard mountain climbers?"[81]

If there was any doubt about the conservative influence shaping the victory against this regulation, the media claimed the successful revision of the highway act as a victory against big government. Marianne Means described the victory as "as an admission that legislating morality simply does not work." "Nobody," she explained, "likes to be forced to do something somebody else says is for his own good, particularly if that somebody else is a heavy handed paternalistic government bureaucracy." The helmet bill, she added, "was only one triumph in the direction of getting government out of individual lives where it has no business being. But every little bit helps."[82] James Kilpatrick was even more explicit in his article titled "The Cycle Helmet Stupidity." The helmet bill, Kilpatrick argued, was one simple way to understand why big government was bad and "to understand this issue," he contended, "is to understand what liberals, in general, support, and what conservatives, in general, oppose." Kilpatrick added that it was "useless to try to delineate these differences on the big bills" and ironically used the example of the national debt to make his argument. "I must have put a million people to sleep over the past 25 years arguing a conservative position on the national debt." "No one," Kilpatrick continued," "gives a hoorah about the national debt [and] no one can comprehend a $75 billion deficit." Kilpatrick made a similar argument about the Strategic Arms Limitation Talks and suggested that the "big issues" were "out there with the Milky Way, among the unreachable stars." "But motorcycle helmets? Here we come down to earth." Kilpatrick argued that as a "matter of law" the requirement that riders wear a helmet was a "gross invasion of both states' rights and personal liberty." "The smothering solicitude of Big Government, as manifested in this pompous compulsion, is what liberals tend to support and conservatives tend to oppose." The proposed amendment to Section 402 of the Highway Safety Act of 1966 specifically prohibited the "imposition of a safety helmet requirement on the states," and its passage was a victory for conservatives. Conservatives, Kilpatrick emphasized, "don't win many battles, but they do win a few. They won this one," he added and concluded his article with a terse but prescient statement about the relationship between motorcyclists and the Right that would only grow more conspicuous as the decade came to an end. "Is it any wonder that candidates who oppose Big Government are pop-pop-popping along?"[83]

Even Democrats recognized the helmet law question as the issue critical in shaping their ideas about federal power. Cranston's support, one contemporary argued, reflected the "principle involved" and not any particular interest in pleasing the motorcyclists. His position was also described as an "all too rare display of opposition to the federal bureaucratic intervention with the rights of the people to self-government," which in Cranston's case was "sparked by a federal mandate for states to adopt laws making the wearing of helmets by motorcyclists mandatory and subject to penalties for violations." "Californians are capable of judging for themselves whether or not to mandate helmets," Cranston was quoted saying, and the general public's safety "is not enhanced by a mandatory motorcycle helmet law."[84]

The flurry of legislative activity that quickly followed the amendment of the highway act also suggests the conservative interest in the helmet question. *Biker News* reported in December 1977 that "two years ago, only two states . . . did not have helmet laws. Now, half of all the states (25) do not." The editor admitted that the repeal effort was "lopsided." The southeastern states of Arkansas, Mississippi, Alabama, or Tennessee were not expected to successfully repeal their helmet laws any time soon because until only recently, the paper argued, there had been very little opposition to helmets, and the author described the Northeast as "having trouble." The "Department of Transportation's (DOT) influence," the author argued, was the culprit, and "the closer the states are to Washington D.C. the tougher the battle." The author suspected that "the last state to repeal will be either immediately adjacent to Washington D. C. or in the Southeastern states." The traditionally conservative West, on the other hand, had experienced tremendous success. "With the exception of five states," the author argued, "every state west of the Mississippi has repealed its helmet law!"[85]

By the end of the 1970s the nonriding majority still associated the term biker with violence and antisocial behavior, and motorcyclists' frustration with the government was more palpable than it had been in previous years. But the negative stereotypes associated with motorcyclists were increasingly competing with a political sensibility that was beginning to attract national attention, and it was one that highlighted the motorcyclists' uncompromising commitment to many of the same values conservatives had become known for championing. Motorcyclists, in sum, had transformed themselves from the "least political of citizens" to some of the most patriotic ones and, by doing so, were challenging age-old stereotypes that were at the root of their exclusion (or at least perceived exclusion) from the nation-state. This trend was particularly noticeable not only as the motorcycle rights movement gained ground in the latter 1970s but also as the Right became a political force to reckon with. Motorcyclist's ideas about freedom and big government overlapped with a resurgent conservatism whose political presence became more conspicuous with the national rise of Barry Goldwater and Ronald Reagan. While conservative politicians often downplayed any recognition of or connection to motorcyclists, whose political goals seemingly contradicted their behavior off their bikes, they recognized the potential political gain from the fight over helmets and assumed an active role in the push against helmet regulation.

Kilpatrick summed it up best when he explained that the helmet issue was one simple way to understand why "big government was bad" and the difference between liberals and conservatives. This alliance was not only conspicuous by the end of the 1970s but also significant enough to convince Becky Dunlop that most nonriders had finally caught up to motorcyclists and were embracing age-old biker values. Motorcyclists were in a key position to lead the fight against "Big Brother," and their values would become increasingly aligned with the Right as Reagan assumed the presidency in 1980.

RONALD REAGAN

Ronald Reagan's rise to power takes shape against the backdrop of one of the worst recessions in the postwar period, during which the Harley-Davidson Motor Company was struggling to remain solvent. After the Indian Motorcycle Manufacturing Company folded in 1953, H-D became the last major American motorcycle manufacturer building heavyweight cycles. As Japanese manufactures entered the market in the 1960s, the number of motorcycles H-D manufactured also increased. Harley-Davidson's sales of motorcycles 1000ccs or bigger nearly tripled between 1969 and the mid-1970s—from around 12,000 to 13,000 bikes a year to about 35,000. By the late 1970s, Harley-Davidson was selling more than 50,000 machines annually.[86] During this expansion, H-D's share of the market fluctuated from fewer than 4 percent to about 7 percent in 1977, and during this period the company was profitable.[87]

By the early 1980s, Harley-Davidson was on the brink of collapse. More than a decade of ownership by American Machine and Foundry, an American company that had grown famous for its sporting equipment, had led to increasing complaints about the machine's quality, and H-D faced competition from Honda, which began building its own heavyweights in the late 1960s: the Honda CB 750 was introduced in 1969 and the now-famous 1000cc Goldwing debuted in 1979. By the early 1980s, Japanese manufacturers had introduced V-twin engine touring cycles, which Harley-Davidson complained copied its basic design and marketing schemes. Because of this competition, Harley-Davidson's production peaked at 50,000 cycles in 1979. By 1982 that figure had slipped to around 30,000, a figure comparable to what Harley-Davidson was manufacturing ten years earlier, and the company recorded what Vaughn Beals, president of Harley-Davidson, described as "major" losses in 1981 and 1982. Most important of all, and what was at the heart of Harley-Davidson's complaint about its Japanese competitors, its share of the heavyweight motorcycle marked slipped from 21 percent in 1977 to just over 13 percent (13.3 percent) in 1982. Japanese manufacturers, Beals contended, had been stockpiling heavyweights, and once they were available for purchase, prices would drop even lower and the resulting loss of market share for Harley-Davidson would adversely affect the company, if not push it out of business altogether.[88]

Indeed, by the end of the 1970s some of H-D's most trusted clients—police departments—were also beginning to buy Japanese. Throughout most of the postwar period, the motorcycle cop's motorcycle of choice had been a rumbler—the Harley-Davidson Electric Glide—a bike that "didn't take no sass," according to Lt. Robert Hall and Patrolman Larry Manit of the California Highway Patrol's Golden Gate Division. During the years around World War II, the typical motorcycle cop was an officer in "knee high, shined black boots with a soft rounded hat and a blue bow tie hiding behind a billboard waiting for speeders," and he was riding a Harley. By the mid-1970s, however, the Japanese "started muscling in" with what one contemporary described as "their tinny-sounding, albeit smooth-running bikes." The California Highway Patrol, for example, purchased 248 Harley-Davidson motorcycles in 1970. For the next three years the department was still purchasing Harleys, but the company was beginning to lose out to Honda and Moto Guzzi (an Italian-made bike). By 1974 the department was buying only Moto Guzzis, which relinquished its control of the market to Kawasaki in 1975. Through the rest of the 1970s and early 1980s the California Highway Patrol was buying only Kawasakis, which would soon capture 65 percent of the U.S. police fleet market. Dick Reiter, director of Harley-Davidson's fleet sales, admitted that Harley "lost its hold" on the police motorcycle market soon after AMF purchased the company and began focusing on sports machines. "It was a forgotten market," he exclaimed, a market that was "taken for granted." From 1975 to 1981, he added, "we had our head in the sand."[89]

Police officers also routinely complained about the Harley's performance. "It was ok on surface streets," stated patrolman Manit, "but once it got up to high speeds it was unstable and not that fast." Manit complained explicitly about what he called the "lock to lock" wobbling a Harley experienced at high speeds "when all you could do was let it go . . . [and] ride it out," and the phenomenon known as black dust, a consequence of black paint that would "literally disintegrate from the shaking." The shaking was so bad that Sergeant Stan Odmann claimed that a Harley could not carry a radar gun. The Kawasaki bikes were "smoother, quieter, [and] easier to maintain," said San Francisco Police Department motorcycle officer Bob

Ryan. A typical Harley had to be serviced every 1,500 miles compared to every 3,000 miles for the Kawasaki. Odmann added that the "Kawasaki was designed as a police motorcycle, whereas Harley simply took a civilian motorcycle and just outfitted it with lights and a siren." Another patrolman added, "If they [Kawasaki] had a problem . . . it would be corrected the next year. With Harley we rode them for years and years and years without any changes. You got what you got because they were the only game in town."[90]

Harley-Davidson's response to its loss of market share often focused less on improving its product and more on the jingoistic appeal of "buy American." According to Dana Frank, the economic malaise of the 1960s and 1970s "produced the third, longest, and deepest wave of buy American sentiment in U.S. history." That sentiment led to campaigns in textiles, automobiles, and other industries. The International Ladies and Garment Workers Union began promoting American-made clothing in the early 1970s, and the auto industry followed suit shortly thereafter, culminating with scenes of overzealous autoworkers using sledgehammers to bash Toyotas to the delight of crowds in parking lots across the country, especially the Midwest.[91] These rallies frequently evoked Pearl Harbor or World War II, and the broader campaign to buy American relied upon age-old stereotypes about evil "foreigners," "Japs," and the image of "floods" of Asians or a "Yellow Peril." Motorcycle manufacturers like Triumph had relied on Asian stereotypes in the 1940s to promote their cycles, and as Japanese manufactures began to dominate the U.S. market in the 1960s Harley riders appropriated the image of a "Japanese invasion," and frequently denigrated all "Jap" bikes as "rice burners." H-D also organized its own "Buy American" campaign that began in 1971 with ads that featured the oversized number one festooned with stars and stripes, and in 1972 "the American Freedom Machine" slogan debuted.[92]

Little evidence suggests that H-D's "buy American" campaigns were initially successful. Fluctuations in its market share were often a reflection of fickle consumers rather than the company's advertising schemes. In 1978 *Business Week* noticed that demand for the Harleys in the 900cc range and above had recently doubled, which helped account for the spike in Harley-Davidson's share of the market toward the end of the 1970s. But that increase was accompanied by a 30 percent decrease in motorcycle sales during the preceding three years. Contemporaries specifically linked this overall decrease to middle-class riders who had eagerly taken up motorcycling and who just as quickly gave it up having faced inclement weather and other road hazards, along with automobilists unwilling to share the highways. Harley riders, some argued, were simply more dedicated to their preoccupation and less likely to be affected by the current trends or fads than their counterparts on Hondas or other Japanese-made motorcycles. Although Americans were increasingly attracted to H-D in the 1970s, the company's share of the market was tempered by the overall slump in motorcycles sales.[93]

As Harley-Davidson's fortunes worsened in the early 1980s, the company looked to the government for help. The company had introduced a 15 percent rebate program to help reduce inventories; laid off 40 percent of its employees from January 1982 to May 1983, from about 3,800 employees down to 2,200; and filed a complaint with the U.S. International Trade Commission (ITC), alleging that Japanese manufacturers had stockpiled as many as a two-year supply of heavyweights that would place Harley-Davidson at a further competitive disadvantage when they became available for purchase. Beals explained that Harley-Davidson was "requesting . . . an orderly market where we can stand on our feet and compete." The trade commission agreed with Harley-Davidson's complaint and recommended that the federal government increase import duties on motorcycles with engines of more than 700 cubic centimeters from 4.4 percent of the cost of the motorcycle to 49.4 percent—an increase of 45 percent. The level of the import duty would then be set at decreasing rates of 35, 20, 15, and 10 percent over the next four years. President Reagan accepted the recommendations and supported the proposed increase to import duties. "The domestic (motorcycle) industry," Reagan explained in a written message to Congress, "is threatened by serious injury because of increased imports" and the increase in tariffs was "consistent with our national economic interests."[94]

Reagan would follow up his support of the tariff with a visit to a Harley-Davidson manufacturing plant in York, Pennsylvania, in May 1987. Against the backdrop of the hearings surrounding the Iran-Contra scandal, Reagan toured the York plant to celebrate the company's comeback after nearly collapsing five years earlier. Reagan spoke to "hundreds of workers," was presented with a Harley-Davidson jacket, and posed for pictures with a test rider who encouraged Reagan to switch on the XL-1100 cycle with an electric starter. "It won't take off, will it?" Reagan asked after having started the cycle. He then "gunned the throttle" and said, "That's quite something for an old ex-horse cavalry man."[95]

The turnaround Reagan celebrated in his visit to the York plant in 1987 was only the beginning of Harley's success. In 1982 and 1983 the company reported no profits, and its share of the market dipped back down to less than 4 percent (3.3 percent in 1983 and 3.7 percent in 1984). But over the

President Ronald Reagan at the York, Pennsylvania, plant to celebrate Harley's comeback in front of a crowd of workers and reporters. Courtesy of the Ronald Reagan Library, Simi Valley, Calif.

next few years the company's fortunes improved significantly, and in 1987 H-D requested that the tariff rate quotas be eliminated. In 1986 H-D's share of the market had increased to 5 percent, and by 1988 it had almost reached double digits—9.4 percent. Within two years (1990) that number would nearly double to 17.8 percent, and in 1997 it reached 27.1 percent—a high for the period from 1970 to 2000, a figure just shy of Honda's market share of 27.9 precent. The market for the biggest bikes also saw significant increases. The 13 percent of market share in 1982 had increased to 23 percent a year later, and by 1990 Harley-Davidson had captured 60 percent of the market share for the biggest cycles.[96]

Doubts about the tariff's efficacy were evident from the start. Critics have charged that the tariff was applied to so few bikes that its impact was negligible and that Harley-Davidson's turnaround reflected a company shakeup, the development of a new management style (influenced by the Japanese), and a better built bike.[97] The tariff was also criticized because it violated Reagan's commitment to free trade; it challenged the United States' international obligations to other countries; it discriminated specifically against the Japanese; and the expected economic gains were marginal at best if not outright adverse.[98] While the tariff would save jobs at Harley-Davidson, economists believed that the tariff would produce a potential decline in revenue for Japanese manufacturers, which were expected to have to lay off about three thousand workers in the United States, more than H-D employed altogether.[99] As one motorcyclist explained his ambivalence about the tariff and his frustration with Reagan, "Unless you are a Harley dealer, the tariff has been nothing but a pain in the backside brought about for Ronnie's own political ends."[100] Paula Stern, an ITC member who voted against the protection, noted that competition, not imports, was H-D's major problem. Both Honda and Kawasaki had plants in the United States and their bikes would not be affected by the tariff. And she added, "the blue-collar workers who buy these things are unemployed."[101]

The pairing of motorcyclists and conservative politicians also smacked of contradiction. The motorcyclist's association with drugs and guns had the potential to conjure up fears about the lawless and disorderly behavior conservatives had been using for political gain during the previous two decades, and the motorcyclist's unconventional lifestyle challenged the family values that had come to dominate conservative thinking. The politics of family that had its origins with Nixon's silent majority found its ultimate expression, Robert O. Self argues, "in opposition to the broad liberal left's idea of expanded citizenship"—a conception of citizenship that included gays, lesbians, feminists, and "nonconformists of all sorts."[102] Those nonconformists included a range of 1960s rebels, but we cannot forget the defining image of the motorcyclist, the Easy Rider: the ionic rebel of the 1960s, also known as a hippie on a bike.

Yet motorcyclists were as likely to affirm these values as challenge them. The motorcycle rights movement did not simply allow riders to assert their rights as citizens but helped them defy age-old stereotypes about violent and disorderly behavior and challenge expanded definitions of citizenship that had evolved out of the fight over gender and sexual identity. Motorcyclists may not have been social conservatives, and their status as breadwinners was always in doubt, but they embraced the conventional male behavior that was at the center of a coalition that developed between social conservatives and neoliberals—motorcyclists were unabashedly patriotic and male, white and heterosexual, and antigovernment and antifeminist—characteristics that conservatives were identifying with in their fight to save the nation.

Indeed, Reagan's role in bringing motorcyclists and conservatives together cannot be overstated. For the generations of Americans who came of age after World War II, the 1970s was not simply a decade when a Cold War consensus began to crumble but a moment when Americans were confronted with the realization that there were limits to U.S. power and influence. A decade that began with the bitter end of a tumultuous war and the shock of an oil embargo (1973) ended with the collapse of America's manufacturing base and a hostage crisis in Iran.[103] Reagan successfully tapped into and played on the frustration Americans had been dealing with to promote his campaign against big government and to promote himself as a champion of freedom—themes central to his campaign and to his presidency.[104] What better way for him to highlight his commitment to these values than to save the last American motorcycle manufacturer, as opposed to the scorn he faced if he let it collapse.[105] During the summer of 1982, and just before the tariff was passed, Willie G. Davidson, chief styling officer at H-D and grandson of cofounder William A. Davidson, summed up the potential political fallout and the tariff's benefits for those support- ers: "The red, white, and blue loyalty of Harley-Davidson's customers is extraordinary."[106]

To be sure, when Reagan first addressed the tariff issue in 1983, his enthusiasm for the company and its riders was subdued—perhaps masked by his concern about the tariff's challenge to his stance on free trade. But as the company became profitable by 1987 and had voluntarily ended the tariff, Reagan embraced H-D as "the home of the all-American A-team," and he thumbed his nose at the naysayers who questioned the wisdom of his decision and the capabilities of Harley-Davidson's workers. "The people who say that American workers and American companies can't compete are making one of the oldest mistakes in the world. They're betting against America itself, and that's one bet no one will ever win." Addressing a warehouse full of workers at the York plant in 1987, Reagan exclaimed, "I'll bet on you," and "on America." Reagan continued by prais- ing the workers' "basic American values of hard work and fair play" and concluded by suggesting that Harley, along with the men who rode the bikes, was an appropriate barometer to gauge the country's progress and its vigor. Reagan noted that, "like America, Harley is back and standing tall," and he concluded his speech by emphasizing two points: "America is a special place," and "We're on the road to unprecedented prosperity in this country—and we'll get there on a Harley!"[107]

Reagan's nationalism neatly pigeonholed with the patriotism David- son suggested was well established among H-D owners, and it publicly acknowledged the administration's connection to age-old biker values and the connection of those values to the broader conservative shift of which motorcyclists were increasingly accepted as a part. After all, other industries were asking for similar types of protectionism, and they were consistently ignored, even though these industries had a much more profound impact on the United States' larger economic outlook than motorcycle manufacturing. The American textile industry, for example, routinely found congressional support for stiffer tariffs, but that support was undermined each time with a presidential veto from Reagan, and the steel industry was desperate for quotas on imported steel to try to save the U.S. industry. Shortly after having approved of the increase in tariffs on imported motorcycles, President Reagan made an appearance in Pittsburgh, Pennsylvania, to defend his free-trade policy while thousands of protestors stood in the rain outside the hotel where he spoke. The jobless rate in Pittsburgh was over 16 percent.[108]

Indeed, Reagan's support for Harley-Davidson highlights his relationship to the working class in the 1980s and his propensity to favor a politics of identity instead of one that valued economic substance for working men and women. Earlier in the decade Nixon had unsuccessfully attempted to win over labor with what Jefferson Cowie describes as his working-class strategy, but the scandal surrounding his administration undoubtedly helped to undermine that effort. Nixon lacked the confidence and personality that Reagan is remembered for, and he was too unsure about his own masculinity to try to appropriate someone else's. But it was the vitality of the working class that was particularly difficult to overcome. The early years of the 1970s was a time of optimism for labor that was marked by the most significant strike wave since 1946, a public discourse dominated by working-class issues, and an unprecedented embrace of the working class in popular culture. By the end of the 1970s, Cowie argues, that optimism would turn to disillusionment and defeat. "After a complex and multilayered revival of working-class issues in the seventies, there was a sense," argues Cowie, "that it was not simply that specific groups of workers were defeated at specific places, but that the very idea of workers as an economic subject in civic and popular discourse was defeated." The response, Cowie continues, was a "reasonable adjustment to dwindling material rewards [on the part of blue-collar white males] by accepting the psychic rewards of cultural authority within the Republican party," what Cowie describes as "sort of white, working-class identity politics with a lot of cultural authority but dwindling economic substance." Cowie notes that the void that developed out of the failure of liberalism to "bolster its social agenda with economic backbone" allowed the Republicans "to fill the gap in people's politics," separate the working class from its traditional home in the Democratic Party, and transform the meaning of class in the post-Vietnam era. "Blue-collar conservatism," Cowie argues, "works for one simple reason: class in

America today is a cultural category not an economic one." The American working class, he adds "doesn't have an economic identity as much as it has one defined by culture, race, and gender."[109]

The shift Cowie describes coincided with and was supported by a motorcycle rights movement that shared an understanding of identity politics that was based in culture, not class experience. The outlaw's emergence in the 1940s would lead eventually to fears about violence and reckless behavior, but from the start small-town America had questions about his link to a work ethic and to the working-class communities of which he was a part. By the 1970s, the idea that the typical motorcyclist was also a worker or had any obvious link to the working class was increasingly difficult to find. While the motorcycle rights movement helped challenge stereotypes about lawlessness and disorder, it promoted a political agenda that lacked a distinct working-class component, even as it embraced a working-class cultural sensibility. The movement not only promoted ideas about freedom and individuality that defied and transcended class boundaries but saw those ideas as fundamental to the experience of riding and not a reflection of the needs of wage earners. By the 1960s and 1970s, the traditional rider's rejection of a class-based identity located in the workplace was becoming more conspicuous as more middle-class riders embraced a version of motorcycling that was firmly embedded in their identity as professionals.

Reagan's attempt to align himself with motorcyclists was a political strategy that suggested a particular affinity for the working class but without all the class-based politics for which working men and women had become known. Should we be surprised that Reagan had gone against his own avowed free-trade ideology to save Harley-Davidson? A former actor who fancied himself a cowboy, Reagan was as conscious of the importance of appearance as any politician of his day and sympathetic to a Cold War toughness that often struggled to recognize any nuance or complexity. Reagan came to power amid a rejuvenated ultranationalistic patriotism that would only intensify with his bitter diatribes against the Soviet Union, an increasingly inflated military budget, and the growing presence of U.S. troops worldwide. The motorcyclist's typical image was one that had been routinely vilified as a threat to all that was good and wholesome (and American) but what now seemed altogether appropriate amid the anxiety of the post-Vietnam era and the economic malaise that had sapped American men's strength and resolve. The ground on which male dominance and gender relations rested had been challenged successfully in the fifties, sixties, and seventies, argues Susan Jeffords, but rather than accept these changes, men simply renegotiated the base on which their dominance rested and worked on what Jeffords describes as "remasculization," a "revival of the images, abilities, and evaluations of men and masculinity in dominant U.S. culture."[110] Motorcyclists were one example of this strategy, which allowed Republicans to meet these different challenges. They were what one of Reagan's staff members referred to as the "bluest of blue" workers[111] who were stridently in support of individual rights, and they were tough, uncompromising, and authentic, values the conservative right was particularly fond of as it attempted to make common cause with the working man and convince him to abandon earlier party affiliations and values. Americans could try to achieve this ideal by voting Republican and by riding a Harley, and they were doing both in the 1980s.

In his discussion about this political transformation, Cowie overstates the degree to which Republicans filled "the gap in people's politics." The rise of an outlaw sensibility was accompanied by the motorcyclist's embrace of freedom and his bitterness over federal encroachment. By the 1960s and 1970s, that connection was more obvious, even as fears about the lawless and disorderly outlaw motorcyclist had become more conspicuous. The motorcycle rights movement brought these issues to bear and provided a link to a conservative movement that had become more vocal about freedom and the need to limit big government. But there is no evidence to suggest that motorcyclists were actively pursuing this alliance. The motorcyclists' focus on votes and constituents often meant alliances with any politician willing to support their agenda, and motorcyclists often viewed themselves as leading the fight for the rights of all Americans. Conservatives, on the other hand, recognized the potential benefits from this relationship. The helmet issue raised questions about the government's role that other Americans could identify with, freedom and patriotism had become a central tenet of the Harley-Davidson brand and fundamental to the motorcycle rights movement, and the motorcyclist's grit and determination made sense in light of the political movements of the period that routinely called into question traditional gender arrangements. Republicans had struggled in the past to successfully attract a working-class constituency and still struggled to fully appreciate a working-class cultural sensibility even though they were beginning to recognize the potential electoral benefits from working-class votes. Motorcyclists forged a political movement that not only successfully challenged federal control of the helmet question but also influenced the ways in which the Right imagined itself in the post-Vietnam era.

Indeed, Harley-Davidson's turnaround was linked more likely to the constituency Reagan and the Right had always found support from but who benefited specifically from this political realignment. The economy in general during the late 1970s and 1980s was undergoing significant reorganization in the wake of out-of-control energy costs, deindustrialization, and competition from foreign manufacturers. In this climate a staggering number of corporations went out of business, moved out of the United States in search of lower labor costs, or were purchased and dismantled or merged with other companies. Markets also fluctuated widely and were unstable, and fortunes were lost and made overnight. But opportunity flourished in the legal profession and in finance. Reagan's cuts to social programs and reductions in taxes for the wealthy and for corporations further exacerbated the disparity between rich and poor. In this atmosphere, conservatives identified the "welfare queen" as the root of all evil and celebrated the yuppie or young urban professional.[112]

The yuppie first attracted attention during the 1984 Democratic primary season and Gary Hart's bid for the nomination. In some stories Hart exhibited characteristics yuppies admired: "independence from old ideas and political structures; a pragmatic, nonideological approach to problems and a rejection of the cynicism that developed in the Vietnam and Watergate eras."[113] There was debate about the title: Were they urban or mobile— hence yumpies? Conservative or liberal? One contemporary, for example, described them as "less concerned about unemployment than other age groups . . . inclined to favor further cuts in Federal spending . . . [and] less likely . . . to favor income maintenance programs." But on social issues, they "strongly favor the equal rights amendment . . . freedom of choice on abortion, and oppose employment discrimination against homosexuals."[114] Others identified an independent streak and saw the rise of the yuppie as a reflection of the disdain for established political parties and their constituents. Deborah Dreyfuss, who worked for the *Chicago Tribune* and was a Hart delegate, explained that "the establishment is Republican, and the working class is Democratic, and being independent sounds a lot cooler."[115] "Whatever we call this political development," argued Deborah J. Knuth in a letter to the *New York Times*, "it comes of not very enlightened self-interest, and in November we may end up calling the group [yuppies] 'Republicans.'"[116]

There was, however, less disagreement about the typical yuppie's income and educational level, which were on the high side, and his or her association with certain consumer tastes: Rolex watches, Gucci briefcases, L.L. Bean duck hunting boots, Perrier and other designer waters, and increasingly Harley-Davidson motorcycles. Indeed, the motorcycle's version of the yuppie was the rich urban biker (RUB), often referred to as a rubbie, who appeared first in the late 1980s. A *Wall Street Journal* reporter noticed the RUB after more than 100 motorcycles roared into a parking garage in 1988. "Hell's Angels on a tear" was her initial reaction, but then she noticed "some of these bikes are baby pink, lilac, and mint green. The black leather jackets look too new, some of the riders too well-coiffed." The riders were RUBs, what Michael Blatter, a thirty-year-old advertising executive, described as a "yuppie in disguise." Another contemporary referred to the "nouveau biker" who wears "leather and jeans," although different from those of the stereotypical motorcyclist. "They're kind of clean," she explained, and "you can smell the conditioner in their hair." A more precise definition described them as "Baby Boomers of the rebellious 60's now in cushy jobs, plus other affluent would-be Brandos," who were "tearing themselves from their *Easy Rider* videos to join trendy new motorcycle clubs."[117] They were engineers, businessmen, politicians, accountants, and even Hollywood actors. One member of the Gotham City Riders Motorcycle Club, which was featured in a *New York Times* piece on RUBs, described his club as "an anti-corporate corporate group" whose newsletter included wine recommendations.[118]

Yet, unlike the middle-class and professional men and women who were attracted to motorcycling in the mid-1960s, these riders agreed that "Harley-Davidson rules." Harleys were the "must-have items for those who must have everything." The slogan "If you don't ride a Harley you ain't shit" required a minor revision to fit well with the RUB: "If you don't ride a Harley, you ain't rich." At a Los Angeles club popular among RUBs, dental assistant Debbie Searcy, who described "guys on motorcycles" as "sexy," made this shift apparent: Bikers "used to be hoods . . . [but] now it's materialistic."[119]

Indeed, in the late 1980s and early 1990s Harley-Davidson's dramatic turnaround was linked to the upscale or gentrified biker. In 1990 the *Wall Street Journal* reported that the "aura of tattooed Hell's Angels and *Easy Rider*–era hippies became as much a liability for Harley-Davidson as an asset." "Hurt by leaky, unreliable bikes and plunging market share, the lone American motorcycle maker was brushing up against bankruptcy." Less than a decade later the company had found a "huge new market" and was busy "enticing white-collar workers to become weekend warriors." "Officials" had successfully targeted what the paper called "the yuppie generation." In 1990 about 60 percent of Harley riders had attended college, up from 45 percent in 1984, one in three was a professional or manager, and the median household income had risen from $36,000 in 1985 to $45,000 in 1990. The author explained that Harley-Davidson had captured these professional riders by broadening the "bike's appeal while keeping them looking big, mean and American" and by improving the engine's reliability and style. Harley's management "realized that although blue-collar buyers, loyal and mechanically inclined, might put up with a bike needing frequent attention, the new generation of Harley riders wouldn't." H-D also "brighten[ed] up their stores with more lights . . . slapped the Harley name on cologne and wine coolers. . . [and] even competed with biker clubs such as Hell's Angels with their own Harley Owners Group [HOG]."[120]

By the early 1990s Harley's turnaround was complete, and the *National Review*'s speculation about the average rider's political transformation was hard to ignore. Although the rebellious outlaw of the 1940s was not forgotten, only more violent in some accounts and seemingly harmless in others—the motorcyclist became identified with the conservative political shift of the postwar years: Harleys were now a status symbol for professional riders. This shift was a reflection not only of the Republican Party's interest in the helmet question but also of its economic policies that favored the wealthy even as it claimed a certain affinity for working-class culture. The broader economic challenges facing Americans in the postwar years translated into very explicit cultural changes that upset motorcycle culture and transformed grassroots politics. Indeed, motorcyclists are an excellent example of the contradictions that make up political coalitions but also the role those contradictions can play in shaping attitudes about image, policy, and identity. In the case of the Republican Party, the contradictions contributed to its political success on the national stage even though the policies it ultimately pursued favored the gentrified motorcyclist over his working-class counterpart, whose role in motorcycle culture was waning. In sum, the Republicans pursued a popular agenda that ultimately undermined the very group they were attempting to be identified with and in some cases emulate. The fight over helmet laws attracted some of the most vocal apologists of the Republican Party, whose pursuit of a political agenda was more of a question of political expedience than a genuine concern for the rights of working men and women or the rights of the two-wheeled enthusiasts who had attracted their attention in the first place.

This shift among motorcyclists also helped them address the questions of citizenship and social belonging that had hounded them throughout much of the postwar period. The middle-class rider of the 1960s and 1970s challenged his exclusion more successfully than his working-class counterpart from earlier decades had done. He was routinely depicted as a clean-cut suburbanite whose consumption helped fuel the nation's prosperity and shaped its national identity. But he also made the outlaw motorcyclist appear to be more of a threat than he was, was denounced for the divide over helmets, and blamed for the end of the golden (working-class) age of motorcycling. The yuppie biker (or RUB) of the 1980s and 1990s emerged out of these conflicts and helped resolve them. Rejecting the Japanese bikes, he preferred the Harley, a bike that embraced a certain ruggedness that defied the malaise of the post-Vietnam era. He also embodied the values that promoted his inclusion: Harleys symbolized patriotism and, being American made, represented an American triumph in an increasingly global and free market. In the immediate postwar years, motorcyclists hinted at their support of free trade and free markets. Brand-name loyalty was denounced as a manipulation of the consumer and the marketplace and a threat to free trade, as was the government's helmet law requirement, which had given helmet manufactures a distinct advantage that undermined consumer choice.[121]

Against the backdrop of Harley's comeback and a developing neoliberal consensus (or imagination), the motorcyclist had become the ideal citizen/ consumer. He was as free as the markets around which he organized his consumption and shaped his identity, and he benefited from a class privilege that was a direct consequence of the disadvantaged working man who at one time had dominated motorcycling. He had the advantage because those free markets were opening up previously untapped cheap and easily exploitable labor that were at the root of his increasingly prosperous lifestyle and advantaged because it ensured the middle-class rider's dominance of motorcycling and its values. The working man's preoccupation for motorcycling was supported by good paying (often unionized) industrial jobs that provided him the wherewithal and leisure time away from work. Indeed, throughout the first few decades after World War II, midwestern states with heavy industry had the highest number of motorcycle registrations in the country (with the exception of California). By the end of the 1980s, deindustrialization had taken its toll, and the unemployed were facing free markets that cared more for the bottom dollar than the men and women who lost those jobs. The beneficiaries were increasingly located in the Sunbelt South, where government-sponsored programs and a perpetual state of military expansion helped nurture the rise of conservatism and a Sunbelt South where growing numbers of motorcyclists resided.[122]

AFTER THE GEORGIA LEGISLATURE's House Motor Vehicle Committee killed a helmet repeal bill in 1977, Big Red, a resident of Martinez, Georgia, and a member of ABATE, explained that "it tears the guts out of me to realize that the government doesn't give a damn what the citizens want" and added that the bill's disappointing defeat and the government's indifference "sure as hell wasn't what I spent 20 years serving in the army to achieve. Just maybe I should have spent those 20 fighting our own government and its officials." Red's frustration was common among riders throughout the 1970s, and it was particularly conspicuous during the early years of struggle against helmet laws. The slogan "Helmet Laws Suck" was a reflection of that frustration, which often revealed a divide within motorcycle culture. One of Red's particular complaints focused on a Representative Lucas, who had offended him when he dismissed "his faithful old hawg" as a machine "that vibrates parts off while running down the road . . . even though he professes to be a motorcyclist [he owned a Kawasaki 900]."[123] After speculating about his missed opportunity to "fight the government," Red made it clear that what really bothered him was Lucas's shortcoming as a representative. "I've informed the bikers around the Macon area that it's up to them to convince him, as their elected representative, that he should be more responsive to their feelings and leave his own personal feelings at home. The word, 'Representative,' doesn't mean philosopher," he argued, "but rather, one who reflects the attitudes and opinions of those who elect him to office. I would doubt rather seriously that the motorcyclists of Macon share in his opinions."[124]

Red's focus on the government and individual rights caught the attention of politicians, and conservatives began to speak out about helmet laws. While this alliance did not break clearly along party lines, especially in states where the movement was strongest, and the Right was often concerned more about the ideological advantage of supporting motorcycle rights than the problems facing riders, by the end of the 1970s and early 1980s this alliance was difficult to ignore, and the AMA was openly (and financially) supporting conservatives. Motorcyclists undoubtedly challenged the Right's fantasy about "law and order" that was becoming more conspicuous at about the same time that the outlaw motorcyclist was attracting national attention. Yet motorcyclists were too promising a political constituency to overlook. Their authenticity was unquestionable, as was their embrace of freedom, and they had an uncompromising toughness Republicans yearned to be identified with as they made a play to gain control of the national political stage.

That toughness directly reflected the efforts to mobilize a grassroots campaign against helmet laws and all the baggage associated with outlaw riders that became even more obvious as middle-class riders began to attract attention. But it was also the product of a much larger political debate about gender and race that are critical to understanding the conservative ascendency of the postwar years. These issues affected motorcycle culture well before helmet laws were passed and are the focus of the next two chapters.

6

THE LAST MALE REFUGE

Women Riders, the Counterculture, and the Struggle over Gender

In October 1965 members of the Oakland chapter of the Hells Angels disrupted a peace march to protest U.S. policy in Vietnam. The Vietnam Day Committee sponsored the march that started in Berkeley and ended at the Oakland boundary some two miles away. The city of Oakland had refused the permit needed for the march, and organizers had agreed to stop the march before it crossed into Oakland. According to the *Los Angeles Times*, eighteen members of the Hells Angels Motorcycle Club, whom the paper described as "unkempt and husky," had gathered at the Oakland-Berkeley boundary as the march began. Oakland police had initially formed a cordon in front of the motorcyclists but left them "unguarded as the parade approached the city line." When the marchers were about two hundred feet from the city limit, the Hells Angels stepped into the street, and several of them moved to the front row of the parade column. The Hells Angels then rushed forward and snatched a protest banner, briefly retreated back, only to return again "shouting obscenities at the marchers." Moments later the cyclists "advanced on the marchers with fists ready to strike." The police immediately intervened and in the "ensuing clash" a police sergeant, Claude D. Glenn, broke his leg, and one member of the Hells Angels, Michael Walter (Tiny), was hospitalized after a police officer struck him in the head with a nightstick. "None of the marchers," the *Times* reported, "was injured."[1]

Scholars and journalists have pointed to incidents like this one and other moments of violence to try to understand motorcyclists, their views about the war in Vietnam, and their relationship to the counterculture.[2] What they have not done is connect this moment to the larger history of motorcycling and to the era's broader political challenges. The Hells

Angels' disruption of the march was not an isolated moment of violence against the counterculture.[3] While violence was the motorcyclist's most potent expression of opposition, it was often articulated in cultural terms, inextricably linked to the larger political movements of the day, and often focused as much on the protestors as on the cause that brought them into contact with motorcyclists.

On the Berkeley-Oakland border that day in 1965, for example, the Hells Angels' patriotism was conspicuous, but they did not simply object to the marchers because they considered their actions disloyal. The motorcyclists belittled the antiwar activists as "cowards" and "yellow," and attempted to stomp them—a most traditional of male prerogatives. Their response provides considerable insight into how issues of gender shaped motorcyclists and their fears about the antiwar movement and the men and women who supported it. The motorcyclists were very conventional in their masculinity—husky, strong, brash, and suspicious of any men who were not. The men they attacked on the Oakland boundary not only defied this basic understanding of gender but also exposed a patriotic side to the motorcyclist that was generally overshadowed by his reputation for disorderly and antisocial behavior.

Conflicts surrounding the Vietnam War and the antiwar movement are the most well-known examples of this phenomenon thanks to the notoriety of the Hells Angels. But conflict involved motorcyclists from all walks of life, and it was just as conspicuous in response to women's rights, gay liberation, and the African American Freedom Struggle.[4] For example, fears about "love beads," "long hair," and homosexuality were just as prominent as the clamor over patriotism and just as critical to understanding the ways in which motorcyclists understood citizenship and what it meant to be an American.[5] Alliances between motorcyclists and these different groups would emerge, but outright opposition to these activists was also just as conspicuous if not the overwhelming response to them. Against the backdrop of these larger social and political movements, the motorcyclist represented a contradiction. The nonriding majority may have identified motorcyclists with hippies and a left-leaning, liberal sentiment—the Easy Rider—but conventional ideas about gender and sexual identity frequently overshadowed the motorcyclist's rebelliousness, and he was as likely to be at odds with the movements he was identified with as to be supportive of them.

These conflicts were also just as prominent within motorcycling. The signature look of rebellion that is identified with Hollister after the late 1940s also became linked to gay men wanting to project a more vigorous image of masculinity. By the 1960s and 1970s, and in light of the gay liberation movement, fears of effeminacy would be more acute than during the preceding two decades and give rise to the stereotype that "all bikers are gay." The overwhelming response from male riders was less of an effort to downplay it than to exaggerate a heterosexual prerogative. Outlaws were in fact notorious for embracing homoerotic play as a way to shock the "squares" even as motorcycle culture was becoming so consciously heterosexual and homophobic. By the 1960s and 1970s, for example, women's participation was growing, but so was the commodification of women's bodies in motorcycle culture, typified by the appearance of the scantily clad motorcycle model. Women openly challenged their subordinate status, but those challenges generally failed to solve the problems women faced. Fears about a predominantly same-sex male culture combined with the growing influence of a motorcycle rights movement that adamantly opposed any and all forms of regulation—be they helmet laws or efforts to censor what became known as the biker chick—undermined women's influence on motorcycle culture even as their participation as motorcyclists empowered them as women and as riders.

GENDER

The cowboy was one of the most important cultural influences shaping American masculinity and motorcycling culture throughout the postwar period. "Over 10 percent of all fictional works published in the 1950s were westerns," according to Michael Kimmel, "and eight of the top ten television shows—a total of thirty prime-time television shows in all—were 'horse operas.'" In 1958 alone, fifty-four western feature films were made. Rodeos also experienced a renaissance during this same time; families headed off to dude ranches; and young boys had their own boy westerns like *Old Yeller* or television shows like *Lassie, My Friend Flicka,* and *Fury*, which generally involved a boy's loving relationship with one or several pets. The western, Kimmel argues, "provide[d] the re-creation of the frontier, the 'meeting point between civilization and savagery,' where real men, men who were good with a horse and a gun, triumphed over unscrupulous bankers and other rogue versions of Self-Made Manhood."[6]

Since at least the 1920s motorcyclists have been compared to cowboys but during the second half of the century those comparisons became commonplace. Gary Kieffner notes that film studios released more than forty biker movies between 1966 and 1973 and describes those films as a "continuation of the cowboy image outside the Western genre." Since the 1970s, Kieffner notes, "bikers have worn boots (often cowboy boots), chaps and big belt buckles over their denim jeans, and bandanas while their steel steeds were equipped with saddles, buckhorn handlebars, latigo saddle-bags, Conchos, and other functional or decorative items that originated with cowboy culture."[7]

By the late 1960s, some evidence suggests that the motorcyclist was beginning to overshadow the cowboy. In a 1968 *Esquire* article, Tom Wolfe claimed that the motorcycle movie, what he referred to as the "groovy movie," had replaced the Western as "Hollywood's staple product for the young." The hero of the groovy movie, he argued, has the "same role as the hero of the western": the "broad shouldered stud like Buck Jones, Gene Autry, Tex Ritter, John Wayne or Bob Steele who would travel through the badlands for you" and "face the bad gangs for you,"—cattle rustlers, cattle ranchers, or Indians. The hero of the groovy movie did the "same thing," according to Wolfe, although with a slightly different cast of characters and a different location. He had "skinny shoulders like Peter Fonda, Arlo Guthrie, Dustin Hoffman, Christopher Jones, Bruce Davidson" and traveled through the badlands, which included "almost any part of America outside of a few groovy sections of Manhattan, San Francisco and Los Angeles." He also faced off against men who were as much of a threat as any outlaw the cowboy faced: "the police, the pigs . . . and those vigilante types who travel around the South in pickup trucks with goiters on their necks and shotguns in the rack across the rear window." This cast of characters stood in sharp contrast to the stock western that Americans had grown accustomed to, but Wolfe argued, "It's all the same, the Western or the Groovy Movie."[8]

Wolfe's version of the motorcyclist is the classic example of the romanticized hero roaming the outer reaches of civilized society to protect those who are least able to protect themselves. The film *Easy Rider* figures prominently in his version of motorcycling, including the cast of criminal types like the "redneck" who appeared in the film and murdered Peter Fonda's and Dennis Hopper's characters as well as the political undertone of his version, which leaned in a similar direction as the hippies in *Easy Rider*. The bad guys were the corporate types, the establishment, and those entrusted to enforce law and order but instead abused it for their own personal or political gain at the expense of our civil liberties and rights. Motorcyclists, in sum, were part, if not a prominent symbol, of a younger generation of Americans who had been emboldened politically in the wake of apparent contradictions surrounding American affluence and power, and that image reflected, in part, the American romance with the cowboy.[9]

During this same time, however, other forces began to eclipse the cowboy's influence on motorcycling, and questions of sexual identity were particularly prominent. The postwar years saw the rise of gay liberation that unsettled gender and sexual identities, and well before that, the gay motorcyclist had become a noticeable influence on all of motorcycle culture. In his fascinating study, *Gay New York*, set during the first half of the twentieth century, George Chauncey notes that as gay men in the mid-1940s became increasingly uncomfortable with charges of effeminacy, they began adopting a more masculine look and style that included, among other things, blue jeans and leather jackets, a style that was also identified with one of the most masculine rebels of the 1940s and 1950s, the motorcyclist.[10] Postwar gay erotica that appeared in the pages of *Physique Pictorial* also featured a host of working-class icons, including the motorcyclist. The photographs and drawings featured men seated on the motorcycle in various stages of undress or using the motorcycle as a makeshift cot they could lay back on—head resting on the gas tank and entirely naked from the waist down. Tom of Finland is the most well-known artist associated with these images, but other artists' drawings of the gay, erotic motorcyclist were also circulating throughout the 1950s and 1960s. A gay leather subculture has also generally been linked to post–World War II motorcycle culture and Los Angeles–based clubs like the Satyrs (1954) or Oedipus (1958). The Satyrs remains an active club to this day, and members describe it as "the oldest, continuously-running gay organization in the world."[11]

Many Americans' introduction to gay culture came from the media's growing interest in homosexuality in the early 1960s in which the gay motorcyclist was prominent. *Harper's* magazine featured a story titled "New York's Middle-Class Homosexuals" in March 1963 that was followed up with a front-page *New York Times* piece on homosexuality in December. Then in June 1964 *Life* magazine ran an article titled "Homosexuality in America" that began by describing homosexuality as a "secret world" that "grows open and bolder." The essay's opening image was a photograph of the Tool Box, a gay motorcycle bar in San Francisco located on the corner of Fourth and Harrison in what is known as South of the Slot or South of Market. The Tool Box was initially funded by a group of Los Angeles investors and quickly became what Martin Meeker describes as the northern home to southern California-based motorcycle clubs like the Satyrs and Oedipus and San Francisco–based motorcycle clubs like the Warlocks. The photograph included men dressed in the familiar Marlon Brando style: leather jackets and caps, blue jeans, and dark sunglasses, against the backdrop of a mural of distinctly masculine-looking men whose features were similar to those men who appeared in the sports pages of newspapers or in department store catalogs that featured men's clothing.[12]

The recognition of gay men in the media and their link to motorcycling was profound and gave rise to an increasingly common stereotype that all motorcyclists were gay. In his correspondence with Peter Tamony about the naming of the Hells Angels, R. W. Burchfield, editor of the *Oxford English Dictionary* supplement, cited a 1967 article by G. Legman, titled "The Fake Revolt," as the earliest usage of Hells Angels. The article refers to the club as "The hoodlum drug-addicts and homosexual motorcyclists."[13] In 1965 a University of Nebraska student contacted the FBI requesting information about the Hells Angels for a term paper, noting that it was "difficult to obtain information about them." J. Edgar Hoover's response avoided specifics, citing Department of Justice regulations about confidentiality, but he did mention the club's link to "various crimes" and noted that "some of the group have been classified as homosexual and as narcotic users."[14] Indeed, "kissing as ritual," as one newspaper headline described the act, became associated with outlaw motorcyclists in the 1960s and undoubtedly contributed to the ambiguity surrounding the motorcyclist's sexuality. In the opening scene of *Hells Angels on Wheels* (1967) two groups of motorcyclists converge on the outskirts of a city—one group led by one of the film's stars (Adam Roarke) and the other headed up by Sonny Barger, then president of the Oakland chapter of the Hells Angels. As the two groups of riders meet, Barger quickly hops off his bike, embraces Roarke, and passionately kisses him on the mouth. He just as quickly jumps back on to his bike, and the two groups head off together.[15] That same year two of the three motorcyclists who were accused of nailing a girl to a tree in Florida "kissed passionately in a court-house hallway . . . to 'snap the minds of citizens' " after a judge ordered them back to jail under bonds raised from ten thousand to fifteen thousand. The paper referred to the jailed cyclists as "smoochers" and claimed that "kissing among male members is part of the motorcyclists' ritualistic mystique."[16]

Some men simply internalized the public's assumptions that "all bikers are gay" and feared their interest in motorcycling was a sign of their homosexuality. Dr. Armand M. Nicholi II of Harvard's Medical School, for example, had been treating college motorcyclists for years for what he diagnosed as a "motorcycle syndrome." In an article that appeared in the *American Journal of Psychiatry*, Nicholi claimed that his patients had a "day-and-night preoccupation with the machine" and "saw their cycles as extensions of their masculine selves." One student described the experience of riding as "a very physical almost sexual feeling. You accelerate fast and there is nothing between you and nature. . . . My new machine has a huge motor. With this under me I feel I can do anything I want to."[17] Off their machines they had an "acute awareness of [their] inadequacy" and a "tenuous masculine identification," which Nicholi linked to the relationship problems they had with their fathers who were successful, demanding, and critical. Nicholi's cyclists found it hopeless to try and be like their fathers, and they used their motorcycles to "compensate for feelings of effeminacy and weakness." They were both "promiscuous" and impotent, Nicholi concluded, but also accident prone and "always worried about being labeled homosexual."[18]

Other men contested the link to homosexuality by targeting the gay motorcyclist. After a viewing of *Scorpio Rising*, an underground film featuring leather-clad bikers and pseudo-Fascist iconography,[19] one biker complained about having "to listen to all this crap about us being queers. Shit, did you see the way those punks were dressed? And those silly goddamn junkwagon bikes? Man, don't tell me that has any connection with us. You know it doesn't."[20]

In 1972 *Easyriders* magazine also addressed the all-bikers-are-gay stereotype with a cartoon featuring the "husky" biker. The cartoon included a man speaking to a bartender unaware of the two bikers standing behind him. The caption below reads, "Personally, I think all those silly bikers are a bunch of queers!" The bikers appear in what had become a typical look by the early to mid-1970s: broad-shouldered and barrel-chested, with a respectable gut (sometimes), especially beefy forearms that are disproportionate to his much skinnier legs, shoulder-length hair (usually helmetless), moustache and beard (or unshaven), and dressed in jeans and a jean jacket with the sleeves torn off. It was a body seemingly fit for the bigger Harleys and custom cycles that graced the magazine's pages and a body that *Easyriders* was convinced was heterosexual. It was often bruised, battered, broken, and possibly disabled. A story that appeared in the *Saturday Evening Post* in 1954 that characterized motorcyclists as the most "unpopular men on the road" argued that motorcycling "seem[ed] to attract a certain number of the handicapped—men with poor sight, no hearing, a missing leg or other physical disabilities."[21] Hunter Thompson made a similar comment about disabled riders in his now famous book about riding with the Hells Angels in the mid-1960s. Hunter notes, "After being around the Angels for a while I became so accustomed to seeing casts, bandages, slings and lumpy faces that I took them for granted and stopped asking what happened."[22] Their bodies were neither refined nor sculpted and certainly not the product of the (industrial) discipline and routinization required of the men who were heading off to weight rooms in the second half of the 1970s and early 1980s.[23] The fine features of the man who made the "all bikers are gay" comment—the elongated face and chin and the delicate manner in which he holds his cigarette—not only stand in sharp contrast to the bikers'—the round faces and fixed unemotional gaze—but he also appears less masculine, more effeminate, and not nearly as heterosexual as the two bikers standing behind him. The diminutive size of the man and the barkeeper is so pronounced, one can only wonder if the two of them could ride a motorcycle if they had wanted to. The outcome of this unfortunate and ill-timed comment is assumed: the bikers effortlessly stomping the much smaller man into the ground. The cartoon plays on the stereotype that all bikers are gay but swiftly challenges it with the assumption of violence and the image of the husky biker.

Indeed, size (and increasingly girth) was one of the easiest ways to counter any suspicion or assumptions the uninitiated may have had about motorcyclists—a sort of "he's so masculine" pretense or bravado that allowed men to more easily cross those (sexual) boundaries if they wanted to, even as they challenged the very idea that they had. To be sure, the bigger Harleys often required bigger riders, and anyone who has ever watched a motorcyclist struggling to pick up a fallen-over motorcycle that can weigh hundreds of pounds can attest to that. But this image was often more imagined than real and the product of the growing acknowledgment of other sexual identities. All men struggled to understand the boundaries surrounding gender and sexuality, but the issue could be especially prominent among men who identified with a culture that was so thoroughly same sex. The "all bikers are queer" stereotype represented very real circumstances (from gay men and gay motorcyclists), and the struggles surrounding it shaped everything from style, body type, and image—hence the pervasiveness of the stereotype and the potential for violence surrounding it.[24]

This particular masculinity and body type was also taking shape at the same time that the gay macho appears first in New York and San Francisco discos. Gay macho was that distinctive look among young gay men in the 1970s—leather jackets and jeans, short hair and a lean, sculpted body from the increasingly popular workout regimes on the new Nautilus weight machines, a body built specifically for the disco scene and for dancing shirtless. Gay men, as Alice Echols argues, had been challenging the association of homosexuality with effeminacy since at least the 1910s. By the postwar period that association began to weaken, and by the mid-1960s "masculine gay men were becoming a discernable presence even beyond

Campsite at City Park, Sturgis, in 1979. Note the artificial limb propped up against a bike's back tire. Courtesy of Michael Lichter.

the gay community." The gay macho, Echols adds, was viewed simultaneously as a parody of conventional or normative masculinity, a masculinity that made "gay men utterly indistinguishable from straight boys," and a masculinity that was "meticulous" and lacked the "casualness that marked the self-presentation of straight men."[25] Regardless of how it was described, it was a masculinity that stood in sharp relief to the image of the biker that was developing during these same years, an image that was certainly not meant for dancing and one motorcyclists equated with heterosexuality. Indeed, if the typical heterosexual style was casual (using Alice Echol's language), the motorcyclist was not—more disheveled, grungier, and what often came off as sloppy.

The image of the husky biker continues to influence popular culture's imagination about size and motorcyclists. Arnold Schwarzenegger, who defined the action star during the last two decades of the twentieth century, became a recognizable Hollywood star as *Conan the Barbarian* (1982), but his most memorable role is that of the *Terminator* (1984), especially *Terminator 2: Judgment Day* (1991). The movie begins with the Terminator traveling to our time, his initial encounter with a biker, and the iconic words that followed: "I need your clothes, your boots, and your motorcycle." The biker laughs and puts his cigar out in Schwarzenegger's bare chest. After the Terminator beats him, he occupies his identity for the remainder of the film and adopts his external appearance: leather pants, jacket, sun glasses, and the big Harley.[26] Schwarzenegger's size may have made the Terminator so intimidating, but his motorcycle made it all seem almost too real.

This new action star also remains conspicuously heterosexual despite the nonstop action and the increasing body count. Susan Bordo argues that the popular version of the action star that became well known in the post-1960s era stood in sharp contrast to the vulnerability that made Marlon Brando so popular and so attractive to women fifteen to twenty years earlier. An endless parade of "car chases, earsplitting explosions, [and] contests with other men" replaced Brando's helplessness, and his dependency defined his style and his "willingness to portray male need." Women were still part of the action hero's repertoire but only to reaffirm his heterosexuality, what Bordo describes as "the quick lay, the dead girl-friend, or the barely visible wife." He was stoic, irreproachable, and with an unassailable masculinity that was particularly noticeable because of his intimidating size. The bigger, the stronger, the more self-assured he seemed, the more confident we were that he was up for any challenge or threat we faced.[27]

The motorcyclist's imagined "queerness" also had much broader political ramifications that shaped his relationship with the counterculture/antiwar movement. In 1966, at what was described as the "largest peace demonstration [against the Vietnam War] in the country since the protests began last year [1965]," violence against demonstrators was ubiquitous. The largest contingent of marchers hailed from New York City (an estimated 20,000 to 25,000). Demonstrations were also organized in San Francisco, Chicago, Washington, Oklahoma City, Detroit, Cambridge, Massachusetts, and "scores of other cities throughout the nation." At all the demonstrations featured in a *New York Times* article, marchers faced hostility from counterdemonstrators, ranging from boos from the crowd, signs expressing support for the war, and contempt for the protestors that often led to violence. In New York, "leading contingents of paraders were showered with eggs and refuse at several points" and when the "supply of eggs was exhausted . . . several dozen spectators lunged through police barricades" to attack the demonstrators. One of the counterdemonstrators was an off-duty fireman, Captain John Galvin, who "circulated among the marchers before the parade started carrying a sign that read 'Thanks

Pinkos, Queers and Cowards.' " In Boston about 700 protestors made their way down Massachusetts Avenue across the Charles River to the Arlington Street Church, across from Boston Common. "A half-dozen motorcyclists harassed the marchers along the three-mile route," and one of the eggs thrown at the demonstrators hit a girl. Once the marchers completed their journey and stopped in front of the Arlington Street Church, a scuffle broke out outside the church. "No arrests and no injuries were reported."[28]

The Hells Angels would also continue their assault against the antiwar movement after their initial attack at the Oakland-Berkeley boundary in 1965. Weeks after the protest, an American government teacher from a Redwood high school invited Sonny Barger to speak to his class about his role in the demonstrations. Barger reaffirmed his critique of the protestors and made it clear that the Hells Angels would "counter demonstrate at all future anti-war demonstrations in the area."[29] About a year later the Hells Angels showed up at San Jose State University, where students were protesting against the use of napalm in Vietnam. The motorcyclists, one paper explained, had become "super patriotic [in] the past year" and upon arriving at the protest "attacked the demonstrators with clubs and baseball bats." Yet despite the zeal with which the motorcyclists expressed their patriotism, the students "overwhelmed" them and "ejected [them] from the scene."[30]

Verbal attacks against hippies, antiwar protestors, and the Left also appeared in mainstream motorcycle publications, and once again ideas about citizenship and patriotism were inextricably linked to gender and sexual identity. In 1970 the editor of *Motorcyclist* made an off-the-cuff jab at what he called the "hippy set" in a discussion about "an eastern dealer friend of ours" who had noticed a slump in sales and receivables. After his friend conducted an investigation he "attributed . . . [the declining sales] to the fact that many of his long-haired (male) customers were spending more and more of their money at the local hair-dresser, and therefore didn't have much left by the time they got to the motorcycle store!"[31] In a 1968 *Cycle* article titled "Flat-Top Haircuts and Gunfighters' Eyes," David E. Davis Jr. took exception to the inclusion of motorcyclists in the counterculture. "Lately, it would seem, the Republic has been filling up with frozen-faced, blue-haired ladies who staunchly believe that Today's Youth (as they call it) is going straight to hell in a hypodermic syringe . . . [and they] have somehow managed to include motorcycling in their list of subversive teenage activities—along with draft card burning, folk singing and free love—but they couldn't be more wrong."[32] Mrs. E. Attard of Brooklyn, New York, made an even more explicit jab at the counterculture and issues of gender in a letter she wrote to *Cycle* after readers objected to the appearance of scantily clad models. Attard explained that she had been looking through some older issues of *Cycle* and noticed that "some mothers were complaining about all the sexy girls in the advertisements." "*Cycle* is obviously a man's magazine," she sharply asserted and noted that "anyone who reads it, is most probably interested in motorcycles and what makes them tick," suggesting that motorcycling and women in various stages of undress had become a well-established pair. "These mothers," Attard continued, "should be thankful their sons are interested in girls and motorcycles," and she bitterly complained about the men who were not. "The only thing they want to do [referring to the motorcyclists] is throw their foot over the seat and ride; not overthrow the government like some of the jelly fish 'males?' of today who are interested only in their love beads and downgrading our great country. . . . As long as my husband is interested in motorcycles," she concluded her letter, "he can subscribe to *Cycle* even with the sexy advertisements in it." "We thank you," the editor announced. "The company thanks you, the industry thanks you. We hope your husband thanks you."[33]

Attard's distinction between motorcyclists and the counterculture is, to say the least, glaring. The men she linked to the counterculture were spineless, or what she described as "jellyfish," even though she accused them of wanting to overthrow the government. Indeed, she had doubts about whether they were, in fact, men—or at least heterosexual ones— hence her use of a question mark after "males?" and the quotes around it in her letter. While she does not explicitly address style, she belittles "love beads" and all she imagined those beads stood for, which at the time raised questions about hair as well as sexual identity, citizenship, and patriotism, the same issues Davis addressed in his *Cycle* article about the counterculture and *Motorcyclist*'s editor's attempt to link beauty shops, long hair, and a disinterest in motorcycling. With Attard, in particular, her fears of homosexuality are so inextricably intertwined with what she means by patriotism and citizenship that it is difficult to separate the two. The respectable motorcyclist Attard and Davis imagined not only stood in opposition to the outlaw biker who was irredeemably violent and rebellious but also a motorcyclist who was suspicious because of his long hair, hippie sentiment, and an assumed left-leaning political sensibility. The rough-respectable divide that separated these two motorcyclists posed a liability to the grassroots motorcycle rights movement that was struggling to establish support and unity among riders. But because both versions of the motorcyclist often stood in diametric opposition to the counterculture and understood his patriotism and citizenship as an expression of his gender and heterosexual identity, the riders Davis and Attard imagined to be respectable may have had more in common with the outlaw motorcyclist than either of them would have initially imagined.

During the first few months of its publication *Easyriders* also included cartoons that presented the biker as a blending of both beatnik and hippie. Beatniks were the commercialized media version of the Beat, generally the lower middle-class rebel from the 1950s and linked to men like poet Alan Ginsberg and Jack Kerouac, who wrote *On the Road*. They embodied what Barbara Ehrenreich described as "two strands of male protest—one directed against the white-collar world and the other against the suburbanized family life that work was supposed to support." The original beats, she adds, "criss-crossed the continent between New York, Mexico City and San Francisco," often on freight trains, shacked up with whomever was available, spent endless hours talking late into the night drinking cheap wine and smoking pot; she describes them as rejecting "the pact that the family wage system rested on"—the breadwinner ethic.[34] Beatniks sported dark sunglasses, goatees, horizontally striped shirts and pinstriped vests, and early illustrations of motorcyclists in the first issues of *Easyriders* magazine mimicked these styles. Motorcyclists also shared with the beatnik a shabbier version of the mop-top hairstyle made famous by the Beatles (more of the Sonny Bono variety—ala Sonny and Cher) and often without beards. The bodies were also similar and distinct from the husky biker—unremarkably average with a boxy midsection and arms that were as skinny and unintimidating as the legs.[35]

Bikers also appeared as stereotypical hippies. If there was any doubt about whom *Easyriders* was trying to emulate, a cartoon from the October 1971 issue literally spelled it out. Awaiting his yearly eye exam at the optometrist's, the biker looks like the run-of-the-mill hippie that was typically pictured in *Easyriders*, although a bit shabbier than usual and with a prominent beaded necklace—or love beads, a particularly notorious and gendered stereotype of the hippie style and as common as sandals, which stood in sharp contrast to the leather boots Merle Haggard sang about in "Okie from Meskogie," his ode to middle America.[36] On the floor and to the right of the hippie/biker lies his motorcycle helmet, and to the left of him is the optometrist, standing with folded arms. The eye chart reads: "D I R T Y H I P P I E L E F T-W I N G R A D I C A L P I N K O."[37]

The hippie was not the only image of the biker featured in *Easyriders*, nor was it even the most prominent, but it attracted enough attention to lead the editor to publish a letter from one reader who objected to it. Duke from Daytona Beach, Florida, accused *Easyriders* of trying to copy *Colors*, a motorcycle magazine that first appeared in May 1970 and is considered a forerunner to *Easyriders* that unabashedly celebrated the outlaw rider. "If you guys is gonna copy 'Colors,'" cried Duke, "you ought to get bikers and better broads in it." "Stop trying," he protested, "to make us out as hippies."[38] By the second year of publication, the hippies Duke referred to had disappeared, and the magazine had replaced him with the bikers we have grown accustomed to in film and in print: big, "husky," irredeemably masculine, and heterosexual.

Some evidence even suggests that the earliest usages of the term "biker" revolved around biker invasions of once-peaceful hippie communities. The article about a hippie community in Atlanta suffering from an invasion of bikers and Sylvan Fox's 1969 *New York Times* piece about the conflict between the Pagans and the Alien Nomads on the Lower East Side are two conspicuous examples. According to Fox, the "bikers" were "the allies of the hippies who had thronged to the East Village that summer." Fox claimed that the "bikers" were "helping to protect the 'flower children' from groups of hostile Negroes and Puerto Ricans," and he added, they "saw the bikers as their constabulary."[39] But as conflict between these two clubs became more common, the entire community felt under siege, and the hippies were increasingly the victims.

Other evidence suggests that the police also recognized the differences between hippies and bikers and may have preferred the latter. In a 1969 letter to the editor of the *San Francisco Chronicle*, William R. Cannon Jr. complained bitterly about what he called "buck-passing." Cannon explained that civil servants from different offices had failed to respond effectively to "an act of violence in a public restaurant in San Rafael involving members of a local motorcycle club" and had simply passed the problem on to the next office. The problem was that "no action has been taken by the police, the district attorney, nor any other government agency to either arrest or bring to trial the participants," even though the police had responded to the call and completed a full report of the incident. After a grand jury considered Cannon's complaint and concluded that the DA's office would prosecute the offenders only if the police "wish to file charges," Cannon dismissed the whole affair as a "clear cut case of buck-passing."[40]

To make matters worse, Cannon also pointed out that the "D.A. is getting in on the act when it comes to the favorable publicity on arrests of nudes at Muir Beach," prompting Cannon to criticize the electors of Marin County for their own buck-passing. "Apparently the electors of Marin County have passed the buck of personal responsibility for the proper government of their homeland to a group of professional buck passers. Buck-passing begets buck passers!" he lamented. "Citizens of California," he warned. "If you want to find an isolated beach for nude sunbathing stay away from Marin County. But if you only want to fracture a few skulls, then Marin County is for you."[41]

In light of the political divisiveness of the late 1960s, the contrast between motorcyclists and nude sunbathers in Marin County is difficult to ignore. Marin County and San Francisco were at the heart of the counterculture and gay liberation in the late 1960s and early 1970s, and by this time conflict was more common and violence on the rise. Were the police facing budgets stretched already too thin to act on both complaints and viewing the motorcyclists as the lesser of two evils? Or was the police's failure to act on Cannon's complaint a reflection of an increasingly divisive political climate and evidence of a conservative shift that blamed America's ills on the counterculture (in this case nude sunbathers)? Some of the earliest usages of "biker" grew out of the contrast between the seemingly peaceful hippie community and the presumably violent motorcyclists, but the growing debate and criticism of motorcyclists suggest that the conflict was not simply the product of location: two different groups with meager resources drawn to the same community in search of cheap housing. The rise of the biker and the violence attributed to him (and against hippies) had deep-seated political meanings that were shaped by events well beyond the hippie's or the biker's control but were nonetheless framed by the biker's conventional ideas about citizenship and masculinity. Whatever the answer, certain divisions were becoming clearer that challenged the biker's automatic association with the counterculture, and examples of his outright opposition to it were plentiful.

Indeed, the motorcyclist's political consciousness often developed in direct opposition to the larger (progressive) political movements that have shaped our understanding of the era. Some comments from motorcyclists suggest that other liberation struggles were never too far removed from the development of a biker political consciousness—a resentment that always seemed to be simmering just below the surface and that became visible at unexpected moments. Wanda Hummel of ABATE of Indiana, for example, embraced very conventional gender roles when she objected to the idea of "equality" to characterize her reason for organizing a chapter of ABATE. The issue came up after some male motorcyclists publicly challenged her leadership role in ABATE and threatened violence against her at an Indiana helmet law protest rally in 1976. Hummel explained that she had organized the ABATE chapter for the same reason other cyclists were organizing: "I'll only give up my freedom, and my bike when they pry my cold dead hands off my handlebars." She then addressed her male critics and alluded to the broader political context that contributed to the anxiety surrounding her leadership: "I don't want to be anything stupid like equal," she protested. "I just want to be left alone to enjoy doing my thing. Since no one else was doing anything here to insure this, I decided to take it on."[42] In another story about helmet laws Charles Clayton explained that motorcyclists were the "first to feel the fetters" of a democracy led astray because motorcyclists were what he described as "the least political of citizens." But it was not long, he argued, before "enough of us realized that if we do not rule government, bureaucrats will control us, and so we learned the ways of politics." That education was quickly put to use, and bikers forced the "Congress to act." It also led them to take part in what Clayton described as "the simplest of political action, backed with a unanimity of belief." "We did it," he stressed, "without violence, without occupying buildings or disrupting events."[43] A more explicit example of the frustration surrounding the other political movements of the 1960s and 1970s comes from the "In the Wind" section of the October 1976 issue of *Easyriders* magazine: a depiction of a billboard that reads "Freedom . . . WE HAVE LOST IT TO THE RADICALS!" No commentary is provided to explain the billboard, only a biker bending over and mooning the crowd. The frustration is apparent; the reason for it missing; the radicals are simply to blame.[44]

Against the backdrop of the 1960s and 1970s, it was clear to whom these different motorcyclists were referring, and their critiques about these movements were not unique. "Law and order" had become the favorite slogan of politicians, who used it to demonize those men and women bold enough to challenge the inequality and injustice they faced, a slogan that blamed activists for the problems they encountered, and one that justified their treatment. In contrast, Clayton argued, motorcyclists viewed themselves as defending a political system that was under attack and suggested the importance of "law and order" to understanding the motorcycle rights movement and his objections to other activists. "The system did not fail us," Clayton proclaimed in another editorial, "for we did not fail the system."[45]

Kevin Kearney of the American Motorcyclist Association (AMA) claimed that motorcyclists were part of the "silent majority," what he described as "one of the few significant political philosophies developed in this century." In the postwar period, the term "silent majority" is generally attributed to President Richard Nixon who used it in a 1969 speech to portray the majority of Americans who had remained apart (and silent) from the larger political movements and demonstrations of the era.[46] The term, according to Kearney, "implied a greater good, a responsibility on the part of the President" to what he characterized as "the true will of the American people." Kearney explained that the phrase was "coined" when the Nixon administration was at "the apex of social change in America," a time when "environmentalists, pacifists, consumer activists and civil rights advocates barraged Washington with petitions and media-oriented marches," people Kearny described as the "few on-the-scene radicals." These "radicals," Kearny added, " quickly learned the political facts of life": they "put down their protest signs, shaved, donned suits and entered the smoke filled world of candidates, primaries, coalitions and elected officials—officials like Jimmy Carter—who are now responsible to them."[47]

Kearney's discussion of these "radicals" hinted at a certain admiration, perhaps because they had successfully effected a political balance that he claimed now favored them. But even as he was suggesting that motorcyclists adopt their political skills and boldness, he challenged any empathy for their progressive political agenda. Instead, he advocated voting as the means by which motorcyclists could shape the political process and challenge the idea of a "silent majority." Kearney admonished motorcyclists to contact the AMA or a local board of elections to find out how to register to vote. He also encouraged them to purchase cards that could be passed on to other cyclists or affixed to the back of a motorcycle that said "REGISTER TO VOTE" just below Kearney's main point about his editorial: "Don't Be Part of the Silent Majority." Motorcyclists were not encouraged to reject what Kearney suggested was their inclusion in the silent majority but to recognize that motorcycling's future was dependent upon a rejection of that silence. Voting was the easiest way to challenge the current political balance that favored the left and a strategy of which these former "on-the-scene radicals" had taken advantage.[48]

The motorcyclist was certainly a recognizable member of the counterculture, if not an important cultural influence on it. But his inclusion did not eliminate the possibility that conflict would develop with the other men and women who were a part of it or that the motorcyclist himself would not contest it. The broader political struggles to which the counterculture was attached raised fundamental questions about the status quo. While motorcyclist's unconventional lifestyle and long hair intimately associated him with the counterculture, his actions off his bike often had the potential to contradict or challenge that image. The struggles surrounding these issues not only placed the motorcyclist at odds with many of the other activists of the period but also served as the root source of the development of a political consciousness that would become increasingly prominent as the battle over helmets picked up steam in the 1970s.

WOMEN AND MOTORCYCLING

Important as sexuality and masculinity may have been to the increasingly political motorcyclist, women have often played an equally conspicuous role in motorcycling. In his *San Francisco Chronicle* article describing the "outburst of terror" at the Hollister Rally in 1947, C. J. Doughty Jr. noted the presence of women riders as active participants: "Riders, both men and *women* [my italics], steered their machines into bars, crashing fixtures, furniture and bottles and mirrors. They defied all traffic regulations, racing full speed through the streets and intersections. Hundreds loosed bottle barrages."[49]

Over the next few decades, this image of the woman rider at Hollister would disappear in most accounts. The *Life* magazine story and the *New York Times* and *Hollister Free Lance* articles that appeared in the days following the rally often referred to motorcyclists and "their friends," noting that "many" motorcycles "carried two riders." When women were mentioned, they were included only in the list of those injured at the rally: Margaret Manning of Hollister and Norma Harmon of Salinas.[50] Yet no mention of women riders appeared in these articles, and motorcycles with "two riders" did not automatically suggest a male rider and female passenger. During the early years after World War II to the end of the 1950s and into the early 1960s, the seat behind the driver was referred to as the "buddy seat," and male riders with their male passengers were common.[51]

Later stories about Hollister contained quotes from Doughty's article highlighting the town's damage along with vivid memories of drunks in the gutters, but the estimated 10 percent of women who attended the rally appeared only as participants or passengers. One longtime Hollister resident recalled a motorcyclist driving his bike "right into the bars" with a "gal . . . standing up on the back of the motorcycle," while another article recalled seeing "girls stripped to the waist throwing beer bottles." Indeed, one of the few memories of women riders at Hollister appeared in a 1951 *Cycle* article titled "Vindication in Hollister," which described the return of motorcyclists four years after the 1947 Hollister Gypsy Tour and included a photo of the Ladi Comets, a "club limited to women." Women were identified as passengers or as participants in the day's activities, but women riders steering their "machines into bars" are missing from accounts of the 1947 Hollister Rally and from its memory.[52]

Immediately after the Hollister Rally, photographs including the Ladi Comets and other female groups were common as motorcycle publications attempted to make motorcycling more respectable. A typical example of the mix of motorcycles and domesticity appears in an article titled "Mama's Day Off," which introduced *Motorcyclist*'s readers to the 49ers, a woman's auxiliary of the AMA. The 49ers "seldom have time for housework on Sundays anymore" because Sunday was their favorite day to kiss their husbands goodbye, climb aboard their favorite two-wheelers, and head for Hansen Dam for a field meet. Yet rather than discuss their skill at riding or their mechanical expertise, their aptitude for motorcycling reflected its compatibility with their domestic skills. The "fellas," the article explained, "have found that a surprising number of the sweeter sex are as much at home . . . spinning do-nuts as they are at dunking, as capable with a handlebar as they are with a frying pan."[53]

In other cases, the motorcycle press tacitly acknowledged that women riders were a diverse lot but celebrated what they hoped was the typical "girl" rider. In 1949 the AMA established the "Most Popular and Typical Girl Rider Contest." Any AMA-affiliated club was eligible to sponsor a female rider. She only had to be a member of the AMA and be able to ride a motorcycle. She did not have to own one. A glossy photograph of the woman in "riding togs" and "mounted on the motorcycle" accompanied the entry. The AMA then published the photographs in *American Motorcycling*, and members voted to determine which "girl" was the most popular and the most typical. "By all rights, a most popular girl rider should be standing right up there beside the most popular man rider," argued a writer in *American Motorcycling*, "and she should be given the same honor and recognition as her masculine counterpart." The AMA explained that the inspiration for the contest came in part from the lack of attention women riders had received despite their "doing many worthwhile things to build up the sport while male riders were honored yearly with the Most Popular Rider Contest." But the AMA's concern about recognition would not have been as pressing if questions about respectability had not been paramount, and that concern was palpable. "When the public sees a large clear picture of the girl voted most representative of all AMA girl riders, they'll understand instantly why she was chosen. They'll say 'Well if that girl rider is typical of motorcyclists, it must be a pretty wonderful sport!' "[54]

To be sure, women riders who appeared in the motorcycle press would serve as an inspiration for women across the country in search of useful role models who defied the conventional role of housewife and mother. Women like Dot Robinson, who served as the head of the Motor

Maids throughout a good portion of the postwar period, was not only a motorcyclist but an accomplished one, and a racer known for besting her male competitors. Indeed, even when the only available images of women showed them participating in a petticoat race or in stories that highlighted their accomplishments as housewives and mothers, they were still pictured atop their favorite (and often large) motorcycles, riding in formation down the highway, or lined up for the start of a race or a road run.[55]

But the published examples of women motorcyclists were also circumscribed in ways that potentially attenuated any challenge to conventional gender roles. The AMA and other industry leaders struggled to come to terms with the line women ambiguously and nervously straddled between rider and housewife that was such a notable feature of motorcycle culture. The pressure on women to adhere to prescribed gender roles after World War II was tremendous, and that tension was palpable in motorcycle publications.[56] In an interview about the Most Typical and Popular Girl Rider contest, Dot Robinson argued, "By impressing on the clubs that this is not a beauty contest but is designed for a real motorcycle rider you give it class that can never be obtained by a queen contest." But in that same interview, and in a moment of speculation about her contributions to motorcycling, Robinson challenged that contention by explaining, "There is a place for us in motorcycling, and as long as we stay in our place I'm sure that we'll be welcome."[57] Women's role in motorcycling was shaped by two different objectives: to promote the sport of motorcycling and to make it respectable. Women offered the AMA its best chance to accomplish both, or, as one editorial explained, "proving . . . that one can be a lady and a motorcycle rider at the same time."[58]

THE SCANTILY CLAD MOTORCYCLE MODEL

By the 1960s and 1970s, examples of respectable, carefree, and domesticated women still appeared in motorcycle publications, and those images helped motorcyclists distance themselves from their outlaw past, but the urgency surrounding women riders had faded somewhat. These positive images of women riders were generally part of a larger discussion about the middle-class motorcyclist, his (and it usually is a "his") clean-cut clothes, smaller and more efficient motorcycles, and suburban roots. The middle-class professional rider did not eliminate the respectable girl rider, but his appearance made it easier for contemporaries to ignore her.[59]

Instead, motorcycling's growth in the 1960s and 1970s and the public's increasing interest in female riders gave rise to two other images that began to overshadow that of the respectable housewife. Conventional wisdom about women in motorcycle clubs presented them as willing sexual partners, who were frequently abused, cast aside, or shared among the club's male members.[60] While that image contradicts the day-to-day experience of most female riders and passengers, it became an increasingly dominant theme within motorcycle culture. It was, for example, in the 1960s that the "buddy seat" evolved into the "pea pad" or "pussy pad."[61] "Pussy pad" left few doubts about women's status in motorcycling. Men were riders; women were not. They were passengers, and their seat behind the male rider affected the public's perception about women in motorcycling. "Is that your bike?" was a question female riders had been hearing for decades. For some women, the question was empowering because it reminded them of their autonomy on the road without a male companion or partner. Other women viewed that question as a challenge to their role in motorcycling because of the associated questions it raised about their status, ownership, competence, and even sexual identity. The only issue that the pussy pad did not ambiguously define was the woman passenger's subordinate status within motorcycling and her sexual objectification.

The evolution of the buddy seat also accompanied the appearance of the scantily clad motorcycle model. The first to adopt this advertising strategy was Norton in the late 1960s, but before long she was appearing in other publications. By the early 1970s, and with the appearance of *Easyriders*, topless models began to make their way into motorcycle publications. *Easyriders*, in particular, was intent on building a world around motorcycling in which women were as conspicuous as they were inconsequential. July 1971 saw the first published issue of *Easyriders,* and within a matter of months, "Booze, Bikes, and Broads" became the magazine's unofficial ethos, although weed could compete against any of these three at about any time (*Biker News* preferred Bikes and Broads).[62] For the first issue the magazine's title was simply *Easyriders*. For the next year and a half (through the February 1973 issue) *Easyriders* included the subtitle *For the Swinging Biker* followed by its current title: *Easyriders: Entertainment for the Adult Biker.*

Over the course of the magazine's first few years of publication, women's presence became increasingly conspicuous. The cover of the first issue features only a picture of a chopper from the perspective of the rider looking down at the handlebars and the gas tank. Over the next year, these types of covers were common or covers featuring pictures of men riding choppers with female passengers. Over the next two years women were becoming more visible than the bikes featured in the magazine. The June

1972 issue sports the first cover where only one side of the chopper's handlebars is visible. By June 1974, the cover has no actual motorcycle, only
a photo of a woman's torso, a Harley-Davidson logo just above her panty
line, and what looks like a film negative of two small choppers on the right
side of the cover. By June 1975, there is no motorcycle or any representation
of a motorcycle (or brand), only a picture of a female model. Similar covers
would become common after that, although with different female poses.
One particularly notorious and common pose is a close up of a woman
who is apparently on her knees with her face tilted upwards as if looking
at the man she is kneeling by with his over-sized belt buckle (and crotch)
next to her face.[63]

Inside the magazine the change was just as noticeable. From the first
issues, women appear in cartoons as available and easily excitable sexual
partners who are often naked. "Miraculous Mutha Tells All" also made her
debut in the first issue. "Miraculous Mutha" was an advice column on a
range of topics: relationships, weed, bikes, and, above all, sex. Early issues
also included the occasional model in a low-cut vest, blouse, or tank top or a
photo essay staged specifically to highlight the woman's body or breasts. The
October 1971 issue features "The Pleasures of Drinking Out of a Wine-Skin,"
which is essentially a photo layout of a woman, Angela, attempting to drink
wine out of a bota bag, "a small, bladder shaped bag, usually made of goat
skin, used to keep liquids in—usually wine." For four pages Angela struggles
to drink wine successfully from the bota bag, although more often than not
she fails and the wine washes down across the front of her tight-fitting tank
top, a sort of wet-T-shirt moment without all the pomp and circumstance of
an actual contest. By the time she is finished with the wine she is "smashed,"
and the front of her shirt is sopping wet with wine. Drinking from a bota bag,
the reader is sure to conclude, is more difficult than it looks.[64]

The first nude shot of a female model appears in August 1972 (just over
a year after the first published issue), although the story was about tattoo
art, and so nakedness may have been unavoidable.[65] The first photograph
of a nude woman who appears solely as an accessory to the featured
chopper appears in February 1973. By the middle of that year, nude layouts
of models become a regular feature of the magazine. The first published
photo of a topless woman to appear in the magazine's "In the Wind" seg-
ment is December 1973.[66]

Over the next few years, "Miraculous Mutha" would become raunchier,
photographs of topless women in "In the Wind" common, and violence
often the root of their sexual objectification.[67] Women were often the butt of
jokes or the foil around which a story develops. The (male) bikers confront

some problem or misfortune that ends with a slap upside a female companion's head or a punch in her face. Violence also appeared in the letters section in response to female complaints or objections. After an article appeared in the June 1973 *Easyriders* in which a woman objected to the use of "chick," the editors published the responses from male and female readers. Some of them praised the article: "Thank you, thank you, thank you," began Ms. Micki Hagen's letter. "That article," she continued, "was the best thing any motorcycle magazine has ever done for us. I ride my own Royal Enfield 700 and I've gotten so frustrated because my brothers continually pass me off as a mere 'chick.'" Most of the published letters, however, were critical and often advocated violence against any women who challenged their treatment or the use of "chick." Carlos of the Grateful Dead Motorcycle Club belittled the discussion as "bullshit" and claimed he had used the term all his life. He "never intended it to be an insult" but could not help but ask, "How many bikers can take a liberated chick, anyway?" Manny of Dayton, Ohio, explained that "If my ol' lady told me that garbage I'd hit her in the back of the head with a piston." "If chicks want to ride on this stud's bike," he continued, "they'll have to remember who's boss, and I'll call my chick a bitch, pussy, or douche bag if I want to. I'll let a chick oil my crank, but not tell me what to do."[68]

Other examples include cartoons in which bikers appear as sexual predators. Rape scenes (presented as "gang bangs") become conspicuous. In pictorials women appear pinned to the ground or leashed, and are routinely presented entirely naked and surrounded by a large group of men, an unusually vulnerable predicament in any context but particularly so given the frequent allusions to rape. In some cases the all-male setting was seemingly innocuous, perhaps a simple example of male culture that highlighted its heterosexual potential. Men in these scenarios are often in a garage or some other workplace or male space—tearing a bike apart or putting one back together—and a woman casually enters the room without any response from the men busily working. Over the course of several photographs, the men continue to work even as the woman proceeds to take off her clothes as she wanders around the shop. Completely naked and unable to distract the men, she leaves abruptly, and only then do the men put their work aside and pursue her. These pictorials hint at sexual play and fantasy, or at least a male version of one, and suggest that the "biker chick" was always available and sexually uninhibited.[69] But even as she was a conspicuous feature of these all-male spaces, her presence did little to change the atmosphere, let alone challenge it. Her intrusion simply reinforced the focus of the all-male space (the motorcycle and not the woman), and her nakedness challenged any assumptions about sexual orientation that often arise in these all-male settings.[70] The scene emphasized the heterosexual potential of these spaces and the heterosexual prowess of the men who occupied them.

Some men responded negatively to the presence of scantily clad women. "Take back your lousy nude with the ink job," complained one 1969 *Cycle* reader who failed to sign his name. "Don't want trash in my cycle books. We buy motorcycles, not prostitutes—which are you selling is hard to tell?"[71] After Eldon L. Maret of Cushing, Oklahoma, had received his first copy of *Cycle*, he was "sorry I ever subscribed." Maret had gotten a peek at what he described as a "nude woman wearing only a safety helmet." His initial thought was to throw away the magazine before his thirteen-year-old son saw it but managed instead to "blot out the picture." Maret asked the editor why he published this type of advertisement and warned that censorship was in the offing "if the trend continues towards publication of sex and profanity." He then reprimanded the editor for making it more difficult to raise his son and admonished him to "pause" and give some thought to what he publishes and what he "sends into peoples' homes."[72] The "vulgar display of filthy female trash" that Russell H. Peel of Richmond, Indiana, found in his January 1968 issue of *Cycle* also shocked him. Peel advised the editor to "throw out that rotten sex goon's display" and described the ads he found as a "disgrace to the good motorcycle riders." "We don't need," he concluded, "any more restrictions on our freedom of choice."[73]

A more common response in some publications was to defend the bawdy behavior as a fundamental part of motorcycle culture that affected men and women equally. In response to the use of nude photographs of women in *Biker News*, B. Wayne Johnson of Mechanicsville, Virginia, explained that " 'Booby' contests, banana-eating contests, skinny-dipping, wet-T-shirts contests, short dick contests, etc. are all part of the runs I have attended." "It's all part of the party," he added. "It offends no one at the scene . . . so to censor your paper in this manner would be unrealistic and in my opinion 'cover up' a part of the biker lifestyle."[74] Frank Motschko of British Columbia, Canada, explained that "biker chicks showing their stuff are as much a part of the biker lifestyle as riding down the road," while Fred Hartman of Columbus, Georgia, claimed that he was not offended by "any photos shown in *Biker* up to now" and admonished the editors not to "worry about those who would cancel because of a few 'tit' pictures. They aren't real bikers anyway."[75]

Still yet others argued that the push to censor was no different from the other more prominent attempt to regulate motorcyclists' rights—helmet laws. J. Schock of Marquette, Michigan, would "cast [his] vote for the lack of censorship in *Biker* for the simple damned reason that nudity and women are a good chunk of our very lifestyle. First the helmet crap, now this garbage." Jingles from Indiana asked, "Bitchin, what the hell is this 'censored' bullshit? You trying to form a government or what? The name of your rag is *Biker* and by God that's who reads it. If a dude is a biker he's probably already seen a set of tits and if they haven't, it's time they did. . . . Keep up the good work, but can the censored bull."[76] After the editor at *Biker* asked for readers' responses about censorship, James D. Han of West Lafayette, Indiana, was confused: "I find your request to comment on censorship puzzling, for obviously your publication promotes freedom— freedom to ride Harleys or Hondas, freedom to wear helmets or not, freedom to use profanity in print if so chosen, freedom to access to state and national parks for cyclists, freedom to buy Plymouths, etc. And then you turn around and curtail *yourselves*, putting yourself at the mercy of our whims, our preferences, or sense of what is offensive. How come? . . . Do you see the incongruities I'm talking about? . . . I fully believe in freedom and I resent your decision to keep from me something you are afraid will offend me. I'm 40. Let me decide if I want to see boobs or not. If I don't I'll look the other way."[77]

Yet even as motorcyclists identified scantily clad models as an issue of censorship and regulation, other deep-seated anxieties about women's role in society and in motorcycling shaped the debates. One example, and one that is familiar to the discussion of motorcycling in the 1970s, is Evel Knievel. His outrageous stunts on his motorcycle were often upstaged by his behavior off his bike. In a 1974 story about Knievel's planned jump over the Snake River Canyon, columnist Wells Twombly summed up the stuntman by noting, "Nobody understood the phrase macho quite as well as he [Knievel] does." Beneath his "surface layer of arrogance," Twombly added, "there exists a man who is cruel, temperamental, sadistic, suicidal and violent." He has "no socially redeeming qualities," Twombly protested, and it would "drive a reporter wild" looking for them.[78] The antisocial behavior to which Twombly referred included, among other things, Knievel's penchant for boasting about his numerous sexual conquests (over 600), his propensity to drink Wild Turkey bourbon, his love of hunting and other dangerous sports, and the brawls he had with other bikers, hippies, and an occasional reporter. Knievel was also known for his verbal assaults against Jews, Native Americans, Italians, Poles, gays, lesbians, and especially feminists.[79] In 1974, for example, he described feminism as a "bunch of horseshit" and claimed that these "Lib-types" "were running all over me asking if I'm a male chauvinist. . . . You're damn right I am," he boasted; "no other kind in my house baby."[80]

Some evidence even suggests that Knievel's vicious diatribes against feminists were not only inextricably intertwined with his reputation for fearlessness but also explain why so many Americans were attracted to the wily stuntman. Wells Twombly made this point clear: "In the dubious era of female liberation he [Knievel] has this unique ability to restore male pride." Another example comes from the preshow hype before Knievel's ill-fated jump over the Snake Canyon River in 1974. A minister, according to a *New York Times* article, gave several "preflight prayers" and used one to thank "the Lord [and apparently Knievel] for helping us become real men," as if Knievel's lone attempt to jump the canyon served as the vicarious dose of courage these men apparently lacked, yet desperately yearned for. The crowd responded to the minister's prayer, according to the reporter, by cheering "lustily."[81]

Knievel was not fearless simply because of his death defying stunts but because of the way he lived his life. He seemed so fearless at a time when so many other men feared they were not. Knievel made this point in 1974 when he said: "I'm doing what every kid's dad wanted to do if he hadn't had momma telling him not to." His comment was undoubtedly another dig against feminism, but it also critically exposed the uncertainty surrounding American masculinity. The debate about sexism in American society coincided with a renewed popularity of motorcycling and motorcycle daredevils like Knievel. But rather than reject Knievel as an outdated example of unrestrained and dangerous bravado, Americans were attracted to him (and to motorcycling), and Knievel played the part for all it was worth.[82] While the number of motorcycle daredevils was on the rise in the early 1970s, Knievel continued to survive his jumps despite the likelihood of a fatal crash. When he did crash, he would literally pick himself up off the pavement and stagger to the microphone or have his entourage carry him to one so he could thank the crowd and apologize for his failure. This spectacle could easily be dismissed as another example of Knievel playing to a crowd that was naïve enough to accept him as genuine. But the spectacle, as Toni Morrison has argued, "is the best means by which an official story is formed and is a superior mechanism for guaranteeing its longevity."[83] In this case the official story men were desperately trying to write favored an understanding of masculinity that was vigorous, determined, and unafraid of any challenge. Knievel was the physical reminder of what masculine men were capable of and why conventional gender roles should be preserved and celebrated.

Other male riders were just as bitter about women and especially their presence in motorcycling. In a column celebrating the differences between men and women, Bob Bitchin addressed women's liberation and the limits of the equality women were striving for that challenged their place in motorcycling. The "world is going to hell in a bread basket," Bitchin argued, "and all this equality horse shit is what's sending it there." Bitchin explained that in "today's sewing circles" women frequently complain about exploitation and of not being "considered man's equal. . . . Except in the divorce court, where they want special compensation. . . . Except when the check comes for dinner, and they coyly ignore the check. . . . Except when they ride their own bike and it has a flat. . . . Except, except, except. Damnit! If you're gonna be equal, don't screw around, be equal." Bitchin asked the magazine's readers if they remembered "a few years back when it was a good thing to be discriminatory? Any man who was discriminating was a man with integrity. Now he's a chauvinist."[84]

This last point about women riders wanting equal opportunity to be motorcyclists but unprepared to fix a flat was particularly problematic for Bitchin. "Every week or so I hear from women who are into *Biker*, asking why they aren't featured with their bikes like the men are. There is at least one very good reason. The men we feature, for the most part, built their own machines and they are a part of the industry." Bitchin added: "The women I have met who putt their own scoots are more than welcome to ride with me, party with me, sleep with me and eat with me. But when I break down on the road I will fix my own scoot. I don't want to have the job of fixing someone else's."[85]

While the ability to "wrench one's own" had become more prominent with the rise of the middle-class rider and the resulting class divisions within motorcycling, the timing of its resurrection, as Bitchin's comments suggest, also contributed to women's exclusion. His approach not only drew upon age-old assumptions about gender and masculinity that divided the sexes but ultimately placed the blame on women riders who failed to live up to certain expectations as opposed to accepting a broader definition of what it meant to be a motorcyclist. After all, most men could do little more than basic maintenance on their own bikes, and the growth of motorcycling in the 1960s and 1970s in part reflected the acceptance that a maintenance-free motorcycle was not a myth.

WOMEN RIDERS

Women's responses to these complaints highlight the degree to which these issues were as divisive within motorcycle culture as outside of it, and they consistently challenged the typical image of the sexually avail-able and scantily clad model. Tally Blaine of Honolulu, Hawaii, had been reading *Easyriders* for a few years when she admitted that she looked for-ward to the magazine each month. But, she asked, "why is *Easyriders* such a put-down to women? Every biker has an ol' lady or even a wife. I imagine they all read your magazine too (as well as pay for it). The only recognition we ladies receive is the space devoted to pictures of naked women or in the ol' ladies contest. . . . What the hell, don't we women have any future?"[86] Another woman, who signed her letter KSRC also admitted that she read the magazine every month, but was much more pointed about the maga-zine's shortcomings than Blaine. KSRC described *Easyriders* as "egotistical, chauvinistic, and unrealistic. Some of your so-called bitches are really dogs, and I can't see how any male in his right mind could get off on such shit. 'Entertainment for Adult Bikers?' No—more like 'Entertainment for Assholes.' "[87] Other women bluntly connected their marginalization to women's sexual objectification. Deidre, from Tucson, Arizona, agreed that *Easyriders* was a " 'great rag' except for the constant put-down of chicks." "Just because I'm not a dude doesn't mean I don't know how to do any-thing except fuck. So cut the shit!"[88]

Admittedly, complaints like these were common enough in *Easyriders* to suggest that the editor was trying to egg on the dispute, and the letters they included from disgruntled women readers were often so sexually explicit that they had the potential to contribute to the idea that "biker chicks" were as sexually available as male motorcyclists imagined them to be. However, other publications provided letters from women readers that were just as critical and which highlighted the transformation tak-ing place. "I would like to say that a motorcycle magazine is not a 'girlie' magazine," objected Mrs. Joan M. Yarbrough in her 1968 letter to *Cycle*. Yarbrough suggested that *Playboy* was a more appropriate venue for these pictures and noted that the magazine included "44 girls" in the "June issue alone." "If your magazine starts to have more girls in it than motorcycles, you can count me out as a regular customer."[89]

Other women focused on their role as riders and the degree to which they had been excluded from motorcycling. Karen Cantrell, who was from Florissant, Missouri, and the president of the Missing Link Dirt Riders, began her letter with "Let's put women in *The Motorcyclist* Magazine." Cantrell emphasized that "we're not a group of Women Liberators," but a "group of women in the greater St. Louis area who truly believe that women do have a place in the world when it comes to motorcycles." Cantrell reminded the magazine's male readers that "for many years . . . we have listened to you and played the role of spectators during your events." But even as she explained that "we don't' intend to take over the spot-light" and that "we will be content to stand on the sidelines," she cautioned the magazine's male readers, only "as long as you guys recognize us and take us seriously."[90] In a letter to *Cycle* in 1971 Cherie Loraine Sullivan made a similar point when she objected to the idea that motorcycling was "the last male refuge."[91] Like Cantrell, Sullivan began her letter by stating, "I'm not pro Lib or anti," but she was "prohuman beings and intelligence, so be forewarned, the next cat I see or hear calling motorcycling 'the last male refuge' gets stabbed to death with my knitting needles."[92] In 1975 a reporter interviewed Catharine Colon about the all-woman cycle club she had recently organized. At the time of her interview, her club had about forty members, ranging in ages from twelve to fifty-six, and Colon was setting up a national listing of first names and phone numbers. She explained that she started the club "when she found that she wasn't able to talk to men about her motorcycle." "I just couldn't understand what one of my friends was saying," she recalled, and "felt enormous tension, enormous anger because I had no technological background." That experience convinced her that "there ought to be a cycle club for women, who could talk with each other on the same level." She claimed her club, named "Uppity Women," did not "want to repeat what we've seen in male clubs." "We're not pack riders," she added.[93]

Other women riders blatantly disregarded the fear of being labeled "feminist" and openly connected motorcycling to women's liberation. In August 1972 women from across the country organized rallies to mark the fifty-second anniversary of the ratification of the Nineteenth Amendment, which gave women the right to vote and to draw attention to the "second of the first Women's Strike for Equality." The demonstrations "stretched from Boston to San Francisco and included marches, workshops, and fair[s] that drew crowds of feminists—and a few male supporters—ranging in size from several dozen to several thousand." Much of the rally's focus was a show of support for the Equal Rights Amendment, which up to that point had already been ratified by twenty states. Feminists in New York "capped their demonstrations with a Friday evening march down Fifth Avenue that drew several thousand." The crowd of women marchers was "led by three women on motorcycles" who frequently shouted to the onlookers: "Join Us Sisters."[94] Margie Siegal, of Piedmont, California, also identified herself as a feminist in a letter to *Biker* in March 1978. Siegal had been riding a motorcycle for over four years and did a "lot of wrenching on both [her] bikes (stock 350 Honda, rat 500 Triumph) and quite a bit of cruising," and wondered, "Does that make me a biker?" she asked. "If it does," she was a biker who "doesn't appreciate a good set of tits." One of her main reasons for writing to *Biker* was to express her opposition to censorship in motorcycle magazines and to emphasize the need for equal rights. "I think if you are going to show naked women you ought to show naked men for the benefit of your women readers who like to look at guys." Siegal preferred "big guys with long hair; athletic (not weightlifter) muscles, furry chests, no beer bellies." She suggested that the magazine "pose em naked on a bike and I'll cut the picture out and put it on my wall."[95]

Her letter also responded to an earlier editorial about joining a motorcycle rights organization (MRO) to support the fight against helmets, and she echoed Sullivan's sentiment about the "last male refuge." Siegal explained that she "would do so [join an MRO] if I thought I would be comfortable around one." Referring to the Modified Motorcycle Association, Siegal noted, "it looks like they don't like women unless they bow and scrape. I'm sorry," she added, "but I won't do that—too much self-respect." She asked the magazine's male readers, "If you want more women bikers around (don't you want more of us around?) you're going to have to act like you want us around. Messing around with women's heads don't make you a man."[96]

The idea of a "last male refuge" was also particularly noticeable to other women riders.[97] Nancy Slechta of College Park, Maryland, claimed that "cycle clubs are some of the most sexist organizations I have ever seen!"[98] Slechta pointed to the unwanted attention with which women riders had to contend from their male counterparts and the problem of them constantly asking, "Is that your bike?" "Women cyclists don't want extra attention," she explained. "We just want to be treated as bikers, not as piston-packing mamas! . . . How many men are willing to treat a chic on a bike with equal consideration as a guy on the same bike?" Slechta concluded her letter by suggesting that men's behavior was "forcing us [women] to unite to form our own clubs." "Good riddance, you say? Well, without the chics on bikes, it is going to get pretty cold out there some lonely night after a long ride. Then it'll be too late. Let's see your bike keep you warm."[99]

Women riders did not simply attend the Hollister Rally in 1947. They participated in the weekend's events with their male counterparts and also earned the label of "outlaw." In the days following the rally, industry leaders struggled to redeem the motorcyclist, whether male or female, in the public's eye and replace it with a domesticated version. Men in this era were idealized as respectable and law abiding, and women motorcyclists were generally cast as wives and mothers first and riders second.

These men and women riders collectively met a Cold War expectation about maturity, responsibility, and a commitment to each other and the community of which they were a part—everything the outlaw at Hollister was not.

By the 1960s, women were still struggling with the expectations surrounding conventional gender norms, but the tension between the sexes was more conspicuous and public than it had been in earlier years. The respectability associated with the middle-class rider translated into the idea that motorcycling was family friendly and suited to women's day-to-day life and needs. Yet even as the face of motorcycling was changing, so were expectations about men's and women's behavior. In the 1960s and 1970s men found their behavior intensely scrutinized as second-wave feminism gained strength against the backdrop of the worst economic malaise since the 1930s and in light of the United States' retreat from Vietnam, which fundamentally challenged a nation and a generation of men and women. Motorcycling's popularity accompanied these larger social and economic changes as increasing numbers of men looked for ways outside of work to shore up any questions about their roles as husbands, fathers, and as men. The culture they found in motorcycling reinforced traditional ideas about difference that revolved increasingly around sexualized and subordinate images of women. This shift captured the attention of men and women alike, and it led to heated exchanges that at times influenced motorcycle culture. But against the backdrop of the motorcycle rights movement that idealized freedom and individual rights, women's objections garnered little support. The bawdy culture that had become more mainstream by the latter 1960s was viewed as a fundamental part of the biker lifestyle, and any compromise to it viewed as a challenge similar to the controversy surrounding helmets and the government's push to regulate motorcycles and the men and women who rode them. If motorcyclists gained mainstream credibility through a motorcycle rights movement that allowed them to reclaim the citizenship that was critical to their inclusion and social belonging, then accepting women who challenged their subordinate role was a compromise that also called into question their understanding of freedom and individual rights.

Yet women motorcyclists remained undeterred. Motorcycling empowered them as women and as riders, and the resistance they faced only seemed to strengthen their resolve. Their determination unnerved motorcycle culture and convinced some to abandon traditional organizations and clubs for their own. Apart from their male counterparts, women's appreciation for motorcycling only intensified and strengthened their idea about what it meant to be a motorcyclist and what it meant to be a woman. These riders were generally not characterized as outlaws, but the challenge they posed to male culture in the 1960s and 1970s was as significant as the sight of women crashing their bikes into bars at Hollister two to three decades earlier, and it was a challenge that would only grow stronger in the years to come.

GENDER AND SEXUAL IDENTITY shaped the image of the motorcycle rebel who emerged out of the Hollister Rally. At times he posed a challenge to small-town America because he was unruly and disorderly on and off his bike. At other times he was surprisingly conventional. Rigid gender roles in motorcycling questioned the very idea of women riders, and motorcycle publications presented the male rider as willingly domesticated and contented.

The social and political movements of the 1960s and 1970s brought that discussion into sharp relief as white heterosexual, male privilege attracted increasing scrutiny. That debate affected Americans from all walks of life and is fundamental to understanding the conservative ascendancy of the postwar years. Motorcyclists were included in the Right's resurgence, and the best example is the fight over regulation that heated up with the passage of helmet laws across the country.

But the Right's interest in motorcyclists preceded the helmet laws and was not limited to the issue of big government. One of the first examples of that interest began on the Oakland-Berkeley boundary in 1965, when an attempted assault by the Hells Angels on antiwar protesters led police to arrest six of the motorcyclists. They would drop the charges against all of them except for the ones against Michael Walter (Tiny), who quickly found support from an unexpected source. In an interview with the *Los Angeles Times*, Fred Ullner, director of the San Rafael–based Republicans for Conservative Action, described the Hells Angels as patriots and announced that the group had established an organization called the "Friends of the Hells Angels" to pay for Walter's bail bond and court expenses.[100]

Different motivations may explain the conservative Republicans' unexpected support for the motorcyclists, but we cannot ignore the ongoing conflict surrounding the counterculture and the broader context of struggle over gender and sexual identity. The key issue—the passage of the Highway Safety Act of 1966—that led to a grassroots motorcycle rights movement and an alliance between motorcyclists and conservatives had not materialized. Yet the clash between motorcyclists and the police on the Berkley-Oakland border and the conservative response to it suggest that this alliance had its roots in the struggles over identity that were especially conspicuous against the backdrop of the liberation struggles of the 1960s. The conflict revolved around the stereotype that all bikers were gay and the increasingly vocal female rider who asserted an alternative understanding of motorcycling that often alluded to (and sometimes explicitly) the broader discussion about feminism that was sweeping the country. The consequence of this struggle was the husky motorcyclist, a biker who was compulsively heterosexual, white, male, antifeminist, and patriotic. Some of these attributes had been visible for decades—topless women appeared in accounts about the Hollister Rally, and the 1%er was linked to Riverside in 1948—but in light of the struggles over gender and sexual identity in the 1960s, these issues became more conspicuous, and conflict surrounded them.

This debate had the potential to further exacerbate the contradictions surrounding the motorcyclist and thus undermine the potential for an alliance with an emerging Right that was increasingly concerned about protecting the family. The husky motorcyclist who appeared at the Oakland-Berkeley boundary and was frequently linked to guns and drugs had little in common with the run-of-the-mill conservative who was out to save the nation from itself. Yet the motorcyclist's actions off his bike still had the potential to attract the political Right. The debate about censoring the scantily clad pinup led motorcyclists to oppose it as another example of government regulation, even though some of the most outspoken critics were other riders. And the female riders who were advocating equal treatment within motorcycling often prefaced their objections with the familiar trope that plagued women's liberation throughout the period, "I'm not a feminist, but." The motorcyclist's transformation from outlaw to biker and from *Easy Rider* to conservative voter was never inevitable nor was it simply about fear and violence. It was, at times, explicitly political and grounded in conflict with the other activists of the era who posed a fundamental challenge to the motorcyclist and in conflict that recast him as surprisingly conventional and mainstream. Gender and sexual identity were fundamental to these struggles, but as the next chapter will show, so was the issue of race.

IT'S A BLACK THANG

Law and (Dis)order and the African American Freedom Struggle

In the late 1960s and early 1970s, two images that were captured on film effectively highlighted the very complicated ways in which race intersected with motorcycling and the larger political drama surrounding the white motorcyclist. The first is *Sweet Sweetback's Baadasssss Song*, which debuted in 1971 and captivated the attention of fans and critics alike. The film, which Melvin Van Peebles wrote, directed, produced, and starred in, revolves around the life of Sweetback, a young black man who finds himself on the run from the law after rescuing a black revolutionary from a beating at the hands of the police. One scene finds Sweetback and a friend asleep in an abandoned garage. They are unexpectedly awakened by a group of white bikers who accuse the pair of trespassing. A biker yells, "They got to pay." Another proposes a duel between Sweetback and the club's "Prez," who arrives moments later dressed in denim, glasses, and a white helmet. As the bikers taunt Sweetback, the "Prez" shows off the strength and prowess that make for a formidable adversary and to suggest an ability to handle any challenge Sweetback posed. Removing the white helmet, the Prez is revealed to be a woman. The room grows silent. Sweetback hesitates for a moment, and says "Fuckin'," an unsurprising response given the film's routine focus on sexual fantasy and Sweetback's sexual agility and skill. As the bikers begin to cheer, the Prez silences them and accepts Sweetback's challenge. Sweetback and the Prez undress. The duel begins before a ring of cheering bikers, and climaxes (literally) with her wild shrieking. Sweetback stands up, demurely puts on a hat, and the scene ends as abruptly as it began.[1]

Reviews of the film focused largely on whether it challenged racial stereotypes or promoted them, but the motorcycle scene did attract the attention of film critic and professor, Don L. Lee. While Lee dismissed the scene

Hells Angels beating concertgoers with pool cues at the Altamont concert in 1969. Courtesy of Photofest, Inc.

as "unnecessary and sheer fantasy," his reasoning suggests that motorcyclists were more important to the film than he was willing to admit. "I don't believe," he insisted, "any group of white boys (especially the prototype of Hell's Angels—who recently killed a brother at a music festival) is going to stand by and let some brother screw one of their women. No! I can't buy that."[2]

Lee's comment about a music festival referred to the second image captured on film that highlights the issue of race and motorcycling—the death of Meredith Hunter, an eighteen-year-old black man who was stabbed by a member of the Hells Angels at the Altamont concert in 1969. The Rolling Stones had organized the concert and hired the Hells Angels to head up security in exchange for five hundred dollars in beer. Hunter was moving toward the stage when Hells Angel, Alan Passaro, repeatedly stabbed him. Hunter's murder was not merely a random act of racially motivated violence by an outlaw biker. Hunter had been brandishing a gun as he approached the stage, and it is clearly visible in the film footage of the concert. But the ease with which Lee connected the event to Van Peebles's critique of race relations further suggests the importance of race to understanding motorcycling and its relationship to the black community.

Hunter would die from his wounds, and a jury would acquit Passaro on murder charges two years later.[3]

The violence at Altamont left an indelible mark on public perceptions of the counterculture. As soon as the Altamont concert was announced, contemporaries had immediately begun to refer to it as "Woodstock West." That comparison quickly faded as stories of the concert's violence circulated and as Hunter's death attracted headlines across the nation and the world. Altamont came to be regarded as the tragic moment that marked the end of the counterculture, in stark opposition to Woodstock's success as a concert and as a representation of the counterculture's values and ideals in full bloom less than four months before Hunter's death at Altamont.[4]

The tendency to link the Altamont tragedy to Woodstock's success has also overshadowed Hunter's death and the importance of race to understanding it. In this telling, Hunter's death was simply the unfortunate moment that marked the end of the counterculture of which, it was assumed, he was a part. Likewise, Van Peebles seemed to suggest that the bikers of *Sweetback* were on the side of the establishment. The unlikely motorcycle scene that begins with Sweetback's duel ends with the bikers taking Sweetback to another supposedly safe building for the night. Unknown to Sweetback, the bikers are in league with the police who arrive shortly thereafter to apprehend him. Sweetback's subsequent fight to save his own life ends with two dead policemen.

Van Peebles defied conventional wisdom about motorcyclists, just as he challenged age-old taboos about white women and black men. Throughout the postwar years the general consensus had imagined the outlaw motorcyclist as a threat to the law and order the police were entrusted to uphold. Van Peeble's version of motorcycling defied simple divisions by ignoring the typical boundaries between law and order and by viewing motorcyclists and the police as a collective threat to Sweetback and to the larger black community. After all, as Van Peebles explains in bold type at the bottom of the movie's first scene, his film is "dedicated to all the brothers and sisters who had enough of the Man."[5] The white outlaw is no longer a threat to the Man but the Man himself.

As *Sweet Sweetback's Baadasssss Song* and Hunter's death at Altamont suggest, race is fundamental to understanding the motorcyclist in the postwar period. The rise of the outlaw at Hollister and his subsequent (and violent) transformation came of age at the same time that the African American freedom struggle captured the nation's attention and challenged its conscience. While a segregated motorcycle culture complicated the points of intersection between these two developments, by the

1960s and 1970s interaction between white motorcyclists and the black community was becoming more common. Indiscriminate violence characterized some of those interactions, but race was generally the motivation, the struggle over racism was often the particular focus, and the white motorcycle cop as prominent a threat to the black community as any other rider. Indeed, by the 1960s the white motorcycle cop was a particularly conspicuous figure policing urban communities and often at the heart of the controversy surrounding the push for liberation that shaped the black community's relationship with law and order and their views of motorcycling.[6]

Race also shaped the rise of a motorcycle rights movement. The black community's fight for civil rights emboldened motorcycle rights activists to challenge the discrimination they faced and to make their own claims about freedom. But they also used that movement to highlight their differences with the black community, to refine an understanding of citizenship and individual responsibility, and to challenge age-old stereotypes about motorcyclists. These struggles not only contributed to a segregation between black and white riders that is still evident but also helped crystallize the relationship between motorcyclists and conservative politicians, who also promoted a conventional (and racialized) vision of freedom, politics, citizenship, and equality that has generally ignored the black community.[7]

At the same time, we cannot forget the important role that black riders played in shaping motorcycling in America. While black men and women were as enthusiastic about motorcycles as their white counterparts, black riders also recognized that the rebelliousness that had its roots at Hollister could also unsettle racialized and gendered assumptions that have contributed to their exclusion from mainstream motorcycle culture. Even *Sweet Sweetback's Baadasssss Song* featured a black motorcyclist (played by John Amos of *Good Times* fame) who aided Sweetback in his escape from the white bikers and the police. The growing visibility of black riders and their relationship to the larger struggle for equality not only shaped motorcycling but also ensured that these divisions based on race would remain prominent. Indeed, by the late 1970s and early 1980s, signs of a black motorcycle culture were more pronounced than ever. Mainstream motorcycle rallies organized by and for black riders were a direct reflection of the role race played in shaping motorcycle culture and of the problems black riders faced from an activity and preoccupation overwhelmingly dominated by white riders. But they also demonstrated how the black community could empower itself even if only for a few moments. Apart from their white counterparts, black motorcyclists would create the space that affirmed their identity as riders and as black men and women and create a space that had the potential to shape all of motorcycle culture once the rally came to an end.

WHITENESS AND WHITE MOTORCYCLISTS

"Since the arrival of Africans on slave ships in the early seventeenth century," argues historian Joe William Trotter Jr., "mobility has been a central theme in African-American history."[8] Fleeing from slavery represented resistance and possible freedom and was a constant challenge that shaped plantation culture and threatened to destroy it. Emancipation only further encouraged mobility. Freedmen by the thousands took to the roads in search of family members or joined the growing numbers of black men and women leaving the South for a better life.

By the twentieth century this trend would only accelerate. World War I restricted the supply of labor from Europe for America's growing industrial base, and set off what became known as the Great Migration—that massive movement of millions of black men and women out of the South. For many of these migrants the promise of a better life and the employment opportunities to support it explain their decision to migrate. Others were driven less by the potential opportunities in the North and West and more by the discrimination they faced from the rise of Jim Crow, the threat of lynching, and disenfranchisement.[9]

Perhaps unsurprisingly, mobility also emerges as a central theme in literature, music, and film where the central protagonists are African American. Migration not only was a popular theme in the blues but also was linked to itinerant musicians who spread their craft well beyond its southern origins. Cities like Atlanta, New Orleans, Dallas, Memphis, and Houston became known for their blues clubs in the first half of the twentieth century, but the recording industry was in the North and West, and fame could be had in cities like New York, Chicago, Los Angeles, or Kansas City.[10] Black writers like Chester Himes, Richard Wright, Farah Jasmine Griffin, and Isabel Wilkerson and poet Langston Hughes highlighted this migration or chose the struggles surrounding mobility as the central themes of their literature. In these novels the plot is often developed around the issue of mobility, or critical scenes often take place in automobiles, streetcars, or on other forms of transit. Richard Wright's *Black Boy* is an autobiographical account of his journey as a young man in the early twentieth century out of Jim Crow Mississippi to the bustling metropolis of Chicago. Even in *Sweet Sweetback's Baadasssss Song* the central theme is escape. The sex and violence that attracted the audience's attention take place against the backdrop of Sweetback fleeing for his life after his first encounter with the police. The film ends with him crossing the desert and escaping into Mexico.

Conflict surrounding transportation has also been a central theme of black life. In the South, some of Jim Crow's most well-known and explosive battles erupted over trains, buses, and other public forms of travel.[11] In the North, conflict and violence were also conspicuous. Subways and streetcars, Brian McCammack argues, not only "expanded the sphere of citizen mobility for work and recreation" but also made "the boundaries of a segregated community more fluid than perhaps many whites would have liked them to be." The unsupervised contacts that public transport promoted (as opposed to work or school) and the degree of bodily contact that at times could escalate into verbal confrontations and violence were issues that routinely attracted attention in northern cities. How often those contacts led to violence is difficult to estimate, but black passengers on public transport became the targets when minor conflicts set off race riots. A riot in Manhattan in 1900 and the Chicago Race Riot of 1919 saw mobs of whites dragging black passengers off of streetcars.[12]

Automobiles privatized mobility but did not eliminate the violence or the importance of race. In his fascinating study of same-sex relationships in Mississippi in the postwar period, John Howard explains how transportation promoted opportunities for intimate and erotic exchanges. But African Americans, as one southerner explained, were generally denied the same courtesies extended to white drivers, and "many deadly altercations between blacks and whites began as or were framed as automobile mishaps."[13] Automobiles offered black motorists autonomy, but their mobility also presented a new challenge that was met with violent resistance.

Motorcycles also promised greater mobility and freedom from scrutiny, but riders also faced similar problems on America's expanding network of roads and highways. While motorcyclists in the post-Hollister era were facing increased scrutiny and were often scorned as a general threat to a community's peace and tranquility, in the South black riders were potentially a challenge to the racial status quo. When facing an accident or crisis, motorcyclists had the advantages of increased agility and speed. But because they were often alone or isolated, especially in rural areas or anywhere outside of a major city, they were a likely target and especially vulnerable to attack. Wendell W. Levister, for example, recalled purchasing a "new motorcycle" and joining a motorcycle club after receiving his first check from a factory job in 1949. As he was riding the bike alone one evening, "a gang of white youths in an auto forced his cycle off the road." His bike a wreck and his pride "bruised," Levister "rounded up" some of his friends, and they went looking for his assailants. The police had apparently been tipped off about the possible confrontation, and when Levister and his companions arrived across town, the police were waiting for them. After it was discovered that two of the young men were armed, "all of the youths were charged with acting in concert," and Levister received a seven-month jail term for his involvement.[14]

Just as important are the repeated attempts to ignore, demonize, or exclude the black motorcyclist. Notable examples like Bessie Stringfield, who attracted attention in the 1930s as a dispatch rider and for riding her motorcycle across the country eight times, and Benny Hardy, who built the choppers made famous in the film *Easy Rider,* are notable exceptions that have attracted some attention and, in Hardy's case, shaped motorcycle culture. Yet black riders have generally been ignored and their contributions generally unacknowledged. Al "Sugar Bear" Myers, a forty-year veteran of motorcycling who learned to build bikes from Hardy explained, "There's always been Black motorcycle clubs, especially in Southern Cali. We've just been ignored."[15] Like mass-circulation magazines and newspapers from the era, motorcycle publications rarely included black men or women, and their occasional appearance prompted an explanation. In a 1951 *Cycle* article about the California Highway Patrol's efforts to control "outlaw" riders, the story included a photo of about a dozen motorcyclists signing safety pledges with a police officer present. A caption explained the unusual appearance of black motorcyclists: "Jolly Riders, a San Diego, California club sign safety pledge as Chuck Pollard (far right) beams satisfaction. Club has clean accident slate, is composed mainly of Negroes."[16] In other cases the appearance of a black rider had little to do with motorcycling and more to do with racial stereotyping. One of the earliest examples of an African American in *American Motorcycling* (the official publication of the American Motorcyclist Association [AMA]) took the shape of a wanted poster in 1959. Under the heading "Wanted" was a picture of John Henry Haywood, who allegedly had shot two people in Flint, Michigan. Presumably, Haywood was included in the magazine because he was an "avid motorcycle enthusiast," although his alleged crime was not connected to motorcycling. Readers were encouraged to contact the FBI if they had any "information which might assist in locating this fugitive."[17]

The general invisibility of black riders reflected the decades of discrimination and segregation against which African Americans struggled. Bessie Stringfield recalled that she was refused a motorcycle license in Miami

Sugar Bear Myers riding one of his choppers in 2012. Courtesy of Michael Lichter.

because the police did not allow "Nigger women" to ride motorcycles. The state of Florida granted Stringfield a license only because of a single officer, Captain Jackson, who was a "white motorcycle cop who worked in what was then known as the Negro precinct." He agreed to give her a riding test at a local park where she completed several figure eights and other tricks. Jackson had never "seen a woman ride like that" and was "amazed."[18] The American Motorcycle Association (later named the American Motorcyclist Association) was formed in 1924, and at the organization's initial meeting black riders were specifically excluded. The association would not accept black members for thirty years (until 1954).[19] In other cases, outright restrictions against riding motorcycles were less of a problem than a particular community's segregation. When asked about motorcycling in the black community where he was raised in North Carolina during the 1960s and 1970s, Kwame Alford recalled one motorcycle dealer, but it was located on the wrong (white) side of town, and violations of the town's segregation could exact a heavy toll.[20]

Toward the end of the twentieth century, the motorcycle industry still had little understanding or connection to the black community and to black riders. In 1995 Ed Youngblood, then president of the American Motorcyclist Association, wrote an article in which he lamented the "prejudice experienced by non-white motorcyclists who feel they are unwelcome within the white motorcycling community." Youngblood explained that he was "taken by the overwhelmingly 'white' makeup of our membership," and after explaining that black riders had the same "government relations [and] travel and social needs as all motorcyclists" asked "why do we see so few black riders at AMA gatherings?" Much of what followed was a push to recognize the "tradition of prejudice" that preceded the current problem he was addressing and an admission of his own ignorance. "I think they are right," referring to the idea that the motorcycle industry has ignored the "black ridership." Youngblood cited a *Washington Times* article about the lack of a black presence in the motor-cycle industry, and noted the almost nonexistent white presence at the National Biker Roundup, a rally organized by black riders (first in 1979) that attracts tens of thousands of black motorcyclists every year. Youngblood had visited the rally a few years earlier and described it as "huge!" "There were over 40,000 motorcyclists on hand. And as far as I could tell, I was the only white guy on the grounds." Youngblood then admitted that the Roundup had "been going on for nearly 15 years and as president of the American Motorcyclist Association, I was embarrassed to realize that I had never heard of it even though it's one of the nation's largest gatherings of motorcyclists." Youngblood added that he was "constantly astonished that such a gulf exists between the black and white motorcycling communities in America. Even though we share the same activities, the same interests and the same needs, we pursue them in separate worlds."[21] More recently, Youngblood has described his attendance at the National Biker Roundup as an example of the AMA "trying to get in touch with the black biker com-munity, and my observation was that it was quite happy doing its own thing without the AMA." Youngblood added that the segregation that is evident was a consequence of the black motorcycling community having grown "tired of discrimination and exclusion a long time ago, and hav-ing developed their own community with their own events, organizations, and communications vehicles." Youngblood did not detect any "bad feel-ings" toward the AMA, but that the AMA was "quite irrelevant to them."[22]

In general, the responses to Youngblood's 1995 editorial recognized that there were differences between black and white riders, although there was no agreement as to why. Marty Joda of Burbank, Illinois, argued that Youngblood's premise based on racial prejudice was a "flawed" one. Joda did not deny that black and white riders had little contact and encouraged the AMA to advertise in publications that catered to a black ridership. "More membership [in the AMA] means more legislative power." But he naïvely argued that the AMA moved beyond prejudice in 1954 (the date the association began admitting black riders), and that about ninety percent of the current membership joined after that date. "They joined a club that was open to all races," and, he asserted, "the other 10 percent who were already members stayed after the change." "They may have even driven the change," he added.[23] Robert Lowery, on the other hand, praised Youngblood's article as "probably the most significant piece of writing in a motorcycle publication I've ever read." Lowery had been asking the same question for several years about his own Harley Owners Group (HOG) in Milwaukee—"Why are our HOG clubs not attracting more black members?" Lowery admitted that he did not "know the answers to the problems" but cited the scarcity of black-owned motorcycle dealerships, the fact that "motorcycle clubs affirm the gulf that exists in society at large," and the failure of white motorcycle clubs to "reach out."[24]

The near invisibility of black riders throughout the postwar years did not, however, translate into the absence of race in motorcycle culture. While black riders are generally missing from accounts about motorcycling, the motorcycle industry and white motorcyclists were certainly conscious of their own (white) racial identity.[25] For example, in a 1950 letter to *Motorcyclist* about the debate over American- and British-made bikes, Dick Ragan of Odessa, Texas, exclaimed that he got "a big charge out of reading your letters to the editor from 'dyed-in-the-wool' 'Honky' riders [which he claimed to be] and 'dyed-in-the-wool' 'Limey' riders."[26] Ragan's letter was too brief to offer any insight into his use of "honky" or "honky rider," and his use of "honky" to distinguish between British- and American-made motorcycles does not show up in any other motorcycle publications. The term's meaning, and perhaps Ragan's use of it, could have reflected its working-class origins. The *Oxford English Dictionary* cites "honky" as a common term for a factory worker at midcentury and provides the line "Man I'm down with it, stikin' like a honky," from Milton Mezzrow and Bernard Wolfe's 1946 book *Really the Blues*.[27] Indeed, after World War II, motorcyclists were typically characterized as "broad-bottomed manual workers" of various sorts, and the derogatory terms applied to them like "hounds," "cowboys," and "roughnecks" referred to rough and rowdy behavior or to specific occupations that were unquestionably working class.[28]

The term "honky" gained national attention two decades after Ragan used the word when Stokely Carmichael delivered a 1967 speech in which he was quoted, "you have to go for the honkies who are keeping you in the ghettos." When asked about "honky," he explained that it was a synonym for "cracker." Carmichael's comment sent contemporaries scrambling to uncover the word's origins. Some of them, as Peter Tamony explained, "assumed this term (honky) is basically a Black/Negro enunciation of 'hunky,' long used as a pejorative for Hungarian and other middle European workmen." Even Stokely Carmichael used the terms interchangeably. In that same 1967 speech he warned that "Whenever the hunkies got injustice we're going to tear their cities apart."[29] Carmichael's comment suggests that he did not accept the gradations of white racial identity as easily as native-born whites from the turn of the century who were suspicious of the racial status of southern and eastern European immigrants.

More recently scholars have located the racial connotations of "hunky" and the word's evolution. While the term "hunky," as David Roediger argues, was a derogatory term for unskilled or semi-skilled workmen, especially Hungarians who were also considered culturally backward, brutish, and stupid, he also notes the common practice in the steel industry of assigning work to hunkies that was thought to be "too damn dirty and too damn hot for a white man." Southern and eastern Europeans in the West were also excluded from a "white man's camp," as were Mexican and Asian miners. Slang terms like "hunky" (and "wop") were commonly associated with "manual types of work" or what was derogatorily called "nigger work." Roediger notes that by the post–World War II period, "hunky" began to lose "some of its negative racial and anti-immigrant connotations" and increasingly was used interchangeably with "honky." The interchangeability of "hunky" and "honky," a practice Carmichael was also guilty of more than twenty years later, marks the beginning of the end of the nonwhite racial identity of eastern Europeans or their descendants. While Roediger argues that terms like hunky "associated new immigrants with nonwhiteness on such multiple fronts," "honky" was typically cast in diametric opposition to blackness. A "honky" was a factory hand to be sure, but he was also what one source described as a "loud mouthed white" whose anger was as hard to understand as his disdain for African Americans.[30]

Indeed, well before Carmichael popularized honky as a term for a cracker and well before Dick Ragan of Odessa, Texas, referred to himself as a "honky rider," the word had other (generally southern) roots in black-white interactions. "Honky" had an "immediate association with honky-tonk, a phrase that dates back to at least the 1880s when it first appeared in print to describe a raucous "dive or booze-joint" that featured "women and music of any type." "Honky" was also used to describe a braying donkey. Another possible meaning refers to the "small-town Southern practice of speeding automobiles through Black/Negro districts or towns with horns honking and blaring." A more specific usage suggests that whites were not simply driving through black communities but cruising in search of black prostitutes. Drivers would honk their horns to "call girls to the window." On hearing the honking of horns, one source explains, bystanders would say, "Here come the Honkies."[31]

Manufacturers also used race to sell their motorcycles. A 1947 advertisement for a Triumph motorcycle featured a drawing of two Asian men in stereotypical fashion with buck teeth and "squinty" eyes, pulling a rickshaw occupied by two British soldiers. The ad does not include a picture of a Triumph motorcycle, only the logo in the ad's bottom left corner along with other information about dealers. Above one of the English officers are the ad's only words "Yes, but I'd prefer a Triumph twin," a reference to the engine's basic design.[32] The ad asserts Western technological and mechanical expertise through the Triumph twin, which stands in bold contrast to eastern ingenuity—the rickshaw.

The contrast between the two directly reflected the decades-old conflict surrounding the Japanese and the broader fears and paranoia surrounding Asian immigrants. Anti-immigrant sentiment on the West Coast had been conspicuous since the mid-nineteenth century and led to waves of violence against the Chinese in the 1870s and 1880s. The influx of Japanese immigrants after 1905 led to renewed fears about a "yellow peril" that found a sympathetic press more than eager to promote the conflict. By the end of World War I, Roger Daniels argues, "a great reservoir of anti-Japanese sentiment had been created throughout the country."[33] This sentiment would only grow more conspicuous during the interwar years, and with World War II it reached unprecedented heights. The war in the East, as John Dower and others have argued, became a race war on both sides, and on the home front Japanese immigrants and Japanese Americans faced internment.[34]

The use of these stereotypical images in Triumph's ads reflected this larger history and the degree to which Americans were familiar with them. In 1947 the influx of Japanese-made Hondas into the American market and Honda's eventual dominance of it was about fifteen years away, and there is no reason to believe that Triumph's management was perceptive enough to predict the industry's future—that Japan's dominance (along with Triumph's own incompetence) would lead to Triumph's demise.[35] Whatever the ad's inspiration, race figured prominently in Triumph's marketing scheme, along with the assumption that the company's general audience was white and sympathetic to a racialized vision of motorcycling. If Triumph was attempting to evoke a particular response or emotion with this ad, it was by highlighting a sense of racial superiority instead of the motorcycle's marketable qualities—agility and speed.

Throughout the 1960s and 1970s race remained prominent in motor-cycle ads even as black riders (and images of them) remained scarce. While motorcycling was becoming popular in the black community and particularly noticeable in magazines that catered to a black middle class, the few ads that appeared in these magazines only reinforced the idea that motorcycling was a white preoccupation. Harley-Davidson has never placed an ad in Jet magazine, and only seven have appeared in *Ebony*, all during a single three-year period, 1960 to 1962.[36] Of these seven ads, only two featured black riders; one of the other five did not feature any riders, and white riders appeared in the other four. In all these ads black and white riders dressed similarly—same khakis or light-colored slacks and loafers—or what had become a signature middle-class and stereotyp-ically white aesthetic. Some of the ads are also strikingly similar to the ads Harley-Davidson had been using since at least the end of World War II that featured a clean-cut male rider and female passenger appropriately riding their Harley with lots of smiles.[37]

These ads were also focused overwhelmingly on Harley-Davidson's increasing interest in lightweights, undoubtedly a reflection of Honda's influence and its popularity among the "nicest people"—white, middle-class men and women. Two of the four ads are montages of differ-ent riders and different bikes. One ad consists of photographs below the heading, "Ride the Sunny Side of the Street." The ad featured the "Super-10," or what H-D described as the "most economical lightweight"—along with the rider dressed in light-colored slacks, sweater vest, and penny loaf-ers surrounded by three admiring co-eds. The New Sprint (another light-weight) is also featured and presented as a "new class of motorcycling" with a young man dressed in light-colored slacks and a vertical-striped shirt charging up the side of a hill on his motorcycle; and Harley-Davidson's new scooter, appropriately named "Topper" because it was the "world's top motor scooter." Perhaps unsurprisingly, a businessman was riding the "Topper" down a busy street, presumably going to work, with several cars following closely behind. The other ad was a cartoon depiction of a Harley-Davidson dealership and an assortment of buyers sizing up the new models for 1962. The top of the ad featured a banner just below sev-eral strings of triangle-shaped (and multicolored) flags that are still typical at car lots. It reads, "Harley-Davidson, 1962 FUN-O-RAMA!" Like the other ad, several different bikes are advertised along with several different types of customers. Two of the sketches depict working men: one with his lunch pail and the other with a mail pouch hanging off of one of his shoulders. The rest emphasize H-D's venture into the off-road market (the sportster

CH) or are stereotypically middle-class and white: the businessman in suit and tie (and pipe) with family admiring the Topper—"Dad, your TOPPER 'H' is an extra set of wheels the whole family can use," and a young couple surrounds the Duo-Glide with the husband asking "How about a deluxe Duo-Glide for our next vacation tour?"[38]

During the 1960s and 1970s, Honda had even fewer ads in publications that catered to a black audience. From the moment Hondas first appeared on the U.S. market in the early 1960s to the end of the 1980s, the company placed no ads in *Jet* magazine and only one in *Ebony*. At a time when Honda was manufacturing a 1000cc motorcycle, the 1980 *Ebony* ad featured a lightweight and asked readers "How about a Honda Express?" The Express was a "step-through scooter" that was "rakishly styled" and the epitome of "simplicity." "No pedals to push. No gears to shift. And it starts with a quick turn of the key, tap of the foot and a squeeze of the lever."[39] The number of Honda ads directed at the black community (which included black actors) was, in fact, so small that a group called the Coalition of Black Stuntmen and Women filed a lawsuit on October 2, 1978, charging Honda Motorcycles with racial discrimination in hiring. The Coalition monitored 27 Honda commercials, and of "about 127 actors used," only 3 were black.[40]

Race was also conspicuous in the immediate postwar years because of a popular style of dress, the Eastern Marcel, also known as the Gestapo Garb. As noted earlier, the Eastern Marcel featured an overdressed rider with a shiny leather jacket fully studded in chrome, wearing a hat, and a motorcycle that was weighed down with an alarming number of chrome-plated attachments. The use of "Gestapo" was no doubt a recognition of the style's prolific use of leather and leather's unfortunate connection to Nazi Germany. In his history of the black leather jacket, Mick Farren bluntly asserts the German influence on leather's history. "Sadly to say," Farren argues, "the Nazis play an uncomfortably major role in any history of the black leather jacket." Farren uncovers the roots of the black leather jacket in Germany during World War I. At the start of the war, the full-skirted leather coat was "standard apparel for both flyers and motorcycle dispatch riders." Aviators adopted a cut-down version of the full-length leather coat, and it soon became standard clothing for aviators and motorcyclists alike. The Nazi Party appropriated various versions of these leather styles, and soon a trademark look had taken shape. Hitler and his henchmen were often seen in full-length leather coats with all the accompanying accessories, and certain units within the Nazi Party became associated with leather. S.S. Panzer divisions, according to Farren, "boosted their world-conquering ambitions with black forage caps, jump boots and natty leather jackets." And the Gestapo, which was "supposed to be a secret police force," made itself conspicuous with its penchant for "slouch hats and ankle-length black cowhide."[41] After the war, these styles became standard issue for rebels of various sorts—the rocker and the motorcyclist are the most well known—hence the rise of the Gestapo Garb.[42]

The Gestapo Garb quickly attracted some attention in motorcycle publications. "Where you get the nerve to refer to motorcycle uniforms as 'Gestapo garb' is more than I can understand," lamented C. W. Conant in a 1950 letter to *Cycle*. Conant described the editor as "way off his beam" and warned that there would be "a great many riders burning after reading this item." Of the dozen or so other letters that were published on the subject, no other rider complained about Gestapo's use.[43] Sergeant Lee E. Davis, who was the secretary of the Luzon Ramblers, preferred "a neat conservative outfit sans studding, jewelry, etc.," but he understood the need for the thick breeches that were part of the Gestapo's look, "especially during spring and fall months when those cold breezes blow."[44]

By the end of the 1950s and early 60s, some evidence suggests that the link between motorcyclists and Nazi paraphernalia was becoming more common. In his coauthored biography of coming of age in postwar America and his membership and eventual leadership of the Oakland chapter of the Hells Angels, Sonny Barger explained that the club's "association" with these symbols started "rather innocently" when another Hells Angel gave him a belt buckle that his father had brought home after the war. "It was a beautiful German World War II military belt buckle, [with] an eagle perched on a swastika." During the immediate postwar years, Barger explained, "it was fairly easy to find authentic captured Nazi war gear at flea markets and gun shops." Barger added that "members who would see my belt buckle would go out and get something with a swastika or an Iron Cross." The "Nazi thing," Barger wrote, "got so out of hand."[45]

Barger described this shift as "innocent enough," but his contemporaries generally identified the paraphernalia with racial intolerance. A 1966 *Ebony* magazine story about a Los Angeles–based, mixed-race motorcycle club called the Chosen Few featured interviews with club members and highlighted a meeting with the Hells Angels, which prompted questions about swastikas. While the author described clubs that were guilty of the "liberal use of Nazi flags and insignias" as " 'way out' motorcycle clubs," like the West Coast's Hells Angels, the Pagans of Washington, D.C., and the Gooses of New Jersey and New York, he also argued that "none" of these clubs "seems to harbor racial animosity." According to "Dougie Poo," a member of the Hells Angels interviewed for the story, "The swastika means, don't mess with us; it has nothing to do with Jews or Negroes." Dougie did add that there were no black Hells Angels and that none had sought membership in the club, suggesting perhaps that these symbols were more complicated than he was willing to admit. "We don't have any Negro members," Dougie added," because we don't know any who could make it," which the author explained referred to mechanical expertise and the Hells Angels' assumption that black men and women had none. According to the author, the "Hell's Angels pride themselves in their performance of enormous mechanical feats, like 'tearing a bike down' and putting it back together in two hours."[46]

Opposition to swastikas and other Nazi symbols was at times conspicuous in motorcycle publications. The Mighty Dugoid, from British Columbia, Canada, asked the question, "Do motorcycles and antisocial behavior (especially in a group or club) go hand in hand?" "I sure hope not," he added, but he emphasized that there "seems to be quite a few zombies on motorcycles, and we'll all suffer because of them. If any of the street clubbers' daddies were ever in World War II and lived to see their sons sporting 'proudly' the Nazi swastika and regalia, they would obviously realize these guys are two bricks short of a fireplace. . . . Best of luck to all of us, brother bikers," he concluded his letter. "We need it now more than ever before."[47] Another letter writer, "The Magic Mountain Man," from Northampton, Massachusetts, explicitly highlighted the contradiction between *Easyriders'* focus on "freedom" and the racial intolerance he associated with swastikas. "You folks have your heads up your collective asses," the Magic Mountain Man began his letter. "How you can throw so much shit about freedom, oppressive bureaucracy, individual rights—just writing it makes me sick, because I've seen too many swastikas, World War II helmets, and other fascist crap among 1%ers—not to mention the way you folks . . . stomp on other people's rights." The Magic Mountain Man admonished the editors to "clean up your act a little and live this freedom your rag keeps talking about (instead of just acting free)—then you'll find out what oppression is. Then I'll be with you."[48]

Easyriders' typical response was to downplay the swastika by describing what one author called the "misconceptions of its [the swastika's] significance to bikers." One writer, for example, argued that the "vast majority of motorcyclists are not sympathetic to Nazism regardless of their own personal prejudices," and explained that these symbols were common because motorcyclists were "theatrical" in their "attitudes and appearance."[49] Another article challenged the swastika's association with bikers by explaining the symbol's larger history. The author acknowledged that the swastika "still conjures up images of the mass hysteria generated by Hitler's impassioned rhetoric—images of extermination camps, of jack-booted troops goose stepping through the streets of Paris, [and] of the devastation of the blitzkrieg." But swastika's association with Nazi Germany was what he described as a "historical coincidence" and provided a concise history of the swastika's link to different cultures and meanings to challenge its negative connotations. *Easyriders* argued that civilizations across North and South America, China, Egypt, Greece, and Scandinavia have used the swastika for centuries. Archaeologists have found it "on textiles made by the Incas, on relics excavated from Troy, and in the catacombs of Rome [to name a few]." The swastika, the author concluded, "has carried a multitude of meanings down through the centuries of its existence . . . and any attempt to insist that its appearance on bikers necessarily means a sympathy with Nazi beliefs or anti-Semitism or the like simply ignores the history of the swastika."[50]

Yet even as *Easyriders* argued that the swastika's broader racial connotations have overshadowed its history, the magazine promoted the intolerance it was trying to downplay. The magazine's very first issue includes advertisements for Nazi belt buckles and other paraphernalia. By the latter 1970s, and just a few months after *Easyriders* argued against the swastika's association with bikers, the magazine began running advertisements for white power patches that featured the swastika or the Confederate flag. The "Ol' Lady Photo Contest" occasionally included photographs of women (in various stages of undress) standing in front of a print of a swastika or Confederate flag, and the magazine even published a favorable interview with David Duke, who at the time was the Grand Wizard of the Knights of the Ku Klux Klan, the largest Klan organization in the United States.[51] The author admitted that the Ku Klux Klan "can be a very touchy subject in many segments of the world" and the organization represented "a lingering hatred kindling deep in the South." "Not so," he emphatically insisted, and explained, "This interview [with Duke] may change many notions and possibly generate some new ones." *Easyriders* described Duke as "a handsome dude. Famous . . . a certified genius . . . young, and successful as most men will never be . . . [who] could probably have any job he wanted." The interview did little more than provide Duke an open forum to advertise the Klan without critically discussing the organization's continued violence. For example, the interviewer alluded to the recent "resurgence of Klan activity" without discussing the Greensboro Massacre in North Carolina where members of the Klan and the American Nazi Party killed five marchers just eight months before the interview. Indeed, the interview was more of a staged audition to figure out if bikers would make good Klansmen. *Easyriders* asked Duke if the Klan "discourage[d] your male and female members from living together?" "Would you say that the Knights of the Ku Klux Klan believe in law and order?" and "Do you believe there should be laws against smoking marijuana?"[52]

The most telling part of the interview was *Easyriders'* question about whether bikers represented a significant number of Klan members. Duke did not think bikers constituted a substantial percentage of the Klan's membership. "But in terms of numbers," he added, "I think there are a lot of bikers or people who are interested in motorcycles who are in the organization." "The average biker today," Duke continued, "is kind of like the knights of old. He is a free spirit. He is usually straightforward. I think most people who ride motorcycles today are courageous. They are tough, they're strong. They are not weak and effeminate like our society is becoming." "You might say," Duke speculated, "they call a spade a spade."[53]

As these examples suggest, race affected motorcycle culture throughout the postwar years. At times it was most conspicuous because of its absence—or, at the least, the absence of black riders, even as a consciousness of race was prominent and, at times, a reflection of the conflict between black and white communities. The appropriation of swastikas and other Nazi artifacts as symbols of conquest and war accompanied a more deliberate use of racial superiority (and inferiority) to sell motorcycles and to shape ideas about motorcycling and motorcyclists. By the late 1960s and 1970s, some evidence suggests that these symbols were more prominent than in earlier years and just as the question of civil rights was gaining ground. Voices of tolerance were heard occasionally over the clamor surrounding these symbols but never loud enough to credibly challenge them or the nonriding public's tendency to associate motorcyclists with racial intolerance.

LAW AND ORDER

During the first half of the twentieth century, the link between motorcycling and police departments was well established. *American Motorcycling* in 1950 claimed that during the decades before World War II, three-quarters of the motorcycles sold were used for service vehicles or by police departments for traffic control.[54] The motorcycle cop, in fact, predates the "outlaw" motorcyclist, emerging shortly after motorcycles appeared and when motorized transportation was still in its infancy. "The two-wheel lawman," argued *Easyriders*, "has as long a history and tradition as any other group of riders in the country. . . . As soon as the first scoots [motorcycles] started

Lineup of motorcycle cops in Washington, D.C., in 1922. Motorcycles were one of the main forms of transportation for police departments in the early twentieth century. Courtesy of the Library of Congress, Washington, D.C.

comin' out of the factories," the author added, "police departments were buyin' 'em, puttin' ridin' officers on 'em, and sendin' 'em out to patrol the streets and highways."[55] Los Angeles organized an eleven-man squad for its first motorcycle corps in 1913. "In those days," explained Anthony Collins, a police inspector who joined the force in 1916, "most roads were just bicycle paths," and the motorcycles "were not equipped with sirens [because] . . . the noise of their own motors was sufficient warning for pedestrians and horses to get out of the way."[56] Charles Silberbauer was New York City's first motorcycle cop. Silberbauer joined the police department in 1900 and was transferred to the motorcycle corps "soon after it was formed in 1917."[57] During these early years, some cities relied exclusively on motorcycle cops until the 1930s. State police in Virginia, according to one source, relied on "some 100" motorcycles "for all purposes," during the "heyday of the motorcycle . . . 1932–36," and did not introduce automobiles into their ranks until 1936.[58]

After World War II, the number of motorcycles for recreational purposes and transportation was on the rise, but the association between motorcyclists and the police remained conspicuous. Photographs in motorcycle magazines throughout the late 1940s and 1950s leave little doubt in the reader's mind about this connection. Motorcyclists are pictured in their Sunday best or club outfits with knee high black boots, dress shirt and tie, jodhpurs, and the police hat (similar to what bikers referred to in the 1970s as a "Gestapo cap)"—nearly indistinguishable from the average police officer's uniform. Indeed, some evidence suggests that the Gestapo Garb so closely resembled a police uniform that there was confusion between the two. In 1950 *Cycle's* editor attempted to explain why "John Q. Public" commonly "frowned" on motorcyclists and the "grand sport of motorcycling?" What he described as the "SEE" side of his editorial focused on the motorcyclist's style, which led to a discussion of the Western Bob and the Eastern Marcel. While the editor complained that the Eastern Marcel was too ostentatious and stood in sharp contrast to the policeman's uniform, which was "simple, neat and pleasing to everyone—except a traffic offender!," he could not help but notice the similarities between the two and suggested that those similarities were conscious. "Surely," the editor reluctantly acknowledged, "the wearers of 'Gestapo Garb' neither intend to emulate policemen nor to try to psychologically affect the habits of Mr. Average Citizen."[59]

The connection between motorcyclists and the police also reflected the push to regulate behavior. In 1947 *American Motorcycling* reported that "fifty members of the Riverside Bombers Motorcycle Club met with the police to have their mufflers checked and to have the Police Department explain regulations that pertained to motorcyclists." They also requested that the local police contact them if any of the club's members were ticketed for violation of the city's muffler ordinance "so that we can take club action against that member in addition to whatever punishment the courts may mete out."[60] The Amarillo Motorcycle Club in Texas began to contact the police to help round up "those bazooka hounds who wouldn't cooperate with the [club's] muffler drive."[61] Other motorcycle clubs organized their own patrol squads, often with the blessing of local law enforcement. The Pasadena Motorcycle Club Inc. of California, which complained of other riders who "muscled in on our meets [to create] disturbances," organized a motorcycle patrol to monitor their major events. The patrol consisted of five or six motorcyclists who acted as citizen policemen at motorcycle rallies and other events. They would "patrol the meets and when a guy gets out of line they'll make a civilian arrest, haul him off to the pokey and sign a complaint against him." The plan was also presented to the chiefs of police in Pasadena, South Pasadena, Monterey Park, and Pomona, and they approved it.[62] Two months later the AMA was boasting about the growth of motorcycle patrol squads. According to the AMA, twenty clubs and dealer organizations from Southern California AMA District 37 had met to discuss a "policing plan" and to organize their own "all-out assault" on what the author called the "undesirable element." As in the Pasadena plan, club members, working with law enforcement agencies, would "exercise civilian police powers, placing under arrest all offenders at motor meets."[63]

Before long the idea of a volunteer patrol of motorcyclists began to spread across the state. In Ventura, a club organized "a snappy, gun-toting outfit" of twenty-five motorcyclists. In Salinas a fifteen-man Sheriff's Motorcycle Squad was drawn "from the local cycle club," and in Oakland the police "depend" on a forty-nine man "cycle auxiliary handpicked from the local club." While their duties varied from city to city, they performed most of the same tasks as regular policemen: handling traffic problems, supervising sports car and motorcycle races, and searching for lost children and escaped criminals. In Ventura each man on the motorcycle squad had graduated from the city's police school, and all of the riders had full police powers, including making arrests anywhere and at anytime in the state.[64]

As these examples suggest, the supposedly lawless Hollister outlaw had a counterpart who was becoming increasingly prominent in the years following the rally. He was respectable and sported a style that reflected leather's utility and a larger, more complicated history that led motorcyclists to use "Gestapo" to describe it. It was a style that might lead bystanders to mistake him for a motorcycle cop. Indeed, this style was so suggestive of a police uniform that even black riders mimicked it to avoid any unwanted scrutiny. According to Sugar Bear, "Some of the earlier clubs dressed like policemen with the pants that bulge so that we wouldn't get hassled by the police." These riders, he added, "didn't want to look like the stereotypical biker," what he described as having "matted hair" and being "greasy," and "dirty." "That would have made us an easy target."[65] Sugar Bear's comment in particularly insightful because he suggests that even black riders could appropriate the Eastern Marcel to ward off any unwanted police scrutiny, and thus defy the stereotypical biker who was "dirty" and "greasy" and perhaps (or at least momentarily) defy their own blackness. Before the civil rights resurgence of the 1950s and 1960s, the black motorcycle cop was virtually nonexistent, and the few black men employed as police officers were generally confined to certain sections of town.

The Gestapo Garb's racial dynamic was further accentuated by the Western Bob and its link to the story of the "greaser," which has its own complicated racial history that dates back to the nineteenth century. The term "greaser" is what dictionaries have labeled a "real Americanism" to describe Mexicans living in what had become U.S. territory after the end of the Mexican-American War. These early racialized origins, David Roediger argues, were as diverse as they were unsettling: linked to "dirty manual work," the "alleged greasiness of Mexican food, skin, and hair" that could also be applied to Indians who greased themselves, and perhaps, Roediger adds, to "black slaves who were greased when sold." Other associations include Anglo settlers' use of the word to characterize the "Tejano Mexican American greaser population of Texas as mongrels with African American and Native American 'blood.'" "Sketches" of the "greaser" also appeared with "tremendous frequency" in the national press and "constantly emphasized mixed-ness and proximity to other people of color."[66]

By the 1950s and 1960s, "greaser" was still commonly used to belittle Mexicans and Mexican Americans, but working-class white ethnics had appropriated it to describe a rebellious and rough attitude characterized by hair tonic, rock 'n' roll, cars, gangs, and motorcycles as well as its own style: greasy or slicked back hair, black leather jacket, and blue jeans. It became an iconic image that has affected our memories of postwar rebelliousness (or at least in the 1950s and 1960s) embodied on screen by Marlon Brando and James Dean and a style known as the Western Bob. The greaser was unambiguously working class and disrespectful but also racially complicated because of the word's origins and (in the Southwest) its sometimes-continued link to Latinos, although perhaps even more so when compared to his counterpart within motorcycle culture—the Eastern Marcel (aka the Gestapo Garb). The Gestapo Garb was a style (and attitude) that was conspicuously respectful, a sign of law and order, and unequivocally white. If motorcycling's "greaser" raised doubts about a nonwhite racial identity, those sporting the Gestapo Garb did not.[67]

MOTORCYCLING IN THE BLACK COMMUNITY

The motorcycle's link to law and order and to police departments across the country would eventually transform the ways in which law enforcement scrutinized urban spaces and the black community. In his now-classic novel, *If He Hollers Let Him Go*, Chester Himes illuminates the role transportation played in shaping the urban setting and the lives of black men and women by exploring a two-day period in the life of Bob Jones, a young black man working in a World War II Los Angeles shipyard. Jones struggles bitterly to negotiate the racism he faces in Los Angeles and what he imagines his future will look like. One of his genuine means of escape is his 1942 Buick Roadmaster. Those brief moments driving across the city not only stand in sharp contrast to his time in the shipyard, where he confronts head on the limits of wage work and intolerance, but also afford him the autonomy he craves to directly confront the boundaries, indifference, and indignities of being black in Los Angeles. The police are never too far removed from Jones's day-to-day experience and often appear in the form of the motorcycle cop. Their scrutiny contributed to Jones's frustration with the city and his struggles to overcome the racism that challenges his humanity.[68]

The motorcycle cop's appearance in Himes's novel reflected larger historical developments that saw white motorcycle cops and African Americans moving into American cities at about the same time. The motorcycle cop who had become a fixture of the American landscape during the early twentieth century saw his role changing in the postwar years. On the one hand, police departments across the country became less dependent on the motorcycle corps. Maryland state police, for example, stopped using motorcycles for highway patrol in 1946, while Virginia's police "retired" the motorcycle officer in 1954. Washington, D.C., began phasing out the motorcycle corps in 1960, citing the "advent of radar," which "rendered the high-casualty motorcycle chasing of speeders a thing of the past."[69] Providence, Rhode Island, on the other hand, did not remove them from freeway patrol until 1965. George E. Healey, head of the Providence Traffic Division, also stressed the "hazards" of trying to catch up to a motorist "exceeding sixty miles an hour."[70]

The motorcycle did not entirely fade from law enforcement, however. While the motorcycle cop would become well known for his role "escorting dignitaries, directing traffic at sports events," or occasionally assisting in an emergency situation, the significant shift in the postwar years was his move from freeways to cities. One contemporary, for example, viewed the motorcycle cop as a "potent weapon" on "city streets," or what Deputy Chief John J. Angew of the Metropolitan Police Traffic Division of Alexandria, Virginia, described as the "city's first line of defense."[71] "It is in the city, in fact," argued a *Washington Post and Times Herald* article in 1955, "that the goggled, leather-booted motorman still retains his old power." Captain George F. Everly of Alexandria summed up the motorcycle cop's effectiveness in an article about its suitability to urban spaces: "The psychological effect of a motorcycle on the average driver," he argued, "is far greater than [that] of a cruiser."[72]

The shift away from freeways and into cities also coincided with two migrations of black Americans from predominantly rural communities to urban centers. The first shift dates back to the Great Migration of the World War I era (1910–30). The increasing violence facing the black community in the South gave it yet another reason to look elsewhere for a better life, and immigration restriction combined with the exigencies of the war dramatically reduced the number of immigrants available as cheap labor. The second period begins with World War II and the growing demands for labor that lasted until about 1970. The second period saw an increase not only in the number of African American migrants but also in the rise of urban communities with a majority black population. Washington, D.C., for example, saw black Americans constitute a majority of the city's population for the first time in 1960.[73]

The increased likelihood of contact between white motorcycle cops and the black community in America's cities was made particularly noticeable against the backdrop of the civil rights and Black Power movements. Throughout the 1950s and 1960s, the motorcycle cop's presence on city streets managing traffic put him in direct contact with the public protests that were becoming increasingly common and in the center of the tragic violence that surrounded the fight over civil rights. Throughout the era, the motorcycle cop was conspicuous escorting the funeral processions for slain civil rights leaders or, more often, in the midst of the battle over segregation. One of the most memorable moments of the civil rights movement is the 1955 Montgomery bus boycott that introduced the nation to Rosa Parks, whose refusal to give up her seat to a white passenger sparked the boycott and boosted the visibility of Martin Luther King Jr., whose leadership of the boycott attracted national and international attention when he was only twenty-six.[74] On the first morning of the boycott, contemporaries noted the "extremely heavy" traffic because so many white employers "were up early, driving to the black community to get their maids and yardmen." The "motorized corps of the police department was [also] out in full force," and the "squads of motorcycles" had a special detail: following empty buses as they made their way through the African American community, it was said, to "protect Negroes" who "wanted to ride."[75] Clyde Sellers, who at the time was the newly elected member of the City Commission and who had charge of the police department, appeared on television on the Sunday after the black community released circulars about the planned boycott to explain the department's response to the expected violence. According to Sellers, "goon squads" made up of black individuals had threatened violence against any black man or woman who failed to support the boycott, and a dozen motorcycle cops had been assigned to accompany all buses that entered into black neighborhoods.[76]

The police's argument that the motorcycle cop was present to protect black riders who were presumably in danger from other African Americans

A motorcycle cop parked in front of the high school at Little Rock, Arkansas, in 1957. Little Rock was the site of one of the first battles over school desegregation. Was the cop there to protect black students attempting to integrate the school or there as a warning to the black community to end its campaign for equality? Courtesy of Ferd Kaufman/AP Images.

supporting the boycott was dubious at best. The boycott was based on King's teaching of nonviolent resistance, and the community's support for the boycott was nearly unanimous. One contemporary, for example, recalled seeing black men and women standing on corners throughout the downtown area. They were generally "silent" as they waited for rides or quietly "moving about to keep warm, but," he added, "few got on the buses."[77]

The motorcycle cops' presence that first morning did little more than signal the police's support of the community's segregation and their role enforcing it. By following buses through the black community, they merely confirmed the boundaries on which segregation was based even as they asserted the right to violate them by crossing into African American neighborhoods. Throughout the struggles over segregation, white privilege was often framed around violations of black community space, and transportation often figured prominently in the struggle. In his study of rural Mississippi after World War II, John Howard argues that altercations between black and white were often initiated on southern roadways, and limits on transportation were critical to the maintenance of white supremacy and the day-to-day ways in which it was experienced.[78] The origin of the term "honky" could have been linked to white motorists honking their horns loudly as they crossed the boundaries surrounding the black community, an aural gesture to assert white privilege and intimidate African American residents.[79] Motorcycles had a similar, if not greater, effect. The loud pipes and trademark sound of a Harley offered the police another conspicuous way to violate the boundaries around which the black community was organized and assert their authority.

In some instances the police also used motorcycles to physically disrupt demonstrations and to punish protestors. In the midst of a 1965 fight over segregation in Jacksonville, Florida, the mayor, Haydon Burns, "vowed to maintain order" even if it "meant crushing the peaceful demonstrations," and he "deputized the all-white 496-man fire department" to "carry out" his threat. His actions were met with increasing support for desegregation, culminating in some two thousand black students descending on the downtown area "shouting 'freedom' and vowing to defy the police." The police "let loose a counterattack . . . to [try to] break up the huge demonstration" by "flailing some of the aggressive students," by "corralling scores of marchers," and by "swerving motorcycles into the crowds" to try to intimidate protestors and break their resolve.[80]

At other moments, the conflict proved fatal. In a 1966 article about demonstrations in Birmingham, Alabama, a *Los Angeles Times* reporter contrasted the current protests with the "situation" in Birmingham in 1963 which was "vastly different."[81] The focus of the demonstrations had shifted from the general issue of segregation to voter registration, and according to the *Times*, violence was largely missing. "Birmingham motorcycle police have accompanied most of the marches," and unlike 1963 when even minor infractions attracted the police's attention, "no notice has been made of the fact that the Negroes often jay-walk, obstruct the traffic or walk against red lights."[82] Two years later in Washington, D.C., a motorcycle cop, Pvt. David A. Roberts, took notice of a twenty-two-year-old black male, Elijah Bennett, jaywalking across a busy intersection in a black neighborhood. A "scuffle" broke out between the two, and Roberts fatally shot Bennett. Roberts was hospitalized with a dislocated shoulder. Word of Bennett's death spread quickly and "a two-hour racial outbreak" erupted. According to the story, "hundreds of youths blocked traffic, hurled rocks through shop windows and burned a police car and a major wholesale auto parts firm."[83]

Much of the conflict that occurred between police and the black community was also initiated during the questioning that followed a simple traffic stop, a situation that attracted increasing attention by the mid-1960s following the Watts rebellion in the summer of 1965 and the fatal shooting of a young black man, Leonard Deadwyler, in Watts the following summer. Both of these events increased the public's scrutiny of law enforcement, and contemporaries argued that the moment of greatest vulnerability to police harassment and brutality often occurred during a traffic stop. As one Watts resident explained, "Most of the trouble with the police in the black community happens behind a car." He specifically cited "Black people" who were "too poor to keep up their cars." They "get stopped, a crowd gathers, and you have potential trouble."[84] In another article about post-Watts Los Angeles, Thomas Pynchon of the *New York Times* made a similar point. The endless search for work, Pynchon noted, was accompanied by the constant "wondering when some cop is going to stop you because the old piece of a car you're driving, which you bought for $20 or $30 . . . makes a lot of noise or burns some oil." "Catching you mobile," he emphasized, "widens The Man's horizons [and] gives him more things he can get you on." Pynchon explicitly cited "excessive smoking [from the car's exhaust]"— what he characterized as "a great favorite with him [the police]."[85]

In this increasingly tense environment, the motorcycle cop did not simply play a role but was central to the growing scrutiny black communities faced and to the process of regulating the streets and black men and women. The Watts rebellion of 1965 that lasted five days and led to thirty-four deaths and about $40 million in property damage began after a motorcycle highway patrolman pulled over a twenty-one-year-old black man, Marquette Frye, for driving under the influence of alcohol. Frye claimed that another patrolman in a squad car arrived at the scene next and as the crowd swelled the patrolman produced a shotgun that he began waving at the crowd. Another account claimed that the next officer on the scene was a second motorcycle cop who was accompanied by a tow-truck and a patrol car.[86] Either way, the police arrested Frye, his brother, and his mother (who showed up shortly after Marquette was pulled over), and they were taken to a police station. Marquette recalled a police officer kicking him as he shoved him into the squad car and at the station a police officer "knocked" him "cold." When he awakened, things had settled down in the station, but outside "something far more violent was brewing."[87]

The conflict *Jet* magazine described as "brewing" outside the station would soon explode, the Watts rebellion would become identified with a divide within the civil rights movement, and the motorcycle cop would play a far more visible role than in the initial arrest of Frye. A year after the uprising the community established the Watts Festival to promote and to celebrate community pride and cultural awareness. *Jet* magazine featured a picture of a white motorcycle cop in attendance at the festival in what the magazine described as a "highly popular display." The officer was apparently on exhibit to explain the "workings of his machine" and thus improve relations between the black community and the LAPD (and motorcycle cops). The photograph showed the motorcycle officer surrounded by several black teens, and the caption below the picture described the moment as "reversing" last summer's role when "white motorcycle cops were chasing Negro youths during violence in Los Angeles' Watts district." The initial arrest involved a single motorcycle cop. The attempt to suppress the rebellion involved many of them.[88]

Seven months after the rebellion, conflict between the police erupted again in Watts, and the police's response to it also suggests the prolific use of motorcycle cops seven months earlier. This uprising began after the LAPD arrested a black student from an area high school for allegedly throwing a brick at a teacher's car. For about four hours, according to the *New York Times*, "gangs of youths moved about a 12-square-block area, throwing bricks at cars and people and looting and burning." The rock throwing would come to an end only after "policemen with shotguns walking shoulder to shoulder in ranks of 12 had cleared the streets." The major difference in tactics, according to a member of the LAPD "riot squad," was the use of a "mobile arrest van," essentially a bus "that cruises the area picking up arrested persons," instead of using motorcycle police. "Last time," this same officer explained, "we used motorcycle officers, who proved very vulnerable." "This time," the LAPD emphasized, "we are sending everybody down in cars."[89]

The Watts uprising would attract considerable attention from urban police departments across the county as well as from federal, state, and local governments. A Congressional Quarterly poll of members of Congress, governors, and mayors found that solutions to the rebellions fell "broadly into two categories—those favoring greater federal, state and local efforts to solve social problems and those favoring stiffer punishment for rioters and for persons inciting to riot."[90] The focus on government efforts to deal with social problems led all of these politicians to single out joblessness as the "major cause of urban ghetto riots this past summer." The emphasis on punishment led authorities to admit that the police's response to the rebellion was largely ineffectual, that the black community's response was unexpected, and that it was perhaps different than in previous conflicts.[91] In the midst of the uprising, Police Chief William Parker described the police department's attempt to control it as a "situation . . . very much like fighting the Viet Cong." He admitted, "We [the police department] haven't the slightest idea when this can be brought under control." Journalist Bill Lance made an equally poignant remark when he described Los Angeles as the "first city I ever saw where citizens quickly rise up, overpower police officers, chase them, take their guns and wreck their cars." Lance provided two examples to make his case and inadvertently illuminated the motorcycle cop's limitations. One of his examples took place two weeks before the uprising and involved a "whole neighborhood of Mexican Americans [who] stormed two white cops who tried to arrest a Mexican housewife on a traffic charge." The other one occurred during the uprising and involved "four Negro women" who "snatched a white cop off his motorcycle, beat him up, took his gun and choked him with a bicycle chain."[92] In the end, the motorcycle cop failed to contain the urban rebellions of the mid- to late 1960s, and that failure contributed to the significant effort to increase the firepower of urban arsenals across the country.[93]

The Black Panthers also had run-ins with motorcycle cops.[94] Huey Newton, one of the founding members of the Black Panther Party, recalled stopping at the side of the road one evening to watch a motorcycle cop "question a citizen."[95] Newton "stood off quietly at a reasonable distance" with his "shotgun in hand." The scene quickly attracted the attention of passersby, Newton explained, which only further agitated the motorcycle cop who was "clearly edgy" at his presence. After issuing the individual a ticket, the officer rode over to Newton and asked him if he "wanted to press charges for police brutality." By this time, Newton recalled, about a "dozen people were standing around watching us." "Are you paranoid?" Newton asked the cop. A heated exchange between the two followed, and the officer rode away "steaming mad." About halfway down the street, he circled back, pulled up close to Newton, and reminded him: "If it was night, you wouldn't do this."[96] The cop's statement, not surprisingly, reaffirmed Newton's argument about the likelihood of police brutality despite arguments from critics that those claims were exaggerated.

One image of law enforcement in the black community that highlighted the motorcycle cop's presence was a 1968 photograph from Howard L. Bingham for *Life* magazine. It was taken from the perspective of the motorcycle cop looking directly ahead at about two dozen Panthers standing in front of a courthouse miming a firing squad. The motorcycle cop is the intended target, and the Panthers are posed as if holding a pistol or aiming a rifle or shotgun in a stance identified with Black Power and armed self-defense.[97]

The motorcycle cop's controversial role in policing urban space also convinced the black community to push to desegregate the motorcycle corps. Throughout the 1960s and 1970s *Jet* and *Ebony* magazine included stories about the "first" black motorcycle cop in cities across the country. In general throughout the period, the black community was pushing to desegregate the police and to give communities more control over law enforcement. The likelihood of police brutality, community leaders argued, diminished if the police were beholden to the communities they patrolled. To a certain extent, the numbers of black motorcycle officers reflected the few black police officers overall. In an article about Houston's abysmal record of police brutality, a journalist noted the disparity between the number of blacks and Hispanics residing in the city and the disproportionately small numbers of them who served as police officers. Blacks and Hispanics made up 26 and 13 percent of Houston's population respectively. But together they made up only about 11 percent of all police officers (each group made up slightly more than 5 percent of Houston's total police force) and historically almost none of its motorcycle officers. At one time, black police officers were assigned to jail duties or to investigations in black neighborhoods. They were not allowed to become motorcycle officers. One black police officer was once reprimanded for riding his motorcycle to work while in uniform. "They might think you're on duty," his supervisor objected.[98] The white motorcycle cop was, in short, a long-standing institution in urban police departments across the country that formalized white privilege, its dominance over law enforcement, and a symbol of the battle over desegregation and resistance to it.

Yet even in communities where the push for desegregating the police force was more successful, the black motorcycle officer was still rare. In Washington, D.C., in 1971, for example, blacks made up over 71 percent of the city's population and 36 percent of its police force (1,797 black police officers out of a total police force of 4,994), a particularly high percentage compared to other cities, especially in 1971. But "in Washington everyone knew a black cop did not join the elite motorcycle units or ride in comfortable squad cars."[99] Indeed, the discrimination facing black officers in Washington, an article in *Jet* magazine maintained, was comparable to the "veiled racial slurs" black officers faced in LA when they took their families to the Police Academy swimming pool, and to the problem black police officers faced in the South where custom prevented them from testifying against whites in court.[100]

Throughout the 1960s and 1970s, the face of law enforcement assumed many forms in the black community, and the motorcycle cop was one of the most conspicuous ones. The motorcycle cop had been an integral part of the urban landscape since first appearing in the early twentieth century but became increasingly identified with city patrol only after World War II. Motorcycles could more easily navigate through congested urban streets than squad cars, and highway travel had become too dangerous for the officers assigned to the motorcycle corps. The motorcycle cop's concentration in urban areas also coincided with an increasingly vocal black freedom struggle that also found its strength in cities. That concentration led inevitably to interaction between the two, but there was nothing inevitable about the conflict that developed. Enforcing the law in police departments was often less of a priority than enforcing segregation, and the motorcycle cop was critical to the divisiveness that was becoming increasingly conspicuous in urban communities across the country in the postwar period.

THE WHITE MOTORCYCLIST

In the black community, the victim of an attack by white motorcyclists was often a single individual. However, in some cases entire communities found themselves under siege.[101] In July 1973 the *Washington Post* reported that "residents of a normally quiet black neighborhood in Northeast Washington" were "angered and frightened" because members of a "white motorcycle gang," the Pagans, had "terrorized" community members and had been "linked to recent incidents of violence in the area." The neighborhood had attracted attention, ironically, after Robert Brown, the thirty-four-year-old leader of the Pagans, died after a brawl involving several residents. The fight began at a local tavern, the RIA, between two women—one white and one black. According to several reports, the Pagans came to the aid of the white woman, and within a short time "15 to 20 individuals [black and white] were involved on each side."[102] Much of the neighborhood's frustration focused on the bar where the brawl erupted. But newspaper stories quoted residents describing their community as an "armed camp" with "turf wars" that extended well beyond the tavern's boundaries, and several sources argued that the violence was racially motivated. The *Washington Post*, for example, described the fear surrounding the "talk of guns, mysterious shots in the night and threat and counter threat" as the product of a "racial vendetta." The fight convinced one black woman from the community that "this whole thing has racial overtones." "They have threatened people by saying 'We are going to get you niggers out of there.'"[103]

Other violence grew out of the conflict surrounding the push for civil rights. In Parkesburg, Pennsylvania, in 1969 one African American man was killed and seven others injured when members of the Pagans Motorcycle

Club "clashed with Negro residents." According to the mayor, Graham Boice, the trouble began at the Parkesburg Arms Hotel where some of the motorcyclists were drinking. "As far as I know," Boice explained, "the Negroes marched on the hotel. That's when it all began."[104] Another police report explained that "the shooting started when a group of Negroes gathered in front of the Parkesburg Arms Hotel where several members of the motorcycle gang were seated on the porch. They said the cyclists shouted racial slurs, and the shooting erupted." The slain man was Harry M. Dickinson, "a spokesman for the black action committee formed several months [earlier] to press housing demands." Four men, including three members of the Pagans motorcycle gang, were arrested and charged for the murder.[105]

In Chicago in 1966, police "were bombarded with curses, bottles, and rocks as they clashed Sunday night with hundreds of whites protesting marches by civil rights supporters." According to the *Lewiston Evening Journal*, sixteen persons were injured and twenty-one arrested. Earlier that day three separate parades were organized by 1,000 civil rights advocates to protest against discrimination by real estate firms. Two of the parades were held "within blocks of Marquette Park," what the report described as "an expanse of grass and playgrounds where whites, spurred by an American Nazi party rally, baited police with chants of 'nigger lover' and stoned automobiles occupied by Negroes." At Marquette Park, "some 70 motorcycles, adorned with American flags, streamed into the park and were applauded by more than a thousand persons who had gathered to protest the [civil rights] demonstration." Hecklers were carrying hundreds of signs bearing a "swastika and the legend 'Symbol of White Power.' "[106]

In Cleveland, Ohio, in the late 1960s, white motorcyclists were also allegedly targeting black nationalists. As the summer of 1967 approached, the nation's attention was riveted on Cleveland because it was expected to be one of the first cities to explode after having experienced "several small incidents of window-breaking and looting." A *Jet* national survey of the "heads of local and national rights groups" found that "the most important factor in preventing future riots will be police-community relations," prompting Reverend Andrew Young of the Southern Christian Leadership Conference to recommend that "the police ... this summer ... show respect towards Negroes." According to the story, "reports" had "circulated that this year's disturbances will not be confined to the Negro areas," and that white motorcyclists were the suspected antagonists. "White motorcycle gangs," the article claimed, "are armed and ready to shoot it out with black nationalists, who also have a supply of weapons and ammunition." No one was sure, the author concluded, "what will happen there this summer," but cited the emergence of bumper stickers that read "Pray for Cleveland."[107]

If there was any doubt about the significance of race to motorcycle culture these encounters did little to challenge it. While much of the conflict was not directly connected to the fight over civil rights, all of it raised questions about equality and discrimination. The violence was certainly similar to its description in other stories about motorcyclists: places of leisure were particularly prominent, the violence was erratic and often spur of the moment, and the outcome was generally predictable. But these encounters also reflected the larger history of motorcycling and the role of race. Questions about racial intolerance accompanied the popularity of swastikas and other symbols of white superiority at a time when the typical response to these symbols was to downplay their significance. The motorcyclist's mobility only increased his threat. The ease with which he could travel significant distances in a short amount of time made the likelihood, or at least the threat, of these encounters more common. As the article about Cleveland made clear, "disturbances" would not be confined to the black community but anywhere black men or women congregated.

Throughout the postwar years, the black community also used motorcycling and motorcyclists as worst-case examples of the racism it faced and its consequences. One of the more prominent examples involved Muhammad Ali. In a 1975 biography about the heavyweight champ, he admitted to throwing the gold medal he won at the 1960 Olympics into the Ohio River after a brawl with a "white motorcycle gang." Ali and a friend first encountered the motorcyclists at a restaurant where they were refused service. As the pair was leaving, one of the motorcyclists called out, "Hey, Olympic nigger! You still tryin' to get a milk shake?" And another threatened to lynch them if Ali did not turn over his medal. Ali and his friend quickly left the parking lot (on their own motorcycles) with the intention of heading back to their own neighborhood. But before they could escape, the motorcyclists caught up to them and the resulting fight left one motorcyclist broken and bloodied against a bridge column and another nearly unconscious after Ali smashed his fist into his face.[108]

His fight with motorcyclists highlights the prominent role they could play in the larger struggle over equality and freedom. As he initially pulled into the restaurant and saw the motorcyclists, Ali immediately noticed the Nazi insignias on their backs and "Confederate flags painted on the front," which Ali claimed was a style popular with "some whites in the East End." Ali's response explicitly challenged simple arguments motorcyclists often made about the presumed innocence of these symbols and their meaning, which was based largely on an imagined history that ignored the recent past. The motorcyclists' mobility was also prominent and another reason they posed such a threat. Ali's initial plan to retreat to the black community to avoid a fight suggests that those neighborhoods still served as the refuge or boundary white motorcyclists crossed only reluctantly. Any black man caught beyond the community's boundary, on the other hand, became an easy target, and one these motorcyclists were already known for singling out. "A good many young blacks," Ali noted, "had already been caught in white neighborhoods by this same gang, beaten, chain-whipped, [and] some almost fatally.[109]

About twenty-five years after the fight, Ali claimed that the incident never happened and that he had lost his gold medal rather than deliberately thrown it into the river.[110] While we cannot ignore his change of heart, the fact that he used a "white motorcycle gang" to explain the racism he faced and to reconcile the loss of his medal is significant. Given the history of race relations in the United States, Ali could have used any one of several caricatures to highlight his experience with racism, especially in the South. The hooded Klansman, the small-town sheriff, the racist cop, and the run-of-the-mill "redneck" were all prominent figures during this period. That Ali chose the motorcyclist suggests that he was as well known, at least in some circles, as these other individuals and perhaps as significant of a threat.

The prominent role the motorcyclist played accentuating race and discrimination was never confined to Ali, however. A story about the trend for northern blacks in the early 1970s to migrate back "home" to the South also described the motorcyclist as a threat. One man interviewed for the story, Elijah Davis, recalls the number of motorcyclists who came through his northern town from time to time. Davis had moved to Gary, Indiana, twenty years earlier and had operated a filling station. But he had decided to move back to his hometown of Jackson, Mississippi, because he simply felt safer back in Mississippi. "Sometimes," he noted in his interview, "there would be 300 to 400 motorcycles moving down Gary's main street. And when they came by everything stopped." The author of the article summarized Elijah's comments by noting, "The traffic stopped, the people stopped, business stopped. Like herds of roaming buffalo, the motorcyclists paralyzed the town."[111]

The black community also used motorcycling to describe the adverse ways in which affirmative action was challenged in response to the "Philadelphia Plan," a federal program established in the late 1960s to try to promote equal job opportunity and to address the disproportionately small number of black workers in the construction trades. The Philadelphia Plan established goals for hiring, what critics complained were quotas, and required contractors to make a "good faith" effort to address these inequalities. Labor leader George Meany described the Philadelphia Plan as a "concoction and a contrivance of a bureaucrat's imagination," but *Ebony* explained that it was difficult to measure the plan's success because of what the author described as the practice of "motorcycle compliance. That is, when inspectors went around to various projects to see if contractors were complying with the federal order, blacks were moved from jobs not covered by the Plan to jobs that came under the order and worked there until the inspection was over."[112]

A 1984 *Ebony* article on "How to Handle a Racist" also included the white motorcyclist to highlight the degree to which racism was still a conspicuous problem for all black Americans and to argue that white Americans were likely to receive preferential treatment regardless of their background or status. Most of the article offered practical advice on how to react to racism and focused on the likelihood of physical threats or discrimination in public places of accommodation. The article began with a story of a U.S. Circuit Court of Appeals judge, Damon J. Keith, and the discrimination he experienced at a restaurant in Cincinnati. At a gathering of black attorneys, the judge recounted the problem he and his law clerk faced at a "posh uncrowded restaurant" where they were seated next to the kitchen door. Keith "asked the maître d' for a better table, and, as he tried to enjoy his meal, watched as rowdy, unshaven and helmeted members of a motorcycle gang were given the best table in the house." "His point," the article emphasized, was that "regardless of who you are and where you are in America, if you are Black, chances are that somewhere along the line you will face racial discrimination."[113] But given the history of motorcyclists and the history of motorcycling in the black community, the point the author was trying to make was as much about the degree of racism as about the fact that it was still a problem. The distinguished U.S. attorney seated near the kitchen would have stood out against any whites enjoying dinner at a restaurant's best table. He chose a motorcycle gang (without noting they were white) and, no less, a group of riders who were unshaven and rowdy, obviously a clear violation of the expected etiquette at a posh restaurant, and one that was particularly glaring given the respectability and stature of the black judge and his law clerk.

As all these examples suggest, motorcycling's popularity in the black community was accompanied by a more complicated struggle over the white motorcyclist's role in those neighborhoods and over the very meaning of what it meant to be a motorcyclist. Words like "motorcycle gang" or "motorcycle gang member" appeared in stories about motorcycling often preceded by "white." Others recounted conflicts revolving around the white motorcycle cop and his intrusion into black communities increasingly leery of his presence and his intentions. If there ever was a difference between outlaws and motorcycle cops, black Americans struggled more to find it than their white counterparts. Mixed-race clubs were certainly part of the motorcycle scene in the immediate postwar years, and scholars have often singled them out to emphasize the degree of fraternity among the two-wheeled set.[114] But the degree to which suspicion, fear, and conflict defined the black community's experience with motorcycling was never isolated or insignificant. That conflict was played out daily across the country's social and cultural landscape, and it helps explain the often unlikely appearance of the motorcyclist in popular culture. It also highlights the seeming contradiction that followed the white motorcyclist: often ambivalent, if not outright opposed, to the changes favored by the liberation movements challenging racial discrimination yet increasingly conscious of their own identity as motorcyclists (and as minorities) and their own fight for freedom from government regulation.

LAW AND ORDER IN THE 1960S AND 1970S

The conflict between motorcyclists and the black community did not, however, attenuate the link between white motorcyclists and the police. The link during the immediate post–World War II period was so complete by the 1960s that the arrival of the middle-class rider was routinely compared to the two groups that had traditionally dominated motorcycling (or at least its image): cops and outlaws. In the motorcycle's long-awaited "social revolution," the middle class had finally "invaded the realm that formerly was dominated by Hell's Angels, traffic cops and the greasy types who hung out at the local gas station."[115] In a 1964 *Esquire* article about the "Upward Mobility of the Motorcycle," Carl A. Gottlieb argued that before the rise of the middle-class cyclist, "if you rode on two wheels you were either a cop or a wild kid looking for trouble."[116] After a reporter in the mid-1970s asked Denise Stekert to describe her "favorite little luxury," she immediately replied, "Riding a Harley-Davidson." Stekert did not own her own motorcycle. She rode her boy friend's "shovel head." It was "the big one," she added. "like [what] the cops have."[117]

Even *Easyriders* admitted to the similarities between cops and bikers in two different illustrations from the early 1970s. The first is of an elderly woman standing in front of a biker seated on a chopper resting back on his sissy bar. The woman is pointing at the rider: "You cops are looking shab-bier every day!" The other illustration features a lineup of five motorcy-cle cops standing next to their motorcycles while two other police officers stand in front and to the left of the lineup with the caption: "Better keep an eye on that new rookie!" At first glance the rookies appear identical: same motorcycle, jacket, and patches and all of them are standing at attention next to their motorcycles. On closer inspection, one of the cops is a bearded outlaw, his motorcycle has slightly extended forks and bigger pipes, and one of his patches is an iron cross.[118]

Other contemporaries focused not only on the similarity in dress and style but also on behavior, what one contemporary described as the "pop-ular stereotype of the pig." At the Speech Communication Association Meeting in 1971, Hunter College professor Lawrence W. Rosenfield gave a paper about the "social function of the Hells Angels" and what he called the "real-life significance of motorcycle gangs"—"their sociological func-tion as masquers." Rosenfield's disdain for both groups was palpable. The police had a "clownish aspect" to their dress, and he belittled the motorcyclist's style as a "getup." Rosenfield argued that the biker's attire and behavior were a "parody of police tactics familiar to television view-ers," and to help make his case, he highlighted the similarities in dress. "Bedecked with chains, mirror sunglasses, profane insignia (usually Nazi swastikas), grimy with filth, slovenly, outfitted mainly in black leather—they [motorcyclists] personify" what he described as "the popular stereo-type of the 'pig' " and, as support, offered a similar, albeit circumscribed, description of the police's uniform. "Motorcycle police [also] wear black leather and reflecting sunglasses and assorted paramilitary patches and equipment."[119]

Indeed, by the second half of the 1960s, the idea that the police and white motorcyclists were working together toward the shared goal of undermin-ing the push for equality was gaining support. Hunter S. Thompson argued that the Hells Angels' relationship with the police was surprisingly positive given the tension that was apparent between the two. Thompson refers to what he called a "psychic compatibility" between the cops and the Hells Angels, who "get along pretty well" and "operate" on what he called "the same motional frequency." Thompson claimed that the Hells Angels and the police "deny this. . . . The very suggestion of a psychic compatibility will be denounced . . . as a form of Communist slander." But he argued that this compatibility was "obvious to anyone who has ever seen a rou-tine confrontation or sat in on a friendly police check at one of the Angel bars. Apart, they curse each other savagely, and the brittle truce is often jangled by high-speed chases and brief, violent clashes that rarely make the papers. Yet behind the sound and fury, they are both playing the same game, and usually by the same rules."[120]

Thompson failed to explain what he meant by the "same game" and the "same rules," but Sonny Barger located it within the broader context of race and the growing divisiveness between blacks and whites. Thompson explained that in Oakland a special four-man detail was assigned to keep tabs on the Hells Angels. They would stop by the "bar now and then, smiling good-naturedly through a torrent of insults, and hang around just long enough to make sure the outlaws knew they were being watched." Thompson claimed that the Hells Angels enjoyed these visits and that the Oakland chapter had a "special relationship with the local law," because of what Barger referred to as a "potential common front against the long-rumored Negro uprising in East Oakland." The cops, Barger pointedly added, were counting on the Hells Angels to "keep the niggers in line. . . . They're more scared of the niggers than they are of us," Barger explained "because there's a lot more of em."[121]

The relationship between the police and the Hells Angels, Thompson explained, was even more surprising given the numbers of politicians who favored law and order but who also failed to single out the Hells Angels as a challenge to it. According to Thompson, much of the public's imagination about the Hells Angels, or at least its initial impression about the club, emerged in 1964 because of the Monterey rape case. That the Monterey case attracted national attention was unsurprising for Thompson, but he was surprised when politicians ignored the alleged crime. Not even Senator Goldwater, Thompson lamented, "seized on the Hell's Angels issue, [and] 'Crime in the streets' was a winner for him."[122] Senator Goldwater was running against Johnson for the presidency in 1964 when the Monterey case broke, and he was part of the initial backlash against the political movements of the 1950s and 1960s. Goldwater voted against the Civil Rights Act of 1964, advocated the use of tactical nuclear weapons in Vietnam, supported privatizing various government programs, and, as noted earlier, urgently began to speak out in favor of "law and order," which would become an increasingly important political slogan over the next few years. Goldwater would lose the election, but he became the first Republican candidate for the presidency since the end of Reconstruction to win five states in the deep South (South Carolina, Georgia, Louisiana, Alabama, and Mississippi).[123]

Capitalizing on the fears of street crime was a political strategy that grew increasingly popular throughout the 1960s because of its link to

African American men. After all, while Thompson mistakenly argued that "crime in the streets" was too vague, his response to Goldwater alluded to the degree to which "law and order" was a potent political slogan and ideal and the degree to which race shaped ideas about it. "Crime in the streets" and the law and order hysteria surrounding it were direct references to the rebellions that erupted in cities across the country throughout the 1960s as more African American men and women became disillusioned about the marginal support for civil rights and frustrated at the increased violence against activists. In short, young black men were a much more potent symbol of violence and perceived to be a much greater threat to white America than motorcyclists who appeared routinely in the media and in film as white, no matter how violent or antisocial they may have been. Political gain was undoubtedly an issue that affected the response to these urban uprisings, but we cannot ignore the very real ways in which race shaped the response to motorcyclists, the day-to-day ways in which race shaped the public's understanding of law and order, and Flamm's argument about "personal security." Understanding personal security was never as simple as deciding who posed a threat to it but who posed a greater threat.[124]

The *Berkeley Barb*, one of the most successful underground newspapers identified with the counterculture, included a similar argument in 1965 about the police, bikers, and the black community. The November 1965 issue of the *Barb* included an excerpt from the *Democrat*, a newspaper for Democrats in the Seventh Congressional District, about "Tension in the East Oakland ghetto" that was "centered on the Hells Angels, who rented headquarters at 32nd Ave. near the Estuary early in October." The larger context, the report suggested, was a protest (what the article described as a riot) organized by students at a junior high school against overcrowded lunchroom conditions. The following weekend the police "routed Negroes from 14th St. bars but did not question a group of [Hells] Angels, standing around 37th St. and E. 14th, though complaints had been made against them." The "Angels" had "cut two Negroes in a barroom fight," but according to some sources, the police "said nothing could be done." These "events have led many Negroes to believe the Angels are working with Oakland police" and compelled the *Democrat* to ask, "Can a Watts happen in Oakland?"[125]

Four years later the Connecticut Commission on Human Rights and Opportunities accused the Rat Pack Motorcycle Club of being a vigilante group working for the police against the black community in Waterbury, Connecticut. The report described the town as "bursting at the seams with tension, fear, extremist groups and the potential for riot." One of the report's conclusions described the relationship between the police and the Rat Pack Motorcycle Club as "unhealthy," included witnesses who claimed that the motorcycle club "patrolled the city's Negro area as a suppressive vigilante group," and contended that the motorcyclists maintained "an arsenal of weapons." The Rat Pack Motorcycle Club consisted of thirty members who wore "black leather, initialed jackets and ride powerful Harley Davidsons." Members had converted a former diner into a clubhouse located on the "edge of town [and] covered with tarpaper." John J. Crafa, the club's president, admitted that "some of the boys were armed last summer [at a time of growing tension surrounding the black community]" but "so was everyone." Crafa added that "half [a] dozen policemen who owned their own motorcycles enjoyed riding, in off-duty hours, with the Pack." But he argued that none of them were club members.[126]

Barger's comments about the relationship between the police and the Hells Angels and the conflict in Berkeley and in Waterbury suggest that concerns about race and the expected uprising in Oakland influenced the police's perception about the Hells Angels and their racial politics and perhaps about motorcyclists in general. In other words, in the midst of tremendous uncertainty, racial conflict, and a broader hysteria about "law and order," a solidarity based on race (or whiteness) not only surfaced but helped reconcile fears the police (and the general public) may have had about biker violence. Whether the Hells Angels and other motorcyclists were as shocking and as antisocial as Thompson claimed—or perhaps because they were—the police and the general public were not ready to abandon them altogether. These outlaws were the frontline of defense the (white) police and their (white) constituents could depend upon to stop the potential rebellion that threatened to spill beyond the boundaries of Oakland's African American community. Barger and the Hells Angels' individual or personal racial politics cannot be ignored. Their racism undoubtedly influenced the cops' understanding of the Hells Angels as well as the public's image of motorcyclists nationwide. Yet the day-to-day way in which the Hells Angels were expected to respond to the African American community also took shape within the much broader context of a nation struggling to come to terms with the issue of civil rights, and that context affected how the nonriding public viewed black versus white violence and the rise of the "biker."

In order to understand questions about citizenship and social belonging, we have to understand the profound influence of race. Race was one of the characteristics motorcyclists were likely to share with the police, and that similarity was reinforced daily on the streets and in popular culture.

To be sure, this relationship was a fragile one, and riders complained constantly about police harassment and its potential to lead to violence. But race also functioned to maintain it, however strained that relationship might be, and proves useful in thinking about the ways in which citizenship was daily understood and practiced. Citizenship, as scholars have reminded us, is both a legal and a cultural construction and was never simply assumed, understood, or agreed on. What Americans have defined as citizenship has always been highly contested and policed according to exclusionary ideas about normative behavior. Often—and the Hells Angels and other motorcyclists are a good example of this—the most marginalized of citizens often participated in policing those ideals and boundaries even if their own citizenship was in question and even if they were (or were perceived to be) a threat to the citizens around them.[127] Because motorcyclists were accused of working with the police, they were no longer simply a threat to those boundaries but responsible for deciding which ones were legitimate and which ones were not. In this context and against the backdrop of the civil rights and Black Power movements, which also directly questioned the meaning of citizenship, motorcyclists could assume a conspicuous role in this conservative political realignment of which they were becoming a part and challenge the contradictions that questioned their own social belonging. Race could expand the meaning of citizenship and simultaneously limit what it meant to be a motorcyclist, especially for racial minorities, gays, and women—individuals generally ignored in motorcycle culture and excluded from popular cultural representations of it.

THE BLACK MOTORCYCLIST

While the fear of another Watts resonated in the late 1960s, challenges to discrimination also came from black riders who appropriated motorcycling as an act of defiance to contest racialized ideas about white superiority and dominance. Motorcycling has been (and for the most part remains) identified with white men, and a "Hells Angels type" has been the dominant image, the type who showed up in increasing numbers of stories in the black media about motorcycle "gang" violence and the type (along with the motorcycle cop) who challenged black opposition to segregation and racism. By simply riding a motorcycle, African American men and women not only challenged this image but also upset the dominant racial discourse that promoted black men's and women's invisibility and defined the typical motorcyclist as male and as white. While motorcycling's popularity in the white community was generally linked to a middle-class rider who made the sport more respectable and conventional, the dynamic shaping motorcycling in the black community revolved around the struggles for equality, and it was a dynamic with the potential for radical change.

Challenges to white stereotypes about African Americans have been prominent throughout the twentieth century and by the 1960s and 1970s athletes were once again at the center of a larger revolt.[128] While this revolt often took the shape of mass protests in opposition to segregation or, in general, focused on the discriminatory treatment of athletes at the amateur and professional levels, individual athletes often attracted most of the attention, and none more so than Muhammad Ali. Thanks in large part to Ali, and his competitors, the 1960s–70s was not simply a period when black heavyweights dominated, but one of the critical moments when boxers shaped the public's consciousness about sport and politics. The dominance of black boxers alone challenged mainstream stereotypical depictions of black men, and against the backdrop of the black freedom struggle that dominance was particularly resonant. But it was also never limited to the ring. Ali, in particular often created more controversy outside the ring than in it. His membership in the Nation of Islam and his refusal to register for the draft compelled Americans across the country to demonize him as a militant, and the latter (in particular) would lead to a three-year suspension from the world of boxing and the relinquishment of his heavyweight title.[129]

Ali was also linked to motorcycling, as were some of his most formidable black opponents. Not only was Ali riding a motorbike when he fought a "white motorcycle gang" that ended with his gold medal at the bottom of the Ohio River, but he was in a motorcycle accident over a decade later. Ali cited the accident to explain his worsening health in the early 1980s, which we now know was the onset of Parkinson disease. One of Ali's main adversaries, Joe Frazier, who beat Ali to retain his heavyweight boxing crown in 1971, recalled Ali's accident in an interview in 1973 in which he revealed his own interest in motorcycles. "For some strange reason," he argued, "Clay has tried to compete with me in everything I'm doing and every time he has bombed out. For years," Frazier added, "I've been riding a heavy weight motorcycle [a Harley] and I have become pretty good at it. So Clay goes out and buys himself a motorcycle, too. The next thing, he falls on his a[ss] and damn near kills himself." Another contemporary of Ali's and also a heavyweight champion, Ken Norton, was also a motorcyclist. Norton, who broke Ali's jaw in a split-decision fight that Norton won, emphasized that he enjoyed "the few material things I have, like my cars [including a Rolls Royce], and van and my motorcycle."[130]

Ali's ties to motorcycling simply suggested the potential for rebellion because he was such an important political and gendered representation of the black community and liberation politics. Other black men more openly appropriated motorcycling as a critical element of their style and politics. Isaac Hayes's early association with motorcycles took place during his appearance at the Watts Summer Festival in 1972, also called the Wattstax festival. Originally a songwriter, producer, and musician at Stax Records, Hayes was one of the most influential figures giving shape to southern soul in the late 1960s and early 1970s. He was also known for a signature look that Alice Echols describes as "the quintessence of black pride and black power." Hayes was one of the first to adopt the style that twenty years later would become the hallmark of male bravado in hip-hop: the bare chest and gold chains.[131] Historian John Smith notes that at the Wattstax festival that summer, Hayes's stage entrance and exit were dramatic and powerful. Hayes was "escorted by two LAPD motorcycle policemen on Harley Davidsons," with "sirens blasting and lights flashing as they rode through the main tunnel entrance into the stadium." People stood up screaming "Black Moses," the label associated with Hayes because of his "philanthropic gestures," an album titled "Black Moses, and his signature look—"a gold chain, shiny bald head, metallic orange pants with black and white fringed cuffs." He left the scene with even greater fanfare: "more motorcycles, minibuses and police escorts" with their motors and sirens "roaring" as they "paraded out the exit." Hayes was not riding a motorcycle, but the scene at Wattstax stood in diametric opposition to the previous years' battles that pitted the black community against the motorcycle cop.[132]

Within a couple years of the festival, Hayes abandoned his signature look in favor of a brawnier more rugged style, which was influenced by his interest in motorcycles. In an interview with *Jet* magazine in 1975 Hayes announced the end of "Black Moses." The new image included his love of target shooting (he had an "outstanding collection of Smith-Wesson pistols") and a rigorous workout schedule in his basement gym every other day. Hayes was a 185-pounder but wanted to "get up to 215 pounds and have a muscular body like Charles Atlas." Photos from the article (and from a *Jet* interview a year earlier) also showed him seated on a Yamaha and a custom chopper. Hayes had joined the Choppers Motorcycle Club in Memphis, Tennessee, which from the picture appeared to be an all-black club. The photographs from both interviews show him in typical biker attire: jeans and a jean vest or jean jacket with the sleeves torn off. In another photo at a recording studio, he is wearing the classic white T-shirt with the traditional Harley logo—the oversized number one festooned with stars and stripes.[133]

Other examples from the 1960s and 1970s were so suggestive of a link between black motorcyclists and Black Power that the nonriding public routinely confused the two. Toby Gene Levingston of the East Bay Dragons Motorcycle Club, probably the best-known all-black club from this era, recalled a comment from Black Panther David Hilliard, who explained that "when the Black Panthers visited cities like New York and Chicago wearing berets and leather jackets they were often mistaken for outlaw California Bikers." According to Levingston, Hilliard recalled having to remind the police and the press "We're not bikers. We're Panthers" when they publicized the opening of new chapters outside of Oakland. Levingston added that the opposite was just as common for his club. "When we'd [the East Bay Dragons] ride down to Los Angeles, the LAPD assumed that any black man wearing a dark leather jacket was a Black Panther ready for a shoot-out. We would tell the cops, Look here. It says 'East Bay Dragons.' Don't say nothing about no Panthers."[134]

Levingston argued that the police's tendency to confuse the two groups or what he described as "drawing heat from nervous police" reflected the Panthers' notoriety, but we cannot underestimate the Panthers' ties to motorcyclists. Some of those ties were perhaps more imagined than real. Marlon Brando's influence on men and women coming of age in the 1950s and 1960s was nothing short of profound. Susan Bordo notes that Bob Dylan "adored" and "idolized" Brando and so did James Dean, who showed "up at a party dressed in an exact replica of Brando's *The Wild One* outfit."[135] Brando was just as influential among many in the black community because of his outspoken support for civil rights and because he embodied a style black men tried to emulate. Billy Dee Williams, who realized mainstream success in film and television in the 1970s and 1980s and who helped define 1970s soul recalled a period in his life when he "wanted desperately to be like Marlon Brando. He tried to mumble like him, walk, act and dress like him." Williams was particularly attracted to Brando as Johnny, "leader of that motorcycle gang in *The Wild One*." He recalled that "Brando . . . understood the dilemma of a person not being able to express himself," and the actor "reflected his dual nature." Williams described himself as "a gentle soul but there was also a strong violence in me."[136]

Brando also had more direct ties to the Panthers. According to Susan Bordo, "Black Panther Leader Bobby Seale" also "idolized Marlon Brando." Seale identified with his "rebellious streak" and "admired Marlon from the time I was sixteen and saw *The Wild One*."[137] Brando also publicly supported the Panthers. In his autobiography Brando recalls wanting to know more about the Panthers after a visit to Harlem in 1968 (shortly after

Martin Luther King Jr.'s assassination). Brando contacted the Panthers and, after speaking with one of them (either Bobby Seale or Eldridge Cleaver), decided to meet with them in Oakland. After spending most of the evening talking with Cleaver, Cleaver's wife Kathleen, and Bobby Hutton, he learned "a great deal about a variety of subjects," especially about the "day-to-day experience of being a black man in Oakland." Two weeks after Brando's visit, Hutton was killed by the Oakland police, prompting Brando to return to Oakland to attend the funeral.[138]

At the same time, motorcyclists like the East Bay Dragons assumed a highly visible presence in the struggle over liberation. Levingston noted that "Dr. King used a 'we shall overcome' approach through peaceful protest and nonviolent civil disobedience." But, he added, "patience" often "ran thin" and "not many of our members bought into the nonviolence of Dr. King." Levingston added that King had been successful at "enlist[ing] black civic leaders, black businessmen, black politicians and black judges to advance his agenda of equality and change." But in Oakland "things were different," and this is what Levingston "really admired about the Black Panthers. They were the first to mobilize ordinary folks in the black community . . . a party made up of working people, laborers, longshoremen, teamsters, the unemployed, gang members, prostitutes, pimps, workers at General Motors, and black bikers." Levingston explained that a "lot of our members attended Free Huey rallies at De Fremery Park" and participated in "weekend rallies to show off their bikes and to listen to speeches given by prominent Black Power movement leaders." Members of the East Bay Dragons "wore their 'Free Huey' badges right next to their peace symbols and Black Power buttons." Levingston attributed Oakland's "bad-boy image" to the Oakland Raiders and the Hells Angels and specifically cited the "Stop the Draft" riots, where members of the Hells Angels beat up protestors. But, he added, "if you were against the war in Vietnam, in favor of your kids getting a decent education, or worried about food and health care, the Panthers spoke for you."[139]

Levingston also suggested that men like the East Bay Dragons shaped Black Power's rise and development. In his autobiography, he reminds readers that the "Panthers' roots in self-defense came out of the South just like us" and suggested that the Dragons were visibly challenging these inequalities before the Black Power movement materialized. While Huey Newton, Bobby Seale, and David Hilliard watched the "racist confrontations" that were attracting more attention in the South by the late 1950s, Levingston emphasized, "we rode our Harley-Davidsons" as if the simple act alone of riding their bikes posed a challenge to white privilege and power. Indeed, Levingston notes that "prior to the Panthers" and when the "gun laws were mellow," he would "stand on East Fourteenth and wait for my friends with my Browning shotgun across my knee." Other members of the Dragons "carried large caliber pistols and thought nothing of snapping a .45 on someone if they pissed him off. . . . On runs to Fresno or L.A. we rolled our guns up inside our sleeping bags strapped on the sissy bars of our motorcycles." The Panthers, Levingston recalls, even invited the East Bay Dragons to accompany them on their now-famous visit to the California State Capital to protest changes to gun laws. Already attracting increasing scrutiny from the police, the club was careful to avoid anything that might attract more unwanted attention and declined the invitation.[140]

The scrutiny Levingston noted was comparable to what white motorcyclists experienced, but in the black community it led to major rebellions. For example, between 1979 and 1989 Miami was the site of three major uprisings, and in two of them the rebellions began after the police killed a black motorcyclist. The first incident was in December 1979 when Arthur McDuffie, a thirty-three-year-old father of three and an insurance executive, was beaten to death by the police after being pursued for speeding and running stop signs.[141] Initial police reports claimed that he had run at least twenty-five stop signs and red lights while traveling nearly 100 miles per hour with his lights turned off (the pursuit took place after dark). McDuffie crashed his motorcycle after hitting a curb and struck his head on the pavement. Despite the injuries, police reports said that McDuffie "jumped up on his feet and struck an unidentified officer." Other officers arrived on the scene and helped "subdue" McDuffie, who "fought violently."[142] Bobby Jones, acting director of the Dade County Public Safety Department, contradicted the police's initial reports by stating that McDuffie's death "may have been caused by police instead of an accident," and Dr. Ronald Wright, chief deputy medical examiner, stated that he "may have died of injuries received in the beating that followed the chase." Four policemen were suspended as a result of an investigation that followed the medical examiner's report and later charged with manslaughter and tampering with or fabricating physical evidence. A fifth officer was also charged with being an accessory and fabricating evidence.[143] At the trial, one of the accused officers who was offered immunity for his testimony explained that McDuffie had voluntarily ended his attempted escape from the police and as the police approached said, "I give up." One of the officers pulled his revolver on McDuffie and said "freeze." McDuffie was handcuffed, and after the officers removed his helmet, they started beating him with flashlights and nightsticks, what one policeman described as a "gang tackling."[144] The officers also "clubbed his motorcycle" and tried to "make the death look like an accident."[145] Less than three hours after an all-white jury of six men acquitted the four officers, a riot erupted in Miami. Eighteen people died and countless buildings were burned or destroyed.[146]

Almost exactly a decade later another Miami police officer killed another black motorcyclist, Clement Lloyd, and his passenger, Allen Blanchard, igniting a riot that lasted three days. The police officer was William Lozano, who said a motorcycle carrying a passenger "veered toward him as he walked onto a street at dusk on Jan. 16." According to one report, the "motorcycle was being chased by a police car for speeding and running stop signs." Lozano explained that as he "turned his body to face the motorcycle, he just came straight at me . . . [and] I was just only able to . . . turn my body, draw my gun and shoot."[147] Witnesses at the scene contradicted his statement and claimed that the cycle had already passed Lozano when he stepped into the street, assumed a "combat stance" and fired a single shot, striking the motorcyclist in the temple. A longshore-man who witnessed the shooting but refused to talk with the authorities because of the fear of retaliation said that Lozano "crouched, then kind of tiptoed out into the street." Once he reached the centerline, he held his pistol with "both hands" and fired "just when the motorcycle came by." "He meant to kill him," he told the reporter. The motorcycle continued down the street for another twenty to thirty yards before veering out of control and striking a car head on. Lloyd and his passenger, Allen Blanchard, were thrown against the oncoming car's windshield. "Blanchard's head struck the windshield before the force of the collision tossed his body back over the car." He would die from his injuries the next day.[148] One report claimed that at least one hundred onlookers ran to the scene where Lloyd's body remained in the streets for over two hours. Individuals from the crowd began pelting the police with stones and bottles, and soon a full-scale rebellion erupted that would last for three days. Nearly thirty buildings would burn, and the police arrested more than 350 residents.[149]

Residents and other contemporaries cited poverty, lack of economic opportunity, and the tensions between black and Cuban/Latino residents to explain the conflict. An *Ebony* article that appeared after McDuffie was slain cited the "dual standard of justice," lack of job opportunities for Blacks, poor housing, and Black resentment over the ease with which Cuban immigrants have advanced up the social and economic ladder while very little has been done to help blacks." Ten years later, these issues were just as prominent, if not more so. Lozano was Nicaraguan and some evidence suggested that police brutality was on the rise in the city. According to one report, complaints of policy brutality had risen from 368 cases in 1987 to 568 during the first three quarters of 1988.[150]

The authorities responded with complaints about violence against both men. Despite McDuffie's injuries, police reports claimed he "jumped up on his feet and struck an unidentified officer." Other officers arrived on the scene and helped "subdue" McDuffie, who "fought violently."[151] At Lozano's trial, his attorneys claimed Lloyd was a drug dealer who was "willing to kill a police officer to avoid arrest." His lawyers also asserted that Lloyd was carrying marijuana, over fifteen hundred dollars, and had alcohol, marijuana byproducts, and traces of cocaine in his blood. The police portrayed both men in stereotypically violent terms and argued that the force they used to subdue them was justifiable.[152]

Yet we also cannot forget the fact that these men were riding motorcycles at the time of their deaths and that their connection to them may have figured into the police's response. McDuffie's mother explicitly blamed the fact her son was on a motorcycle for the police's response and his death. "They beat him just because he was riding a motorcycle and because he was black," she said to a reporter after evidence implicated the police. Lloyd's connection to motorcycling was not highlighted by the police other than the speed he was going when he first attracted their attention and the suggestion that the motorcycle's speed and agility made it a threat to Lozano. But the bike was critical to Lloyd's presence in the neighborhood and his identity, and it was a bike that was beginning to attract attention. Lloyd was riding a Kawasaki Ninja, a new breed of sport bike noted for its speed and maneuverability that appeared first in 1984. Bikes with lower handlebars, foot pegs positioned toward the back half of the bike, and a small fairing had been visible on bikes for years. But as superbike racing became more popular, manufacturers began to build production bikes with similar specifications (e.g., Honda Interceptors, Yamaha FZRs, Suzuki GSX-Rs, and Kawasaki Ninjas). These bikes, as Sonny Barger recently explained in his *Guide to Motorcycling*, are "better left to the race track."[153] Ads for the Ninja in 1984 described it as the "fastest production motorcycle in the world," and the company boasted a one-quarter-mile track speed of 10.55 seconds. In their study of consumer brands, which included a section on motorcycles, Bernard Cova, Robert V. Kozinets, and Avi Shankar note that in their "experience as ethnographers it appears that American youth, especially among whites, Asians and African-Americans, have embraced sport bikes and racing styles and have largely turned an indifferent ear towards the traditional Harley-Davidson style of motorcycles and riding."[154]

Popular culture would soon pick up on the use of sport bikes and the diversity of their riders. Women on these bikes have appeared in a number of films (*Lora Croft, Charlie's Angels*, and *The Matrix: Revolutions*), and both young men and men of color have been featured on sport bikes in *Black Rain, Top Gun*, and *Biker Boyz*. In these movies riders are seen blasting down highways without a care in the world or breezing through unimaginably heavy traffic sporting brightly colored helmets and leather pants. Lloyd mimicked these styles, or perhaps this was a case where film was mimicking reality. He rode a red Kawasaki Ninja with a matching red helmet and red jump suit—a style that set him apart from other riders and one that made him easily recognizable in the neighborhood in which he was killed. One report stated that Lloyd and his "blood red Kawasaki were familiar figures in Overtown" and that few of the neighborhood's residents "paid much attention as he gunned it" through the neighborhood earlier that day. Given the larger history of motorcycling and the meaning of motorcycling in the black community, the police may not have overlooked Lloyd as easily as Overtown's residents, especially on that particular bike. It was increasingly identified with men of color.[155] Kawasaki touted its motorcycle as the fastest production bike in the world, and Lloyd's style and dress made him stand out in the community. A current (2013) ad for the Kawasaki Ninja takes place at a police academy. The instructor stands in front of a classroom full of cadets whose attention is focused on a poster-sized picture of a Kawasaki Ninja.[156]

The growing scrutiny surrounding black motorcyclists and the black community perhaps explains the establishment of rallies intended for the black motorcyclist. The National Biker Roundup was organized in 1977 to "bring black motorcyclists together in the region surrounding Kansas City." Only forty-nine riders attended the first gathering. Today, and for much of the rally's history, it attracts upward of thirty thousand to forty thousand motorcyclists at a time.[157] Three years after motorcyclists established the Roundup, Black Bike Week debuted at Atlantic Beach in South Carolina. Atlantic Beach, according to Sherry A. Suttles, was a "mecca for African American vacationers in Myrtle Beach and other East Coast communities during segregation, [and] remains one of a few African American owned and governed oceanfront resorts in North America. Bikers, she adds, "were coming to the beach in the 1960s and 1970s, long before the now famous BikeFest." The first Atlantic Beach Rally that included "parade floats and biker contests was in 1980 and grew from an initial 100 bikers to nearly 400,000" participants.[158]

In their discussions about these all- or nearly all-black biker rallies, black riders often defended motorcycling against charges of discrimination. Herb Dorsey of Pemberton, New Jersey, admitted that he was "the only black member in one club I belong to" and that at "some of the events I attend, I'm the only black rider there." But he challenged the idea that these rallies were a "white thang.'" "We all know what the government thinks about motorcyclists," he continued, admonishing all motorcyclists to "join and ride together." "Let's forget about the concept that this is for us and that is for them. Instead, I think it's better to say that united we ride, divided we walk."[159] The idea of the Roundup argued two of the event's founders, Dallas Thibodeaux and Rozell Nunn Jr., was "simple": "Give motorcyclists a yearly gathering place to meet new friends, see old ones, and have a good time." "We don't care about your color, your religion or anything else," emphasized Billy Walker, the Roundup's chairman in 2001. "You're a biker—that's good enough for us."[160]

Other letters from African American riders were just as careful about the issue of discrimination but nonetheless recognized the significance of race in motorcycle culture and the importance of these rallies to understanding motorcycling in the black community. One rider called such rallies "our family reunion," a concept not all that different from Earl Lewis's concept of segregation as congregation. In his study of Norfolk, Virginia, in the early twentieth century, Lewis argued that as blacks in the postwar South struggled to "secure the range of improvements desired," they worked to "frame their own reality," and "modified the political language so that segregation became congregation." Congregation, Lewis argued, suggested a degree of autonomy and an "act of free will," which stood in stark opposition to segregation, which was the "imposition of another's will." Congregation, he adds, "produced more space than power," but they "used this space to gather their cultural bearings, to mold the urban setting."[161] In his discussion about motorcycle rallies and the issue of discrimination, Harold A. Black, from Knoxville, Tennessee, concluded his letter to *American Motorcyclist* by emphasizing that he had encountered "very few cases in which all bikers I've encountered weren't brothers." But he also noted that he was "always struck by the paucity of black faces" at the different rallies he attended every year and asked the magazine's editor to "give me the addresses for Black Riders magazine and the National Round-up. Then once a year," he emphasized, "I can be among the majority."[162] J. Green of San Diego, California, also noted that "the prejudice you speak of within the motorcycle community is not widespread," but, he admitted, "it is there and often subtle." Green explained that the prejudice that did exist "may be part of the reason why the National Biker Round-up . . . came to be. . . . It is one place where black riders can come together and not have to deal with the color barrier. I have been to several, and I love it." "To be honest," he added, "I hope it stays that way—a 'black thang.' It's about people, mainly black, coming together with peace and love in our hearts to enjoy our common bonds—motorcycles and each other." Green added, "If we wanted it to be known to the whole motorcycle community, we know how to publicize it. We keep it quiet for a reason. It's our family reunion."[163]

THE MOTORCYCLE RIGHTS MOVEMENT AND RACE

Throughout the debates over regulation, motorcyclists specifically cited the struggles against racial and ethnic discrimination to suggest what might be possible in their own fight for liberation and to inspire others to action. In an article about the possibility of brotherhood, Rogue explained, "The blacks and other minority groups were suppressed for so long it could make you puke. They rose up and fought and are now finally making some headway. . . . Now the bikers," he added, "are up in arms and united and they [the government and bureaucrats] aren't going to get away with any more bullshit with them."[164] Lane Campbell also noted the success African Americans had realized to emphasize the average motorcyclist's potential in an article about "bike power" (a phrase clearly inspired by Black Power). Campbell explained that he had been told repeatedly that bikers were doomed to failure because they "are too dumb . . . [and] too individualistic to organize . . . too cheap [and] too poor; that bikers don't vote and don't give a damn; that bikers are too busy playing with their toys . . . [and] so shaggy and gross that they'll always alienate non-riders . . . I don't waste my breath denying any of it," he explained, "except to say, 'Yeah sure, all Blacks used to shuffle and say 'yowsah.' "[165]

Other motorcyclists were more explicit about the similarities between their movement and the black community's and the shared struggles they faced, even appropriating the term "minority" to describe their experience with discrimination. In 1972 *Motorcyclist*'s editor Bob Greene began an editorial about helmet laws with "Minorities suffer." Greene's editorial focused overwhelmingly on the issue of helmets and safety, paying particular attention to the government's discriminatory attitude toward motorcyclists. While the government failed to address the number of motorists killed because of fatal head injuries, Greene explained that helmet advocates argued in support of regulation because motorcyclists were "not old enough to know better" and thus required "government protection. . . . Ironically," he admitted, "they're right much of the time." But, he asked, "whose obligation is it to save them, if not their own?" "Motorcyclists are a minority," proclaimed Greene who described the helmet law debacle as a struggle about "constitutional rights against discrimination."[166]

Over twenty years later motorcyclists were still making comparisons between the discrimination facing the black community and the prejudice they experienced. In a 1995 editorial, Ed Youngblood recounted his thoughts about prejudice and motorcycling after reading the book, *South of Haunted Dreams*, a travelogue written by a black man, Eddie Harris, who rode his motorcycle across the south to "discover the roots of racism in America." Harris's book, Youngblood explains, is as much an internal exploration of racism and its effect on Harris as it is about the racism that is still "real and present in our society." Youngblood admits that "Harris learns that not everyone will be his friend but that many people will accept him if he is open to them." "What has all this got to do with motorcycling?" he asks about half way through his editorial. "On the most obvious level," Youngblood explained, motorcyclists could learn how racism shaped Harris's fear of strangers and hopefully convince other motorcyclists not to "pass up encounters with potential friends of motorcycling." But, Youngblood added, "there's a deeper way in which I think Harris' story can mean something to the rest of us who ride motorcycles." Although Youngblood admitted that he "can't see his journey through the eyes of a black American, Harris' message transcends racism and speaks to the larger theme of prejudice as a whole—including the prejudice many of us experience as motorcyclists."[167]

The similarities motorcyclists described, however, did not always translate easily into an acceptance of the other minority-led movements and their goals, which became increasingly central to the ways in which helmet opponents understood their movement and citizenship. In his editorial that began with "Minorities suffer," Bob Greene reminisced about his experiences in World War II to highlight the dramatic—and what he perceived to be the adverse—changes that had developed in the United States since the end of the war and how those changes had led to the rise of government regulation. "Like thousands of others," he complained, "I ducked bullets in Burma for three years, sometimes with a helmet, sometimes without—fighting for rights that are now being thrown away by 'representatives of the people.'" By placing the helmet law debate against the backdrop of World War II and an era of what was perceived to be the unconditional unity and cohesiveness of the American people, Greene conjured up a "golden age" that following generations of Americans failed to live up to. During those three decades, the government had lost sight of the values Greene and his cohort had fought to defend, and the nation's wartime unity had degenerated into divisiveness as unprecedented numbers of activists took to the streets. In his editorial Greene offered few details about these activists and the conflict surrounding them. But in light of the "golden age" he imagined, he suggested that a discernible gap had developed between these different groups. On one side of the gap stood motorcyclists and the values they had been defending for more than three decades and on the other side stood an undefined assortment of activists implicitly connected to these adverse changes. Greene did suggest that the trust between the government and its troops reflected the war's demands and the desperate need for manpower. "They didn't make us wear a hard hat to keep those high-speed 20-calibers out of our hair," he said. "They didn't have time to hassle the troops, and they needed us too urgently." But he also argued that the whole helmet debacle "was a laugh" because motorcyclists had "been fingered" by a government that had lost sight of the liberties motorcyclists were now fighting to restore.[168]

His claim, "minorities suffer," is particularly ironic because he wanted motorcyclists to be accepted as minorities even as he refused to acknowledge the larger significance of that experience. Nowhere in his editorial does he deal with the problems so-called minorities were facing nor does he make any attempt to link motorcyclists to the larger minority-led political movements of the preceding two decades. Was his use of "minority" the best way to energize motorcyclists to organize against helmet laws because it effectively highlighted the discrimination they faced? Or did he choose such a politically charged word because of the ambivalence (or rage) white Americans were expressing about the direction the country was heading and used that tension to build his own movement? Either way, his claim that "minorities suffer" and their invisibility in his editorial reinforced his belief in the ideological distance between motorcyclists and other minorities, what he imagined these activists stood for, and why motorcyclists had so little in common with them.

That difference also highlighted the degree to which motorcyclists claimed they were not dependent on the government for their rights and other minorities were. Biker rights, what motorcyclist Kelley Wendeln defined as constitutional rights, were guaranteed in the Bill of Rights and were "rights we citizens have which cannot be infringed [upon] no matter what laws are passed." Wendeln did not object to the label minority and evoked it to describe the average motorcyclist's experience. He explained that participation in the motorcycle rights movement had been a valuable education, and he now realized that the "American people have been taught several misconceptions. . . . That many people think our government is, or is supposed to be, a democracy, when in fact, we have, and are supposed to have a constitutional republic" was one of the most "outstanding ones." Wendeln added that if "we really have a democracy," which he equated with "majority rule in this country," then the question of repealing helmets should have been voted on by all its citizens. "Since most citizens do not own, ride or care about motorcycles, and the majority of the general public favors helmet laws, bikers would have lost."[169]

Yet even as Wendeln concluded that a democracy "is oppression of the minorities by majorities," he explained that some minorities had a more legitimate claim to their rights than other minorities. Unlike the constitutional rights motorcyclists claimed, Wendeln argued that the "word 'civil' implies that the government gave them to you" and cautioned activists to understand that "that which the government gives it can also take away."[170] Motorcyclists and other "minorities," Wendeln argued, shared a history of discrimination that could potentially unite them, but that shared sense of discrimination was the extent to which they were similar. Those distinctions reflected the subtle differences he saw between civil and constitutional rights that reflected larger (and gendered) distinctions about their relationship with the government. Black Americans and the success of their movement for civil rights were, in Wendeln's way of thinking, dependent upon a government for the gains they had made, and motorcyclists were not. In other words, the political realities of the motorcycle rights movement did not simply allow motorcyclists to claim their citizenship but to claim their identity as white citizens who were not dependent on the state for their rights or welfare and whose freedom, however marginal it may have appeared, was in no need of state measures to protect it.[171]

Indeed, by the time the fight over regulation began to make headway, a politicized version of the "biker" that bridged the gap between the movement's ideological shift from "Helmet Laws Suck" to "Let Those Who Ride Decide" was visible. This motorcyclist exhibited a clear sense of the government's proper role and had an uncompromising and tough attitude that was based to a large degree on (and in diametric opposition to) the stereotypes about African Americans. In an article about the media's portrayal of bikers, one rider described motorcyclists as the type who would "stand up" to "the system" and "shout FUCK OFF," no matter "the consequences." The nonriding masses, he complained, had already accepted the media's portrayal of motorcyclists, barely pausing to question what they viewed in primetime, and he suspected the public would do the same unless motorcyclists quit "backing down" and quit "kissing ass," what he described as "yessiring and nosirring, jiving and shuffling," words historically (and stereotypically) used to belittle African Americans and to justify their treatment. His understanding of these stereotypes made race critical to the differences between men and women who rode motorcycles and those who did not, and words that suggested that motorcyclists were more deserving of their rights than other "minorities." The motorcyclist's courageousness was, in this line of thinking, his political consciousness and his whiteness, which made him distinct from the nonriding masses, whom he also envisioned as weak, dependent, and given to "jiving and shuffling."[172]

By the 1970s the AMA was also more openly supporting the Right, and race was once again prominent. The AMA bitterly attacked George McGovern for his tireless support of "increased government interference in the marketplace and greater Federal authority." Examples included mandatory gasoline rationing, support for the Department of Transportation's push for airbags and seatbelt interlock systems, and federal guidelines for no-fault insurance—issues particularly relevant to motorcyclists, and issues reminiscent of the fight against government regulation. But the AMA also discredited McGovern as an "outspoken leader of ultra-liberal causes, very few of which originate in South Dakota," who seemed to favor "as his constituency" the "left wing radicals of the American political system" rather than the farmers and ranchers in South Dakota. The AMA highlighted "his efforts . . . toward more and more food stamps and greater Federal control over local school systems and the food industry in general." South Dakotans want their "Senator to battle red tape," the author complained, "not create it." Yet the AMA argued that "McGovern constantly advocates for increased government interference in the marketplace, greater Federal authority and more tax dollars" for what the organization described as "costly social welfare legislation."[173]

The AMA's critique of McGovern took a swipe at an undefined Left, but the comment about "social welfare legislation" raises questions about race. Susan Douglas notes the degree to which the media's coverage of the war on poverty in the early 1960s focused on the poor whites in Appalachia and other rural communities, people she describes as "left behind when mines or factories closed and no other employers came to replace them." These images were familiar and recalled the depictions of poverty in the 1930s that highlighted the plight of migrants to California (e.g., *The Grapes of Wrath*) and the photos of the Dust Bowl. With the urban uprisings in the mid- to late 1960s, however, "the news media began to rely almost exclusively on pictures of African Americans to illustrate stories about welfare, thus reinforcing the stereotype that most welfare recipients are black," even though a majority of recipients is not.[174]

By 1980 that association was indisputable. Increasingly the focus was on black women—welfare queens—and Reagan, Douglas argues, was the "politician most responsible for promoting the gendering of welfare in the popular imagination."[175] Reagan's contempt for welfare dates back to his time as governor of California in the 1960s, but welfare became the basis for his campaign rhetoric as he ran for president in 1976. Reagan became linked with the term "welfare queen" because of his lengthy diatribes about abuses of the welfare system and specifically his comments about a "woman in Chicago," whom he claimed had "80 names, 30 addresses, 12 Social Security cards and [was] collecting veterans' benefits on four nonexisting deceased husbands."[176] During Reagan's successful bid for the presidency in 1980, the issue of welfare was again conspicuous, although debate about its effects had surfaced early in the primary season. Reagan's campaign manager, John Sears, had initially "sacked" the "welfare queen" strategy in an attempt to broaden Reagan's appeal and to direct more attention to his economic policy. But when Reagan lost the Iowa primary, the resulting tension within his election camp led to Sears's dismissal and the revival of the "welfare queen," which remained conspicuous through-out the election cycle and his presidency.[177]

During George H. W. Bush's 1988 campaign, questions of race and class remained conspicuous. A 1992 *New York Times* piece noted that Bush was "the first scion of the old-line Eastern establishment to run the country since Franklin D. Roosevelt," and he saw a "sharp distinction between politics and governing." But in his successful bid for the presidency in 1988 against Democrat Michael Dukakis, Bush was willing to court "Joe Six pack" (not Joe the plumber). The author described him as "willing to surround himself with operatives who had sandpaper personalities and middle-class backgrounds," and he worked with political strategist and consultant Lee Atwater who helped court a working-class constituency. Atwater, known best for his negative campaigning and for his ability to connect with average Americans, had successfully promoted the idea that pork rinds were a staple of Bush's diet. Bush also attempted to ally himself with Harley-Davidson, even though he failed to make an appearance at one of the company's manufacturing plants and even though Harley first attracted attention during the campaign season from his Democratic opponent, Dukakis. In 1988 Harley-Davidson's turnaround was apparent and against the backdrop of the country's economic woes emerged as the poster boy for American competitiveness in a global marketplace. Dukakis mentioned the company in his acceptance speech at the Democratic National Convention in July, having toured the Milwaukee plant earlier in the year while campaigning for the presidency. Dukakis cited Harley-Davidson as an example of the benefits of cooperation between labor and management that brought the company back to life and saved twelve hundred good jobs. "We are all enriched and ennobled," Dukakis stated in his speech, "when a dedicated new management team and a fine union in Milwaukee work together to turn Harley-Davidson around and help it come back to life"[178] Bush wasted no time responding to the Democratic hopeful by describing Dukakis's mention of Harley as "odd, since we were the ones who helped the company." During a five-hour campaign swing in Milwaukee, Bush stopped first at Festa Italiana to meet with festival workers, then spoke at a Republican fund-raiser at the March Plaza hotel. Harley-Davidson's turnaround, he emphasized, was the product of "Reagan-Bush administration politics." Bush stressed that he and President Reagan had a close working relationship and that he often talked with and advised the president. While he added that he did not reveal the substance of these meetings to the press or that he had talked with the President and gave him advice, he emphasized that Harley-Davidson's success was "an example of exactly what our trade policies are supposed to do."[179]

Bush's attempt to court the working class and Harley-Davidson have for good reason been overshadowed by the larger role race played in the 1988 election, but again motorcyclists were conspicuous. In that same piece about Bush's attempt to court the working class, the *Times* explained that in recent years the Republican Party had tried to "escape its elitist image as the party of big business and country clubs" by co-opting "the symbols and issues of populism from the Democrats": "flags, country music singers," and what the author described as "racially tinged messages" like, for example, speeches on the death penalty and law and order. The best example is the campaign ad Atwater crafted that introduced the nation to Willie Horton, the black man who stabbed a man and raped his girlfriend while out on a prison weekend furlough approved by Michael Dukakis when he was governor of Massachusetts. The ad begins by emphasizing Bush's and Dukakis's sharp disagreements about the death penalty and argued that Dukakis had allowed "first-degree murderers to have weekend passes from prison." Willie Horton had been granted ten weekend passes, the ad continues, despite his conviction and imprisonment for "stabbing a boy nineteen times." He fled while on one of these furloughs, kidnapped a young couple, stabbed the man, and raped his girlfriend. The ad includes repeated images of Horton's mug shot and ends with (in bold letters) "Weekend Prison Passes: Dukakis On Crime." The ad has become a symbol of racist campaigning and fear mongering. Atwater argued that neither he nor Bush had any knowledge of the ad before it debuted, but in 1992 the *New York Times* claimed otherwise, reporting that as Bush's chances for reelection were dimming, Atwater created the ad and found support for it when he "ventured into a bikers' gathering in Luray, VA., in the spring of 1988 to test out on the Harley-Davidson crowd the story of Willie Horton."[180] After the motorcyclists responded favorably to the ad, it was released to the nation as a whole.

That the "Harley-Davidson crowd" found the ad compelling may not be surprising given the growing divisiveness surrounding race over the previous three decades and the developing relationship between motorcyclists and Republicans since the mid-1970s. What is more surprising is Atwater's decision to try the ad out among motorcyclists. After the ad aired and attracted the notoriety that still follows it, Atwater described the motorcyclists as middle class and suggested that they were more palatable to the conservative base than the general public might assume and sympathetic to a politics of "law and order" that focused overwhelmingly on black men. Was the motorcyclist still the rebel who first attracted national attention forty years earlier? Or had the motorcyclist become so integrated into this new conservative movement that his or her opinions offered critical insight into the likes and dislikes of mainstream, conservative America. The Bush administration's campaign strategy suggests that we cannot overlook the latter possibility. While motorcyclists had cut their political teeth on the fight over regulation, which highlighted a conservative slant Republicans found appealing, the issue that continued to push that relationship forward was race, and Atwater's ability to recognize it explains Bush's electoral victory in 1988.

Events like the airing of the Willie Horton ad have also attracted increasing scrutiny from historians of the Right who have argued that scholars have exploited these spectacular moments of racial demagoguery at the expense of the white voters whose voices have been overlooked or ignored.[181] While this critique has compelled us to more carefully consider all of our sources, it ignores the extent to which these images grew out of the grassroots experience historians have encouraged us to include. The attraction of the Willie Horton ad began several decades earlier with the development of a segregated motorcycle culture and the rise of the outlaw motorcyclist whose lawless and disorderly behavior challenged motorcycle culture. These two issues would routinely intersect in the following decades and only reinforce the segregation and the urgency surrounding the outlaw rider. To be sure, other issues besides race shaped these points of intersection. The motorcyclist's connection to law and order grew out of the rough-respectable divide that was associated with Hollister (or the 1%er), and it was often at the root of the conflict between motorcyclists and the counterculture. But the importance of the other factors shaping law and order should not challenge the very fundamental ways in which race shaped motorcycling, the nonriding public's understanding of motorcyclists, and the relationship between riders and the Right.

IN THE DECADE AFTER HOLLISTER to the 1960s–70s motorcycles would become more noticeable in the black community and their increased appearance followed a pattern similar to the growth of motorcycling among white Americans. The rise of the Japanese Honda affected both communities, and this shift was particularly noticeable among middle-class men and women whose increasing prosperity shaped their consumption of motorcycles. Motorcycles were another marker of class and status, and the black community as eagerly embraced them as did their white counterparts. Yet, despite these similarities, a sharp divide among motorcyclists and among black and white communities was visible. Phrases like "motorcycle gang" or "motorcycle gang member" appeared in stories about motorcycling but were almost always preceded by "white." Or the conflict revolved around the white motorcycle cop and his intrusion into black communities increasingly leery of his presence and his intentions. Violence was often the end result of these encounters and often against the backdrop of the broader fight against discrimination and the questions of citizenship that were at stake. Indeed, if there ever was a difference between outlaws and motorcycle cops, black Americans struggled more to find it than their white counterparts. Mixed-race clubs were certainly part of the motorcycle scene in the immediate postwar years, and scholars have singled them out to emphasize the degree of fraternity among the two-wheeled set. But the black community's relationship with motorcycles was often shrouded in fear, conflict, and suspicion that was reflected in popular culture (as in the film *Sweetback*) but was based on real day-to-day struggles. Motorcyclists were not only part of a status quo the African American community was struggling against, but their machines were one of the instruments of oppression used to support it.

The turmoil surrounding civil rights and the counterculture brought this perception into sharper focus, but it did not originate at this particular moment. Race had long shaped the motorcyclist's self-perception, and a defense of "law and order" developed alongside the "outlaw" rider's supposed lawlessness. The rise of the outlaw in the 1940s had in fact created two images that were distinct, different, and seemingly at odds with one another. One embodied the clean-cut image of law and order, and the other did not. The Hollister Rally not only encouraged the outlaw's image but placed motorcyclists in direct conflict with the police. While these two images raced along on seemingly different trajectories, when they intersected, the similarities between the two were difficult to deny and highlighted the importance of race to motorcycle culture and its development.

By the 1960s–70s the distance between cops and motorcyclists only seemed to grow. The motorcyclist was increasingly identified with drugs and guns, and the sensationalized stories that appeared in the press only confirmed the public's fears about the motorcyclist's potential for violence. Yet the further the motorcyclist moved away from his roots in law and order, the stronger his link with the police became because of a shared sense of racial identity. Unkempt and disheveled, dirty and greasy, sexually promiscuous and bawdy, and opposed to the world of work and an industrial sense of time and order, the biker was more akin to those men and women who have transgressed the boundaries of middle-class respectability and whiteness than those who did not. The "squares" found motorcyclists repulsive yet were strangely attracted to them, and that dynamic helps explain the crowds of curious onlookers who often accompanied motorcyclists wherever they gathered, even though many of these men and women had never ridden a motorcycle and had no intention of ever doing so. The biker represented every pent-up urge respectable (and white) America ever had about sex, drugs, indecency, bodily functions, and laziness, and a dynamic not all that different from the one historian George Rawick observed in his studies of race and identity. When thinking about the legacy of slavery and racism, Rawick envisions that "the Englishman met the West African as a reformed sinner meets a comrade of his previous debaucheries. The reformed sinner very often creates a pornography of his former life. He must suppress even his knowledge that he had acted that way or even that he wanted to act that way."[182]

This identity held out the possibility of alliances with other Americans who have been ignored or consciously pushed to the margins, but those alliances generally failed to materialize. The rise of the outlaw also coincided with a renewed consciousness of the biker's racial identity that is generally identified with the appropriation of swastikas and other symbols of white power. But it was also a consciousness that was evident when the outlaw first attracted national attention at Hollister in 1947 and one that reflects a history of "law and order" that became more conspicuous in light of the political movements of the 1960s and 1970s. The prominence of this racial identity is certainly debatable, but it was prominent enough to convince the nonriding public not to abandon bikers altogether. The public feared and loathed the biker because he represented everything it struggled to reject but was drawn to him because of a sensibility of race and all the privileges it associated with a white racial identity. During the 1960s and 1970s, bikers may have seemed as far removed from law and order as any time in the postwar period, but in an increasingly divisive political climate, the relationship between the police and motorcyclists grew stronger even as it grew more bitter, and the issue of race was central to understanding this dynamic.

Every president from Ronald Reagan to George W. Bush and numerous other national political candidates have visited a Harley-Davidson manufacturing plant, made an appearance with motorcyclists at some other public gathering, or claimed some affinity or allegiance to the company and its workers. Many of them have used that visit to highlight trade issues and the possibility of American success in an increasingly global market. President Bill Clinton, for example, visited a Harley-Davidson plant in York, Pennsylvania, in 1999 just before he was scheduled to meet with the Chinese about trade negotiations. Like other presidents, he donned a leather jacket and even talked about "becoming a biker at the end of his presidency." He visited the plant to emphasize trade restrictions facing the United States and highlighted H-D's experience in Japan where "archrival" Honda is based but "remains barred from the Chinese market." The President offered a "series of arguments about why trade helps American workers and consumers, and he cited Harley-Davidson, which exports 66,000 cycles a year."[1]

Trips to Harley-Davidson have also become a standard event for Republican politicians eager to talk about American manufacturing but in far greater numbers than their Democratic counterparts and also to highlight their conservative politics and the values of freedom and patriotism they claimed to share with motorcyclists. Recall, for example, a January 2006 speech by Vice President Dick Cheney at a Harley-Davidson manufacturing plant on the outskirts of Kansas City, Missouri. The speech emphasized the president's economic policies but included discussions about the war in Iraq and a brief aside when the vice president was presented with a leather jacket, which he would still be wearing a few days later when he spoke to U.S. troops at Fort Leavenworth. "The Harley-Davidson brand," Cheney proudly asserted in his speech, "is known around the world as a symbol of the American values of freedom and independence," values the president also highlighted in his defense of the war.[2]

More recently, John McCain made an appearance at the 2008 Sturgis Rally. His wife Cindy introduced the presidential candidate to the crowd, describing him to the thousands of motorcyclists in attendance as the "only man that can keep us free." McCain followed up by suggesting that Cindy participate in the Miss Buffalo Chip contest, a beauty contest featuring the "hottest girls in Sturgis," and then launched into his own appropriation of freedom.[3] McCain emphasized that this was his first visit to Sturgis, but he told the crowd that he recognized the "sound of freedom"—a reference to the tens of thousands of motorcyclists revving their engines as he made his way to the stage. McCain also used the roar of the motorcycles to criticize the roar of the crowd at a speech Obama gave in Berlin earlier that summer to 200,000 Germans. "As you may know," McCain said to the crowd of motorcyclists at the Buffalo Chip fairgrounds, "not long ago a couple hundred thousand Berliners made a lot of noise for my opponent. I will take the roar of 50,000 Harleys any day, any day my friends." McCain concluded with a discussion of the current war in Iraq and the need for victory rather than a date of withdrawal Obama was advocating. "We owe victory to the courage and love of this country by people who are here [in Sturgis]," McCain proclaimed, and described the motorcyclists as the "Heartland of America," and as the "soul of America."[4]

One journalist argued that the appearance was McCain's way of making Obama appear as an "out-of-touch celebrity," who had little in common with average Americans. In the context of the Sturgis Rally, though, Obama clashed with McCain's focus on freedom and with the freedom of the fifty thousand riders present to see the presidential hopeful. The crowd and the bikes roared with approval in response to McCain's comments, and one particularly enthusiastic woman pulled up her shirt to reveal a picture of a bald eagle painted across her breasts.[5]

McCain's appearance at Sturgis speaks to the degree to which motorcyclists have become a recognizable political constituency worth soliciting. Clearly, there were many motorcyclists at Sturgis who were Democrats and just as many who were indifferent to the political system or likely to vote for a different politician. But appearing at Sturgis was different from a simple photo opportunity at a Harley-Davidson manufacturing plant where the focus was often as much about American manufacturing as the other values associated with H-D and its workers. McCain's appearance suggests that Republicans were welcome at major motorcycle rallies, and he was taking advantage of that opportunity to advance his candidacy to a sympathetic crowd.

McCain's appearance is also one more example of the ways in which culture has shaped political life and of the contradictions surrounding the political realignments of the postwar years. The motorcyclist's opposition to helmets was grounded in an ideological embrace of freedom and individuality that promoted limited government and the expansion of the private sphere, but it also restricted the roles gays, women, and men and women of color could play in motorcycle culture. Reagan promoted a free-trade ideology throughout his campaigns and his presidency, but he supported protective tariffs for Harley-Davidson because of the machine's and the motorcyclist's patriotism. The Right's increasing interest in the American family took shape against the backdrop of a motorcyclist who offered a distinct challenge to work and heteronormative family arrangements. And the broader left-leaning political movements of the era that embraced alternative ideas about gender, sexual identity, and citizenship often stood in stark opposition to the motorcyclist's surprisingly conventional behavior, even though he had become a symbol of the counterculture and its rebellion against the broader consensus of the postwar era—the Easy Rider. The motorcyclist's appeal was in part a reflection of these contradictions or perhaps his ability to represent different things to different constituencies. Whatever the reason, his political activism had become a part of mainstream politics, and he continues to affect U.S. culture and society.

The extent to which the relationship between the Right and motorcyclists will endure is hard to say. Recent events suggest that the public continues to struggle to accept the motorcyclist despite the ways in which he has challenged his marginal status over the years and is particularly visible on America's streets and highways—the same issue that was attracting attention before the Hollister Rally in 1947 and one that is absolutely critical to understanding contemporary complaints about motorcyclists. The stories that have garnered the most attention are the ones where a group of motorcyclists are responsible for a confrontation and where the motorcyclists have successfully compromised the automobilist's autonomy on the road. Nowhere is that more evident than the recent incident involving a group of motorcyclists and the driver of a Range Rover in New York City in 2013. The incident, which was videotaped by one of the motorcyclists with a helmet camera, begins with a Range Rover moving along a highway with what appears to be several dozen motorcyclists cruising along at the same speed. One of the motorcyclists pulls in front of the moving Range Rover and decelerates just enough that the SUV bumps into the motorcycle's back tire. The driver of the SUV, Alexian Lien, eventually pulls to the side of the road and is quickly surrounded by motorcyclists who begin hitting the

SUV with their helmets and slashing its tires. At this point Lien, who was in the car with his wife and two-year-old child, abruptly drives away from the scene and in the process runs over one of the motorcyclists, Edwin Mieses Jr., whose legs were broken. Mieses also suffered a spinal injury, which has left him paralyzed from the neck down. Lien was chased by the motorcyclists for a couple miles before leaving the highway and eventually coming to a halt because of traffic. The video shows two motorcyclists pounding on the driver's-side window and breaking the glass. The video ends at this point, but, according to witnesses, the motorcyclists pulled Lien from the SUV and beat him.[6]

The motorcyclists who were filmed chasing Lien were part of planned ride involving hundreds of riders who started the day outside of Manhattan and planned to finish the ride en masse in Times Square. The ride the year before had "succeeded in snarling Midtown traffic . . . with well over a thousand motorcycles, dirt bikes, quads, four-wheel vehicles." To counter the impact of so many motorcyclists, the police in 2013 established check points to inspect the bikes and the motorcyclists before they descended into the city. At least fifteen arrests were made, and fifty-five motorcycles were confiscated.[7]

The press response to the incident with Lien was to immediately target the motorcyclists without asking any critical questions about how it started, relying primarily on the video for its stories. The press described the incident as a "motorcycle Road Rage Case."[8] The motorcyclists were characterized as a mob and as a swarm, and the incident was labeled a melee and a brawl. The seven men implicated in the attack, none of whom appeared to be white, were charged on various counts, including assault, criminal mischief, and most notably gang assault, and the prior criminal records of two of the men were made known.[9]

The stories about the Range Rover also led to a broader discussion about the motorcyclists and what was presented as the growing problems the nonriding majority faced on the country's roads and highways. One story featured a New Yorker who recalled his experience on the highway with a group of motorcyclists, and the author used the term commandeer to describe the experience and to suggest that motorcyclists had inappropriately seized control of the road, even though they were simply riding in a group. Other articles legitimized the public's fear of the motorcyclist with statistics that suggested a growing problem. One story noted that as of May 2013, for example, New York Police had seized 1,440 motorcycles and about 450 motorcyclists had been arrested, 187 of them for reckless driving or reckless endangerment. In July 2013 New York State Police also arrested eight people who had participated in a "street stunt ride" that involved about one hundred motorcycles. "The police said many were seen driving into on-coming traffic, forced vehicles from the road, and riding on side-walks."[10] A related story about the relationship between cops and bikers argued that in recent years, "sport bike enthusiasts have begun forming impromptu packs, sometimes assembled via social media, for massive 'runs' that clog highways and can intimidate motorists."[11]

The discussion about the Range Rover incident in 2013 also led a New York City Council member to propose legislation that would essentially criminalize riding a motorcycle. The article cited one council member, Melissa Mark-Viverito, a Democrat representing the Eighth District and currently council speaker, whose car was struck by a motorcyclist who was part of a group that "roared" down Third Avenue in June 2013. Mark-Viverito described the experience as "really scary" and claimed that police officers said large groups of motorcycles like this were a "constant" problem. Another council member, James Vacca, a Democrat representing the Thirteenth District, described New Yorkers as "shocked" by what happened on the West Side (the Range Rover incident) and proclaimed, "It's time for action, time to cut these guys off at the legs." A new bill that was under consideration by the city council, which presumably would require motorcyclists to present their ID every time they purchased gas, would target gas station owners who sold fuel to riders with illegal and unregistered dirt bikes. Another bill would ban from roadways "large groups of riders unless they had a permit," which had the potential to make all motorcyclists lawbreakers for simply riding their bikes.[12]

What the incident in New York did not lead to, though, was a broader discussion about motorcycle safety and the extent to which the automobilist is still the most significant threat to the motorcyclist. The cases against the seven motorcyclists in New York have yet to be resolved, but after the initial outrage had subsided, a lawyer for one of the motorcyclists, Gloria Allred, claimed that "Lien bumped another motorcyclist while changing lanes on the highway two to three miles before his SUV knocked into biker Christopher Cruz" and several minutes before the motorcyclist with the helmet camera started taping the chase after Lien.[13]

The incident in New York was not the first one to attract the media's attention, nor will it be the last. Motorcyclists have long questioned whether they had the same rights as automobilists, and a significant history of being run off the road or crowded out of their lanes by automobilists suggests that they do not. The conflict over who controls America's roadways gave rise to the outlaw rider and the public's fears about motorcyclists even though the typical rider is always at a distinct disadvantage when facing a several-thousand-pound automobile and a driver who does not care. The outlaw who burst on to the scene at Hollister and Riverside and established the look and style of the 1950s rebel attracted attention because of his unruly behavior not only off his bike but also on it—crashing into bars, riding on the sidewalks, drag racing down Main Street, and consciously blocking traffic to perform stunts in the middle of the intersection. Motorcyclists had taken over the town and had become a threat to the motorist, or so the press claimed, and they did it with their motorcycles.

Nearly seven decades after Hollister motorcyclists' behavior on their bikes and the larger struggle over their rights on the road remain critical to understanding their behavior and the public's perception of them. It was not a small-town invasion like it was in Hollister but a planned descent into Times Square. Differences between these two events are obvious. The incident occurred during what was initially a planned ride to celebrate the end of the year and turned into an across-the-city chase after the driver of a Range Rover turned violent. But questions about what constitutes appropriate roadway behavior shaped both events and the responses to them. Motorcyclists have always performed stunts wherever they rode their bikes in part because they could and it was fun, but against the backdrop of a history of an indifferent automobilist and a history of conflict on the road, the actions of these riders cannot simply be dismissed as unruly and disorderly. These rides are planned out in advance and often with a particular goal in mind. The day-to-day experience of a motorcyclist who uses his bike on a routine basis is generally not in a group of riders, and hence he has to struggle to negotiate traffic and drivers who routinely push him out of his lane or off the road altogether. Riding in a group is one of the few opportunities motorcyclists have to control the pace and rhythm of the road, challenge their exclusion from it, and deal with the frustration of being a second-class citizen simply because they prefer two wheels to four, even though the stunts they perform are dangerous and the potential for conflict is ever present. Given the increasing hostility all motorists face on today's highways, these incidents will not only continue but also guarantee that the outlaw will remain as conspicuous today as in previous decades and continue to shape our discussion about U.S. culture and society. As much as motorcycling has changed, it remains the same and remains as hotly contested as it was when the outlaw first rose to national fame in the postwar period.

At the same time, the relationship between Republicans and motorcyclists has the potential to change because the Republicans have started to realize that future electoral success may be possible only if they successfully attract groups outside their core constituency. Ron Brownstein, columnist and editorial director for the *National Journal*, recently argued in an NPR interview that the United States is in "the midst of the most profound demographic change since the turn of the twentieth century." What Brownstein refers to as the "brown and the gray" highlights a youth population that will be a majority minority by the end of the decade and a senior population that is 80 percent white. Today almost 47 percent of Americans below 18 are minority or nonwhite and about 40 percent of Obama's support came from minorities in the 2008 election compared to about 10 percent for McCain.[14] In the 2012 election Obama received 55 percent of the female vote (11 points higher than Romney), 93 percent of the African American vote, and 71 percent of the Hispanic vote. The president received only 39 percent of the white vote, down from 43 percent in 2008.[15]

Brownstein also noted a significant divide between these two groups when it comes to the government's role and hence very potentially different ideas about the meaning of freedom. Despite the numerous advantages the largely white, aging baby boom population receives from government programs like Social Security and Medicare, it is increasingly skeptical of government, according to Brownstein, and increasingly opposed to paying taxes for government services. Minorities, on the other hand, view government support as key to their future success. Those families "believe they need public investment, particularly in schools and in health care to help their kids ascend into the middle class." The two groups, Brownstein adds, make up the "core" or "anchor" of each political party. The older, white population is at the center of the Republican Party, and the Democrats are increasingly dependent upon votes from minorities.[16]

In his interview Brownstein compared the past few decades to understand the extent to which the country was divided along racial lines and the extent to which it is changing. In the 1970s "racially overt issues" like affirmative action, crime, welfare, and busing served to polarize the country along racial lines. This divisiveness would diminish to a certain extent as these issues receded from the national debate. Crime rates dropped precipitously over the next two decades, busing and affirmative action were either amended or ignored, and the Clinton administration ended welfare "as we know it" in 1996. The political climate during the period from 1992 to about 2008, what Brownstein refers to as the post–Willie Horton era, was "less racially . . . explosive." That has started to change, he argues, and nowhere is that change more evident than in the discussion about government, "even if there is no racial language." Brownstein has found that "whites who say they are troubled by the pace of racial change express conservative views on a whole series of other issues particularly the role of government" and these debates about the government's role "are now reacquiring a racial content to them even if there is no racial language."[17]

The motorcycle industry began looking for ways to increase its percentage of underrepresented groups a few years before the current Republican scramble, but the problems facing motorcycle manufacturers are just as significant. The industry remains largely segregated nearly twenty years after Ed Youngblood called for greater inclusion in the mid-1990s, and black and Latino riders remain surprisingly inconspicuous despite their growing influence on motorcycle culture. In an *Ebony* article about the thirtieth anniversary of the National Bikers Roundup, the "largest gathering of Black riders" in the country, the author admitted that "no statistics detail the numbers of Black riders," although he suggested that they made up what appeared to be an ever-growing share of the market.[18] That statistics regarding the number of black riders is unavailable is especially glaring when considering that the Motorcycle Industry Council, a trade association for manufactures and others involved in the marketing and selling of motorcycles, publishes a yearly statistical analysis (called the *Motorcycle Statistical Annual*) that breaks down nearly every facet of the motorcycle industry, including gender, economic status, age, and type of bike. The *Annual* does not include information about riders' race.

Charges of discrimination have also surrounded Black Bike Week. During the period from 1999 to 2003, lawsuits were filed against the city of Myrtle Beach and area businesses for discrimination against African Americans attending the rally. Plaintiffs complained that the event "has been marred by excessive police force, intrusive traffic laws and a hostility that flows from the shell-encrusted fringes of the Atlantic Ocean to the doors of the local Denny's." Myrtle Beach hosts two biker rallies back-to-back each spring—Harley Week, primarily attended by white riders, and Black Bike Week. The city was charged with discriminatory behavior because officials changed the streets to a one-way system for Black Bike week and maintained two-way traffic during Harley Week, and because it employed 550 police officers and only 300 when the white bikers were in town. Twenty-eight Myrtle Beach restaurants were also named in various lawsuits for shutting their doors or reducing their hours of operation during Black Bike Week but remaining open during Harley Week. As one police detective who is a motorcyclist explained: "When the white bikers come to Myrtle Beach, the town rolls out the red carpet. When the black riders come, they roll it right up."[19]

The history of racial conflict that Brownstein suggested was beginning to shape the debate about government's role has also shaped motorcycling even though there is no racial language. The Rat Pack Motorcycle Club that was accused of patrolling black neighborhoods in Waterbury, Connecticut, "as a suppressive vigilante group" in the late 1960s reemerged in the national spotlight in 2009 as an escort for the Tea Party Express, "a national bus tour of protest against what organizers consider excessive government spending, taxes and intervention." More than two dozen Rat Pack members participated in the escort and also helped organize a rally in their hometown of Waterbury.[20]

The situation for women riders also seems to have changed very little since women objected to motorcycling as the "last male refuge" in the 1960s and 1970s. The scantily clad model, "bikini babe," or biker chick not only remain prominent at rallies and on other biker paraphernalia, but the general bawdiness that characterized motorcycle culture in previous decades also has been replaced with one that focuses almost exclusively on women's bodies. Images of topless women riding pillion at Hollister were accompanied by charges of indecent behavior on the part of male participants and, throughout the following decades, skinny dipping at a lake near an overnighter and other forms of public nudity generally accompanied the increasingly common "show me your tits" mantra that has become the common refrain among male motorcyclists. One longtime rider who has attended the Sturgis Rally for twenty years running seemed confused when I asked him if he had ever seen a naked man at Sturgis. "Never," he quipped, but "lots of naked women."[21]

There is also no reason to think this is going to change anytime soon. When women objected to the presence of the scantily clad model in the 1960s and 1970s, men overwhelmingly objected to censoring those images because censorship was too intimately connected to fears of regulation. Toward the latter half of the 1970s, the Highway Safety Act of 1966 would be amended, the debate about helmets would shift back to the states, and a flurry of legislative activity would follow and lead to the repeal of helmet laws across the country. While only twenty states currently have helmet laws, most of the states without helmet laws consistently face efforts to reestablish them.[22] In this climate, like in the mid-1970s, any efforts to regulate motorcycling or motorcyclists face an uphill climb.

Even Harley's efforts to attract a new clientele remain bogged down by simplistic ideas about male culture and motorcycling. One of H-D's attempts to retool its marketing and attract more younger riders was the development of its Dark Custom line of bikes, which featured a "stripped-down look that was purposely light on the chrome and heavy on the black steel" and a price tag of about $8,000, considerably less than one of the company's other motorcycles. The ad compared the cost to "about six bucks a day" and listed other daily expenses Harley-Davidson's customers might be willing to sacrifice for a motorcycle: "smokes, a six-pack, *a lap dance* [my italics], a bar tab, another tattoo, a parking ticket, a gas station burrito, bail, cheap sunglasses or more black T-shirts."[23]

Plenty of evidence exists to suggest that women riders remain ambivalent about this excess if not outright opposed to it. In a recent story about attracting more women to Sturgis, Rick Barrett of the *Journal Sentinel* described the rally as a "male dominated event" and suggested that female motorcyclists may be offended by scantily dressed women who pose for cheesy photos with men twice their age," but he argued "that most women who get into motorcycle riding just look the other way." Barrett quoted Genevieve Schmitt, founder and editor of WomenRidersNow. com, an online source for women motorcyclists, and her comments suggested that women riders were more complicated than Barrett was willing to admit. Schmitt encourages women riders to attend the Sturgis Rally but admits that if they "are offended by that [the bikini babe], then perhaps they wouldn't feel welcome at Sturgis."[24] A recent story celebrating women motorcyclists made this point clear by noting that the growing number of women riders was accompanied by the establishment of "dozens of female-only motorcycle clubs" that have "joined more established groups like Women on Wheels or Ladies of Harley"—the same response from women in the 1960s and 1970s.[25] Indeed, the simple theme of empowerment has framed efforts to increase women's participation and their testimonials about riding. Harley-Davidson has used the slogan "It's Your Life, Don't Just Go Along For the Ride" to encourage women to test out their jumpstart model, and their "No Cages" ad has often focused on women riders. No Cages is a reference to the automobile as a cage but also the other restraints all of us face—a particularly resonant theme for women and motorcycling and one that clashes with the dominant culture that continues to thrive among male motorcyclists.[26]

The other current trend that is picking up steam is the establishment of clubs that are explicitly multiracial, and nowhere is this trend more evident than among black and Latino riders. Probably the best example is the Latin American Motorcycle Association (LAMA). The association was founded in 1977 "in Chicago's notorious Humboldt Park neighborhood." The club would not establish a chapter until 1995, and a year later elected a national president. Since then the association has grown precipitously with nearly four dozen chapters across the Midwest, southern and eastern portions of the United States, and in Puerto Rico, Mexico, Cuba, Spain, Australia, Uruguay, Argentina, and Venezuela. LAMA describes itself as a "club of the 21st century" and as an "International Humanist Association." The association makes it clear that it accepts "working people from all walks of life regardless of nationality, race, color, religion, social class, gender, age, brand of motorcycle. etc." But its website emphasizes, "We believe that it is more important to be human than to be Latin, Asian, black, white, etc!"[27]

The Latin American Motorcycle Association also stands apart because of its transnational understanding of motorcycling and motorcycle clubs. It describes itself as a club without borders and stresses the need to cross them and associate with other motorcyclists. Riding is still the fundamental issue that defines these motorcyclists, and the club emphasizes long-distance runs that challenge the stamina and perseverance of its participants. But its focus is often on the destination as much as on the ride itself. The association describes itself as a "work in progress" that would be "continued" by the "flow and ideas of new members in near and far off lands," and its website stresses that to know LAMA is to "visit the other chapters, especially chapters in other nations." The club currently has a fund-raiser organized for a children's hospital near Medellin, Columbia.[28]

The future of American motorcycling and American manufacturers has also become increasingly dependent on overseas sales, and those sales have the potential to change the face of American motorcycling. In 2010 sales abroad accounted for 30 percent of the motorcycles Harley-Davidson produced and in 2011 that number had increased to about 36 percent. The overseas motorcyclist hails from a wide variety of countries, but India and China have attracted much of the focus in recent years because of a growing middle class in both countries. In the *Wall Street Journal*, David Foley, Harley-Davidson's Asia-Pacific chief, said that the company was "expecting sales outside the United States to exceed 40 percent of the total by 2014."[29] At the current rate of increase, the number of motorcycles for consumers abroad will be a majority of new Harley Riders in the not too distant future.

H-D also seems to be gearing up to support this change. The company opened an assembly plant in Brazil in 1999 and in 2010 another one in India. Both plants assemble Harleys from parts that are produced in the United States and then shipped abroad, significantly reducing the amount of tariff added to each bike and hence a cheaper market price. Recent reports have even suggested that the day a Harley is built (including parts) in another country is closer than any of us may have imagined. According to *Motorcycle News*, Harley-Davidson is "now deciding to virtually 'junk' plans" for a mere assembly plant and instead build what the author called a "mother plant" or an entire factory that would build bikes from the ground up. According to the *Financial Express*, an Indian paper cited by *Motorcycle News*, the company's declining sales prompted this "development." Between 2006 and 2010, sales of Harleys in the United States decreased 52 percent, and the company produced more than 100,000 fewer cycles in 2006 (349,196) than in 2011 (233,117).[30] H-D's India spokesperson did "not confirm or deny the development" and would only emphasize that "Harley-Davidson is committed to global growth." The *Financial Express* added that tariffs on imported motorcycles are 110 percent of the cost of the bike and 60 percent on motorcycles that are shipped in parts and assembled in India.[31]

The company insists that its customers would not tolerate production overseas, but the threat of moving production has arisen in recent years. In the midst of H-D's reorganization in the early 1980s and as the company was getting tariff protection from the Reagan administration, a bargain was struck with Harley-Davidson's unions—the International Association of Machinists; the Paper, Allied-Industrial, Chemical and Energy Workers; and the United Steel Workers—that required "labor and management to agree on decisions affecting workers." This agreement allowed the unions to have some say in the selection of a new assembly plant site (Kansas City, Missouri) in the mid-1990s, and it recognized that the company's management "cannot transfer 'core production' overseas without union consent . . . [or] lay off workers unilaterally."[32]

But as sales began to drop by the early 2000s, conflict between workers and management became more conspicuous. The relationship between labor and management that took shape in the mid-1980s and revolved around the principle of "made in America" was dependent on the balance between the need to increase production and sell more Harleys, the growth of (and cost associated with) automation, and maintaining job security for H-D's workers. But that balance quickly fell apart as Harley-Davidson's sales dropped. The strikes and contract negotiations in 2007, 2008, and 2010 that accompanied this decline saw union workers and management arguing over pensions, health care costs, and the prospect of a two-tier employee system that would lead to permanent layoffs of full-time union workers for part-time employees (or what have been called "casuals") to allow the company to deal with seasonal slowdowns. In "years past," the *New York Times* argued, employers have used "two-tiered

Ron Milam alone in a sea of bikes at Sturgis, 2014. Courtesy of Uyen Nguyen.

systems" to drive down costs but primarily at companies already in trouble and with the assumption that these systems would expire in a few years. In recent years, those attempts have been successful at companies like GM, Chrysler, Delphi, and Caterpillar, and it appears that the shift is permanent. During the negotiations over a new contract in Milwaukee, union employees were upset with the prospect of a pay freeze, the elimination of hundreds of production jobs, and the establishment of a two-tiered system but begrudgingly approved of a new contract that would start in April 2012 after the company threatened to move its factories out of the state. "This is absolutely a surrender for labor," said Mike Masik Sr., president of the United Steel Workers of America, who added that the union's support for the contract did not guarantee that the company will stay in Wisconsin until the contract ends—"only that the company would stop searching for alternate sites." A similar agreement at Harley-Davidson's York, Pennsylvania, plant that went into effect about a year earlier shrunk the core workforce "by more than half, to nearly 800 full timers, while adding 300 'casual' employees, who are union members [but] without benefits." The Milwaukee agreement will also reduce the full-time payroll significantly.

Already down to 1,250 from 1,600 before the recession began, the new agreement would shrink it further to 900.[33]

In two decades the youngest members of the baby boom generation will be seventy years old. The number of them riding Harleys since the end of World War II has often constituted a marginal percentage of the total number of motorcyclists, but their influence has never been doubted. They were part of and shaped the rise of the outlaw rider and his more violent counterpart (the biker), organized a grassroots movement against helmet laws, helped transform the motorcyclist into the ideal citizen-patriot, and played a particularly conspicuous role in the larger social, cultural, and political movements of the postwar era. Indeed, conflict surrounding race, gender, and sexual identity shaped a biker "type" in the 1960s and 1970s and simultaneously limited the roles gays, women, and minorities were permitted to play in biker culture. As the baby boom generation moves into retirement, those issues will not only remain important but also emerge as fundamental issues that will affect the future of motorcycling at home and abroad. In sum, an expanding consumer base abroad and a growing body of riders at home who have represented a marginal number of motorcyclists increases the likelihood of more women riders and more men and women of color. These groups have embraced motorcycle culture as enthusiastically as the traditional outlaw, but their experiences on and off their bikes suggest that, in the decades to come, the basic themes on which motorcycle culture has been based may not remain as influential as they had been. The Easy Rider that the *National Review* objected to in 1980 because of a left-leaning political sentiment may be as important to motorcycle culture in the years to come as he was when he first attracted national attention in the 1960s and 1970s.

Introduction

1. "Don't Shoot the Easy Rider," *National Review*, October 31, 1980, 1309; "Looking toward November," *American Motorcyclist*, November 1980, 12–13; *Easy Rider*, directed by Dennis Hopper (Columbia Pictures, 1969).

2. For an *Easy Rider* trailer, see https://www.youtube.com/watch?v=UjlxqANj68U (accessed September 3, 2014).

3. Osgerby, *Biker*, 26.

4. See Wood, "Hell's Angels." On motorcyclists in film, see Seate, *Two Wheels*. On social deviance, see Ingebretsen, *At Stake*. See also Fine, *Difficult Reputations*.

5. Zaretsky, *No Direction Home*, 2; see also Cowie, *Stayin' Alive*. For an overview of the social protests of the 1960s–70s, see Anderson, *Movement and the Sixties*.

6. C. J. Doughty Jr., "Havoc in Hollister," *San Francisco Chronicle*, July 6, 1947, 1, 11; "Motorcyclists Put Town in an Uproar," *New York Times*, July 7, 1947.

7. "Motorcyclists' Convention Terrorizes Town," *Life*, July 21, 1947, 31.

8. On the speculation about Eddie Davenport, see Yates, *Outlaw Machine*, 19; see also "Forty Hours in Hollister," *Cycle*, August 1987.

9. On general histories of memory, see Halbwachs and Coser, *On Collective Memory*; Nora, "General Introduction"; Linenthal, *Unfinished Bombing*; and Bodnar, *Remaking America*.

10. Michael Taylor, "Scary Memories of a Bikers' Holiday," *San Francisco Chronicle*, July 4, 1979, "motorcycles" file, in Peter Tamony Collection, Western Historical Manuscript Collection, University of Missouri–Columbia (hereafter Tamony Collection); see also John Dorrance, "Forty Hours in Hollister," *Cycle*, August 1987, 50–54, 87.

11. The Hells Angels official website notes that the first Hells Angels Motorcycle Club was founded on March 17, 1948, in the Fontana/San Bernardino area. See http://affa .hells-angels.com/hamc-history/ (accessed September 9, 2014).

12. Michael Taylor, "Scary Memories of a Bikers' Holiday," *San Francisco Chronicle*, July 4, 1979, "motorcycles" file, Peter Tamony Collection.

13. Thompson, *Hell's Angels*; Alford and Ferriss, *Motorcycle*.

14. No one has been more important to this shift than Suzanne Ferriss. In March 2005 she and Wendy Moon started an online journal, *The International Journal of Motorcycle Studies*, that covers all aspects of motorcycling and motorcycle culture. Other important books on motorcycling are Wolf, *Rebels*; Hall, *Riding on the Edge*; Levingston, *Soul on Bikes*; Joans, *Bike Lust*; Pierson, *Perfect Vehicle*; Bishop, *Riding with Rilke*; Pirsig, *Zen and the Art of Motorcycle Maintenance*; and Crawford, *Shop Class As Soulcraft*.

15. On the larger history of migrants or itinerant workers, see Herndon, *Unwelcome Americans*; McCurdy, *Citizen Bachelors*; Higbie, *Indispensable Outcasts*; Chudacoff, *Age of the Bachelor*.

16. For a general history of suburbanization, see Jackson, *Crabgrass Frontier*, and Flink, *Automobile Age*, 175–76.

17. Heitmann, *Automobile and American Life*, 150.

18. See Avila, *Popular Culture*.

19. Nader, *Unsafe at Any Speed*; Lewis S. Buchanan and Herbert R. Miller, "Recent Developments in Traffic Safety Programs for Motorcyclists," in *Proceedings: International Motorcycle Safety Conference* (Washington, D.C.: National Highway Traffic Safety Administration, 1975), 329; see also Flink, *Automobile Age*, 384–85.

20. Motorcycle Industry Council, *1977 Motorcycle Statistical Annual* (Newport Beach: MIC, 1977), 7.

21. Becky Norton Dunlop, "Turning the Tide," *American Motorcyclist*, November 1980, 14.

22. Under "Government Briefs," *American Motorcyclist*, November 1984, 30.

23. Cowie, "From Hard Hats to the Nascar Dads," 13.

24. On the Right, see Kruse, *White Flight*; Lassiter, *Silent Majority*; Carter, *Politics of Rage*; McGirr, *Suburban Warriors*; on the idea of backlash, see Formisano, *Boston against Busing*.

25. On the counterculture, see Sides, *Erotic City*.

26. Studies about the black rider are scarce compared to those on the white motorcycling community. See, for example, Levingston, *Soul on Bikes*; for travel literature featuring a black rider, see Harris, *South of Haunted Dreams*.

27. *Sweet Sweetback's Baadasssss Song*, directed by Melvin Van Peebles (1971).

Chapter 1

1. "A Violent New Opera on Motorcycle Gangs," *San Francisco Chronicle*, March 26, 1971, and "Hell's Angel Opera is Tough," *San Francisco Chronicle*, March 26, 1971, "motorcycles" file, Peter Tamony Collection, Western Historical Manuscript Collection, University of Missouri–Columbia (hereafter Tamony Collection).

2. "A Violent New Opera on Motorcycle Gangs," *San Francisco Chronicle*, March 26, 1971, and "Hell's Angel Opera is Tough," *San Francisco Chronicle*, March 26, 1971, "motorcycle" file, Tamony Collection.

3. Seate, *Two Wheels on Two Reels*; Thompson, *Hell's Angels*.

4. On the term "gypsying," see Kieffner, "Riding the Borderlands," 34. Kieffner notes that a "gypsying" subculture was evident by the 1920s and that motorcyclists adopted the term from nonriders who used it negatively.

5. St. Clair and Anderson, *Images of America*, 7; "History of the Sturgis Motorcycle Rally," www.sturgismotorcyclerally-info/timeline-and-photo-gallery.

6. Gypsy tours were generally off the beaten path, and in 1955, the AMA suggested that more were taking place. See *American Motorcycling*, May 1955, 15.

7. See the AMA website, www.americanmotorcyclist.com/about/history (accessed June 12, 2014). The AMA was originally called the American Motorcycle Association.

8. John Dorrance, "Forty Hours in Hollister," *Cycle*, August 1987, 87.

9. See Osgerby, *Biker*, 28.

10. Doughty, "Havoc in Hollister," *San Francisco Chronicle*, July 6, 1947, 1.

11. *Motorcyclist*, August 1947, 8; see also "Let's Take Inventory!," *American Motorcycling*, August 1947, 11.

12. "Let's Take Inventory!," *American Motorcycling*, August 1947, 11; *Motorcyclist*, August 1947, 8. For other descriptions of the individuals involved, see "Cyclists Face Bar of Justice during Three-Day Meeting," *Hollister Free Lance*, July 7, 1947, 1; see also "County Jail Jammed with Law-Breakers; Night Court Held," *Hollister Free Lance*, July 5, 1947, 1.

13. "Let's Take Inventory!," *American Motorcycling*, August 1947, 11; *Motorcyclist*, August 1947, 8; C. J. Doughty Jr., "Havoc in Hollister," *San Francisco Chronicle*, July 6, 1947, 1. See also L. S. Storrs, "Grand-Dad Rides a Thirty-Fifty," *Cycle*, July 1952, 19.

14. "Let's Take Inventory!," *American Motorcycling*, August 1947, 11.

15. Ibid.; *Motorcyclist*, August 1947, 8.

16. "Let's Take Inventory!," *American Motorcycling*, August 1947, 11; "All Right! Riders, Clubs, Dealers, Importers, and Factories. Let's Face It!," *Motorcyclist*, August 1947, 8.

17. "Motorcyclists Riot Again in California," *Daytona Beach Morning Journal*, September 2, 1947.

18. On Riverside in 1947, see "Motorcyclists Riot Again in California," *Daytona Beach Morning Journal*, September 2, 1947; and "Cyclists on Rampage at Riverside, Calif.," *Lewiston (Me.) Daily Sun*, September 2, 1947. On the incident in 1948, see "Cyclists Rule Town; 28 Held in Disorders," *New York Times*, July 5, 1948, 16; "One Killed, 54 Are Arrested as Motorcyclists Plague Town," *Washington Post*, July 6, 1948, 6; and "46 Jailed in Riverside Cycle Riots," *Los Angeles Times*, July 5, 1948, 1.

19. "Regardless of What You Have Read or Heard, Here's the Truth about Riverside," *Motorcyclist*, July 1948, 14.

20. "Regardless of What You Have Read or Heard, Here's the Truth about Riverside," *Motorcyclist*, July 1948, 14.

21. "The City of Riverside Reports," *Motorcyclist*, August 1948, 36.

22. "Regardless of What You Have Read or Heard, Here's the Truth about Riverside," *Motorcyclist*, July 1948, 14.

23. "The City of Riverside Reports," *Motorcyclist*, August 1948, 36.

24. "Best Wheel Forward AMA Theme," *American Motorcycling*, February 1961, 15.

25. Letters to the Editor, *Hollister Free Lance*, July 7, 1947, 4.

26. Ibid., July 9, 1947, 4.

27. Ibid.

28. Ibid.

29. John Dorrance, "Forty Hours in Hollister," *Cycle*, August 1987, 87. On the point about merchants welcoming the rally, see, for example, "Motorcyclists May Return for Race This Fall," *Hollister Free Lance*, July 16, 1947, 1.

30. Gorn, *Manly Art*; Gilfoyle, *City of Eros*; see also Moore, *Cow Boys and Cattle Men*; Linderman, *Embattled Courage*; and Chauncey, *Gay New York*.

31. Doughty, "Havoc in Hollister," *San Francisco Chronicle*, July 6, 1947, 1.

32. "Cyclists Face Bar of Justice during Three-Day Meeting," *Hollister Free Lance*, July 7, 1. For the various terms used to described motorcyclists, see also "Battle of Hollister Ends

as Wild, Celebrating Motorcyclists Leave City," *Hollister Free Lance*, July 7, 1947, 1; and "County Jail Jammed with Law-Breakers," *Hollister Free Lance*, July 5, 1947, 1.

33. C. J. Doughty Jr., "Havoc in Hollister," *San Francisco Chronicle*, July 6, 1947, 1, 11.

34. "Battle of Hollister Ends as Wild, Celebrating Motorcyclists Leave City," *Hollister Free Lance*, July 7, 1947, 1.

35. "The City of Riverside Reports," *Motorcyclist*, August 1948, 36.

36. "County Jail Jammed with Law-Breakers," *Hollister Free Lance*, July 5, 1947, 1; see also "Battle of Hollister Ends as Wild, Celebrating Motorcyclists Leave City," *Hollister Free Lance*, July 7, 1947, 1.

37. Beier, *Masterless Men*, 3–9.

38. Cresswell, "Vagrant/Vagabond," 248–49.

39. Rogin, *Ronald Reagan, the Movie*, 45–46, 64.

40. Cresswell, *On the Move*, 160–61.

41. Higbie, *Indispensable Outcasts*, 134–72; see also "County Jail Jammed with Law-Breakers," *Hollister Free Lance*, July 5, 1947, 1.

42. On the Dust Bowl, see Bonnifield, *Dust Bowl*; Gregory, *American Exodus*; Shindo, *Dust Bowl Migrants*; and Egan, *Worst Hard Time*.

43. Avila, *Popular Culture*, 31.

44. Higbie, *Indispensable Outcasts*, 5, 12–13.

45. Ibid., 12.

46. May, *Homeward Bound*.

47. C. J. Doughty Jr., "Havoc in Hollister," *San Francisco Chronicle*, July 6, 1947, 1, 11.

48. Michael Taylor, "Scary Memories of a Bikers' Holiday," *San Francisco Chronicle*, July 4, 1979, "motorcycle" file, Tamony Collection.

49. United States, *United States Census of Population, 1950. Number of Inhabitants, California. Total for Cities, Small Areas, Counties, Urban & Rural* (Washington, D.C.: U.S. Government Printing Office, 1951), 5–135 United States, *United States Census of Housing: 1950. General Characteristics, California.* (Washington, D.C.: U.S. Government Printing Office, 1950), 5–186.

50. See, for example, "Visiting Cyclists Hurt in Accidents," *Hollister Free Lance*, July 5, 1947, 1.

51. Kieffner, "Riding the Borderlands," 80.

52. On the exclusion of black riders from the AMA, see Ed Youngblood, "Moving Beyond Prejudice," *American Motorcyclist*, March 1995, 15.

53. C. J. Doughty Jr., "Havoc in Hollister," *San Francisco Chronicle*, July 6, 1947, 1, 11.

54. Bordo, *Male Body*, 134; *A Streetcar Named Desire*, directed by Elia Kazan (Warner Bros. Pictures, 1951).

55. Stansell, *City of Women*, 90; Kelley, *Race Rebels*, 161–82; Peiss, *Zoot Suit*.

56. Kelley, " 'We Are Not What We Seem,' " 75–112.

57. *The Wild One*, directed by László Benedek (Columbia Pictures, 1953).

58. Hunnicutt, *Free Time*, 119–21.

59. Discussions about Hollister by academics and others have been all over the place. Brock Yates goes to considerable length to show that the *Life* magazine photograph was staged and that the rally was sensationalized. But he also says of the rally, "Brawls were unrelenting, and Hollister's five-man police force was quickly overwhelmed." See Yates,

Outlaw Machine, 16. Jeremy Packer (*Mobility without Mayhem*, 117) argues that "two members [of a motorcycle gang] were charged with raping a young Hollister girl." Paul Garson (*Born to be Wild*, 52) downplays the Hollister Rally but connects the term "outlaw" with mayhem. See also Osgerby, *Biker*, 31. Other scholars have been much more precise about Hollister and its impact. Alford and Ferriss (*Motorcycle*, 89–93), address the sensationalism and use the rally (and the subsequent film representations of it) to explore issues of identity and rebellion. Gary Kieffner ("Riding the Borderlands," 134–42) explores the myth of Hollister and downplays the sensationalism surrounding the weekend's events, but he focuses more on the popular cultural representations of motorcyclists that were influenced by the rally than the rally itself.

60. The most detailed description of the use (and misuse of the picture) is Yates, *Outlaw Machine*, 17–20. The picture was taken by Barney Peterson. According to Yates, Jerry Smith of Coos Bay, Oregon, investigated the photograph and two others taken of Davenport on the bike by Peterson. In one of the photographs, the beer bottles are standing upright, and in the one published in *Life*, they are scattered about the ground. Smith and historian Daniel Corral also interviewed Gus DeSerpa, who was at the rally and who confirmed that the picture was posed.

61. On the different types of handlebar styles, see "The Story of the Three Bars," *Cycle*, October 1951, 14–15, 32.

62. On images of working men before and after World War II, see Freeman, "Hardhats," 728–30; on images of farmers, see David, *North Carolina during the Great Depression*, and Schulz, *Michigan Remembered*.

63. "Editor's Viewpoint," *Cycle*, June 1950, 4.

64. Mail Pouch, *Cycle*, March 1954, 7.

65. Youngblood, "Birth of the Dirt Bike."

66. Mail Pouch, *Cycle*, March 1954, 7.

67. "Motorcycling—California Style," *Motorcyclist*, September 1949, 20, 26.

68. "The Press and Radio Rub Salt 'Riverside' Brand in the Hollister Wound," *Motorcyclist*, October 1947, 17.

69. Ibid.

70. Alford and Ferriss, *Motorcycle*, 19–26; Osgerby, *Biker*, 14–15.

71. For a discussion of lightweights before the war, see Fred Woll, "A Lightweight Sales Manager Sounds Off," *Motorcyclist*, August 1951, 14–15, 29; see also "Publisher's Page," *Motorcyclist*, January 1948, 7. Some motorcyclists were talking about their British bikes before Hollister; see, for example, "Bench Racing," *Motorcyclist*, February 1947, 19; and Letters, *Motorcyclist*, June 1947, 3; on the push to minimize tariffs, see Michael Emmett, "Lightweights and the American Market," *Motorcyclist*, November 1954, 6–7.

72. *Easyriders*, June 1971, 22.

73. For the use of the expression "crouching forward," see "Rider Writings," *Cycle*, December 1952, 6.

74. "A Limey Wants to Know," *Cycle*, November 1952, 28.

75. "Rider Writings," *Cycle*, December 1952, 6.

76. "56 Are Charged in Cycle Gang Stabbings," *San Francisco Chronicle*, March 10, 1971, "motorcycle" file, Tamony Collection; see also "5 Sleeping Motorcyclists Massacred," *San Francisco Chronicle*, July 5, 1979, "motorcycle" file, Tamony Collection.

77. "'Galloping Geese' Are Unhorsed," *San Francisco Chronicle*, January 18, 1972, "motorcycle" file, Tamony Collection.

78. Bill Dobbins, "Biker and the Law," *Biker News*, no. 11, 1974, 14.

79. "Price of a Baby . . . One Motorcycle," *San Francisco Chronicle*, January 4, 1969, "motorcycle" file, Tamony Collection.

80. "Hoods Attach Shotgun Shells to Motorbikes," *San Francisco Examiner*, October 9, 1972, "motorcycle" file, Tamony Collection. Bitchin made the same point about motorcycles being made into weapons in "Just Puttin," *Biker News*, no. 5, 1974.

81. "Mystery Shot Kills Woman," *San Francisco Chronicle*, July 6, 1972, "motorcycle" file, Tamony Collection.

82. "Hint of 'Reprisal' In Girl's Torture," *New York Times*, November 16, 1967; "Florida Fighting Motorcycle Gang," *New York Times*, November 19, 1967, 22; "Not Guilty Pleas on Girl's Crucifixion," *San Francisco Chronicle*, November 28, 1967; "Three Cyclists Sentenced for 'Crucifixion,'" *San Francisco Chronicle*, July 26, 1968, all "motorcycle" file, Tamony Collection.

83. See Phil Finch, "Cycle Stunt Riding Popularized," *San Francisco Examiner*, November 12, 1971, "motorcycle" file, Tamony Collection.

84. For a recent biography of Knievel, see Montville, *Evel*.

85. Mandich, *Evel Incarnate*.

86. "Cycle Jumping Slaughter of Men," *San Francisco Chronicle*, July 6, 1972, "motorcycle" file, Tamony Collection.

87. "Evel's Rival Dies in Crash," *San Francisco Chronicle*, August 6, 1974, "Evel Knievel" file, Tamony Collection.

88. "Cycle Jumping Slaughter of Men."

89. "Stuntman's Hectic Adventure," *San Francisco Examiner*, January 24, 1970, "Evel Knievel" file, Tamony Collection; see also Gordon Martin, "Knievel's Record Is Target Tonight," *San Francisco Chronicle*, December 11, 1971, "Evel Knievel" file, Tamony Collection.

90. "They Rode That Children May Walk!," *American Motorcycling*, August 1948, 14; some clubs organized "child welfare" programs. See, for example, "Rider Writings," *Cycle*, February 1951, 6.

91. Mile Ottenheimer, "Motorcycle Club's Good Image," *San Francisco Examiner*, August 21, 1970, "motorcycle" file, Tamony Collection.

92. Robert Ruark, "He Says Jackets, Jeans ARE Uniform of Hoods," *San Francisco News*, March 2, 1958, "motorcycle" file, Tamony Collection.

93. "Editor's Mail Box," *San Francisco Examiner*, December 5, 1966, in "motorcycle" file, Tamony Collection.

94. Dick Alexander, "Another Daredevil Wants Evel to Level with Kids," *San Francisco Examiner*, September 3, 1975, "motorcycle" file, Tamony Collection.

95. Wolf, *Rebels*, 218–19; see also Massad Ayoob, "Outlaw Bikers," *Police Product News* 6, no. 5 (May 1982): 27–28.

96. Hall, *Riding on the Edge*, 62.

97. Mail, *Cycle*, September 1967, 16.

98. Letters, *Cycle*, July 1971, 10.

99. Bill Dobbins, "Biker and the Law," *Biker News*, no. 11, 1974, 14.

100. Gordon Jennings, "Speaking Out," *Cycle*, September 1967, 8.

101. Mail, *Cycle*, January 1968, 14.

102. Cosell, *Like It Is*, 97–98.

103. David Lyle, "Cup of Anguish," *Esquire*, January 1969, 89.

104. Palladino, *Teenagers*, 159.

105. Phillips, "Blue Jeans, Black Leather Jackets, and a Sneer."

106. Michael J. Gittens, "Special Motorcycle Patrols Cut Accidents in Pittsburgh," *American City* 67 (November 1952): 159; "Craftsmen on Wheels," *Popular Science* 52 (January 1948): 198; James A. Hoye, "One Motorcycle Is Worth Six Cars in Traffic Control," *American City* 66 (August 1951): 135; "Motorcycles Save Policeman Power," *American City* 70 (November 1955): 171.

107. "Young Cyclist," *Life*, December 1, 1947, 73–74; also on Donny, see "The American Way," *American Motorcycling*, August 1947, 12.

108. Andrew R. Boone, "How They've Halted Delinquency on Wheels," *Popular Science*, March 1955, 99–102, 258.

109. See "Hell's Angels: Their Naming" in "motorcycle" file, Tamony Collection; see also R. W. Burchfield, "Hell's Angels: Content and Continuum," October 1969 in "motorcycle" file, Tamony Collection.

110. Thompson, *Hell's Angels*, 35.

111. "New Films," *Newsweek*, December 14, 1953, 88; *New Statesmen and Nation*, April, 9, 1955; *New York Times*, December 31, 1953, 9:2; *Time*, January 18, 1954, 100, 102; *Catholic World*, January 1954, 304.

112. *Catholic World*, January 1954, 304.

113. "Reign of Terror Jails 92 Cyclists," *San Francisco Examiner*, August 22, 1960, "motorcycle" file, Tamony Collection.

114. Ibid.

115. Ibid.

116. Linda Moran, "State Laws: What You Need to Know Before You Go Riding," *Cycle*, May 1972.

117. "One Road Leads to a Promised Land!," *American Motorcycling*, October 1948, 7.

118. Letters, *Cycle*, July 1975, 10.

119. Mail, *Cycle*, March 1968, 15.

120. "Florida Fighting Motorcycle Gang," *New York Times*, November 19, 1967, 22, "motorcycle" file, Tamony Collection.

121. Flamm, *Law and Order*, 2–4.

122. Ibid., 8–9.

123. Wells Twombly, "Easy Rider Makes Money, Not Enemies," *San Francisco Examiner and Chronicle*, January 27, 1974, "motorcycle" file, Tamony Collection.

124. *Random House Historical Dictionary of American Slang* (New York: Random House, 1994), 1:156; the dictionary also defines "biker" as a motorcycle gang member.

125. "The Black Hats," in Mail, *Cycle*, March 1968, 15.

126. "Motorcycle" file, Tamony Collection.

127. Hal Burton, "The Most Unpopular Men on the Road," *Saturday Evening Post*, September 25, 1954, 130.

128. L. S. Storrs, "Grand-Dad Rides a Thirty-Fifty," *Cycle*, July 1952, 19.

129. Letters, *Motorcyclist*, January 1948, 3; "This May Be of Interest To YOU!" *American Motorcycling*, September 1947, 9, 32. The term "sporting life" comes from studies of late

nineteenth- and early twentieth-century male culture. See Gorn, *Manly Art*, and Gilfoyle, *City of Eros*.

130. See Orsi, "Religious Boundaries of an Inbetween People"; see also Jacobson, *Whiteness of a Different Color*; and Roediger, *Working toward Whiteness*.

131. On the eugenics movement in the United States and its connection to IQ tests and immigrants, see Kline, *Building a Better Race*; on Mexicans and eugenics, see Stern, *Eugenic Nation*.

132. "How the 'Thunder Herd' Boss Brought a Honda Boom to U.S.," *Newsweek*, July 6, 1964, 66–67; Chas Cruttenden, "Cycles in Social Revolution," *San Francisco Examiner and Chronicle*, June 19, 1966, "motorcycle" file, Tamony Collection.

133. Chas Cruttenden, "Cycles in Social Revolution," *San Francisco Examiner and Chronicle*, June 19, 1966, "motorcycle" file, Tamony Collection.

134. Tom Beesley, "Dallas Is Motorcycle Country," *Dallas Times Herald*, classified display, March 7, 1971, 11.

135. David Kleinberg, "Super Joe Flies over Cars; Sometimes He Makes It," *San Francisco Examiner and Chronicle*, December 5, 1971, "motorcycle" file, Tamony Collection.

136. "What Makes Evel Jump?," *San Francisco Chronicle*, July 31, 1974, "Evel Knievel" file, Tamony Collection.

137. Dick Alexander, "Another Daredevil Wants Evel to Level with Kids," *San Francisco Examiner*, September 3, 1975, "Evel Knievel" file, Tamony Collection.

138. See "What Makes Evel Jump?," *San Francisco Chronicle*, July 31, 1974, "Evel Knievel" file, Tamony Collection.

139. Sylvan Fox, "Crime and Violence Are Commonplace in Nether World of Lower East Side," *New York Times*, March 20, 1969, 40.

140. "A Decaying District's Terror," *San Francisco Chronicle*, February 12, 1971, "motorcycle" file, Tamony Collection.

141. Sylvan Fox, "Crime and Violence Are Commonplace in Nether World of Lower East Side," *New York Times*, March 20, 1969, 40.

142. "2 Youth Clubs Fight in Richmond," *San Francisco Examiner*, November 19, 1971, "motorcycle" file, Tamony Collection.

143. *Shoemaker v. Trompen*, 326 Mich. 120, 40 N.W. 2d 92, Mich., December 7, 1949; *City of Dalton v. Cochran*, 80 Ga. App. 252, 55 S.E. 2d 907, GA. App. October 29, 1949.

144. *People v. Reagan*, 128 Cal. App. 3d 92, 180 Cal. Rptr. 85, Cal. App. 4 Dist., January 20, 1982.

Chapter 2

1. On law and order and the fears about urban unrest, see Flamm, *Law and Order*.

2. "Freedom of Information and Privacy Acts, Subject: Hells Angels, Part 2 of 2," "The Hells Angels Part 4 of 6," vault.fbi.gov/The%20Hells%20Angels/The%20Hells%20Angels%20Part%204%20of%206/view (accessed April 2, 2014).

3. Ibid.

4. "Revoke the Licenses of Rioting Motorcyclists?," *San Francisco Examiner*, August 10, 1965, "motorcycles" file, in Peter Tamony Collection, Western Historical Manuscript Collection, University of Missouri–Columbia (hereafter Tamony Collection).

5. Ibid.

6. See Flink, *Automobile Age*, 175–76; Avila, *Popular Culture*, 186, 198, 203. See also Kruse and Sugrue, *New Suburban History*, 1–3; Jackson, *Crabgrass Frontier*; and Nicolaides, *My Blue Heaven*, 1–8.

7. See Avila, *Popular Culture*, 161–84, for the history of struggle over highways and the destruction of communities; see also Avila, *Folklore of the Freeway*, and Norton, *Fighting Traffic*, 4–17.

8. Avila, *Popular Culture*, 203–4; on the highway act, see ibid., 206; Schlosser, *Fast Food Nation*, 40.

9. Motorcycle Industry Council, *1977 Motorcycle Statistical Annual* (Newport Beach: MIC, 1977), 7.

10. "This May Be of Interest to You!," *American Motorcycling*, September, 1947, 9, 32.

11. Ibid., 32. On other complaints about "boulevard cowboys," see "Don't Judge All by One," *American Motorcycling*, October 1949, 7. See also "Take It Easy Fella! Play it Safe," *Motorcyclist*, June 1949, 21; "O.K. Fellas and Girls, Don't Let Your Sport Down by Noisy, Reckless Motorcycling," *Motorcyclist*, March 1949, 17; "Ride Safely and Live," *Motorcyclist*, October 1949, 21; and "All Eyes Are on Cyclists," *American Motorcycling*, August 1949, 7. For other complaints about daredevils, see "We Lead with Our Chin," *Motorcyclist*, October 1947, 19.

12. See, for example, Hal Burton, "The Most Unpopular Men on the Road," *Saturday Evening Post*, September 25, 1954, 32, 128, 130; "One Road Leads to a Promised Land," *American Motorcycling*, October 1948, 7. Mention of restrictions are also found in "Quoting a Friend," *American Motorcycling*, February 1947, 5. At Laconia in 1948 noisy pipes could lead to the authorities impounding the motorcycle, and, depending upon the violation, the state's Commissioner of Motor Vehicles could in turn deny "the right of the offender to operate in this state for a period of 10 to 30 days." See "We're Welcome at Laconia but 'Pipes' Are Banned," *American Motorcycling*, May 1949, 22.

13. Hal Burton, "The Most Unpopular Men on the Road," *Saturday Evening Post*, September 25, 1954): 130.

14. Coffee Break with the Editor, *Motorcyclist*, November 1959, 4. Motorcyclists were initially denied use of the New York State Thruway when it was opened in 1954. See "Motorcyclists Denied Use of New York's Super Cross-State Highway," *Motorcyclist*, August 1954, 8; and "New York Thruway Opens to Motorcycle Traffic, *Motorcyclist*, December 1954, 18.

15. "Life Goes Motorcycling," *Life*, August 1947, 112–14.

16. "Regardless of What You Have Read or Heard, Here's the Truth about Riverside," *Motorcyclist*, July 1948, 14; reprinted from the *Pasadena California Independent*.

17. Motorcycle Industry Council, *1977 Motorcycle Statistical Annual* (Newport Beach: MIC, 1977), 7.

18. See "suburbia" file, Tamony Collection.

19. Cycle Chatter, *American Motorcycling*, November 1948, 16; "Why Motorcycling?," *American Motorcycling*, July 1947, 7. On the freedom and modernity associated with autos, see Rajan, "Automobility and the Liberal Disposition," 113–29; on automobility and the contested nature of roads, see Newman and Giardina, *Sport, Spectacle, and NASCAR Nation*, 19–30.

20. Avila, *Popular Culture*, 221.

21. Clark Trumbull, "It's *You*—Not the Motorcycle that Is 'Dangerous,'" *Motorcyclist*, April 1947, 14; on women and automobiles, see Scharff, *Taking the Wheel*.

22. Rider Writings, *Cycle*, February 1951, 6.

23. Letters, *American Motorcycling*, October 1948, 5.

24. Letters, *Motorcyclist*, November 1949, 3.

25. Clark Trumbull, "It's *You*—Not the Motorcycle that Is 'Dangerous,'" *Motorcyclist*, April 1947, 14.

26. Letters, *American Motorcycling*, April 1949, 5.

27. "Motorcycling—California Style," *Motorcyclist*, September 1949, 20, 26.

28. *American Motorcycling*, May 1950, 10.

29. Hal Burton, "The Most Unpopular Men on the Road," *Saturday Evening Post*, September 25, 1954.

30. Ibid.

31. "Over 200 Million Miles, But '48 Accident Rate Dips," *American Motorcycling*, February 1948, 10.

32. Letters, *American Motorcycling*, March 1949, 4.

33. For statistics on highway safety issues, see www.fhwa.dot.gov/policyinformation/ statistics/2010/fi210.cfm; and www.fhwa.dot.gov/policyinformation/statistics/2010/vmt421 .cfm; see also *Statistical Abstract of the United States, 1977; National Data Book and Guide to Sources* (Washington, D.C.: U.S. Government Printing Office, 1977), 635.

34. "A Gory Traffic Anniversary Near," *San Francisco Chronicle*, July 28, 1973, "traffic" file, Tamony Collection.

35. Nader, *Unsafe at Any Speed*; other books on Nader include Pertschuk, *Revolt against Regulation*, 30–33, 40–41; Holsworth, *Public Interest Liberalism*; and Packer, *Mobility without Mayhem*.

36. Nader, *Unsafe at Any Speed*, 77–78.

37. Ibid., 78.

38. Ibid., 67.

39. Ibid., 4.

40. Ibid., 80.

41. See Cohen, *Consumers' Republic*, 357–63; on the broader history of consumer activism, see Glickman, *Buying Power*.

42. "New Auto Safety Standards Urged," *Spokane Daily Chronicle*, December 3, 1966, 9.

43. On bad drivers, see Anthony Tramondo, "Female Drivers: Less Deadly than the Male," *New York Times*, March 27, 1955, SM 26; "Doctors Link Bad Driving to Unhappy Childhoods," *New York Times*, November 24, 1953; Bert Pierce, "Automobiles: Attitudes, Good Drivers Become Bad Drivers When Their Emotional Responses Are Wrong," *New York Times*, October 25, 1953, X28; and Burton W. Marsh, "Older Drivers Pose a Safety Problem," *New York Times*, April 2, 196, A13.

44. "States Examine Driver Standards," *Spokane Daily Chronicle*, March 16, 1967, 42.

45. Ibid.

46. *The People of the State of New York, Plaintiff v. Warren F. Bielmeyer, Richard J. Ball, James T. Dommer, Jerome A. Mingle, David J. Pyc, Robert Cullen, Thomas J. Bojarski, David L. Masters, Gary J. Wesolowski and Fred Scinta, Defendants; City Court of New York, Buffalo*; 54 Misc. 2d 466; 282 N.Y.S.2d 797; 1967 N.Y. Misc. LEXIS 1282; August 28, 1967.

47. "Texans Going for Gas-Stingy Motorcycles Despite Risks," *Dallas Times Herald*, May 24, 1974, 6.

48. "Motorcycle" file, Tamony Collection.

49. Ibid.; for the movie trailer, see www.youtube.com/watch?v=byxXwgvonHE.

50. "Motorcycle" file, Tamony Collection.

51. "Newsmen's Party Caught in Shootout," December 17, 1979; "motorcycle" file, Tamony Collection.

52. "All Right! Riders, Clubs, Dealers, Importers, and Factories. Let's Face It!," *Motorcyclist*, August 1947, 8.

53. "Meeting Set by Knowles on 'Outlaws,'" *Milwaukee Journal*, June 4, 1966, 1.

54. "56 Motorcyclists Charged in Killings," *St. Petersburg Times*, March 10, 1971, 17-A; see also "4 Cyclists Shot in Gun Battle; Police Nab 25," *Miami News*, October 9, 1967, 7C.

55. On different aspects of suburbanization, see Kruse and Sugrue, *New Suburban History*; see also Nicolaides, *My Blue Heaven*.

56. "Lakes Luring Holiday Visitors," *Lawrence Journal World*, May 27, 1972, 1.

57. "Motorcyclists, Youths Clash," *Evening Independent*, September 7, 1971, 12-A; see also "Rock Festival Brawl Leaves 1 Man Dead," *News and Courier*, September 8, 1971, 11-A.

58. "Revoke the Licenses of Rioting Motorcyclists?" *San Francisco Examiner*, August 10, 1965, "motorcycle" file, Tamony Collection.

59. "Motorcyclists Ravage Town in Michigan," *Morning Record*, August 8, 1966, 7.

60. "Black Angels" (advertisement), *San Francisco Chronicle*, January 22, 1971, "motorcycle" file, Tamony Collection.

61. Ibid.

62. Avila, *Popular Culture*, 6, 186.

63. "Cyclists Killed, 10 Wounded at Rock Festival," *Lewiston (Idaho) Morning Tribune*, September 8, 1971, 1.

64. "Small Town Terrorizes Motorcycle Gang," "motorcycle" file, Tamony Collection. An article in *Easyriders* tells the story of a motorcyclist who was chased for three miles before he was rammed by a car, killing the motorcyclist. See "Father/Son Biker-Killers Sentenced to Life," *Easyriders*, October 1983, 43.

65. Bill Hampton and Bill Stermer, "Staying Alive on Two Wheels," *Popular Mechanics*, April 1981, 80.

66. Dan Watson, "Spring Is Joyous—but Deadly—Time for Cyclists," *Dallas Morning News*, April 14, 1980, D1.

67. "How to Kill a Motorcyclist," *Dispatch*, August 18, 1977, 6; see also "Kill a Biker Go to Jail," *Easyriders*, July 1983, 11. *Easyriders* was advocating a nationwide protest movement to ensure that drivers who kill bikers are punished accordingly.

68. R. B. Read, "Twice the Fun and Twice the Risk," *California Living* in *San Francisco Sunday Examiner and Chronicle*, December 11, 1966, 22.

69. "Advice on Traffic Laws from Connecticut State Police," *American Motorcycling*, June 1960, 28.

70. Wirt Gammon, "Just Between Us Fans," *American Motorcycling*, June 1963, 5.

71. "You Can't Judge a Motorcyclist," *Sarasota (Fla.) Herald-Tribune*, November 12, 1970, 1B.

72. "Victim Denies Firing Gun at Motorcyclists," *Evening Independent*, June 4, 1969, 3-A; Keith Gabler and Richard Morgan, "Motorcyclists Deny They Make Trouble," *St. Petersburg (Fla.) Times*, June 4, 1969, 4-B.

73. "Victim Denies Firing Gun at Motorcyclists," *Evening Independent*, June 4, 1969, 3-A.

74. Ibid.

75. "Bikers Lose in Red River Showdown," *San Francisco Examiner*, July 4, 1978, "motorcycle" file, Tamony Collection.

76. There are disputes about the definition of road rage. Some specifically use the term "deliberate" and others talk of a more general behavior that has the potential to endanger other motorists or pedestrians. See Packer, *Mobility without Mayhem*, 238–40; see also Rothe, *Driven to Kill*, 38, 123–24.

77. Avila, *Popular Culture*, 203.

78. "Motorcycle" file, Tamony Collection; *Smokey and the Bandit*, directed by Hal Needham (Universal Pictures, 1977).

79. This observation is based on my own and my dad's experience watching the film.

Chapter 3

1. Michael Sumner, "Varoom at the Top: The Madison Avenue Motorcycle Club," *Esquire*, November 1965, 141.

2. On the idea of class consumption, see Benson, *Household Accounts*; see also Cohen, *Consumers' Republic*; McGovern, *Sold American*; and May, *Recasting America*.

3. Motorcycle Industry Council, *1977 Motorcycle Statistical Annual* (Newport Beach: MIC, 1977), 7.

4. Garson, *Born to Be Wild*, 116.

5. "Wooing the 'Mild Ones,'" *Business Week*, March 30, 1963, 26–27; "How the 'Thunder Herd' Boss Brought a Honda Boom to U.S.," *Newsweek*, July 6, 1964, 66.

6. Walter Carlson, "Advertising: V-r-r-room in Honda's Sales," *New York Times*, July 29, 1966, 38.

7. "Twice the Fun, Twice the Risk," *California Living* in *San Francisco Sunday Examiner and Chronicle*, December 11, in "motorcycle" file, Peter Tamony Collection, Western Historical Manuscript Collection, University of Missouri–Columbia (hereafter Tamony Collection).

8. "The World's No. 1 Thunderer," *Reader's Digest*, December 1966, 13–14, 17–18, 20.

9. "How the 'Thunder Herd' Boss Brought a Honda Boom to U.S," *Newsweek*, July 6, 1964, 66.

10. Moskowitz, "The U.S. Craze for Japan's Motorcycles," *California Living* in *San Francisco Sunday Examiner and Chronicle*, December 11, 1966, "motorcycle" file, Tamony Collection.

11. Chas Cruttenden, "Cycles in Social Revolution," *San Francisco Sunday Examiner and Chronicle*, June 19, 1966, "motorcycle" file, Tamony Collection.

12. Ibid.

13. Michael Sumner, "Varoom at the Top: The Madison Avenue Motorcycle Club," *Esquire*, November 1965, 141.

14. Albert G. Maiorano, "A Motorcycle Offers Fun, Thrift—and Respectability," *New York Times*, April 2, 1967, A27.

15. See, for example, "Motorcycling Is a Family Affair," *American Motorcycling*, April 1963, 12.

16. "Wooing the 'Mild Ones,'" *Business Week*, March 30, 1963, 27.

17. Robert Reinhold, "New Breed of Motorcycle Buff Is Businessman 5 Days a Week," *New York Times*, June 16, 1969, 59; "New Breed of Motorcyclists," *San Francisco Examiner*, November 29, 1966, "motorcycle" file, Tamony Collection; Lyn Billingsley, "Blonde on Motorcycle Is Secretary, Mother of Two," *American Motorcycling*, April 1965, 16.

18. Lyn Billingsley, "Blonde on Motorcycle Is Secretary, Mother of Two," *American Motorcycling*, April 1965, 16. For a more general discussion of women motorcyclists, see Ferrar, *Hear Me Roar*, and Joans, *Bike Lust*.

19. Letters, *American Motorcycling*, March 1949, 3.

20. Walter Carlson, "Advertising: V-r-r-room in Honda's Sales," *New York Times*, July 29, 1966, 38.

21. "The Uneven Race to Take Over Honda," *Business Week*, May 25, 1975, 156.

22. "50 Eligible Bachelors: Singles Search for the Girl with 'Soul,'" *Ebony*, June 1969, 62–65, 68–70, 72.

23. See www.youtube.com/watch?v=QWQkfow5JR4&feature=results_video&playnext=1&list=PL4C7A31F9ECB52.

24. *Easyriders*, October 1972, 24.

25. "We Lead with Our Chin," *Motorcyclist*, March 1947, 7; for a history of auto mechanics, see Borg, *Auto Mechanics*.

26. Letters, *American Motorcycling*, September 1950, 6.

27. Ibid., March 1949, 3.

28. "Rider Writings," *Cycle*, January 1953, 6.

29. Letters, *Motorcyclist*, June 1947, 7.

30. Ibid., February 1948, 3, 6.

31. Jack Jamison interview by author, June 5, 2010, audiotape in author's possession.

32. *Motorcyclist*, May 1949, 3.

33. Letters, *Motorcyclist*, August 1947, 3.

34. "Rider Writings," *Cycle*, December 1952, 6.

35. Letters, *Motorcyclist*, February 1949, 3.

36. Ibid., March 1949, 3.

37. Ibid., October 1947, 3.

38. Ibid.; for a rider's critique of Francis, see Letters, *Motorcyclist*, February 1948, 3.

39. Letters, *Motorcyclist*, December 1947, 6.

40. Letters, *Cycle*, June 1973 and November 1973.

41. "Bikers Fail to Stir Sex, Violence," *Dallas Morning News*, July 28, 1979, 1D.

42. "Motorcycle Renaissance," *Business Week*, September 18, 1948, 91.

43. Bob Olmstead, "Macho Machine," *San Francisco Examiner*, August 19, 1977, 25, "motorcycle" file, Tamony Collection; see also Moskowitz, "The U.S. Craze for Japan's Motorcycles," *California Living* in *San Francisco Sunday Examiner and Chronicle*, December 11, 1966, "motorcycle" file, Tamony Collection.

44. Michael Sumner, "Varoom at the Top: The Madison Avenue Motorcycle Club," *Esquire*, November 1965, 141.

45. *Playboy*, September 1966, 128.

46. Erik Arctander, "Civilized Cycles: Everybody Rides 'em Now," *Popular Science*, July 1965, 68–72.

47. Mail, *Cycle*, April 1968, 12.

48. *Cycle*, January 1968, 14.

49. *Cycle*, April 1973, 30.

50. Barry Boesch, "Bikers Fail to Stir Sex, Violence," *Dallas Morning News*, July 28, 1979, 1D, 8D.

51. Mail, *Cycle*, February 1968, 14.

52. Ibid., April 1968, 12.

53. Ibid.

54. Hunter S. Thompson, "Man's Best Friend Is His Hog," *Los Angeles Times*, February 26, 1967, A36; *History of the Chopper* (Discovery Channel, 2007).

55. Mail, *Cycle*, February 1968, 14; Hunter S. Thompson, "Man's Best Friend Is His Hog," *Los Angeles Times*, February 26, 1967, A36.

56. McGovern, *Sold American*, 2–6.

57. Cohen, *Consumers' Republic*, 7.

58. Benson, *Household Accounts*, 7–8.

59. Hunter S. Thompson, "Man's Best Friend Is His Hog," *Los Angeles Times*, February 26, 1967, A36; Benson, *Household Accounts*, 7–8.

60. Mail, *Cycle*, February 1968, 14.

61. Barry Boesch, "Bikers Fail to Stir Sex, Violence," *Dallas Morning News*, July 28, 1979, 8D.

62. Letters, *Cycle*, December 1968, 19–20.

63. *American Motorcyclist*, October 1961, 40; *American Motorcyclist*, September 1964, 22; see also Hook, *Harley Davidson*, 240.

64. *American Motorcyclist*, October 1961, 40.

65. Holmstrom, *Harley-Davidson Century*, 127. Holmstrom makes a similar argument, noting that "kick starting had always been an honored rite of passage among Big Twin riders. The standard answer to a son's/little brother's/nephew's/neighborhood pest's longing pleas of 'When can I ride it?' were answered (in condescending tones) with, 'Maybe some day—if you can kick start it.' "

66. Biker Views, *Biker*, February 23, 1977, 13.

67. *Cycle*, June 1973, 30.

68. *Cycle*, July 1972, 10.

69. G. A. Trump, "Myths & Legends," *Biker*, vol. 2, no. 3, 1975, 21.

70. *Easyriders*, June 1982, 24.

71. *Cycle*, June 1950, 4.

72. "Let's Keep It a Clean Sport," *American Motorcycling*, April 1950, 9.

73. Letters to the Editor, *Cycle*, September 1950, 34.

74. Ibid.

75. Merritt H. Barnum, "New Image in Motorcycling: The Score in Clothes for Men," *American Motorcycling*, August 1963, 5.

76. "Motorcycles Roar at Cal," "motorcycle" file, Tamony Collection.

77. "Why Motorcycling," *American Motorcycling*, July 1947, 7; see also "Cycle Chatter," *American Motorcycling*, November 1948, 16.

78. *American Motorcycling*, January 1947, 5.

79. "How to Avoid Killing Yourself," *Esquire*, November 1965, 140.

80. "Pleasure Principle on Wheels," *Esquire*, April 1976, 99.

81. "Twice the Fun, Twice the Risk," *California Living*, December 11, 1966, "motorcycle" file, Tamony Collection.

82. "Watch Out! The Straights Are Coming!," *Easyriders*, June 1971, 18–19, 51.

83. Ibid.

84. Carl A. Gottlieb, "The Upward Mobility of the Motorcycle," *Esquire*, November 1965, 138–39.

85. Ibid.

86. Ibid.

87. Ibid.

88. Ibid.

89. Ibid.

90. Michael Sumner, "Varoom at the Top: The Madison Avenue Motorcycle Club," *Esquire*, November 1965, 141; see also Chas Cruttenden, "Cycles in Social Revolution," *San Francisco Sunday Examiner and Chronicle*, June 19, 1966, "motorcycle" file, Tamony Collection.

91. Letters, *American Motorcycling*, November 1966, 7.

92. Steven V. Roberts, "Roughing It Can Be Soft in a Camper," *New York Times*, April 2, 1967; on consumption in the postwar years and critiques of it, see Horowitz, *Anxieties of Affluence*.

93. Chas Cruttenden, "Cycles in Social Revolution," *San Francisco Sunday Examiner and Chronicle*, June 19, 1966, "motorcycle" file, Tamony Collection; "Light Bikes Sell Big to Young," *Sunday Examiner and Chronicle*, July 14, 1968, "motorcycle" file, Tamony Collection.

94. "Motorcycle Scavenger Hunt," *Playboy*, September 1966, 128; on critiques of *Playboy*, see Ehrenreich, *Hearts of Men*, and Fraterrigo, *Playboy and the Making of the Good Life*.

95. Hal Burton, "The Most Unpopular Men On the Road," *Saturday Evening Post*, September 25, 1954, 128.

96. Ann Landers, "All Family Profits Go on Hubby's Motorcycle," 1956, "motorcycle" file, Tamony Collection.

97. John Kifner, "Motorcycling Takes on Touch of Chic," *New York Times*, April 4, 1965, A15.

98. "Surgeon Rides Motorcycle to Relax," *American Motorcycling*, June 1963, 5.

99. Robert Reinhold, "New Breed of Motorcycle Buff Is Businessman 5 Days a Week," *New York Times*, June 16, 1969, 59.

100. Michael Sumner, "Varoom at the Top: The Madison Avenue Motorcycle Club," *Esquire*, November 1965, 141.

101. Robert Reinhold, "New Breed of Motorcycle Buff Is Businessman 5 Days a Week," *New York Times*, June 16, 1969, 59.

102. "The Man in the Grey Flannel Helmet," *Motor Trend*, June 1974; see also "The Uneven Race to Take Over Honda," *Business Week*, May 25, 1975, 156.

103. "Civilized Cycles," *Popular Science*, July 1965.

104. "The Man in the Grey Flannel Helmet," *Motor Trend*, June 1974, 88–89.

105. "Motorcycle club" file, Tamony Collection.

106. On the oil embargo and the larger conflicts in the Middle East, see Farber, *Taken Hostage.*

107. "Parks against Motor Sports Commissioner," *San Francisco Chronicle*, January 22, 1974, "motorcycle" file, Tamony Collection. Other benefits included easier access to gas pumps. According to one report, "motorcyclists were able to forego long, frustrating waits by using the central pumps of gasoline islands." See "The Man in the Grey Flannel Helmet," *Motor Trend*, June 1974.

108. "30% Jump in Deaths of Cycle Riders," *San Francisco Examiner*, August 2, 1974, "motorcycle" file, Tamony Collection. Toward the end of the 1970s, as gas prices continued to rise, dealers also noted the growing popularity of motorcycles. See John Klustner, "Gasoline Crunch Fueling Sales of Motorcycles," *Dallas Morning Herald*, May 27, 1979, 1.

109. "Speaking Cycle," *Cycle*, February 1952, 4.

110. "Promoting Endless Thrills," *San Francisco Examiner*, July 19, 1971, "motorcycle" file, Tamony Collection.

111. Nancy Smith, "Wheels Keep Turning," *Dallas Morning News*, June 17, 1976, 1.

112. Robert Reinhold, "New Breed of Motorcycle Buff Is Businessman 5 Days a Week," *New York Times*, June 16, 1969, 59.

113. Fraterrigo, *Playboy and the Making of the Good Life*, 49.

114. Whyte, *Organization Man*; other literature includes Yates, *Revolutionary Road*, and Wilson, *Man in the Gray Flannel Suit.*

115. Letters, *Cycle*, July 1971, 10.

116. Michael Sumner, "Varoom at the Top: The Madison Avenue Motorcycle Club," *Esquire*, November 1965, 141.

117. On oppositional cultures, see Rosenzweig, *Eight Hours for What We Will.*

118. Barger, *Hell's Angel*, 27.

119. Thompson, *Hell's Angels*, 59.

120. "Motorcycle Madness," *Southwest Scene*, July 1, 1973, 9.

121. Jim Pisaretz, "Whatza Matter with Bikers?," *Biker*, September 6, 1978, 19.

122. On the term "mystique," see "Motorcycle Madness," *Southwest Scene*, July 1, 1973, 9; and Margaret Downing, "Courthouse Gears Up for Biker Club Fight Trial," *Dallas Times Herald*, May 9, 1978. On "macho mystique," see "Zen and the Art of Cyclemakers," *Forbes*, April 19, 1984, 158–59; see also Bob Bitchin, "The Harley Mystique—An Introduction," *Biker*, October 5, 1977, 13.

123. Thompson, *Hell's Angels*, 271.

124. "Motorcycle Madness," *Southwest Scene*, July 1, 1973, 9.

125. Michael Sumner, "Varoom at the Top: The Madison Avenue Motorcycle Club," *Esquire*, November 1965, 141.

126. "Why Motorcycling?," *American Motorcycling*, July 1947, 7.

127. "The Big Swing to Motorcycles," *California Living* in *San Francisco Examiner and Chronicle*, December 11, 1966.

Chapter 4

1. See chapter 2.

2. Beth Magid, "Danger Rides on Two Wheels," *Parents Magazine*, September 1963, 68–69, 106–8.

3. Ibid.

4. Ibid.

5. Harris Edward Dark, "Your Youngster and the Motorcycle," *Today's Health*, May 1967, 24.

6. "Death Rides on Two Wheels," *Reader's Digest*, October 1967, 152.

7. Harris Edward Dark, "Your Youngster and the Motorcycle," *Today's Health*, May 1967, 24.

8. Ibid., 21–24; "Death Rides on Two Wheels," *Reader's Digest*, October 1967, 151–52.

9. Beth Magid, "Danger Rides on Two Wheels," *Parents Magazine*, September 1963, 108.

10. "Motorcycle Policemen Issued Crash Helmets," *Los Angeles Times*, December 9, 1955, A1.

11. Beth Magid, "Danger Rides on Two Wheels," *Parents Magazine*, September 1963, 108.

12. Harris Edward Dark, "Your Youngster and the MOTORCYCLE," *Today's Health*, May 1967, 21–22.

13. Ibid.

14. "A Heavy Toll for Small Cycles," *San Francisco Chronicle*, July 28, 1966, "motorcycle" file, Peter Tamony Collection, Western Historical Manuscript Collection, University of Missouri–Columbia (hereafter Tamony Collection).

15. Harris Edward Dark, "Your Youngster and the Motorcycle," *Today's Health*, May 1967, 21.

16. "A Heavy Toll for Small Cycles," *San Francisco Chronicle*, July 28, 1966, "motorcycle" file, Tamony Collection.

17. Chas Cruttenden, "Cycles in Social Revolution," *San Francisco Examiner and Chronicle*, June 19, 1966, 1P, "motorcycle" file, Tamony Collection; see also "Tips for your Home and Family," *Today's Health*, October 1966, 85.

18. Beth Magid, "Danger Rides on Two Wheels," *Parents Magazine*, September 1963, 152.

19. "Save Our Young Men For War!," *Easyriders*, February 1972, 26.

20. Laurie Cray Sadler, "Motorcycling: A Hazardous Two-Wheel Ride," *Today's Health*, July/August 1975, 28–29.

21. "Dangers of Riding on Two-Wheelers," *San Francisco Chronicle*, October 2, 1972, "motorcycle" file, Tamony Collection.

22. "A Heavy Toll for Small Cycles," *San Francisco Chronicle*, July 28, 1966, "motorcycle" file, Tamony Collection.

23. Ibid.

24. Harris Edward Dark, "Your Youngster and the Motorcycle," *Today's Health*, May 1967, 22.

25. Ibid.

26. Laurie Cray Sadler, "Motorcycling: A Hazardous Two-Wheel Ride," *Today's Health* July/August 1975, 28.

27. Ibid.

28. Harris Edward Dark, "Your Youngster and the Motorcycle," *Today's Health*, May 1967, 21; see also "How to Avoid Killing Yourself," *Esquire*, November 1965, 140–41.

29. Will Bernard, "The Family Lawyer," *Southeast Missourian*, April 28, 1970, 16; see also Knudson et al., "Motorcycle Helmet Laws"; French and Homer, "Motorcycle Helmet Laws"; and Charlie Williams, "The Next Era: A Helmet Law History," The Motorcycle Riders Foundation, September 1995, 1–2, http://www.abate-wa.org/Legislative/DocumentsAndForms/LAO%20Articles%202010/06-10%20LAO%20report%20part-2.pdf (accessed August 6, 2014).

30. "Helmet Law Unenforced," *Spokane Daily Chronicle*, July 29, 1969, 6.

31. "Helmet Law Enforcement Begins," *St. Petersburg (Fla.) Times*, May 30, 1968, 14C. On examples of state studies of helmets and motorcycle accidents, see pamphlets located at the Library of Congress: Illinois Department of Transportation, "Motorcycle Accident Facts 1978"; Iowa Department of Transportation, "Iowa Motorcycle Accidents, 1974–1976"; Virginia Highway and Transportation Research Council, "Final Report, Repeal and Modification of Mandatory Motorcycle Helmet Legislation," January 1978; Harry E. Balmer Jr., "Analysis of the Mandatory Motorcycle Helmet Issue, August 1977 (Pennsylvania)"; and Arkansas, Legislative Council, "Informational Memo, No. 34," May 10, 1966.

32. "Helmet Law," *Spartanburg (S.C.) Herald-Journal*, September 20, 1970, B8.

33. "Most Cycle Helmets Unsafe," *Beaver County (Pa.) Times*, October 14, 1972, A2; see also Ada Carr, "In a Nutshell," *Biker News*, no. 6, 1974.

34. *Reading (Pa.) Eagle*, November 30, 1967, 50.

35. "Cyclists Need Not Wear Helmets," *Gettysburg Times*, July 3, 1969, 19.

36. "Motorcyclists Rally to Protest Helmet Ruling," *Toledo Blade*, July 12, 1970, 55.

37. "Cyclists Go to Capitol for Helmet Protest," *Dallas Morning News*, 16 August 1968, 18.

38. "The Public Speaks," *Evening Independent*, December 28, 1967, 10A; see also Ed Armstrong, "One Temporarily Down," *Biker*, December 10, 1975, 16.

39. Bob Gustin, "SB Man Fights Nebraska Helmet Law," *Biker*, December 10, 1975, 16; see also Earl Golz, "Judge Estes Rules against Helmet Suit," *Dallas Morning News*, September 22, 1970, 1.

40. "Libertarians OK Bashing One's Head," *Lodi (Calif.) News-Sentinel*, April, 3, 1972, 8.

41. "Case: Motorcyclists vs. U.S. D.O.T. and N.H. T. & S. A.," *Biker*, no. 19, 1975, 10.

42. "Government by the People," under Biker Views, *Biker News*, no. 6, 1974.

43 "Motorcycle Helmets CAUSE Accidents Not Prevent Them," *Biker News*, no. 13, 1975, 6; Bob Gustin, "SB Man Fights Nebraska Helmet Law," *Biker*, December 10, 1975, 16; on the helmet's deficiencies, see also Bulletin Board, *Biker*, January 10, 1979, 2; and "Legalities," *Biker*, no. 6, 1974.

44. "Legalities," *Biker*, November 12, 1975, 22.

45. Ada Carr, "In a Nutshell," *Biker News*, no. 6, 1974.

46. Will Bernard, "Law Protects Man from Self," *Sarasota (Fla.) Journal*, April 24, 1970, 9A.

47. For this quote, see "Why Motorcycle Deaths Are Soaring," *U.S. News & World Report*, September 4, 1978, 36.

48. "Make Motorcyclists Wear Helmets?," *U.S. News and World Report*, July 18, 1977, 39–40. Some contemporaries added up what the costs were in a typical state. Dr. R. Adams Cowley, director of the Maryland Institute for Emergency Medical Services, for example, gave the case of Maryland in 1977 to support the case for helmets. According to Cowley, sixty-five badly injured cyclists were admitted to Maryland hospitals in 1977. Of those, twenty-six were not able to or did not pay their medical bills, which cost the state or tax-payers $256,592.96.

49. Kelly Wendeln, "The Motorcycle Helmet Law Success Story," *Biker*, April 21, 1976, 20.

50. "Outside Opinions," *Biker*, vol. 2, no. 2, 1975, 16–17.

51. Ibid.

52. Letters to the Editor, *Biker*, March 8, 1978, 19.

53. Coffee Break with the Editor, *Motorcyclist*, December 1972, 2.

54. "Helmet Law Draws Protest," *Dallas Times Herald*, August 30, 1989, A24. On helmet laws and the availability of organs, see "Cycle Helmet Use Is Gearing Down," *Dallas Morning News*, June 18, 1977, 4.

55. "Outside Opinions," *Biker*, vol. 2, no. 2, 1975, 16–17.

56. Letters to the Editor, *Biker*, June 28, 1978, 19.

57. This figure is comparable to the number of fatalities today; see Jones and Saravanan, "Who, What, When and Where."

58. Coffee Break with the Editor, *Motorcyclist*, July 1972, 2. Bob Bitchin (aka Bob Lipkin) also complained about tickets for no helmet but no seatbelt requirement for automobilists; see "Just Puttin," *Biker News*, July 15, 1974.

59. Rogue, "How to Protest," *Biker News*, no. 14, 1975, 3.

60. "Connecticut Bikers—All of Us Get the Shaft," *Easyriders*, April 1972, 43–44.

61. "A Federal Case," Coffee Break with the Editor, *Motorcyclist*, December 1972, 2.

62. "Will the Feds Kill Freedom?," *Motorcyclist*, May 1973, 73.

63. Bob Bitchin, "Just Puttin," *Biker News*, July 15, 1974.

64. Ibid.

65. Bob Bitchin, "Just Puttin," *Biker News*, August 1, 1974.

66. Ibid., July 15, 1974; see also Bitchin's editorial in ibid., August 1, 1974.

67. "Make Motorcyclists Wear Helmets?," *U.S. News and World Report*, July 18, 1977, 39.

68. *San Francisco Chronicle*, August 17, 1967, "motorcycle" file, Tamony Collection.

69. "HARLY" Walker, Duquesne, Pa., *Cycle*, January 1968, 14.

70. Letters to the Editor, *Biker*, June 28, 1978, 19.

71. Ibid., August 9, 1978, 27.

72. "Vital Info for All Motorcycle Owners!," *Easyriders*, June 1972, 24–26, 52, 53–58, 60–61; motorcyclists still blame "yuppie riders" for the helmet issue. In a 2007 issue of *Playboy*, a reader objected to the previous month's article about the rise in motorcycle fatalities in Florida after the helmet law was repealed by noting that the real danger is "yuppies who buy powerful bikes but never take a safety course" (*Playboy*, February 2007, 12).

73. "Here, at Last, Is a Sound Program for Fighting Anti-bike Legislation," *Easyriders*, June 1972, 36–37.

74. "Will the Feds Kill Freedom?," *Motorcyclist*, May 1973, 73.

75. Bob Bitchin, "Just Puttin," *Biker News*, August 1, 1974.

76. Ibid.

77. "Get in the Wind," *Biker News*, no. 4, 1974.

78. Thompson, *Hell's Angels*, 58.

79. Ibid., 61.

80. *Cycle*, May 1973, 110; see also *Cycle World*, August 1976, 29, in which another motorcyclist also reminisced about "turning back the clock."

81. "Less Noise, He Says," *American Motorcycling*, July 1948, 7.

82. *American Motorcycling*, January 1948, 5; see also "Rochester Finds a Heart in Her Motorcycle Riders," *American Motorcycling*, March 1948, 12.

83. Letters, *Motorcyclist*, January 1948, 3. A letter from Mr. and Mrs. Lloyd Carlock from Kansas City, Missouri, that appeared in the December 1948 issue of *American Motorcycling* (p. 5) also suggests a "stage of the lifecycle" understanding of these issues.

84. Letters, *Cycle*, July 1972, 10.

85. "'Decent' Family Sport," *San Francisco Chronicle*, July 16, 1974, "motorcycle" file, Tamony Collection.

86. "Motorcycling—California Style," *Motorcyclist*, September 1949, 20, 26; see also Youngblood, "Birth of the Dirt Bike."

87. See also Laco Bob Lawrence, "In the Wind," *Biker News*, August 1, 1974.

88. Kelly Wendeln, "The Motorcycle Helmet Law Success Story," *Biker*, April 21, 1976. 20.

89. For more on the issue of a slogan, see "Robert Friedrich, "Let's Come up with a New Helmet Repeal Slogan," *Biker*, November 29, 1978, 17.

90. Bailey and Farber, *America in the Seventies*.

91. For a picture of the tattooed lip, see *Easyriders*, December 1975, 15, and *Easyriders*, September 1978, 61.

Chapter 5

1. On the Bob Dara posters, see http://nostalgiaonwheels.blogspot.com/2010/07/bob-dara-posters.html (accessed August 4, 2014); see also the Yankee Poster Collection at the Library of Congress. There is one other poster by Dara of Spiro T. Agnew on a motorcycle. It can be also be found at the Library of Congress. The poster is nearly identical to the poster of LBJ on a bike and is dated 1965. Dara created a poster of Agnew overpowering the statue of liberty in 1969 after he claimed in a speech that the press was practicing liberal censorship. The year 1965 seems early for larger political critiques of Agnew, who became governor of Maryland in 1966 and became the vice president in 1969.

2. "Motorcyclists Form Political Committee for Reelection of President," *American Motorcyclist*, October 1972, 39.

3. Ed Youngblood, "Overcoming the Silence," *AMA News*, December 1972, 44.

4. "Turning the Tide," *American Motorcyclist*, November 1980, 14; "Looking toward November," *American Motorcyclist*, November 1980, 12.

5. At the time of the article's publication Magnuson was running unopposed.

6. "Turning the Tide," *American Motorcyclist*, November 1980, 14.

7. "Don't Shoot the Easy Rider," *National Review*, October 31, 1980, 1309; "Turning the Tide," *American Motorcyclist*, November 1980, 14; "Looking toward November," *American Motorcyclist*, November 1980, 12.

8. For a discussion of the Right in the postwar years, see McGirr, *Suburban Warriors*; see also Cunningham, *Cowboy Conservatism*.

9. Kelly Wendeln, "The Motorcycle Helmet Law Success Story," *Biker*, April 21, 1976, 20; *Congressional Quarterly Weekly Report*, vol. 33, no. 51, December 20, 1975 (Washington D.C.: Congressional Quarterly Inc., 1975), 2786, 2826.

10. "ABATE Members in 44 States Have Started Working toward Our Freedom of the Road," *Easyriders*, February 1972, 26–27.

11. *Easyriders*, October 1971, 16–17; "ABATE Members in 44 States Have Started Working toward Our Freedom of the Road," *Easyriders*, February 1972, 26–27.

12. "Warren Bennett Interview," *Biker*, June 15, 1977, 8.

13. Coffee Break with the Editor, *Motorcyclist*, April 1972, 10; see also "Political Frontier Series Opens with Detroit Workshop," *AMA News*, March 1972, 22–23.

14. Ibid.

15. "Will the Feds Kill Freedom?," *Motorcyclist*, May 1973, 73; *Biker* also applauded the AMA. See "Senate Action Marks 'Victory for Motorcyclists,'" *Biker*, January 28, 1976, 17.

16. "The Washington State Penitentiary Motorcycle Association," *Biker*, June 29, 1977, 4.

17. Biker Views, *Biker*, February 23, 1977, 13.

18. *Easyriders*, August 1971, 23.

19. "New York Bikers Hold 'Helmet Law' Protest," *Biker News*, no. 7, 1974, 4.

20. "ABATE Members in 44 States Have Started Working toward Our Freedom," *Easyriders*, February 1972, 26.

21. Laco Bob Lawrence, "Get in the Wind," *Biker News*, no. 19, 1975, 6.

22. Gino Sheridan, "Freedom to Choose," *Biker*, June 30, 1976, 3.

23. Gordon Martin, "Daylight Motorcycle Lights Wouldn't Reduce Accidents," *Biker News*, no. 24, 1975, 3.

24. Letters to the Editor, *Biker*, under "Freedom's defenders," November 2, 1977, 8.

25. *Easyriders*, March 1979, 69 (all pages in this issue are 69).

26. Ibid.

27. For more on the issue of a slogan see Robert Friedrich, "Let's Come up with a New Helmet Repeal Slogan," *Biker*, November 29, 1978, 17.

28. Charles Clayton, "Image—the New 'One Percent,'" *Biker*, March 24, 1976, 2; see also "Outlaws," under "Just Puttin'," *Biker News*, no. 14, 1975, 2.

29. "California's First Helmet Law Protest," *Biker News*, no. 16, 1975, 10.

30. Post Entry, *AMA News*, June 1977, 6.

31. McGirr, *Suburban Warriors*, 145–52; see also Kruse, *White Flight*; Lassiter, *Silent Majority*; and Dochuk, *From Bible Belt to Sunbelt*. For a discussion about paleo-conservatives and neo-conservatives, see Newman and Giardina, *Sport, Spectacle, and NASCAR Nation*, 47–66. For a general overview of the literature on the Right, see Phillips-Fein, "Conservatism."

32. McGirr, *Suburban Warriors*, 149–76.

33. Ibid.

34. Carter, *Politics of Rage*, 218; see also Perlstein, *Before the Storm*.

35. Carter, *Politics of Rage*, 106, 160–61, 226, 345–47, 382–83, 424, 460–61.

36. Lipsitz, *Rainbow After Midnight*, 245, 255–262; see also Lipsitz, *American Studies*, 244–248; Brown, *Race, Money, and the American Welfare State*, 135–40.

37. Robert Montemayor, "State Legislature May Reconsider Motorcycle Helmet Law," *Dallas Times Herald*, August 26, 1978, 1.

38. "Senate Action Marks 'Victory for Motorcyclists,'" *Biker*, January 26, 1976, 17.

39. Ibid.

40. "Legislators May Resume Motorcycle Helmet Law Debate in Next Session," *Dallas Times Herald*, August 26, 1978, 1, 4.

41. "California Tells DOT Where to Get Off!," *Biker News*, no. 14, 1975, 7.

42. "New York Bikers Hold 'Helmet Law' Protest," *Biker News*, no. 7, 1974, 4.

43. "Presidential Candidate Blasts Helmet Laws, 55 mph Limit Speed," *Easyriders*, June 1976, 22.

44. *American Motorcyclist*, October 1980, 15.

45. Ibid., December 1984, 10.

46. Ada Carr, "In a Nutshell," *Biker*, April 21, 1976, 2.

47. *Easyriders*, February 1972, 26.

48. *Biker*, December 10, 1975, 16.

49. *Easyriders*, February 1978, 6. Motorcyclists also discussed Orwell's 1984; see "Just Puttin," *Biker News*, no. 18, 1975, 4. On Brandeis, see Ed Armstrong, "One Temporarily Down," *Biker*, December 10, 1975, 16.

50. On the founders, see "Land of the Free," *Biker*, vol. 2, no. 2, 1975, 2; ABATE of New York, "New York Helmet Law Protest," *Biker*, December 10, 1975, 3; "From the Inside," under Biker Views, *Biker News*, no. 6, 1974; for an example of the "founders" as outlaws, see *American Motorcyclist*, January 1989, 13.

51. Charles Clayton, "Congress to Buchanan: 'Alright Lowey, Drop the Gun,'" *Biker* January 28, 1976, 3.

52. Post Entry, *American Motorcyclist*, April 1977, 6.

53. "A Conversation with Thomas Jefferson," *American Motorcyclist*, March 1980, 40, 45.

54. ABATE of New York, "New York Helmet Protest," *Biker*, December 10, 1975, 3.

55. Yates, *Outlaw Machine*, 13–14.

56. See, for example, *American Motorcycling*, September 1961, 36; June 1982, 40; October 1966, 10; and January 1964, 24.

57. Rogue, "Memorial Day: A Day Set Aside to Honor the Dead of Any American War," *Biker*, June 30, 1976, 5.

58. Paul Hodge, "400 Motorcyclists Protest Helmet Law," *Washington Post*, September 2, 1975, C3.

59. "PEACE: Restoring the Margin of Safety," speech given at Veterans of Foreign Wars Convention, Chicago, Illinois, August 18, 1980, http://www.reagan.utexas.edu/archives/reference/8.18.80.html (accessed December 13, 2013).

60. *Easyriders*, April 1981, 39; November 1980, 54; April 1982, 79; October 1981, 51; September 1981, 42.

61. Ibid., October 1980, 19.

62. Letters, *Cycle World*, August 1983, 13.

63. For the Run for the Wall website, see http://www.rftw.org/index.asp?lg=1&w=pages&r=0&pid=1 (accessed December 7, 2013).

64. The Patriot Guard website is http://www.patriotguard.org/content.php?1-the-front-page (accessed December 7, 2013). See also Dorothy Masters, "This 'N' That," *Wabaunsee*

County Signal-Enterprise, December 8, 2005, 10; *Congressional Record*, 2006, 11877–81, http://books.google.com/books?id=wWZaPbgTsu4C&pg=PA282&dq=%22patriot+guard%22&hl=en&sa=X&ei=t4t3UsDfMazNsQSVzYDABQ&ved=0CDgQ6w-EwAQ#v=onepage&q=%22patriot%20guard%22&f=false (accessed December 8, 2005); "Straight Allies: Biking to Block Phelps," *The Advocate*, March 28, 2006, 22.

65. On the issue of race and the question of backlash, see Sugrue, *Origins of the Urban Crisis*; Self, *American Babylon*; and Durr, *Behind the Backlash*. For examples of backlash, see Edsall, *Chain Reaction*, and Rieder, *Canarsie*.

66. Kruse, *White Flight*, 8–9; see also Turner, " 'Specter of Environmentalism,' " 139–41.

67. "Where It's At," Letters to the Editor, *Biker*, January 11, 1978, 24.

68. David S. Mangeim, "New York Anti-Motorcycle Law," *Biker*, September 20, 1978, 16.

69. "Regardless of What You Have Read or Heard, Here's the Truth about Riverside," *Motorcyclist*, July 1948, 15.

70. Laco Bob Lawrence, "Get in the Wind," *Biker News*, no. 19, 1975, 6.

71. Lifestyle, *Biker*, January 10, 1979, 16.

72. Sandbrook, *Mad as Hell*.

73. "Cycle Helmet Passage Stirs Outburst," *Telegraph-Herald*, April 2, 1975, 16.

74. "Motorcyclists Cheer Helmet Bill Defeat," *The Bulletin*, June 27, 1972, 8.

75. *Easyriders*, October 1976, 11.

76. "State Panel Protects Repeal of Helmet Law," *Dallas Morning News*, March 10, 1977, 11.

77. "Now Can We Take Our Helmets Off?," *Baltimore Sun*, July 23, 1976, A14.

78. Ibid.

79. North Carolina's first protest would be on April 25, 1976; see "Protests Around the Nation," *Biker*, June 2, 1976, 5. Motorcyclists in South Carolina participated in a national helmet law protest in June of 1975, but only five bikers showed up at the capitol. See "Helmet Law Protests Stun Nation," *Biker*, vol. 2, no. 1, 1975, 6.

80. "Legalities," *Biker*, vol. 2, no. 5, 1975, 4–5.

81. "Cranston Joins Reagan in War on Helmet Law," *Modesto Bee*, December 9, 1975, A3.

82. Marianne Means, "Cycle Helmet on Way Out!," *Kentucky New Era*, May 26, 1976, 3.

83. James Kilpatrick, "The Cycle Helmet Stupidity," *Evening Independent*, July 1, 1976, 18A.

84. " 'Protect Me from Me Ways of Washington," *Lodi News-Sentinel*, December 19, 1975, 4; see also "Cranston Joins Reagan in War on Helmet Law," *Modesto Bee*, December 9, 1975, A3.

85. Kelly Wendeln, "Lid Law Battle: How the West Was Won," *Biker*, December 14, 1977, 23.

86. Robert W. Stewart, "Survival Is at Stake, U.S. Motorcycle Firm Warns," *Los Angeles Times*, May 1, 1983, G1.

87. Bob Olmstead, "Macho Machine," *San Francisco Examiner*, August 19, 1977, 25.

88. Ibid. For a general overview of the problems facing Harley-Davidson, see Reid, *Well Made in America*.

89. Devin's Beatniks, "Harley Police Bike 'Best in Years,' but Will Cops Buy It?," *San Francisco Examiner*, September 30, 1983, A1, A20.

90. Ibid.

91. Frank, *Buy American*, 132–34, 160–62, 225–26.

92. Ibid., 162–63.

93. See "Harley-Davidson: A Revival as Macho Motorcycles Take Off," *Business Week*, August 21, 1978, 108.

94. George Skelton, "Tariffs Imposed on Motorcycles Made Abroad," *Los Angeles Times*, April 2, 1983, D16; Penny Pagano, "Reagan Urged to Hike Tariff on Japanese Cycles," *Los Angeles Times*, January 26, 1983, E1.

95. *Lewiston (Me.) Daily Sun*, May 5, 1987, 11.

96. Robert L. Rose, "Vrooming Back: After Nearly Stalling, Harley-Davidson Finds New Crowd of Riders," *Wall Street Journal*, August 31, 1990, A1; Motorcycle Industry Council's *Motorcycle Statistical Annual* for 1990 (p. 17) and 1999 (p. 4).

97. On Japanese management styles, see Reid, *Well Made in America*, 63–64.

98. David Klein, Cato Institute Policy Analysis No. 32, "Taking America for a Ride: The Politics of Motorcycle Tariffs," January 12, 1984, http://www.cato.org/pubs/pas/pa032.pdf (accessed August 4, 2014).

99. "Helping the Hogs," *Time*, April 11, 1983, 74. For a brief discussion of Reagan's opposition to helmets while governor of California, see "California Tells DOT Where to Get Off," *Biker News*, no. 14, 1975, 7.

100. "Helping the Hogs," *Time*, April 11, 1983, 74; Letters, *Motorcyclist*, October 1985, 5.

101. "Visit to Harley-Davidson Plant—York PA (5)," box 318, Speechwriting Research Office, Ronald Reagan Library, Simi Valley, Calif.

102. Self, *All in the Family*, 6.

103. Zaretsky, *No Direction Home*. On foreign policy, see McCormick, *America's Half Century*, 216–36; see also Lekachman, *Visions and Nightmares*, and Phillips, *Politics of Rich and Poor*.

104. See Jacobs and Zelizer, *Conservatives in Power*; Courtwright, *No Right Turn*; Reeves, *President Reagan*; Wilentz, *Age of Reagan*; and Schneider, *Conservative Century*.

105. Roderick Oram, "Riding Free Again; Harley-Davidson," *Financial Times*, April 2. 1987, 24, in "Visit to Harley-Davidson Plant—York PA (5)," box 318, Speechwriting Research Office, Ronald Reagan Library, Simi Valley, Calif.

106. David Klein, Cato Institute Policy Analysis No. 32, "Taking America for a Ride: The Politics of Motorcycle Tariffs," January 12, 1984, http://www.cato.org/pubs/pas/pa032.pdf (accessed August 4, 2014).

107. "Radio Address to the Nation on Free and Fair Trade and the Budget Deficit," May 16, 1987, The American Presidency Project, http://www.presidency.ucsb.edu/ws/?pid=34290 (accessed October 3, 2014).

108. Steven Roberts, "At Harley Plant, Reagan Defends Trade Policy," *New York Times*, May 7, 1987, D8.

109. Cowie, "From Hard Hats to the Nascar Dads," 10, 13, 15–16; see also Cowie, *Stayin' Alive*.

110. Jeffords, *Remasculinization of America*, xii.

111. See "Visit to Harley-Davidson Plant—York PA (5)," box 318, Speechwriting Research Office, Ronald Reagan Library, Simi Valley, Calif.

112. On the collapse of America's manufacturing base, see Cowie, *Capital Moves*; see also Cowie and Heathcott, *Beyond the Ruins*.

113. Steven V. Roberts, "Hart Taps a Generation of Young Professionals," *New York Times*, March 18, 1984, 26; see also Hans Fantel, "Yuppies at Home—A Hi-Fi Habitat," *New York Times*, June 10, 1984, H23.

114. "The Year of the Yuppies," *New York Times*, March 25, 1984, E20.

115. Steven V. Roberts, "Hart Taps a Generation of Young Professionals," *New York Times*, March 18, 1984, 26.

116. Deborah J. Knuth, "A.K.A. Republicans," *New York Times*, July 15, 1984, 185.

117. Kathleen A. Hughes, "In Beverly Hills, the Wild Ones Aren't Hell's Angels," *Wall Street Journal*, October 7, 1988, A1. Famous celebrity RUBs include Malcolm Forbes (*Playboy*, April 1979, 75); Jay Leno (*Playboy*, December 1990, 57); and Mickey Rourke (*Playboy*, February 1987, 43). For a more detailed discussion of Forbes, see "Malcolm Forbes," *American Motorcyclist*, March 1980, 59–61, 72.

118. "Recall Brando? The Wild One? Bet They Do, Too," *New York Times*, November 17, 1990.

119. Ibid.

120. Robert L. Rose, "Vrooming Back: After Nearly Stalling, Harley-Davidson Finds New Crowd of Riders," *Wall Street Journal*, August 31, 1990, A1.

121. See, for example, "We Lead with Our Chin," *Motorcyclist*, June 1947, 15. After critiquing nameplate loyalty, the editor emphasized that he was not "anti-business." "Business," he wrote, "performs a valuable and essential function, namely: That of developing, manufacturing, marketing, and servicing. The profit angle is strictly essential and legitimate unless held at exorbitant levels by monopolized controls and restraint of free trade." See also Bob Bitchin, "Just Puttin," *Biker*, February 11, 1976, 2.

122. Michigan reached its peak for motorcycle registrations in 1980 with 254,129 registered motorcycles. By 1990 Michigan's number of registered motorcycles had dropped to 134,319. Florida's total number of registered bikes surpassed Michigan in 1983 (Florida had 224,965; Michigan had 219,929). Texas's total number of registered motorcycles surpassed Michigan in 1979 (the same year the state's numbers surpassed Ohio). In 1979 Texas had 291,510 registered motorcycles; Michigan had 251,290; and Ohio had 267,100. For these figures see the Motorcycle Industry Council's *Motorcycle Statistical Annual* for 1979 (p. 8), for 1988 (p. 10), and for 1991 (p. 10).

123. "Hear the Rider's Horse Approaching," Biker Views, *Biker*, March 23, 1977, 16.

124. Ibid.

Chapter 6

1. Daryl E. Lembke, "Hells Angels Attack Peace March at UC," *Los Angeles Times*, October 17, 1965, 1; "700 Stage Peaceful Viet Protest March in S.F.," *Los Angeles Times*, October 18, 1965, 3. For other conflicting accounts see the transcripts of the Vietnam Day Committee's suit against the City of Oakland: *Hurwitt v. City of Oakland*, D.C.Cal. 1965, 247 F.Supp. 995.

2. Wood, "Hells Angels." Jefferson Cowie (*Stayin' Alive*, 189–90) briefly discusses the motorcyclists in *Easy Rider*; see also Veno and Gannon, *Brotherhoods*, 5; Charters, *Portable Sixties Reader*, 220–21; Thompson, *Hell's Angels*, 245–55; and Roszak, *Making of a Counter Culture*.

3. For general overviews of the period, see Braunstein and Doyle, *Imagine Nation*, and Kurlansky, *1968*. On the politics of the Left and Right, see Klatch, *Generation Divided*. On the counterrevolutionary response to the counterculture, see Sides, *Erotic City*.

4. On women's liberation in the 1960s and 1970s, see Echols, *Daring to Be Bad*; Cobble, *Other Women's Movement*; Rosen, *World Split Open*; and Chafe, *Paradox of Change*.

5. For examples of the scholarship on citizenship, see Marshall, "Citizenship and Social Class." For an example of scholarship that considers the legal and cultural dimensions, see Gordon, *Pitied but Not Entitled*; Lee, *At America's Gates*; Ngai, *Impossible Subjects*; and Canaday, *Straight State*. See also Shah, *Contagious Divides*, and Manalansan, *Global Divas*.

6. See Kimmel, *Manhood in America*, 252–53; see also Wills, *John Wayne's America*.

7. Kieffner, "Legend Unknown," 30–32.

8. Tom Wolfe, "Sissy Bars Will Be Lower This Year," *Esquire*, February 1971, 60.

9. Wills (*John Wayne's America*, 13) describes John Wayne as the cowboy who was "usually on the sheriff's side."

10. Chauncey, *Gay New York*, 358.

11. See the Satyrs website for information about their history, www.satyrsmc.org. See also Meeker, *Contacts Desired*, 158; Hennen, *Faeries, Bears, and Leathermen*, 102, 135, 137, 139; and Rubin, "Valley of the Kings." For examples of these images, see Waugh, *Out/Lines*, 154, 168, 169, 170, 171, 259, 265. Some of these images are explicitly cited as "bikers." Others are not, but the dress and style suggests leather men/bikers. See also Bob Mizer, *Physique Pictorial*. On gay motorcycle clubs in the south, see Sears, *Rebels*.

12. Meeker, *Contacts Desired*, 151–59.

13. "Motorcycle" file, Peter Tamony Collection, Western Historical Manuscript Collection, University of Missouri–Columbia (hereafter Tamony Collection).

14. "Freedom of Information and Privacy Acts, Subject: Hells Angels, Part 2 of 2," "The Hells Angels Part 4 of 6," vault.fbi.gov/The%20Hells%20Angels/The%20Hells%20Angels%20Part%204%20of%206/view (accessed April 2, 2014).

15. *Hells Angels on Wheels*, directed by Richard Rush (Fanfare Films, 1967).

16. "Motorcyclists Kiss as Ritual," *Evening Independent*," November 28, 1967, 2-A.

17. "The Motorcycle Syndrome," *Time*, December 1970, 65.

18. Ibid.

19. *Scorpio Rising*, directed by Kenneth Anger (Puck Film Productions, 1964).

20. Thompson, *Hell's Angels*, 87.

21. Hal Burton, "Most Unpopular Men on the Road," *Saturday Evening Post*, September 25, 1954, 130.

22. Thompson, *Hell's Angels*, 93–93.

23. On bodies see, Kasson, *Houdini, Tarzan, and the Perfect Man*, 21–76; and Ronald Boyd, "Bodybuilding Muscle Its Way to Respectability," *St. Petersburg (Fla.) Times*, July 23, 1980, 1D.

24. On the development of gay liberation, see White, *Pre-Gay L.A.*; Carter, *Stonewall*; and Duberman, *Stonewall*.

25. Echols, *Daring to Be Bad*, 132.

26. *Terminator 2: Judgment Day*, directed by James Cameron (Carolco Pictures, 1991).

27. Bordo, *Male Body*, 111.

28. Douglas Robinson, "Thousands on Fifth Ave. March in Vietnam Protest," *New York Times*, March 27, 1966, 1.

29. "Hell's Angels Will Picket Viet Marchers," *Los Angeles Times*, November 4, 1965, A9.

30. "DISSENT: Collegiate War against Napalm," *Los Angeles Times*, November 26, 1967, P5.

31. Coffee Break with the Editor, *Motorcyclist*, January 1970, 4, 14.

32. David E. Davis Jr., "Flat-Top Haircuts and Gunfighters' Eyes," *Cycle*, December 1967, 52–53.

33. Letters, *Cycle*, February 1969, 13.

34. Ehrenreich, *Hearts of Men*, 53.

35. *Easyriders*, August 1971, 55, 60.

36. For the song's lyrics, see http://www.metrolyrics.com/okie-from-muskogee-lyrics-merle-haggard.html (accessed December 12, 2013).

37. *Easyriders*, October 1971, 54.

38. "Wordmonger's Word-Hoard," *Easyriders*, December 1971, 6.

39. Sylvan Fox, "Crime and Violence Are Commonplace in Nether World of Lower East Side," *New York Times*, March 20, 1969, 40. See also John Kifner, "Hippies Fading from City Scene," *New York Times*, August 26, 1968, 41; James T. Wooten, "Motorcycle Gangs Terrorizing Once-Calm Atlanta Hippie Area," *New York Times*, January 3, 1971; and "A Decaying District's Terror," *San Francisco Chronicle*, February 12, 1971, "motorcycle" file, Tamony Collection.

40. "Buckpassing," Letters to the Editor, *San Francisco Chronicle*, September 26, 1969, "motorcycle" file, Tamony Collection.

41. Ibid.

42. Wanda Hummel, "Stupid Bikers Disrupt Indiana Helmet Law Protest," *Biker*, July 28, 1976, 9.

43. Charles Clayton, "Congress to Buchanan: 'Alright Lowey, Drop the Gun,'" *Biker*, January 28, 1976, 3.

44. *Easyriders*, October 1976, 43.

45. Ibid., 3.

46. For a general biography of Nixon that includes his views on several 1970s issues, see Perlstein, *Nixonland*.

47. Kevin Kearney, "The Vote: A Powerful Political Tool," *American Motorcyclist*, October 1979, 32.

48. Ibid.

49. C. J. Doughty Jr., "Havoc in Hollister," *San Francisco Chronicle*, July 6, 1947, 1, 11; "Motorcyclists Put Town in an Uproar," *New York Times*, July 7, 1947.

50. See "Visiting Cyclists Hurt in Accidents," *Hollister Free Lance*, July 5, 1947, 1.

51. Kieffner, "Legend Unknown," 156.

52. "Vindication in Hollister: Successful Gypsy Tour Earns Cyclists Welcome," *Cycle*, August 1951, 16–17, 31, 35. See also "Motorcyclists Put Town in an Uproar," *New York Times*, July 7, 1947; Michael Taylor, "Scary Memories of a Bikers' Holiday," *San Francisco Chronicle*, July 4, 1979, "motorcycle" file, Tamony Collection; John Dorrance, "Forty Hours in Hollister," *Cycle*, August 1987, 50–54, 87.

53. "Mama's Day Off," *American Motorcycling*, January 1953, 26–27.

54. "The Most Popular and Typical Girl Rider!," *American Motorcycling*, May 1949, 11.

55. On Dot Robinson, see "Bike-ographies," *American Motorcycling*, May 1950, 17.

56. See May, *Homeward Bound*.

57. "Bike-ographies," *American Motorcycling*, May 1950, 17; "The Most Popular and Typical Girl Rider!," *American Motorcycling*, May 1949, 32.

58. "An All-American Girl," *American Motorcycling*, January 1947, 27.

59. For an excellent overview of the different images of motorcycling during the post-war years, see Alford and Ferriss, *Motorcycle*, 117–60.

60. See Rosemarie Santini, "Touch Me, Feel Me, Spank Me," *Playboy*, January 1977, 178.

61. Kieffner, "Legend Unknown," 156.

62. See, for example, Bob Bitchin, "Just Puttin'," *Biker*, April 21, 1976, 2.

63. See *Easyriders*, February 1977, front cover.

64. "The Pleasures of Drinking Out of a Wine Skin," *Easyriders*, October 1971, 44–47.

65. See *Easyriders*, February 1973, 48. The picture is of a topless woman with her hair covering up part of her breasts, and below is the caption "Meet Our Cover Girl," which provides the standard details of a pin-up: measurements, weight, aspirations, etc.

66. "In the Wind," *Easyriders*, December 1973, 34.

67. "Southern Sausage Suckers," *Easyriders*, June 1980, 32–35; "Here's Mud In Your Eye," *Easyriders*, January 1982, 18–23.

68. See "The Term 'Chick' Is an Insult to Liberated Women," *Easyriders*, June 1973, 55–56, and "Readers React to 'Chick' Article," *Easyriders*, October 1973, 18. "I know a lot of heavy biker males, and I know they usually think the People's Revolution is so much shit, but the Revolution is happening now, brothers, and it would be really great if everyone could help (the People's Revolution includes bikers ya know) and maybe all people could be considered people and there'd be no more niggers, chicks, fags, spicks, etc."

69. "Joan's Pocket," *Easyriders*, December 1977, 74–77.

70. "Eyestrain in the Garage," *Easyriders*, March 1980, 32–37.

71. *Cycle*, July 1969, 12.

72. Ibid.

73. Mail, *Cycle*, March 1968, 25.

74. *Biker*, December 14, 1977, 28.

75. *Biker*, January 11, 1978, 25.

76. All of these are in *Biker*, December 14, 1977, 22.

77. *Biker*, January 11, 1978, 25; *Biker*, December 14, 1977, 28.

78. Wells Twombly, "A Man without Redeeming Values," "Even Knievel" file, Tamony Collection.

79. John Nordheimer, "Knievel to Leap Today: He and Promoter Tense," *New York Times*, September 8, 1974, 48. See also Tom Irish, "Daredevil 'Evil' Knievel: IS HE THE WORLD'S MOST FEARLESS MAN?," *For Men Only* 15, no. 7 (July 1968): 78; Wells Twombly, "Knievel's Projected Leap the Last Great Youth Orgy," *San Francisco Examiner*, September 5, 1974, "motorcycle" file, Tamony Collection; and Wells Twombly, "Knievel: A Man without Redeeming Values," "motorcycle" file, Tamony Collection; and "Evel: High Noon for a Gunfighter," *Los Angeles Times*, February 9, 1973, 10.

80. Mandich, *Evel Incarnate*, 60–61; "Evel Knievel—A Modern-Day Houdini," *San Francisco Examiner*, August 20, 1974, "motorcycle" file, Tamony Collection.

81. "To Garden Fans, the Show Is a 'Rip-Off,'" *New York Times*, September 9, 1974; Barbara H. Settles and Dene G. Klinzing, "Young Children's Perceptions of a Public Figure: Evel Knievel," *Young Children*, March 1975, 184–88.

82. "Evel Knievel—A Modern Day Houdini," *San Francisco Examiner*, August 20, 1974, "motorcycle" file, Tamony Collection.

83. Morrison, "Official Story," xvi–xvii.

84. "Viva la Woofie," *Biker*, March 8, 1978, 32.

85. Ibid.

86. "Wordmonger," *Easyriders*, January 1979, 10; the editor responded to Blaine with: "Buy a woman's mag—get outta our hair."

87. "Wordmonger," *Easyriders*, February 1979, 10.

88. *Easyriders*, May 1976, 10.

89. *Cycle*, September 1967, 16.

90. "On the Line," *Motorcyclist*, March 1975, 6.

91. *Cycle*, February 1971, 16.

92. Ibid., 15.

93. "Starts Women's Cycle Club," *Youngstown (Ohio) Vindicator*, July 11, 1975, 25.

94. "Thousands of Women Stage Rights Protests," *Los Angeles Times*, August 26, 1972, A20; Louise Cook, "Statistics Show Mixed Success," *Tuscaloosa News*, August 27, 1972, 9A.

95. "Women's Lib in Biker?," Letters to the Editor, *Biker*, March 8, 1978, 19.

96. Ibid.

97. Grace Butcher, "So Much Depends Upon a Red Tent," *Sports Illustrated*, February 1975, 63–68.

98. *Cycle*, June 1972, 18.

99. Ibid.

100. Daryl E. Lembke, "Hells Angels Attack Peace March at UC," *Los Angeles Times*, October 17, 1965, 1.

Chapter 7

1. *Sweet Sweetback's Baadasssss Song*, directed by Melvin Van Peebles (1971). For more information on the response to *Sweetback* among African American and white audiences, see Bogle's synthesis of African Americans in film, *Tom, Coons, Mulattoes, Mammies, and Bucks*.

2. See, for example, Huey P. Newton, "He Won't Bleed Me: A Revolutionary Analysis of *Sweet Sweetback's Baadasssss Song*," *The Black Panther*, June 19 1971; Don L. Lee, "The Bittersweet of Sweetback/or, Shake Yo Money Maker," *Black World/Negro Digest*, November 1971, 47.

3. *Gimme Shelter*, directed by Albert Maysles and David Maysles (Maysles Films, 1970).

4. For a discussion of books that define Altamont as the end of an era, see Eisen, *Altamont*. For an example of a challenge to this view, see Delhomme-Cutchin, "Altamont Festival Revisited." See also Steigerwald, *Sixties and the End of Modern America*.

5. *Sweet Sweetback's Baadasssss Song*, directed by Melvin Van Peebles (1971); Formisano, *Boston against Busing*; Edsall, *Chain Reaction*; Carter, *Politics of Rage*.

6. For a general analysis of "law and order" during the 1960s, see Flamm, *Law and Order*.

7. General surveys of the civil rights movement can be found in Williams, *Eyes on the Prize*, and Weisbrot, *Freedom Bound*.

8. Trotter, *Great Migration in Historical Perspective*, 1.

9. See also Painter, *Exodusters*. For more information on the Great Migration and urban life for African Americans after World War II, see Grossman, *Land of Hope*; Trotter, *Great Migration in Historical Perspective*; and Baldwin, *Chicago's New Negroes*. For the most significant work on the creation and consequences of ghettoization, see Hirsch, *Making the Second Ghetto*.

10. Gregory, *Southern Diaspora*, 139.

11. Abel, *Signs of the Times*, 5, 130.

12. McCammack, "'My God, They Must Have Riots on Those Things All the Time,'" 973–74, 980–82.

13. Howard, *Men Like That*, 104; Griffin, *Black Like Me*.

14. Art Peters, "High-Flying Soldier of Fortune," *Ebony*, June 1964, 42, 44.

15. Adrienne P. Samuels, "Black Bikers: The Rides and the History," *Ebony*, October 2007, 98–104.

16. *Cycle*, September 1951, 13.

17. "Wanted," *American Motorcycling*, June 1959, 37.

18. *American Motorcycling*, June 1996, 31; "The Motorcycle Queen of Miami: Bessie Stringfield," *American Motorcyclist*, March 2003, 36–39.

19. Ed Youngblood, "Moving Beyond Prejudice," *American Motorcyclist*, March 1995, 15.

20. Notes from Kwame Alford interview by author, June 2, 2006.

21. Ed Youngblood, "Moving Beyond Prejudice," *American Motorcyclist*, March 1995, 15.

22. Ed Youngblood email to author, July 24, 2013.

23. Post Entry, *American Motorcyclist*, May 1995, 4–5.

24. Ibid., 4.

25. On whiteness, see Roediger, *Wages of Whiteness*.

26. Letters, *Motorcyclist*, September 1950, 3.

27. Mezzrow and Wolfe, *Really the Blues*, 216. See also "honky" file, Peter Tamony Collection, Western Historical Manuscript Collection, University of Missouri–Columbia (hereafter Tamony Collection). Tamony explains that in this context, honky is self-defined as a white factory worker.

28. See chapter 1.

29. See "honky," file, Tamony Collection, esp. "Rights Leaders Fear Another Summer of Violence in Big Cities," *San Francisco Sunday Examiner*, April 23, 1967, 10.

30. Roediger, *Working toward Whiteness* 45–50; see also "honky" file, Tamony Collection.

31. "Honky" file, Tamony Collection.

32. The Triumph ad can be found in *Motorcyclist*, August 1947, inside back cover.

33. Frank, *Buy American*, 74–75, 139.

34. See, for example, Linderman, *World within War*, and Dower, *War without Mercy*.

35. See, for example, Koerner, *Strange Death of the British Motorcycle Industry*.

36. See *Ebony*, May 1962, 17; December 1962, 11; October 1960, 16; June 1962, 6; November 1962, 14; November 1961, 92, and October 1961, 63. The number of ads is based on a search of Google Books, which has digitized copies of *Ebony* from November 1959 to December 2008 and copies of *Jet* from November 1951 to October 2008.

37. For an example of one of these ads for Harley-Davidson, see *American Motorcycling*, March, 1957, 20–21.

38. *Ebony*, October, 1960, 16; October 1961, 63.

39. *Ebony*, December 1978, 109.

40. *Jet*, July 10, 1980, 61.

41. Farren, *Black Leather Jacket*, 22–27.

42. Ibid.

43. Letters, *Cycle*, August 1950, 34.

44. *Cycle*, September 1950, 34. See also Editor's Viewpoint, *Cycle*, June 1950, 4.

45. Barger, *Hell's Angel*, 38–39.

46. "Rebels on Wheels," *Ebony*, December 1966, 64–66, 68, 70–71.

47. "Wordmonger," *Easyriders*, March 1979, 70–71.

48. "Wordmonger," *Easyriders*, April 1978, 10.

49. David S. Mangeim, "Wearing the Swastika: A Viewpoint," *Easyriders*, September 1978, 14–15, 86.

50. Tex Campbell, "The Swastika: Its Origin and History," *Easyriders*, February 1979, 15, 81–84.

51. For pictures of women in front of swastikas, see "In the Wind," *Easyriders*, September 1978, 94; for pictures of confederate flags see ibid., July 1980, 42; for swastika belt buckle, see ibid., August 1972; for Nazi and white power patches, see ibid., December 1979.

52. "An Interview with David Duke: The Grand Wizard of the Knights of the Ku Klux Klan," *Easyriders*, July 1980, 25, 78, 81–87, 89–90.

53. Ibid.

54. "What the AMA Means to You," *American Motorcycling*, January 1950, 12.

55. "Gotcha!," *Easyriders*, December 1982, 25–27. See also Zonker, *Murdercycles*, 83–88.

56. "City's First Motorcycle Squad Had 11 Officers," *Los Angeles Times*, May 15, 1950, A2.

57. "1st Motorcyclist of City Police Dies," *New York Times*, May 22, 1953, 27. In *Murdercycles* (86–87) Patricia Zonker notes that Charles Murphy of Flushing, New York, was the first motorcycle officer in the United States.

58. Wendell P. Bradley and Elihu Ben Klein, "Radar Outmodes Police Motorcycles," *Washington Post and Times Herald*, February 21, 1955, 20.

59. Editor's Viewpoint, *Cycle*, June 1950, 4.

60. "AMA Clubs Meet the Law More Than Halfway!," *American Motorcycling*, December 1947, 9.

61. "Muffler Campaign Helps Amarillo MC Hike Membership, Increase Prestige," *American Motorcycling*, February 1950, 17.

62. Letters, *Motorcyclist*, July 1948, 3.

63. See "'Rider Police' Movement Grows," *American Motorcycling*, September 1948, 7. See also "District 37 Leads the Way!," *American Motorcycling*, August 1948, 3.

64. "'Rider Police' Movement Grows," *American Motorcycling*, September 1948, 7.

65. Adrienne P. Samuels, "Black Bikers: The Rides and the History," *Ebony*, October 2007, 103.

66. Roediger, *Working toward Whiteness*, 40–43.

67. Ibid.

68. Himes, *If He Hollers Let Him Go*, 10.

69. Alfred E. Lewis, "Accident Squad Police to Ride White Cruisers," *Washington Post, Times Herald*, May 12, 1960, C28.

70. "Motorcycle Police Bow to Speed Peril," *New York Times*, June 20, 1965, 49.

71. Wendell P. Bradley and Elihu Ben Klein, "Radar Outmodes Police Motorcycles," *Washington Post and Times Herald*, February 21, 1955, 20.

72. Ibid.

73. On migration, see Grossman, *Land of Hope*; Trotter, *Great Migration in Historical Perspective*; and Baldwin, *Chicago's New Negroes*.

74. For more general information on the Montgomery Bus Boycott, including some references to the use of motorcycle cops, see Burns, *Daybreak of Freedom*, and Garrow, *Walking City*.

75. Lerone Bennett Jr., "The Day the Black Revolution Began," *Ebony*, September 1977, 54–56, 58, 60, 62, 64.

76. Garrow, *Walking City*, 6, 210–11.

77. Lerone Bennett Jr. "The Day the Black Revolution Began," *Ebony*, September 1977, 54–56, 58, 60, 62, 64.

78. Howard, *Men Like That*, 104.

79. See "honky" file, Tamony Papers.

80. Simeon Booker, "Shocking Police Action Spurs Negro Students to Strike Back," *Jet*, April 9, 1964.

81. For general information on the African American Freedom Struggle in Birmingham, Alabama, see McWhorter, *Carry Me Home;* and Garrow, *Birmingham*.

82. Sterling G. Slappey, "Birmingham Marches Taking Different Tone," *Los Angeles Times*, January 9, 1966, 23.

83. *Jet*, October 24, 1968, 8.

84. John C. Waugh, "Negro Patrol Offers Police-Ghetto Go-between in Watts," *Christian Science Monitor*, July 28, 1967, 7.

85. Thomas Pynchon, "A Journey into the Mind of Watts," *New York Times,* June 12, 1966, 80.

86. Cinoglu, "Analysis of Major American Riots," 18–19.

87. Louie Robinson, "'. . . IF THEY HADN'T KICKED THAT MAN': Police Action Ignited Fiery L.A. Riot," *Jet*, October 1965, 114–24.

88. "Ride Baby Ride," *Jet*, September 1, 1966.

89. Peter Bart, "New Riot in Watts Kills 2, Injures 25; 200 Police Quiet Negro Teen-Agers," *New York Times*, March 16, 1966, 1.

90. "Joblessness Top Cause in Riots," *San Francisco Chronicle*, September 24, 1967, "Watts" file, Tamony Collection.

91. Ibid. See also Jack Welter, "Reagan's 'Watts Plan' for Minorities Jobs," *San Francisco Examiner*, December 27, 1966, "Watts" file, Tamony Collection.

92. Horne, *Fire This Time: The Watts Uprising and the 1960s*, 64–65.

93. Ibid. See also Jack Welter, "Reagan's 'Watts Plan' for Minorities Jobs," "Watts" file, Tamony Collection, for a discussion of the emphasis on private efforts to deal with joblessness. Then lieutenant governor–elect Robert Finch explained, "What we have in mind is not creating jobs at all, but recognizing that a great many jobs are going unfilled and matching available skills to available jobs."

94. There are several recent books on the significance of Black Power and the various Black Panther Party organizations. One of the most important early works on Black Power is Van Deburg, *New Day in Babylon*. For the most recent works on Black Power, see Jeffries, *Black Power in the Belly of the Beast*, and Joseph, *Neighborhood Rebels*. For a local view of the Black Panther Party, see Murch, *Living for the City*.

95. For general information on Huey P. Newton including some of his experiences with motorcycles and motorcycle cops see biographical and autobiographical works, Hilliard and Zimmerman, *Huey: Spirit of the Panther* and Newton, *Revolutionary Suicide*.

96. Newton, *Huey P. Newton Reader*, 62.

97. Bingham, *Black Panthers 1968*, 27.

98. *Ebony*, July 1978, 140, 142.

99. Alex Poinsett, "The Dilemma of the Black Policeman," *Ebony*, May 1971, 123–24.

100. Ibid.

101. *Jet*, April 20, 1967, 55.

102. Kirk Scharfenberg and Alfred E. Lewis, "NE Residents Claim 'Pagans' Terrorize Neighborhood," *Washington Post*, July 21, 1973, D1.

103. John Saar, "Violence Feared in Woodridge," *Washington Post*, July 23, 1973, C1.

104. "Negroes, Motorcyclists Clash," *Chicago Tribune*, September 2, 1969, A4.

105. "Cop, Woman Slain in Camden Disorders," *Chicago Tribune*, September 3, 1969, 6.

106. Dick Ciccone, "Rioting Whites Protest Negro Marches in Chicago," *Lewiston (Me.) Evening Journal*, August 15, 1966, 1, 6.

107. Frederick Graves, "How Cities Can Avoid Another Long Hot Summer," *Jet*, May 18, 1967, 14–18.

108. Ali, *Greatest*, 63–77.

109. Ibid.

110. Remnick, *King of the World*, 89–91.

111. "It's Good to be Home Again," *Ebony*, August 1971, 66–71.

112. Alex Poinsett, "Watchdog for U.S. Labor," *Ebony*, April 1971, 102–3.

113. "How to Handle a Racist," *Ebony*, November 1984, 51.

114. Kieffner, "Riding the Borderlands," 94–97.

115. "Cycles in Social Revolution," *Sunday San Francisco Examiner and Chronicle*, June 19, 1966, 1P.

116. Carl A. Gottlieb, "The Upward Mobility of the Motorcycle," *Esquire*, November 1965, 138.

117. "Question Man," "Your Favorite Little Luxury?," *San Francisco Chronicle*, November 4, 1977, "motorcycle" file, Tamony Collection.

118. *Easyriders*, October 1971, 8; February 1972, 8.

119. "The Social Function of Hell's Angels," *San Francisco Chronicle*, December 31, 1971, "motorcycle" file, Tamony Collection.

120. Thompson, *Hell's Angels*, 37.

121. Ibid., 236–37.

122. Ibid., 36.

123. For a recent biography of Goldwater, see Perlstein, *Before the Storm*.

124. Flamm, *Law and Order*, 8–9.

125. "Hells Angels Rumor Bugs Ghetto," *Berkeley Barb*, November 19, 1965, back page.

126. John Darnton, "Charge of Racism Tarnishes Waterbury's Yankee Image," *New York Times*, March 24, 1969, 47.

127. For examples of the scholarship on citizenship, see Marshall, "Citizenship and Social Class"; Gordon, *Pitied but Not Entitled*; Lee, *At America's Gates*; Ngai, *Impossible Subjects*; Canaday, *Straight State*; Shah, *Contagious Divides*; and Manalansan, *Global Divas*.

128. On Jack Johnson, see Ward, *Unforgiveable Blackness*; see also Edwards, *Revolt of the Black Athlete*, and Bass, *Not the Triumph but the Struggle*.

129. For a general reader on Ali, see Gorn, *Muhammad Ali*.

130. "Ken Norton: Best Bet to Succeed Ali," *Jet*, December 15, 1977, 55; Joe Frazier, "Cassius WHO?," *Ebony*, May 1972, 72.

131. Echols, *Hot Stuff*, 26–27.

132. Tyler, "Rise and Decline of the Watts Summer Festival," 71.

133. "What's Happening to Marriage and Career of Isaac Hayes?" *Jet*, June 26, 1975, 54–58.

134. Levingston, *Soul on Bikes*, 123.

135. Bordo, *Male Body*, 133.

136. Ponshitta Pierce, "A Look Into the Private Life of Billy Dee Williams," *Ebony*, April 1974, 56.

137. Bordo, *Male Body*, 133.

138. Brando, *Brando*, 300–301.

139. Levingston, *Soul on Bikes*, 125–26.

140. Ibid.

141. On Duffie, see Buchanan, *Corpse Had a Familiar Face*, 217–41.

142. "Miamian's Luck Ended in Death Laid to Officers," *New York Times*, January 1, 1980, 6.

143. "4 Policemen Suspended in Death," *New York Times*, December 28, 1979, A14.

144. "Ex-Policeman Describes Beating of Florida Black," *New York Times*, April 23, 1980, A16; "Policemen Beat Black to Death after He Shouted, 'I Give Up,'" *Los Angeles Times*, A8; "Dade Officers Charged with Man's Beating Death," *Palm Beach Post*, December 29, 1979, A2.

145. *Palm Beach Post*, December 29, 1979, A2; "4 Policemen Suspended in Death," *New York Times*, A14.

146. Mike Clary, "Police Officer Convicted of Killing 2 Miami Blacks," *Los Angeles Times*, December 8, 1989, A1, A32.

147. "Miami Officer Defends Shot that Sparked Riot," *Chicago Tribune*, December 1, 1989, A3; Jeffrey Schmalz, "Officer Arrested in Miami Death That Began Riot," *New York Times*, January 24, 1989, A1.

148. Michel Marriott, "Miami Officer Disputed on Shot That Led to Riot," *New York Times*, January 22, 1989, 18.

149. Ibid.

150. "Miami: Roots of Rage," *Ebony*, September 1980, 137, 140–45; "Police Deadly Force: A National Menace," *Ebony*, March 1981, 46–52; see also Jeffrey Schmalz, "More Than 200 Arrested in Miami in 2d Night of Racial Disturbances," *New York Times*, January 18, 1989, A1, A10.

151. "Miamian's Luck Ended in Death Laid to Officers," *New York Times*, January 1, 1980, 6.

152. Jeffrey Schmalz, "Miami Officer Tells Jurors Motorcyclist Aimed for Him," *New York Times*, December 1, 1989, A28.

153. Barger and Holmstrom, *Let's Ride*, 88.

154. Ninja advertisement, www.ebay.com/itm/1984-KAWASAKI-NINJA-900-ORIGINAL-2-PAGE-AD-/370919317975?pt=LH_DefaultDomain_0&hash=item565c83a1d7 (accessed December 8, 2013); *Cycle World*, January–December, 2009, 74; Cova, Kozinets, and Shanker, *Consumer Tribes*, 68–69.

155. Cova, Kozinets, and Shanker, *Consumer Tribes*, 68–69.

156. For this ad, see www.coloribus.com/adsarchive/prints/kawasaki-ninja-zx-12r-classroom-2054055/ (accessed December 8, 2013).

157. *American Motorcyclist*, December 2001, 30.

158. Suttles, *Atlantic Beach*, 54.

159. Post Entry, *American Motorcyclist*, June 1995, 6.

160. *American Motorcyclist*, December 2001, 30.

161. Lewis, *In Their Own Interests*, 90–92.

162. Post Entry, *American Motorcyclist*, May 1995, 4.

163. Ibid.

164. Rogue, "Memorial Day: A Day Set Aside to Honor the Dead of an American War," *Biker*, June 30, 1976, 5.

165. Lane Campbell, "Bike Power—Where Is It Now?" *Biker*, vol. 2, no. 6, 1975, 21; see also David Mangeim, "New York Anti-Motorcycle Law," *Biker*, September 20, 1978, 16.

166. Bob Greene, "I'll Save You Poor Devil!," *Motorcyclist*, July 1972, 2.

167. Ed Youngblood, "A Journey into Prejudice," *American Motorcyclist*, November 1994, 8.

168. Coffee Break with the Editor, *Motorcyclist*, July 1972, 2.

169. Kelly Wendeln, "Do We Have a Democracy or a Constitutional Republic?," *Biker*, October 4, 1978, 22.

170. Ibid.

171. Robert O. Self makes a similar argument in *All in the Family*, 399.

172. Bill Dobbins, "Bikers and the Media," *Biker News*, no. 7, 1974, 10.

173. "Don't Shoot the Easy Rider," *National Review*, October 31, 1980, 1309; "Turning the Tide," *American Motorcyclist*, November, 1980. 14; "Looking toward November," *American Motorcyclist*, November 1980, 12.

174. Douglas and Michaels, *Mommy Myth*, 184–85.

175. Ibid.

176. "'Welfare Queen' Becomes Issue in Reagan Campaign," *New York Times*, February 15, 1976, 51.

177. Rowland Evans and Robert Novak, "What Sacking Sears Won't Fix," *Washington Post*, February 29, 1980, A13. See also Jay Mathews, "Reagan's Words on Welfare Rolls Raise Hackles," *Washington Post*, September 26, 1981, A10; Eleanor Clift, "Reagan Condemns Welfare System, Says It's Made Poverty Worse Instead of Better," *Los Angeles Times*, February 16, 1986, 27; Robert Pear, "Reagan Seeks Change in Welfare System," *New York Times*, December 13, 1986, 12; Spencer Rich, "'Safety Net' Strands Thinner under Reagan," *Washington Post*, November 27, 1988, 1.

178. "Not Enough: Harley Compliment Won't Sway Vote," *Milwaukee Journal*, July 22, 1988, 4A.

179. Ibid.

180. Maureen Dowd, "Adrift in Bush's Circle Seeking the Common Man," *New York Times*, December 1, 1991, 28. See also the transcript for the documentary *Boogie Man: The Lee Atwater Story*, http://www.pbs.org/wgbh/pages/frontline/atwater/etc/script .html (accessed July 13, 2014). On the motorcyclists at Luray, Virginia, see "Proceedings" 1988–1989," Institute of Politics, John F. Kennedy School of Government, Harvard University, www.iop.harvard.edu/sites/default/files_new/Proceedings/1988-1989.pdf (accessed July 13, 2014).

181. See Kruse, *White Flight*, 10.

182. Rawick, *From Sundown to Sunup*, 132.

Epilogue

1. "Clinton Cites Harley in Pushing His Trade Policy," *New York Times*, November 11, 1999, www.nytimes.com/1999/11/11/business/international-business-clinton-cites-harley-davidson-in-pushing-his-trade-policy.html (accessed December 8, 2014).

2. Garance Burke, "Cheney Tours Kansas, Missouri," *Topeka Capital-Journal*, January 7, 2006, cjonline.com/stories/010706/kan_cheney.shtml (accessed January 29, 2013).

3. "Miss Buffalo Chip, 2014," www.buffalochip.com/EVENTS (accessed June 13, 2014).

4. For a glimpse of McCain's speech at Sturgis, see http://www.youtube.com/watch?v=sK-LEyyf7d4 (accessed January 28, 2013).

5. Ibid. Photograph of woman in author's possession.

6. See "Land Rover Driver Caught on Video Mowing Down NYC Motorcyclist," http://www.autoblog.com/2013/09/30/land-rover-driver-caught-on-video-mowing-downnyc-motorcyclists/ (accessed June 15, 2014).

7. J. David Goodman, "After Motorcyclist Is Struck, Driver Is Pulled From S.U.V. and Beaten, the Police Say," *New York Times*, September 30, 2013, http://www.nytimes .com/2013/10/01/nyregion/motorcyclists-assault-suv-driver-after-chase-uptown-police-say.html (accessed June 15, 2014).

8. "Another Biker Arrested, Charged in Road-Rage Melee," CBS New York, October 19, 2013, http://newyork.cbslocal.com/2013/10/19/another-biker-arrested-charged-in-road-rage-melee/ (accessed June 15, 2014).

9. "Road Rage Case Breakdown: Who's Who in Manhattan Motorcycle Melee," October 23, 2013, CBS New York, http://newyork.cbslocal.com/2013/10/23/road-rage-case-break-down-whos-who-in-the-motorcycle-melee/ (accessed June 15, 2014).

10. Tina Susman, "New York Biker Bash and Attack on SUV Polarizing Event," *Los Angeles Times*, October 10, 2013, http://www.latimes.com/nation/la-na-biker-suv-attack-20131011-story.html (accessed June 15, 2014).

11. Lisa Riordan Seville and Hannah Rappleye, "Lines Blur Between Cops and Bikers Across the Country," NBC News, October 9, 2013, http://www.nbcnews.com/news/other/lines-blur-between-cops-bikers-across-country-f8C11364142 (accessed June 15, 2014).

12. "Biker Accused of Triggering Motorcycle Melee Speaks Out," CBS New York, October 7, 2013, http://newyork.cbslocal.com/2013/10/07/nypd-2-persons-of-interest-sought-in-manhattan-motorcycle-melee/ (accessed June 15, 2014).

13. "SUV Driver Seen for First Time Since Biker Melee," CBS New York, October 13, 2013, http://newyork.cbslocal.com/2013/10/13/suv-driver-see-for-first-time-since-biker-melee/ (accessed June 15, 2014).

14. "Do America's Changing Demographics Impact Politics?," NPR News, July 4, 2011, http://www.npr.org/2011/07/04/137609363/do-americas-changing-demographics-impact-politics (accessed January 28, 2013).

15. "Divided America Revealed as Women, Hispanics Back Obama," http://www.bloomberg.com/news/2012-11-07/divided-america-revealed-in-exit-polls-of-voters.html (accessed January 17, 2013).

16. "Do America's Changing Demographics Impact Politics?," NPR News, July 4, 2011, http://www.npr.org/2011/07/04/137609363/do-americas-changing-demographics-impact-politics (accessed January 28, 2013).

17. Ibid.

18. Adrienne P. Samuels, "Black Bikers: The Rides and the History," *Ebony*, October 2007, 99–105.

19. "Operation Bike Week Justice," www.naacp.org/legal/cases/docket/bikeweekcases/JeffreyGettleman (accessed February 9, 2013); "Suit Charges Bias at Rally for Black Bikers," *New York Times*, May 21, 2003, A22.

20. Paul Hughes, "Bikers Show up for Tea Party at the Capitol," *Republican-American*, September 12, 2009, 1A; Frances Chamberlain, "Tough Exteriors, Hearts of Gold," *New York Times*, December 3, 2000, http://www.nytimes.com/2000/12/03/nyregion/tough-exteriors-hearts-of-gold.html?pagewanted=all&src=pm (accessed January 26, 2013).

21. Ron Milam interview by author, January 23, 2013, audiotape in author's possession.

22. Insurance Institute for Highway Safety, http://www.iihs.org/laws/helmet_history.aspx (accessed February 9, 2013).

23. Brian Quinton, "Screw It, Let's Ride: Harley-Davidson Retools Its Marketing," *Chief Marketer*, June 1, 2009, http://www.chiefmarketer.com/database-marketing/demographics/screw-it-lets-ride-harley-davidson-retools-its-marketing-01062009 (accessed September 10, 2014).

24. Rick Barrett, "Harley Aims to Make Women Feel Welcome at Sturgis," *Milwaukee Journal Sentinel*, August 7, 2012; Genevieve Schmitt telephone interview by author, April 22, 2014, audiotape in author's possession.

25. Kitty Hall-Thurnheer and Leanne Italie, "Women and Motorcycles: Ridership Is on the Rise," *Elmira (N.Y.) Star Gazette*, www.stargazette.com/article/20120820/NEWS01/308200050/Women-motorcycles-Ridership-rise?odyssey=nav/head (accessed January 22, 2013).

26. For commercial about "No Cages," see http://www.youtube.com/watch?v=ubgJklZ6UAE (accessed January 28, 2013).

27. Latin American Motorcycle Association, http://www.lamausa.org/ (accessed October 6, 2014).

28. Ibid.

29. Amrit Raj, "Harley Sales Cruise; Will Momentum Last?," http://www.livemint.com/Home-Page/dDL68j4Jp9evQvG5HY3rnN/Harley-sales-cruise-will-momentum-last.html (accessed October 6, 2014). In 2011, Harley-Davidson sold 83,505 bikes overseas, about 36 percent of its total sales; "Revving Up in Asia's Emerging Market," *Wall Street Journal*, July 4, 2011, http://online.wsj.com/articles/SB10001424052702304450604576417172290719458 (accessed December 9, 2014).

30. "Harley-Davidson to Set up First Factory Outside US," http://www.aimag.com/2011/02/motorcycle-news-harley-factory-in-india/ (accessed December 9, 2014); "Harley-Davidson Reports 2009 Results," *Financial News*, http://investor.harley-davidson.com/phoenix.zhtml?c=87981&p=irol-newsArticle&ID=1573916 (accessed December 9, 2014); Shawn Langlois, "Harley Profit Drops 84%; Buell Shut Down," http://www.marketwatch.com/story/harley-posts-84-profit-drop-shuts-down-buell-2009-10-15 (accessed December 9, 2014); James B. Kelleher, "UPDATE 2-Harley-Davidson Profit Rise Fails to Rev Up Investory," Reuters, http://www.reuters.com/article/2014/01/30/harleydavidson-results-idUSL2N0L40LL20140130 (accessed December 9, 2014).

31. "Harley-Davidson to Set up First Factory Outside US," http://www.aimag.com/2011/02/motorcycle-news-harley-factory-in-india/ (accessed December 9, 2014).

32. Louis Uchitelle, "If You Can Make It Here . . . ," *New York Times*, September 4, 2005, http://nytimes.com/2005/09/04/business/04manu.html?pagewanted=all&_r=0 (accessed September 11, 2014).

33. Louis Uchitelle, "Unions Yield on Wage Scales to Preserve Jobs," *New York Times*, November 19, 2010, http://www.nytimes.com/2010/11/20/business/20wages.html?scp=14&sq=harley davidson and york&st=nyt&pagewanted=1 (accessed December 8, 2014).

Periodicals

The Advocate
AMA News
American City
American Motorcycling
American Motorcyclist
Baltimore Sun
Berkeley Barb
Biker News
The Black Panther
The Bulletin (Bend, Ore.)
Business Week
Catholic World
Chicago Tribune
Christian Science Monitor
Cycle
Cycle World
Dallas Morning News
Dallas Times Herald
Daytona Beach Morning Journal
The Dispatch
Easyriders
Ebony
Elmira (N.Y.) Star Gazette
Esquire
The Evening Independent
   (St. Petersburg, Fla.)
Hollister Free Lance
International Journal of Motorcycle Studies
Jet
Kentucky New Era
Lawrence (Kans.) Journal-World
Lewiston (Idaho) Morning Tribune
Lewiston (Me.) Daily Sun
Lewiston (Me.) Evening Journal
Life

Los Angeles Times
Miami News
Milwaukee Journal
Modesto Bee
The Morning Record
The Motorcyclist
Motor Trend
National Review
The News and Courier
New Statesmen and Nation
New York Times
Newsweek
Palm Beach Post
Parents Magazine
Playboy
Popular Science
Reader's Digest
St. Petersburg (Fla.) Times
San Francisco Chronicle
San Francisco Examiner
Sarasota (Fla.) Herald-Tribune
Saturday Evening Post
Spartanburg (S.C.) Herald-Journal
Spokane (Wash.) Daily Chronicle
Sports Illustrated
Telegraph-Herald (Dubuque, Iowa)
Time
Today's Health
Tuscaloosa News
U.S. News & World Report
Wall Street Journal
Washington Post
Wabaunsee County Signal-Enterprise
   (Alma, Kans.)
Youngstown (Ohio) Vindicator

Secondary Sources

Abel, Elizabeth. *Signs of the Times: The Visual Politics of Jim Crow*. Berkeley: University of California Press, 2010.

Alford, Steven E., and Suzanne Ferriss. *Motorcycle*. London: Reaction Books, 2008.

Ali, Muhammad, with Richard Durham. *The Greatest: My Own Story*. New York: Random House, 1975.

Anderson, Terry H. *The Movement and the Sixties: Protests in America from Greensboro to Wounded Knee*. New York: Oxford University Press, 1996.

Avila, Eric. *The Folklore of the Freeway: Race and Revolt in the Modernist City*. St. Paul: University of Minnesota Press, 2014.

———. *Popular Culture in the Age of White Flight: Fear and Fantasy in Suburban Los Angeles*. Berkeley: University of California Press, 2004.

Bailey, Beth, and David Farber, eds. *America in the Seventies*. Lawrence: University Press of Kansas, 2004.

Baldwin, Davarian. *Chicago's New Negroes: Modernity, the Great Migration, and Black Urban Life*. Chapel Hill: University of North Carolina Press, 2007.

Barger, Ralph, and Darwin Holmstrom. *Let's Ride: Sonny Barger's Guide to Motorcycling*. New York: William Morrow, 2010.

Barger, Ralph "Sonny," with Keith and Kent Zimmerman. *Hell's Angel: The Life and Times of Sonny Barger and the Hell's Angels Motorcycle Club*. Perennial: New York, 2000.

Bass, Amy. *Not the Triumph but the Struggle: 1968 Olympics and the Making of the Black Athlete*. Minneapolis: University of Minnesota Press, 2004.

Beier, L. *Masterless Men: The Vagrancy Problem in England, 1560–1640*. London: Methuen, 1985.

Bingham, Howard. *Black Panthers 1968*. New York: Ammo Books, Popular Edition, 2010.

Bishop, Ted. *Riding with Rilke: Reflections on Motorcycles and Books*. New York: W. W. Norton, 2007.

Bodnar, John. *Remaking America: Public Memory, Commemoration, and Patriotism in the Twentieth Century*. Princeton: Princeton University Press, 1993.

Bogle, Donald. *Tom, Coons, Mulattoes, Mammies, and Bucks: An Interpretative History of Blacks in American Films*. New York: Continuum, 2001.

Bonnifield, Paul Matthew. *The Dust Bowl: Men, Dirt, and Depression*. Albuquerque: University of New Mexico Press, 1979.

Bordo, Susan. *The Male Body: A New Look at Men in Public and in Private*. New York: Farrar, Straus and Giroux, 2000.

Borg, Kevin L. *Auto Mechanics: Technology and Expertise in Twentieth-Century America*. Baltimore: Johns Hopkins University Press, 2010.

Brando, Marlon, with Robert Lindsey. *Brando—Songs My Mother Taught Me*. New York: Random House, 1994.

Braunstein, Peter, and Michael William Doyle. *Imagine Nation: The American Counterculture of the 1960s and 1970s*. New York: Routledge, 2002.

Brown, Michael K. *Race, Money, and the American Welfare State*. Ithaca, N.Y.: Cornell University Press, 1999.

Buchanan, Edna. *The Corpse Had A Familiar Face: Covering Miami, America's Hottest Beat*. New York: Random House, 1987.

Burns, Stewart, ed. *Daybreak of Freedom: The Montgomery Bus Boycott*. Chapel Hill: University of North Carolina Press, 1997.

Canaday, Margot. *The Straight State: Sexuality and Citizenship in Twentieth-Century America*. Princeton: Princeton University Press, 2009.

Carter, Dan. *The Politics of Rage: George Wallace, the Origins of the New Conservatism, and the Transformation of American Politics*. 2d ed. Baton Rouge: Louisiana State University Press, 2000.

Carter, David. *Stonewall: The Riots That Sparked the Gay Revolution*. New York: St. Martin Griffin, 2010.

Chafe, William H. *The Paradox of Change: American Women in the Twentieth Century*. New York: Oxford University Press, 1991.

Charters, Ann. *The Portable Sixties Reader*. New York: Penguin Classics, 2002.

Chauncey, George. *Gay New York: Gender, Urban Culture, and the Making of the Gay Male World, 1890–1940*. New York: Basic Books, 1995.

Chudacoff, Howard P. *The Age of the Bachelor*. Princeton: Princeton University Press, 2000.

Cinoglu, Husey. "An Analysis of Major American Riots: Issues in Riots and Riot Control." Master's thesis, University of North Texas, 2001.

Cobble, Dorothy Sue. *The Other Women's Movement: Workplace Justice and Social Rights in Modern America*. Princeton: Princeton University Press, 2005.

Cohen, Lizabeth. *A Consumers' Republic: The Politics of Mass Consumption in Postwar America*. New York: Vintage Books, 2003.

Cosell, Howard. *Like It Is*. Chicago: Playboy Press, 1974.

Courtwright, David T. *No Right Turn: Conservative Politics in a Liberal America*. Cambridge, Mass.: Harvard University Press, 2010.

Cova, Bernard, Robert V. Kozinets, and Avi Shankar, eds. *Consumer Tribes*. New York: Routledge, 2007.

Cowie, Jefferson. *Capital Moves: RCA's 70-year Quest for Cheap Labor*. New York: New Press, 2001.

———. "From Hard Hats to the Nascar Dads." *New Labor Forum* 13, no. 3 (Fall 2004): 9–17.

———. *Stayin' Alive: The 1970s and the Last Days of the Working Class*. New York: New Press, 2010.

Cowie, Jefferson, and Joseph Heathcott, eds. *Beyond the Ruins: The Meanings of Deindustrialization*. Ithaca, N.Y.: ILR Press, 2003.

Crawford, Matthew B. *Shop Class As Soulcraft: An Inquiry Into the Value of Work*. New York: Penguin Press HC, 2009.

Cresswell, Tim. *On the Move: Mobility in the Modern Western World*. New York: Routledge, 2006.

———. "The Vagrant/Vagabond: The Curious Career of a Mobile Subject." In *Geographies of Mobilities: Practices, Spaces, Subjects*, edited by Tim Cresswell and Peter Merriman, 1–18. London: Ashgate, 2011.

Cunningham, Sean. *Cowboy Conservatism: Texas and the Rise of the Modern Right*. Lexington: University of Kentucky Press, 2011.

Davis, Anita Price. *North Carolina during the Great Depression: A Documentary Portrait of a Decade*. Jefferson, N.C.: McFarland, 2003.

Delhomme-Cutchin, Claudine. "The Altamont Festival Revisited: Myth, Reality, and the Uses of the Past." Ph.D. diss., Southern Illinois University Carbondale, 2002.

Dochuk, Darren. *From Bible Belt to Sunbelt: Plain-Folk Religion, Grassroots Politics, and the Rise of Evangelical Conservatism*. New York: W. W. Norton, 2010.

Douglas, Susan J., and Meredith W. Michaels. *The Mommy Myth: The Idealization of Motherhood and How It Has Undermined Women*. New York: Free Press, 2004.

Dower, John. *War without Mercy: Race and Power in the Pacific War*. New York: Pantheon, 1987.

Duberman, Martin. *Stonewall*. New York: Plume, 1993.

Durr, Kenneth D. *Behind the Backlash: White Working-Class Politics in Baltimore, 1940–1980*. Chapel Hill: University of North Carolina Press, 2003.

Echols, Alice. *Daring to Be Bad: Radical Feminism in America, 1967–1975*. Minneapolis: University of Minnesota Press, 1989.

———. *Hot Stuff: Disco and the Remaking of American Culture*. New York: W. W. Norton, 2010.

Edsall, Thomas Byrne, with Mary D. Edsall. *Chain Reaction: The Impact of Race, Rights, and Taxes on American Politics*. New York: W. W. Norton, 1991.

Edwards, Harry. *The Revolt of the Black Athlete*. New York: Free Press, 1970.

Egan, Timothy. *The Worst Hard Time: The Untold Story of Those Who Survived the Great American Dustbowl*. New York: Houghton Mifflin, 2006.

Ehrenreich, Barbara. *The Hearts of Men: American Dreams and the Flight from Commitment*. New York: Anchor Press, 1983.

Eisen, Jonathan, ed. *Altamont: Death of Innocence in the Woodstock Nation*. New York: Avon, 1970.

Farber, David. *Taken Hostage: The Iran Hostage Crisis and America's First Encounter with Radical Islam*. Princeton: Princeton University Press, 2006.

———, ed. *The Sixties: From Memory to History*. Chapel Hill: University of North Carolina Press, 1994.

Farren, Mick. *The Black Leather Jacket*. New York; Abbeville Press, 1985.

Ferrar, Ann. *Hear Me Roar: Women, Motorcycles, and the Rapture of the Road*. 2nd ed. Conway, N.H.: Whitehorse Press, 2001.

Fine, Gary Alan. *Difficult Reputations: Collective Memories of the Evil, Inept, and Controversial*. Chicago: University of Chicago Press, 2001.

Flamm, Michael W. *Law and Order: Street Crime, Civil Unrest, and the Crisis of Liberalism in the 1960s*. New York: Columbia University Press, 2005.

Flink, James J. *The Automobile Age*. Cambridge, Mass.: MIT Press, 1988.

Formisano, Ronald P. *Boston against Busing: Race, Class, and Ethnicity in the 1960s and 1970s*. Chapel Hill: University of North Carolina Press, 1991.

Frank, Dana. *Buy American: The Untold Story of Economic Nationalism*. New York: Beacon Press, 2000.

Fraterrigo, Elizabeth. *Playboy and the Making of the Good Life in Modern America*. Oxford: Oxford University Press, 2011.

Freeman, Joshua. "Hardhats: Construction Workers, Manliness, and the 1970 Pro-War Demonstrations." *Journal of Social History* 26 (4) (Summer 1993): 725–39.

French, Michael, and Jenny Homer. "Motorcycle Helmet Law in the United States from 1990 to 2005: Politics and Public Health." *American Journal of Public Health* 99 (3) (January 2009): 415–23.

Garrow, David J. *Birmingham, Alabama, 1956–1963: The Black Struggle for Civil Rights*. New York: Carlson, 1989.

———. *The Walking City: The Montgomery Bus Boycott, 1955–1965*. New York: Carlson, 1989.

Garson, Paul, and the editors of *Easyriders*. *Born to Be Wild: A History of the American Biker and Bikes, 1947–2002*. New York: Simon & Schuster, 2003.

Gilfoyle, Timothy. *City of Eros: New York City, Prostitution, and the Commercialization of Sex, 1790–1920*. New York: W. W. Norton, 1994.

Glickman, Lawrence B. *Buying Power: A History of Consumer Activism in America*. Chicago: University of Chicago Press, 2009.

Gordon, Linda. *Pitied but Not Entitled: Single Mothers and the History of Welfare, 1890–1935*. Cambridge, Mass.: Harvard University Press, 1994.

Gorn, Elliott J. *The Manly Art: Bare-Knuckle Prize Fighting in America*. Ithaca, N.Y.: Cornell University Press, 1986.

———, ed. *Muhammad Ali, the People's Champ*. Urbana: University of Illinois Press, 1995.

Gregory, James. *American Exodus: The Dust Bowl Migration and Okie Culture in California*. New York: Oxford University Press, 1989.

———. *Southern Diaspora*. Chapel Hill: University of North Carolina Press, 2007.

Griffin, John Howard. *Black Like Me*. Boston: Houghton Mifflin, 1961.

Grossman, James. *Land of Hope: Chicago, Black Southerners, and the Great Migration*. Chicago: University of Chicago Press, 1989.

Halbwachs, Maurice, and Lewis A. Coser. *On Collective Memory*. Chicago: University of Chicago Press, 1992.

Hall, John. *Riding on the Edge: A Motorcycle Outlaw's Tale*. Minneapolis: Motorbooks, 2008.

Harris, Eddie. *South of Haunted Dreams: A Memoir*. New York: Holt Paperbacks, 1997.

Heitmann, John A. *The Automobile and American Life*. Jefferson, N.C.: McFarlan, 2009.

Hennen, Peter. *Faeries, Bears, and Leathermen: Men in Community Queering the Masculine*. Chicago: University of Chicago Press, 2008.

Herndon, Ruth Wallis. *Unwelcome Americans: Living on the Margin in Early New England*. Philadelphia: Pennsylvania University Press, 2001.

Higbie, Frank Tobias. *Indispensable Outcasts: Hobo Workers and Community in the American Midwest, 1880–1930*. Urbana: University of Illinois Press, 2003.

Hilliard, David, and Kent Zimmerman. *Huey: Spirit of the Panther*. New York: Thunder's Mouth Press, 2006.

Himes, Chester. *If He Hollers Let Him Go*. New York: Thunder's Mouth Press, 1945.

Hirsch, Arnold. *Making the Second Ghetto: Race and Housing in Chicago, 1940–1960*. New York: Cambridge University Press, 1983.

Holmstrom, Darwin. *Harley-Davidson Century*. Minneapolis: Motorbooks, 2004.

Holsworth, Robert D. *Public Interest Liberalism and the Crisis of Affluence: Reflections on Nader, Environmentalism, and the Politics of a Sustainable Society*. Cambridge, Mass.: Hall, 1980.

Hook, Patrick. *Harley Davidson: The Complete History*. New York: Barnes & Noble, 2004.

Horne, Gerald. *Fire This Time: The Watts Uprising and the 1960s*. Charlottesville: University Press of Virginia, 1995.

Horowitz, Daniel. *Anxieties of Affluence: Critiques of American Consumer Culture, 1939–1979*. Amherst: University of Massachusetts Press, 2004.

Howard, John. *Men Like That: A Southern Queer History*. Chicago: University of Chicago Press, 2001.

Hunnicutt, Benjamin Kline. *Free Time: The Forgotten American Dream*. Philadelphia: Temple University Press, 2013.

Ingebretsen, Edward. *At Stake: Monsters an the Rhetoric of Fear in Public Culture*. Chicago: University of Chicago Press, 2001.

Jackson, Kenneth. *Crabgrass Frontier: The Suburbanization of the United States*. Oxford: Oxford University Press, 1987.

Jacobs, Meg, and Julian E. Zelizer. *Conservatives in Power: The Reagan Years: 1981–1989*. Boston: Bedford/St. Martins, 2010.

Jacobson, Matthew Frye. *Whiteness of a Different Color: European Immigrants and the Alchemy of Race*. Cambridge, Mass.: Harvard University Press, 1998.

Jeffords, Susan. *The Remasculinization of America: Gender and the Vietnam War*. Bloomington: Indiana University Press, 1989.

Jeffries, J. L. *Black Power in the Belly of the Beast*. Urbana: University of Illinois Press, 2006.

Joans, Barbara. *Bike Lust: Harleys, Women, and American Society*. Madison: University of Wisconsin Press, 2001.

Jones, Steven L., Jr., and Saravanan Gurupakian. "The Who, What, When and Where of Motorcycle Crashes in Alabama." *International Journal of Motorcycle Studies* 8, no. 1 (Spring 2012), ijms.nova.edu.

Joseph, Peniel. *Neighborhood Rebels: Black Power at the Local Level*. New York: Palgrave Macmillan, 2010.

Kasson, John F. *Houdini, Tarzan, and the Perfect Man: The White Male Body and the Challenge of Modernity in America*. New York: Hill and Wang, 2001.

Kelley, Robin D. G. *Race Rebels: Culture, Politics, and the Black Working Class*. New York: Free Press, 1996.

———. " 'We Are Not What We Seem': Rethinking Black Working-Class Opposition in the Jim Crow South." *Journal of American History* 80 (1) (June 1993): 75–112.

Kieffner, Gary L. "Legend Unknown: A Cultural, Gendered History of Motorcyclists in the American Southwest." M.A. Thesis, Northern Arizona University, 2003.

———."Riding the Borderlands: The Negotiation of Social and Cultural Boundaries for Rio Grande Valley and Southwestern Motorcycling Groups, 1900–2000." Ph.D. diss., University of Texas at El Paso, 2009.

Kimmel, Michael. *Manhood in America: A Cultural History*. New York: Free Press, 1996.

Klatch, Rebecca E. *A Generation Divided: The New Left, the New Right, and the 1960s.* Berkeley, Calif.: University of California Press, 1999.

Kline, Wendy. *Building a Better Race: Gender, Sexuality, and Eugenics from the Turn of the Century to the Baby Boom.* Berkeley: University of California Press, 2001.

Knudson, Margaret M., et al., "Motorcycle Helmet Laws: Every Surgeon's Responsibility." *Journal of the American College Surgeons* 199 (2) (2004): 261–64.

Koerner, Steve. *The Strange Death of the British Motor Cycle Industry.* Lancaster: Crucible Books, 2012.

Kruse, Kevin. *White Flight: Atlanta and the Making of Modern Conservatism.* Princeton: Princeton University Press, 2007.

Kruse, Kevin M., and Thomas J. Sugrue, eds. *The New Suburban History.* Chicago: University of Chicago Press, 2006.

Kurlansky, Mark. *1968: The Year that Rocked the World.* New York: Random House, 2005.

Lassiter, Matthew. *The Silent Majority: Suburban Politics in the Sunbelt South.* Princeton: Princeton University Press, 2007.

Lee, Erika. *At America's Gates: Chinese Immigration during the Exclusion Era, 1882–1943.* Chapel Hill: University of North Carolina Press, 2003.

Lekachman, Robert. *Visions and Nightmares: America after Reagan.* New York: Collier Books, 1987.

Levingston, Tobie, with Keith and Kent Zimmerman. *Soul on Bikes: The East Bay Dragons MC and the Black Biker Set.* Minneapolis: Motorbooks, 2004.

Lewis, Earl. *In Their Own Interests: Race, Class, and Power in Twentieth-Century Norfolk.* Berkeley: University of California Press, 1993.

Linderman, Gerald. *Embattled Courage: The Experience of Combat in the American Civil War.* New York: Free Press, 1989.

———. *The World within War: America's Combat Experience in World War II.* New York: Free Press, 1997.

Linenthal, Edward. *The Unfinished Bombing: Oklahoma City in American Memory.* New York: Oxford University Press, 2003.

Lipsitz, George. *American Studies in a Moment of Danger.* Minneapolis: University of Minnesota Press, 2001.

Manalansan, Martin. *Global Divas: Filipino Gay Men in the Diaspora.* Durham: Duke University Press, 2003.

Mandich, Steve. *Evel Incarnate: The Life and Legend of Evel Knievel.* London: Macmillan UK, 2000.

Marshall, T. H. "Citizenship and Social Class." In *The Citizenship Debates: A Reader*, edited by Gershon Shafir, 93–112. Minneapolis: University of Minnesota Press, 1998.

May, Elaine Tyler. *Homeward Bound: American Families in the Cold War Era.* New York: Basic Books, 1990.

May, Lary. *Recasting America: Culture and Politics in the Age of Cold War.* Chicago: University of Chicago Press, 1988.

McCammack, Brian. " 'My God, They Must Have Riots on Those Things All the Time': African American Geographies and Bodies on Northern Urban Public Transportation, 1915-1940." *Journal of Social History* 43 (4) (Summer 2010): 973–88.

McCormick, Thomas. *America's Half Century: United States Foreign Policy in the Cold War and After*. Baltimore: Johns Hopkins University Press, 1995.

McCurdy, John. *Citizen Bachelors: Manhood and the Creation of the United States*. Ithaca, N.Y.: Cornell University Press, 2009.

McGirr, Lisa. *Suburban Warriors: The Origins of the New American Right*. Princeton: Princeton University Press, 2002.

McGovern, Charles F. *Sold American: Consumption and Citizenship, 1890–1945*. Chapel Hill: University of North Carolina Press, 2006.

McWhorter, Diane. *Carry Me Home: Birmingham, Alabama, The Climactic Battle of the Civil Rights Revolution*. New York: Simon & Schuster, 2001.

Meeker, Martin. *Contacts Desired: Gay and Lesbian Communications and Community, 1940s– 1970s*. Chicago: University of Chicago Press, 2006.

Mezzrow, Milton "Mezz," and Bernard Wolfe. *Really the Blues*. Citadel Underground, 2001.

Mizer, Bob. *Physique Pictorial: The Complete Reprint, 1951–1964*. Taschen: Cologne, 1997.

Montville, Leigh. *Evel: The High-Flying Life of Evel Knievel: American Showman, Daredevil, and Legend*. New York: Anchor, 2012.

Moore, Jacqueline M. *Cow Boys and Cattle Men: Class and Masculinities on the Texas Frontier, 1865–1900*. New York: New York University Press, 2009.

Morrison, Toni. "The Official Story: Dead Man Golfing." In *Birth of a Nation'hood: Gaze, Script, and the Spectacle in the O. J. Simpson Case*, edited by Toni Morrison and Claudia Brodsky, vii–xxviii. New York: Lacour, 1997.

Murch, Donna Jean. *Living for the City: Migration, Education, and the Rise of the Black Panther Party in Oakland, California*. Chapel Hill: University of North Carolina Press, 2010.

Nader, Ralph. *Unsafe at Any Speed: The Designed-in Dangers of the American Automobile*. Massachusetts: Knightsbridge, 1991.

Newman, Joshua I., and Michael D. Giardina. *Sport, Spectacle, and NASCAR Nation: Consumption and the Cultural Politics of Neoliberalism*. New York: Palgrave Macmillan, 2011.

Newton, Huey P. *Huey P. Newton Reader*. New York: Severn Stories Press, 2002.

———. *Revolutionary Suicide*. New York: Harcourt Brace Jovanovich, 1973.

Ngai, Mae M. *Impossible Subjects: Illegal Aliens and the Making of Modern America*. Princeton: Princeton University Press, 2003.

Nicolaides, Becky M. *My Blue Heaven: Life and Politics in the Working-Class Suburbs of Los Angeles, 1920–1965*. Chicago: University of Chicago Press, 2002.

Nora, Pierre. "General Introduction: Between Memory and History." In *Conflicts and Divisions*. Vol. 1 of *Realms of Memory: The Construction of the French Past*, edited by Lawrence D. Kritzman, 1–20. New York: Columbia University Press, 1997.

Norton, Peter D. *Fighting Traffic: The Dawn of the Motor Age in the American City*. Cambridge: MIT Press, 2008.

Orsi, Robert. "The Religious Boundaries of an Inbetween People: Street Feste and the Problems of the Dark-Skinned 'Other' in Italian Harley, 1920–1990." *American Quarterly* 44 (September 1992): 313–47.

Osgerby, Bill. *Biker: Truth and Myth: How the Original Cowboy of the Road Became the Easy Rider of the Silver Screen*. Guilford: Lyons Press, 2005.

Packer, Jeremy. In *Mobility without Mayhem: Safety, Cars, and Citizenship*. Durham, N.C.: Duke University Press, 2008.

Painter, Nell Irvin. *Exodusters: Black Migration to Kansas After Reconstruction*. New York: W. W. Norton, 1992.

Palladino, Grace. *Teenagers: An American History*. New York: Basic Books, 1997.

Pierson, Melissa Holbrook. *The Perfect Vehicle: What It Is About Motorcycles*. New York: W. W. Norton, 1998.

Peiss, Kathy. *Zoot Suit: The Enigmatic Career of an Extreme Style*. Philadelphia: University of Pennsylvania Press, 2011.

Perlstein, Rick. *Before the Storm: Barry Goldwater and the Unmaking of the American Consensus*. New York: Hill and Wang, 2001. Reprint, New York: Nation Books, 2009.

———. *Nixonland: The Rise of a President and the Fracturing of America*. New York: Scribner, 2008.

Pertschuk, Michael. *Revolt against Regulation: The Rise and Pause of the Consumer Movement*. Berkeley: University of California Press, 1983.

Phillips, Kevin. *The Politics of Rich and Poor: Wealth and the American Electorate in the Reagan Aftermath*. New York: Random House, 1990.

Phillips, Lily. "Blue Jeans, Black Leather Jackets, and a Sneer: The Iconography of the 1950s Biker and Its Translation Abroad." March 2005, ijms.nova.edu.

Phillips-Fein, Kim. "Conservatism: A State of the Field." *Journal of American History* 98, no. 3 (December 2011): 723–43.

Pirsig, Robert M. *Zen and the Art of Motorcycle Maintenance*. New York: Perennial Classics, 1999.

Porter Benson, Susan. *Household Accounts: Working-Class Family Economies in the Interwar United States*. Ithaca: Cornell University Press, 2007.

Rajan, Sudhir Chella. "Automobility and the Liberal Disposition." In *Against Automobility*, edited by Steffen Böhm, Campbell Jones, Chris Land, and Matthew Paterson, 113–30. Malden, Mass.: Blackwell, 2006.

Rawick, George. *From Sundown to Sunup: The Making of the Black Community*. New York: Greenwood Press, 1973.

Reeves, Richard. *President Reagan: The Triumph of Imagination*. New York: Simon & Schuster, 2005.

Reid, Peter C. *Well Made in America*. New York: McGraw-Hill, 1990.

Remnick, David. *King of the World: Muhammad Ali and the Rise of an American Hero*. New York: Random House, 1998.

Rieder, Jonathan. *Canarsie: The Jews and Italians of Brooklyn against Liberalism*. Cambridge, Mass.: Harvard University Press, 1985.

Roediger, David. *The Wages of Whiteness: Race and the Making of the American Working Class*. New York: Verso, 1993.

———. *Working toward Whiteness: How America's Immigrants Became White: The Strange Journey from Ellis Island to the Suburbs*. New York: Basic Books, 2005.

Rogin, Michael. *Ronald Reagan, the Movie: And Other Episodes in Political Demonology*. Berkeley: University of California Press, 1987.

Rosen, Ruth. *The World Split Open: How the Modern Women's Movement Changed America*, Rev ed. New York: Penguin, 2006.

Rosenzweig, Roy. *Eight Hours for What We Will: Workers and Leisure in an Industrial City, 1870–1920*. Cambridge: Cambridge University Press, 1985.

Roszak, Theodore. *The Making of a Counter Culture: Reflections on the Technocratic Society and Its Youthful Opposition*. Garden City, N.Y.: Anchor Books, 1968.

Rothe, John Peter. *Driven to Kill*. Alberta: University of Alberta Press, 2008.

Rubin, Gayle. "The Valley of the Kings: Leathermen in San Francisco, 1960–1990." Ph.D. dissertation, University of Michigan, 1994.

St. Clair, Charlie, and Jennifer Anderson. *Images of America: Laconia Motorcycle Week*. Charleston, S.C.: Arcadia, 2008.

Sandbrook, Dominic. *Mad as Hell: The Crisis of the 1970s and the Rise of the Populist Right*. New York: Anchor, 2012.

Scharff, Virginia. *Taking the Wheel: Women and the Coming of the Motor Age*. Albuquerque: University of New Mexico Press, 1992.

Schlosser, Eric. *Fast Food Nation: The Dark Side of the All-American Meal*. New York: Houghton Mifflin, 2001.

Schneider, Gregory L. *The Conservative Century: From Reaction to Revolution*. Lanham, Md.: Rowman & Littlefield, 2009.

Schulz, Constance B. *Michigan Remembered: Photographs from the Farm Security Administration and the Office of War Information, 1936–1943*. Detroit: Wayne State University Press, 2001.

Sears, James. *Rebels, Ruby Fruit, and Rhinestones: Queering Space in the Stonewall South*. New Brunswick, N.J.: Rutgers University Press, 2002.

Seate, Mike. *Two Wheels on Two Reels: A History of Biker Movies*. Center Conway, N.H.: Whitehorse Press, 2001.

Self, Robert O. *All in the Family: The Realignment of American Democracy Since the 1960s*. New York: Hill and Wang, 2012.

———. *American Babylon: Race and the Struggle for Postwar Oakland*. Princeton, N.J.: Princeton University Press, 2003.

Shah, Nayan. *Contagious Divides: Epidemics and Race in San Francisco's Chinatown*. Los Angeles: University of California Press, 2001.

Shindo, Charles. *Dust Bowl Migrants in the American Imagination*. Lawrence: University Press of Kansas, 1997.

Sides, Josh. *Erotic City: Sexual Revolutions and the Making of Modern San Francisco*. New York: Oxford University Press, 2009.

Stansell, Christine. *City of Women: Sex and Class in New York, 1789–1860*. Urbana: University of Illinois Press, 1987.

Steigerwald, David. *The Sixties and the End of Modern America*. New York: St. Martin's Press, 1995.

Steinbeck, John. *The Grapes of Wrath*. New York: Penguin Classics, 2006.

Stern, Alexandra. *Eugenic Nation: Faults and Frontiers of Better Breeding in Modern America*. Berkeley: University of California Press, 2005.

Sugrue, Thomas J. *The Origins of the Urban Crisis: Race and Inequality in Postwar Detroit*. Princeton, N.J.: Princeton University Press, 1996.

Suttles, Sherry. *Atlantic Beach*. Charleston, S.C.: Arcadia, 2009.

Thompson, Hunter. *Hell's Angels: A Strange and Terrible Saga*. New York: Modern Library, 1999.

Trotter, Joe William, ed. *The Great Migration in Historical Perspective: New Dimensions of Race, Class, and Gender*. Bloomington: Indiana University Press, 1991.

Turner, James Morton " 'The Specter of Environmentalism': Wilderness, Environmental Politics, and the Evolution of the New Right." *Journal of American History* 96, no. 1 (June 2009): 123–49.

Tyler, Bruce M. "The Rise and Decline of the Watts Summer Festival, 1965–1986." *American Studies* 31, no. 2 (Fall 1990): 61–81.

Van Deburg, William. *New Day in Babylon: The Black Power Movement and American Culture, 1965–1975*. Chicago: University of Chicago Press, 1992.

Veno, Arthur, and Ed Gannon. *The Brotherhoods: Inside the Outlaw Motorcycle Clubs*. 3d ed. Chicago: Allen and Unwin, 2010.

Ward, Geoffrey C. *Unforgiveable Blackness: The Rise and Fall of Jack Johnson*. New York: Vintage, 2006.

Waugh, Thomas. *Out/Lines: Gay Underground Erotic Graphics from before Stonewall*. Vancouver: Arsenal Pulp Press, 2002.

Weisbrot, Robert. *Freedom Bound: A History of America's Civil Rights Movement*. New York: Norton, 1990.

White, Todd. *Pre-Gay L.A.: A Social History of the Movement for Homosexual Rights*. Urbana: University of Illinois Press, 2009.

Whyte, William H., Jr. *The Organization Man*. Garden City, N.Y.: Doubleday, 1957.

Wilentz, Sean. *The Age of Reagan: A History, 1974–2008*. New York: Harper Perennial, 2008.

Williams, Juan. *Eyes on the Prize: America's Civil Rights Years, 1954–1965*. New York: Viking, 1987.

Wills, Garry. *John Wayne's America: The Politics of Celebrity*. New York: Simon & Schuster, 1997.

Wood, John. "Hell's Angels and the Illusion of Counterculture." *Journal of Popular Culture* 37, no. 2 (2003): 336–51.

Wolf, Daniel R. *The Rebels: A Brotherhood of Outlaw Bikers*. Toronto: University of Toronto Press, 2000.

Yates, Brock. *Outlaw Machine: Harley Davidson and the Search for the American Soul*. Boston: Little, Brown, 1999.

Yates, Richard. *Revolutionary Road*. Boston: Little, Brown, 1961.

Youngblood, Ed. "The Birth of the Dirt Bike: Technology and the Shift in Attitude toward American Motorcyclists in the 1970s." *International Journal of Motorcycle Studies*, July 2007, http://ijms.nova.edu.

Zaretsky, Natasha. *No Direction Home: The American Family and the Fear of National Decline, 1968–1980*. Chapel Hill: University of North Carolina Press, 2007.

Zonker, Patricia. *Murdercycles*. Chicago: Nelson-Hall, 1978.

African American freedom struggle:
and Watts rebellion, 61, 253–55; and
Montgomery bus boycott, 250–51;
and Little Rock, Arkansas, 251; and
motorcycle cops, 253–55; and Black
Panthers, 255–56; and Philadelphia
Plan, 260–61; and motorcycle
compliance, 261

African American motorcyclist: and
segregated motorcycle culture, 230;
and AMA, 233; Benny Hardy, 233;
Bessie Stringfield, 233; Al "Sugar
Bear" Myers, 233–34, 247; dressed
like motorcycle cop, 247; motorcycles
as liberation for, 267–72; East Bay
Dragons Motorcycle Club, 270–72;
and police brutality, 272–74; and
sport bikes, 274–75; and rallies,
275–77

African Americans: and the blues, 231;
migration of, 231–32, 249–50; and
mobility-related conflict, 232–33; use of
term "honky," 236–37

Ali, Muhammad, 268–69

Altamont, 228–29; and Meredith Hunter,
228; compared to Woodstock, 229

American International Pictures, 77–78

American Motorcyclist Association
(AMA): Hollister and Riverside and,
18; and gypsy tours, 70; and dress of
cyclists, 107; survey of membership,
119; and politicians, 154–55; and
elections of 1980, 154–56; and "political
frontiers," 158–59; and Thomas
Jefferson, 167–68; exclusion of blacks,
233–36; critique of McGovern, 281–82.
See also Youngblood, Ed

Automobiles, 53, 61, 65, 258; triumph
of, 63; as cages, 67; compared
to motorcycles, 67; and gender
conventions, 67; threat to
motorcyclists, 68–69; and Nader,
73–74; and buy-American campaigns,
180; and black community, 231–32;
and segregation, 237; and motorcycle
cops, 245

Automobilists, 127, 137, 180; and
motorcyclists, 11, 68–70, 84–89, 293;
and triumph of automobile, 63; and
formation riding, 71; discussions
about bad drivers, 74–75; and power
chauvinism, 85; and road rage, 87; and
head injuries, 140, 160

Barger, Sonny: on consumption, 120–21;
in *Hells Angels on Wheels*, 198; attacks
against antiwar protestors, 203; and
Nazi paraphernalia, 241; and race, 264;
and sport bikes, 274

Beats, 105, 205

Bikers, 3–4, 52–53; and hippies, 10, 56–57,
205–7; origins of term, 11, 53; rich urban
biker (RUB), 13, 156, 188–91; as gay, 14,
195, 198–200; films featuring, 18, 77;
associated with violence, 40–41, 44,
56–59, 177; and police, 45; stereotypical
description of, 52; as "dumb old
biker," 55; link to working class, 55–56;
"subway" bikers, 58; as type, 58; as
victims of violence, 83; targeted on
highways, 84–86, 89; and trucker's
revenge, 88; and consumption, 92; and
leisure, 122; and age-old values, 155,
178, 184; as politically unorganized,

linked to rebelliousness, 248; Western Bob as, 248

Great Depression, 3, 6, 28, 33, 105, 162

Hardy, Benny, 233

Harley-Davidson motorcycles: declining sales of, 100–101, 178–79; complaints about, 102; defense of, 102–3; American Machine and Foundry, 178; criticized by police, 179–80; complaints about Japanese manufacturers, 181; economic turnaround of, 181–82; and advertising to the black community, 238–39; Brazil plant, 299–300; overseas market for, 299–300; India plant, 300; and union strikes, 300–301. *See also* Reagan, Ronald

Hayes, Isaac: at Wattstax festival, 269

Hells Angels: and antiwar protests, 193–94, 203, 224; husky image of, 194; relationship with police, 264–65; as type, 267. *See also* Motorcyclist, outlaw

Helmets, 7, 12–13, 91; and Highway Safety Act (1966), 74; laws and constitutional issues, 75–76, 135–36; motorcycle cops first to wear, 127; and middle class, 127–34, 143–45; air force requirement, 130; and Vietnam, 132; concerns about quality of, 135–36; challenges to laws requiring, 136–41; and broken necks, 138; and self-protection laws, 138–40; and public burden theory, 139–40, 175; suggested for automobilists, 140–41; and "Helmet Laws Suck" slogan, 151–52; and the Right, 156, 173–77; and Nader, 175; and Reagan, 175, 177. *See also* Motorcycle rights movement

Helms, Jesse, 174–75

Highways: in 1960s and 1970s, 72–73; Highway Safety Act of 1966, 74; and citizenship, 88–89

Highway Safety Act (1966), 74; amended, 156–57; challenges to, 156–57; and conservatives, 175–76

Himes, Chester, 248–49

Hippies: perceived as homosexual, 203–4; as pinkos, 205; criticized by motorcyclists, 205–6; biker invasions of hippie communities, 206; and police, 206–7. *See also* Counterculture

Hollister Rally, 4; media's portrayal of, 4–5, 20–21, 30–31; memories of, 5–6; and community ties, 6–7, 26–29; attendees viewed as outlaws, 14, 18; and Bolado Park gypsy tour, 19; as pattern for other rallies, 19; attendance at, 20; events at, 20; outside participants, 20; barkeepers at, 20–21; highway patrol at, 20; support from residents, 23–25; and vagrants, 27–28; women riders at, 29, 210–11, 222–24; challenge to work ethic, 29–33; Hispanic participants, 29; and *Life* magazine photograph, 30–31; *The Wild One*, 30; and bobbed cycles, 34–37

Homosexuality: Satyrs Motorcycle Club, 197; Tool Box bar, 197; and Marlon Brando look, 197–98; and middle class, 197–98; and "kissing as ritual," 198; and stereotype of motorcyclists, 198–99; fear of, 198–99; in *Scorpio Rising*, 199; and biker stereotype, 199–200; and heterosexual bodies, 199–200; gay macho, 200–201; girth as counter to assumptions about, 200–201; and politics, 202–3. *See also* Masculinity

Honda, Soichiro, 93, 101, 114

Honda motorcycles, 40, 45, 55, 91; growing popularity of, 92–93, 100, 131; and "nicest people" slogan, 93–94; as family friendly, 94, 113; and women, 94–95; and African Americans, 95; and "Pepsi generation," 95; as civilized, 101; as maintenance-free, 101, 114; defense of, 102; criticism of, 102; and masculinity, 106, 111; as second car, 117; and advertising to black community, 240. *See also* Middle class

"Honky": term used by motorcyclist, 236; factory worker referred to as, 236–37; compared to "hunky," 237; southern roots of, 237–38; and automobiles, 237–38. *See also* African Americans

Hound, 11, 37, 63, 236, 246,

International Trade Commission (ITC), and tariffs, 181

Jamison, Jack: in hill-climbing competitions, 5; on motorcycle maintenance, 97; in races, 98

Kawasaki Ninja, 274; and Clement Lloyd, 273–75

Kelley, Robin D. G.: on infrapolitics, 30–32

Knievel, Evel, 42; and wage work, 55; on feminists, 217–18. *See also* Stunt riders

Laconia, N.H., 19, 45, 119; Weirs Beach, 61–62, 311 (n. 12)

Landers, Ann, 84, 89, 114–15

Latin American Motorcycle Association (LAMA), 298–99; transnational nature of, 299

Law and order, 41, 51–52, 264; motorcyclists challenge to, 192, 229; motorcyclists support for, 208; and the black community, 230, 244; and Gestapo Garb, 248; and race, 265–66, 284–85; and the Republican Party, 283

"Let Those Who Ride Decide" slogan, 8, 161–62, 280. *See also* Motorcycle rights movement

Lien, Alexian, 291–93

Masculinity, 25–26, 30, 33, 37, 106, 185, 187, 194–95, 200–202, 207, 218–19

Masterless men, 27–28

McCain, John: visit to Sturgis Motorcycle Rally, 290–91; appropriation of freedom ideal, 290; praise of motorcyclists, 290; and 2008 election, 295

Middle class: and dress, 108–9, 110–11, 117, 125; motorcycling as status symbol of, 112–13; and consumption, 112–14; fear of

association with motorcycles, 114–16; motorcycles as cheap transportation for, 117–18; and work, 117–20; and motorcycle accidents, 128–29, 130–34

Mobility: viewed as threat, 7, 62–63, 82, 87, 259–60; associated with transients, 19, 27, 33, 62; compromised by police, 45; ; in films, 77–78, 82; among African Americans, 231–32

Moron stereotype, 54–55; and "dumb old biker," 55, 143

Motorcycle, bobbed, 34–36, 103; as California style, 36–38; as representing leisure, 37; as American style, 38–39; and "sit up and beg" posture, 38–39; and off-road riding, 70. *See also* Chopper

Motorcycle cop: origins, 244–45; after World War II, 245–46; uniforms of, compared to Gestapo Garb, 245–46; and city patrol, 249; and highway patrol, 249; as threat to black communities, 251–52, 253–54; opposition to desegregation, 252–53; and Watts rebellion, 253–54; and desegregation of Motorcycle Police Corps, 256–57

Motorcycle rights movement, 141–42, 145–46, 191–92; and independent spirit of motorcyclists, 142–43; divisions in, 145–46; and golden age of motorcycling, 146–50; growing unity in, 161–62; and Black Power, 277; compared to civil rights movement, 277–78; and civil rights vs. constitutional rights, 279–80; use of black stereotypes, 280–81

Motorcycles: numbers of registered, 7, 11; bobbed, 34–38; and off-road riding, 36; British, 38–39, 68; as weapons, 41; straight pipes on, 47, 51, 64, 69, 143, 149; compared to automobiles, 67; and highways, 67; growing popularity of, 92–93; and families, 94; and women, 94–95; and African Americans, 95; and riders' mechanical skill, 96–97;

middle-class fear of being associated with, 116, 119, 126; and golden age, 147; and homoerotic play, 195, 198; women as, 222; and politics, 225; and Altamont, 228; and black community, 229, 262, 266; and police, 263–64, 285–86

Rat Pack Motorcycle Club: and vigilante violence, 265–66; and Tea Party, 297

Reagan, Ronald, 1, 3, 178; support from motorcyclists, 2; and working class, 8–9, 186–87; visit to Harley-Davidson in York, Pennsylvania, 9, 181–82; and helmets, 13, 175, 177; Veterans of Foreign Wars speech, 169; and tariffs, 181, 185–86; and International Trade Commission, 181; and free trade, 182–83, 291; and age-old biker values, 183–84, 186; and nationalism, 184–85; and yuppies, 188; and "welfare queen," 188, 282–83

Regulation, motorcycle: linked to violence, 51; prior to Highway Safety Act, 129; and New York City Range Rover incident, 293

Rich urban biker (RUB), 156, 188–90

Riots: and civil rights, 61; and motorcyclists, 61–62

Riverside Rally: and emergence of outlaw, 18, 21–23; participants as lunatic fringe, 22–23; participants as 1%ers, 23

Road rage, 87–88; and New York City Range Rover incident, 292

Robinson, Dot, 211–12

Safety: highway, 7; motorcyclists threat to, 11–12, 50, 52, 63, 65–66, 108, 122, 127, 138; and citizenship, 88–89; and middle-class riders, 127–35, 152. *See also* Helmets

Seale, Bobby, and Marlon Brando, 270–71; and East Bay Dragons, 271. *See also* African American motorcyclist

Simon, Charles: challenge to helmet laws, 141–42

Sporting culture, 25–26; women's presence in, 26

Stunt riders, 42–43, 63–64; women as, 42; as product of wage work, 55–56

Suburbs, 79; motorcyclists connection to, 48, 82, 87; growth of, 63, 78; complaints about, 66–67, 87

Swastika: in 1950s, 241; sign of racial intolerance, 241–42; and Hells Angels, 241–42; opposition to by motorcyclists, 242; *Easyriders'* defense of, 242–43

Sweet Sweetback's Baadasssss Song (film), 227–28, 230; and Melvin Van Peebles, 227, 229; reviews of, 227–28; and Altamont, 228–29

Tamony, Peter: study of Hells Angels, 48; descriptions of motorcyclists, 53, 198; on origins of term "honky", 236–37

Tariffs: target Japanese, 8–9; and Reagan, 181–83, 185, 291; and Harley-Davidson, 181–84; and India, 299–300. *See also* Reagan, Ronald

Thompson, Hunter, 6, 103–4, 124, 199

Tramp. *See* Vagrancy

Troop, Jack, on bobbed cycle, 36; as stunt cyclist, 64; maintaining bikes, 97

Vagrancy: "tramp scare," 6, 19, 27, 32; laws regulating, 27–29; as consequence of capitalism, 28

Western Bob, 34–35, 107; as rebel, 37; and greaser, 247–48

Wild One, The (film), 46, 48–49; challenge to outlaw image, 48–49

Women, 94, as domestic, 14, 211; and sexism, 14, 67, 68, 211, 213, 214–16; absent from male culture, 26; as vagrants, 27; at Hollister, 29, 210; in the workplace, 31–32; referred to as "mammas," 150; Most Popular and Typical Girl Rider Contest, 211; as motorcycle models, 212–16, 297–98;

and *Easyriders*, 213–14; violence
against, 214–16; and heterosexual
space, 215–16; and misogyny, 217–18;
and lack of mechanical know-how, 219;
critiques of motorcycle publications,
219–21; as feminists, 221–22; and last
male refuge, 221–22; as outlaws, 222–23;
women-only motorcycle clubs, 298;
"No Cages" ad, 298
Women's liberation, 13, 194; motorcyclists'
critique of, 207–8
Working class: and Right, 8–9;
motorcyclists' connection to, 11, 53–54,
95, 110, 186; in contrast to middle class,
12; sporting culture and, 25–26; and
wage work, 28–31; as rebels, 30–31,
33; and drugs, 44; as morons, 54; as
roughnecks, 54; link to garages, 55; as
daredevils, 55–56; and consumption,
92, 104, 113, 116; stigma associated

with, 116–17; link to Democratic Party,
156, 188; George Wallace and, 164–65;
and corporate liberalism, 165–66;
and rights-based activism, 172; and
Reagan, 185–87, 190; and identity
politics, 185–86; and golden age of
motorcycling, 191; and sunbelt South,
191; and gay erotica, 197; and origins
of term "honky," 236; and greaser, 248;
and George H. W. Bush, 282–83

Young urban professionals (yuppies), 188;
and Gary Hart, 188; and consumption,
188–89; and Harley-Davidson
motorcycles, 189
Youngblood, Ed: and AMA support of
Nixon, 154; on Jeffersonian principles,
167; on racism in motorcycling,
234–36, 278, 296. *See also* American
Motorcyclist Association